The Price of Victory

The Price of Victory

Michael Charlton

BRITISH BROADCASTING CORPORATION

Acknowledgements

Associated Press 45, 76, 260; Bahamas News Bureau 282; BBC Hulton Picture Library 35, 77, 81, 135 (left); Crown Copyright 225, 279 (bottom); Churchill Archives, Churchill College, Cambridge 41; *Daily Mail* 217; The Commission of the European Communities 91, 101, 102, 193, 204, 219; *Evening Standard* front cover, 177, 185, 238; Imperial War Museum 13, 16, 30; Keystone Press 39, 74, 127, 130, 135 (right), 153, 230, 237, 279 (top), 302; *New Statesman* 189, 216; Popperfoto 160, 201, 303; Sport and General Press Agency 47, 56; Syndication International 203.

The cartoons on the front cover and pages 189, 203, 216 and 238 are by Vicky, on pages 177 and 185 by Sir David Low and on page 217 by Emmwood.

Published by the
British Broadcasting Corporation,
35 Marylebone High Street,
London W1M 4AA

ISBN 0 563 20055 3

First published 1983
© Michael Charlton and the Contributors 1983
Set in 10/11pt Linotron Ehrhardt
by Phoenix Photosetting, Chatham
Printed in England
by Mackays of Chatham Ltd

Contents

Introduction

THIS IS THE ACCOUNT, as it was told to me in their own words, by surviving former British Prime Ministers, Foreign Secretaries, their Cabinet colleagues, and the political advisers of the time in Whitehall – particularly those in the Foreign Office and Treasury who were most influentially concerned – of Britain's diplomacy in Europe after the last war. What they had to say was broadcast originally by the BBC's Radio 3 as a series of nine programmes, each of some sixty minutes' duration, produced by Anthony Moncrieff for the Talks and Documentaries Department, and called 'The Price of Victory'. Subsequently, extracts from some of these programmes were published in the magazine *Encounter* under the title 'How (& Why) Britain Lost the Leadership of Europe'.

The choices made in a period which ended in 1963 with President de Gaulle's 'veto' of Harold Macmillan's attempt – the first – to make Britain a member of the European Community were prophetic of British destiny. They were choices which either lay, to a very large extent, with the men in the following chapters, or which were intimately observed by them at first hand while they were being made.

In accepting the BBC's invitation to go over the ground again – this time for the public record as 'oral history' – the participants provide in their recollections their own explanation of why they decided as they did. They tell how an accumulation of events in Europe, some of which are still hardly known in any public or popular sense, were opposed during a crucial period – only to be accepted in the end – as calling for a historic reversal of the United Kingdom's traditional policy over 'Europe'. The British recollections are complemented throughout by those of their counterparts in the making of policy in the United States and in Europe, whose own decisions, at the relevant times, became powerful considerations in the evolution and formulation of British policy.

When it comes to this troubled question of themselves and 'Europe', and the sharing of a measure of sovereignty with former rivals and partners, it is the agreed convention that the British public find 'little difficulty in restraining their enthusiasms within the bounds of decorum!' – as Churchill once remarked about a different and unrelated matter. However, the pervasive 'consumerism' of the present day, and its attitudes, have unduly reduced and narrowed the range of considerations involved in both the earlier rejection and the later acceptance of the logic of 'Europe' by British governments. It tends to obscure the engrossing story of its very considerable 'pre-history' as an issue. Important aspects of this are, I think, placed in the public arena for the first time during the course of these interviews.

The series of documentary programmes for Radio 3 set out to explore, in general, the extent to which there had been a failure of British policy over Europe in the vital decade of the 1950s and, above all, to enquire into one so-called 'missed opportunity' in particular. This was the consequence of Britain's self-willed exclusion from the outcome of the Messina Conference in Sicily in 1955, which went on to establish the beginnings of federation among six powers in Europe with the Common Market. The other chapters of this book, as was the intention of the original broadcasts, are the overture and the aftermath of this crucially important event, 'Messina'.

Why was it that the British politicians and their advisers were, on the whole, unprepared for the success of the Continental Europeans in achieving a degree of common purpose which vitally affected British interests? Why was it that they were so consistently dismissive of the enduring significance of those spasms of ardour on the Continent which called into being the European Community, and at a time when there was the coincidentally accelerating decline of the substitute concept of Britain as the hub of an expanding Commonwealth?

That cardinal date in contemporary European history, the invasion of Russia by Hitler on 22 June 1941, had marked the emergence of a world dominated by two great powers, both with access to and control of vast resources and able to exploit them, albeit in wholly opposed ways, within the theories and the framework of the large internal market. In the enforced contemplation of that prospect lay the genesis of the post-war endeavours to forge a more comprehensive and effective unity in Western Europe. When the first photographs of the Americans and the Russians embracing on the Elbe, at the end of the war against Hitler, were published, Fernand Spaak remembers his father, the Belgian Foreign Minister, ruefully asking, 'Where are the Europeans?' The British veneration for their customary role of qualified detachment from Europe kept them aloof, in the most important respects, from any whole-hearted commitment to the answer Spaak implied and practised.

Viewed from the vantage point of a great historian, Arnold Toynbee (who did a stint in the Foreign Office as a planner in the wartime years), it was plain that from the time of the First World War – as he wrote in the 1920s – Britain was being grafted progressively, following her protracted absence from the Continent during the period of Empire overseas, once more on to the body politic in Europe. The great laureate of Empire, Kipling, had after all foreshadowed the need for radical adjustments. He had felt in his bones what was coming – long before the fall of Singapore in 1942 flashed its unequivocal warning.

> Far called our navies melt away;
> On dune and headland sinks the fire:
> Lo, all our pomp of yesterday
> Is one with Nineveh and Tyre!

If Kipling had such deeply sensitive premonitions, why did not the political class in Britain? Why, as his forebodings were manifestly coming to pass, did not the Colonial Office and the Foreign Office? These are among the principal themes which 'The Price of Victory' endeavoured to address. Harold Macmillan's application for membership of the European Community put the European question into the public domain in Britain for the first time in 1962. It appeared with an abruptness which had the appearances of a rush to judgement. As an issue it had, of course, been present, mostly out of sight, for many years. They were the years, particularly in the 1950s, when it did not fill the newspapers or haunt the conversation. It shows up in those Foreign Office files which are open to inspection like a barium meal! It is there surprisingly early when, almost at once after the war, Britain was being presented, in embryo form, with the challenge she eventually accepted of new forms of political cooperation with the European nations as an aid to general recovery after war. This is the time when decisions were taken which to a considerable extent pre-disposed all that followed. It is this course which the succeeding chapters have tried to retrace.

It has been possible to include in book form a good deal of material from the fifty or so interviews which, given even the great generosity of the time allowed, it was not possible to include in the Radio 3 broadcasts. The original interviews usually occupied upwards of an hour and were recorded in the course of 1980, an important – and the only – exception being the extracts from an interview with Harold Macmillan which the former Prime Minister gave to the late Robert McKenzie for the BBC after Mr Macmillan had written about the European issue in his own memoirs, *Riding the Storm*. In advance of each inter-view the participant was advised of the areas of questions only. Thereafter it took the form of a conversation, as though for a 'live' broadcast.

'Oral history' is of course susceptible of an important challenge – of which I believe all were, no doubt, aware – that it is given to 'rear vision', and to the infinite wisdoms of hindsight. However, in important instances, while relying for the most part on simple memory, those taking part were able to consult the diaries they kept at the time (which yield the views of the moment), and in others they took the trouble to look up the official record – still publicly unavail-able – in preparation for the interviews. If I may intrude a personal prejudice, I formed the opinion that they answered with a disarming frankness and clarity about the events of many years ago which, for the most part, seemed to come readily enough to their minds.

To a certain extent I was able to put questions based upon what is so far available, under the thirty-year rule, from the official archives. It is impossible, in my view, to read from among that mass of documentary evidence without sensing the feeling of political excitement which it engenders. There, on the harsh, 'austerity' notepaper of wartime (which was carried over into many of the peacetime years – paper which itself is redolent of that total mobilisation for the European War which bankrupted Britain, and of the financial impotence which was its consequence), is laid bare the painful odyssey of a civilised nation-state and the quickening 'Recessional' from its marvellous achievement of the trans-plantation, all around the globe, of representative democracy. There, too, one can discern the inexorable return to a former constituency among the small and medium-sized states of the European peninsula. And there also, in the cautious sobriety of the Foreign Office and Treasury judgements, stylishly written and elegantly composed, are all the national doubts and hesitations and the begin-nings of the resolute rearguard action which contested the relevance of the European 'idea' for Britain. In the margins of those papers is Bevin's decisive imprint in his huge and all but indecipherable fist, in which the pen was plainly an alien implement, and Eden's elegant flourishes in red ink before the closed period of the thirty-year rule conceals the later history and puts it out of reach.

Out of reach, that is, other than by appealing directly to those who helped to make it!

Here, then, is a momentous journey by Britain, recalled by, and in company with, the chief lieutenants of Churchill and Attlee, of Eden and Bevin, down to the time of Macmillan. These are the 'footfalls echoing in their memories, down the passage Britain did not take, to the door it did not open . . .' in the vital years of the 1950s; and why, partly in consequence, instead of finding the rose garden, the British seem persuaded they see, rather, a bed of nails!

I would like to record my gratitude to Michael Cullis for having concentrated my mind; to my colleagues Anthony Moncrieff and Richard Ellis for the mounting of the original programmes; and to George Fischer, the Head of Talks and Documentaries, and Ian McIntyre, the Controller of the BBC's Radio 3, for their cultivation and preservation of that stimulating constituency in a 'mass medium' where, by devoting the time and the space, it is possible to explore the arts of diplomacy and strategic politics out of the mouths of those who swayed a momentous choice by an old nation state.

1

Churchill's 'Morning Thoughts'

WHEN, IN 1945, the elated British went down in their thousands to Piccadilly Circus to celebrate victory – rationed as they were on diets of 'Spam' and 'powdered egg' throughout five long years of privations and endurances – the foundations of Britain's former power and position were already cracked and broken. For a long time to come the dazzling influence of victory hid from sight the full extent of that condition. Victory shone so brightly that, most importantly of all, the British themselves did not see it.

Alone among the old nation states of Europe Britain emerged from the Second World War with an experience which was fundamentally different. Victory meant that the British held a different view of themselves – it was a national attitude of mind – which reinforced the more obvious historical differences. 'We were alone', 'We fought on', and, in the end, 'We won'. It would transpire that we too, however, were ruined. It was victory which induced Britain to misinterpret and to misjudge the strength and relevance to her of the movement for unity in Western Europe. In the beginning Britain was asked to lead this movement; at various stages to participate in it; throughout she tried to stop it taking the direction it did; and finally felt compelled to join it.

The refusal to take part in the formative years proved to be at the cost of any decisive British influence in moulding the eventual outcome, in shaping that specific nature and character which the European Community assumed at the start and which we find painful to live with today.

That was the Price of Victory.

THIS STORY of our European diplomacy is told for the most part by those senior Foreign Office officials and politicians who either made, or were present looking over the shoulders of those who *did* make, the principal decisions in the years of Churchill and Eden and Attlee and Bevin and Macmillan. It concerns those twenty years after the war which saw the planless agglomeration of empire dissolved with grace and dignity; when Britain lost the initiative over events which decided her post-war destiny; and membership of the European Community became the serious considered thought of the nation.

The dawn of this historical change in British diplomacy begins with Winston Churchill and what he set down in the middle of the war as his 'Morning Thoughts'. Therein were the origins and consequences of his personal dream of a United States of Europe. For it was Churchill's voice which animated Western Europe in its first days of reconstruction as it had aroused Britain in war. He gave a powerful impulsion to the forces in favour of Continental unity with which, at the end of the day, Britain had to find a place herself. But

Churchill's call for a United States of Europe contained also the first of those major ambiguities concerning Britain and Europe which afflicted the formulation of British policy.

Harold Macmillan, who many years later, when Prime Minister himself, took the plunge over the Common Market, was Churchill's resident Minister at Allied Headquarters in North Africa during the war. Macmillan has this memory of an occasion when Churchill, freed for a moment from the day-to-day conduct of the war by Britain's first victories, turned his mind to what would follow final victory.

MACMILLAN: I was in with Churchill at the beginning of the founding of what we called the European Movement, which began in 1947 with the first meetings at Strasbourg of the Council of Europe. That was based upon his extraordinary power always to look forward, never back. Sometimes he would say things that took me a long time to know what he meant. It was because he was casting that strange, brooding mind forward. So unlike de Gaulle, who always looked back. I'll give you an example. He said to me in 1943 at the Cairo conference – he was at a meeting with the President and came back in a bad mood, tired, and suddenly turned to me and said, 'Cromwell was a great man!' And I said, 'Yes, Prime Minister'. 'Aaah,' he said, 'he made one fatal error. Born and bred as a child in the fear of the strength and power of Spain, he failed to see that Spain was finished and France was rising, hence the Marlborough wars, hence the century of war. Will that be said of me?' But after a little thought I knew what he meant. He meant that he'd lost interest in the Germans. Might take one year, might take two years, might take three years, but they were beaten. From the time America came in and we cleared them out of Africa, they were beaten. But *what would Russia be.* Hence all these attempts to get further on, and so on.

SO, AS HAROLD MACMILLAN SAYS, long before the war itself was ended Churchill saw the prospect of a new conflict, that would become the cold war, beginning. The last two years of the war were as much concerned with the future of the world as with the battles being fought.

Today we know that even earlier than the conversation with Macmillan, as early as the autumn of 1942, by which time events were moving quickly in our favour, Churchill was thinking privately far ahead while speaking publicly about the present, as on this occasion in November 1942 at the Mansion House.

CHURCHILL: I have never promised anything but blood, tears, toil and sweat. Now, however, we have a new experience, we have victory ... General Alexander with his brilliant comrades and lieutenant, General Montgomery, have gained a glorious and exciting victory in what I think should be called the 'Battle of Egypt'. Rommel's army has been defeated, it has been routed, it has been very largely destroyed as a fighting force. ...

THREE WEEKS BEFORE that speech in which he saluted the Alamein victory, Churchill had sent a remarkable secret minute to Anthony Eden, his Foreign Secretary. It was dated 21 October 1942, that is two days before Montgomery and Alexander opened the desert offensive – the Battle of El Alamein. What Churchill set down to Eden sounds like both will and testament.

Churchill framed in the cockpit of the Liberator bomber which flew him to Turkey in January 1943, after Alamein and at the time of Stalingrad.

CHURCHILL: I must admit that my thoughts rest primarily in Europe, in the revival of the glory of Europe, the parent continent of modern nations and of civilisation. It would be a measureless disaster if Russian barbarism overlaid the culture and independence of the ancient states of Europe. Hard as it is to say now, I trust that the European family may act unitedly as one, under a Council of Europe in which the barriers between nations will be greatly minimised and unrestricted travel will be possible. I hope to see *the economy of Europe studied as a whole* [author's italics]. Of course we shall have to work with the Americans in many ways, and in the greatest ways, but Europe is our prime care . . . It would be easy to dilate upon these themes. Unhappily, the war has prior claims on our attention.

THAT WAS WRITTEN by Churchill to Eden before the end of 1942! It therefore complements what he said to Macmillan when he used his analogy about Cromwell. Churchill saw Russia about to become the dominant European power. Therefore Britain must make the cause of European unity and Europe her, as he put it, 'prime care'.

In January 1943 Churchill and Roosevelt met secretly at Casablanca. Their joint declaration that 'unconditional surrender' would be the only terms for Germany meant, in effect, that the Russian armies would decide by their presence the future of an unknown extent of Europe. And therefore in January 1943, with the Russians on the Eastern front yet to make certain of the outcome at Stalingrad, the battle which decided the war, Churchill undertook one of his extraordinary wartime journeys. He flew from Casablanca on the west coast of Africa the length of the Mediterranean to Turkey, to make a start on the organisation of post-war Europe at its most Eastern outposts.

His doctor, Lord Moran, has described him at this time, at the age of sixty-eight and wearing only a silk vest, crawling on his hands and knees around the fuselage of an unheated bomber trying to stuff blankets in the cracks of the hatches and bomb bays to stop the icy whistling draughts! The aircraft landed at Adana in Turkey. There he confided his innermost thoughts about the post-war order to the Turks. What he proposed aroused the strong opposition of both the Foreign Office and the Americans. With Churchill throughout the war and on this trip was the then military assistant secretary to the War Cabinet, Sir Ian Jacob.

JACOB: You've got to start off by realising that the Foreign Office and Eden did their utmost to stop him going there, and said, 'Really, we don't think it would be at all a good idea to go and see the Turks.' Well, then we had very good talks with the Turks. They were quite pleased to find they weren't going to be pushed to make up their minds to come into the war. And Winston I remember drawing the conclusions about this. He said, 'You know, you really ought to be in on our side because at the end of the war there will be the victors on the bench and the losers will be in the dock, and there will be a shadowy bunch of people in the body of the court who will be the neutrals. You'd be much better off if you were sitting on the bench with us.' They were extremely friendly and the only thing they were rather frightened of, I think, was Russia. They said they regarded us as the absolutely essential bulwark for Europe against Russia.

THE CONFERENCE with the Turks took place in railway carriages drawn up near the airfield. Sir Ian Jacob kept a diary of this and other meetings through-out the wartime years.

JACOB: Here we are: 'I woke at 8 o'clock after an excellent sleep. The wagon-lit was, I suppose, one of those normally employed on the Orient Express from the Wagon-Lit company, it was comfortable and clean. I found no "travelling companions". The dawn was cloudy, the mountains being only intermittently visible. After breakfast I arranged for Loxley and Co., the Foreign Office people, to translate into French the conclusion that I had drafted the previous night. I got Alan Brooke's [chief of the Imperial General Staff] approval of the draft and then took it in to the Prime Minister who was lying in bed in his coach, the walls of which, all around him, were hung with red silk. He too had been busy and had dictated a paper on political subjects, dealing with some of the post-war fears of the Turks. He called it "Morning Thoughts".'

WE MAY TAKE Churchill's 'Morning Thoughts', sent off to the Cabinet in London, as a convenient dawn of political argument and the beginning of Britain's long post-war European odyssey. In it Churchill emphasised his interest in *regional* forms of organisation rather than that *world* government under the United Nations favoured by the Americans. For this the Americans proceeded to demonstrate a semi-religious faith, regarding their abandonment of the old League of Nations as a sort of sin for which they would, this time, make amends. Churchill, in his 'Morning Thoughts', as he had done to Eden in the minute of October 1942, again called for a Council of Europe and said he had agreed with Roosevelt that an 'instrument of European government' should be established which would 'embody the spirit but not be subject to the weaknesses' of the former League of Nations.

The Foreign Office considered Churchill's ideas at this stage to be romantic and impracticable. Where specific, in the opinion of Lord Gladwyn (then Gladwyn Jebb in charge of the small policy-planning department in the Foreign Office), his ideas hardly merited serious consideration.

GLADWYN: He hadn't really got the time to bend his great intelligence to these projects of the future because he was running the war. And why should he? He couldn't really, anyhow. But when he did he had views which I think were unsustainable in practice. He did, of course, discuss to a certain extent with President Roosevelt the future of the world, but President Roosevelt's views at that time were very hazy, I think, and Roosevelt of course was only anxious to get on good terms with the Russians. Roosevelt didn't think anything, as you know, of the British Commonwealth and Empire, and that was evident ultimately. No, he just wanted to make a deal with Uncle Joe over a division of the world as far as I can make out – which was, of course, disastrous. Churchill didn't agree with that, of course. But I don't think that Churchill's talks with Roosevelt on the future of the world led to anything very much.

CHARLTON: But what were the Foreign Office's alternatives to Churchill? If there could not, in your view, be regional councils subordinate to a world organisation, what was the alternative?

GLADWYN: We thought there might be regional councils of some kind – not a Council of Asia . . . Good God, what could it turn out to be? We thought there might well be some kind of European entity including ourselves and that was a possibility. But we always thought that if there was going to be any organisation including the Russians (as most people thought that there should be), it would have to be, obviously, a *world* organisation. There could be a regional element in it, but we never denied that. I'm afraid what we didn't want was for the regional elements to be the *only* thing and to have no world organisation at all. If we did we thought the Russians would organise their own – as indeed they have, I expect! We didn't want that to happen. We wanted the Russians to come in to some kind of world organisation on a reasonable basis. The quarrels, I think, were between those who thought that there should be nothing but regional organisations and, in the end, no world organisation at all.

CHARLTON: That was your chief objection to Churchill's proposition, was it?

GLADWYN: I think so, yes. That was probably the chief objection we had.

CHARLTON: Now in the 'Morning Thoughts' which Churchill confided to the Turks, to the Foreign Office's horror, the principal proposal appears to be his wish to establish an instrument of European government.

GLADWYN: Yes.

CHARLTON: Now what inherently in that was to be opposed as far as the Foreign Office was concerned?

GLADWYN: Well, it wasn't clear. It wasn't clear whether Great Britain should be part of the instrument of government, you see. And if it was to be an instrument of government without Great Britain, was it going to include Russia? That was quite unclear. And what did he mean? Did he mean that there should be an instrument of government including France and what remained of Germany? It wasn't clear what he wanted really.

Churchill and President Inönü on the train in Turkey in which he dictated his 'Morning Thoughts' to Sir Ian Jacob about the future design of Europe.

CHARLTON: I wonder whether it might have been the fear that, as you later put it, what eventually did happen might happen? That it really was the creation of an ideological bloc, of a regional bloc in the west, implicit in Churchill's idea?
GLADWYN: Well, if he'd wanted a bloc organised by us that was one thing. But he really couldn't maintain that we must have an entity on our own with the Commonwealth behind us and the Empire which we always insisted on *and* be members of a bloc and in conjunction with the Russians. It hadn't been thought out.
CHARLTON: I just wonder whether we're not very close here to what he was shortly to proclaim publicly, his call, which he reiterated several times in the early post-war years, for a United States of Europe?
GLADWYN: Well, again it was never clear. I think he was, in doing this, un-consciously deluding people.

LORD GLADWYN, incidentally, drafted for Eden the dismissive Foreign Office alternative to Churchill's 'Morning Thoughts'. Gladwyn's paper was circulated in that great Victorian building across the street from No. 10 under the title '*Early* Morning Thoughts'!
   The formulation of our post-war European policy had begun. Mr Eden, says the Foreign Office historian of this period, was able to balance and often correct Winston Churchill's 'rapid approach and equally rapid conclusions'. From the beginning the Foreign Office showed itself wary of the innovations Churchill had in mind; and not just because they were incompletely thought out. The evidence suggests that they thought him wayward, a compendium of

vision and irrationality who needed close watching! In particular his notions about 'instruments of European government' were thought to be 'romantic'. One has the feeling that there was an important extra dimension to the Churchill/Foreign Office relationship. While he was, of course, admired for the inspiration of his wartime leadership, he seems never totally rehabilitated from his past in the Foreign Office mind. His sense of adventure and his judgements were suspect. A penumbra of doubt stretching back perhaps to the Dardanelles, and to the landings in Archangel to oppose the Bolshevik revolution in 1919. Considering where he had just been, in Turkey, a residual memory of both was probably to the fore in 1943!

JACOB: You have to realise the Foreign Office were always a very awkward department. They hated anybody writing anything about their subjects. And I think they would criticise the details of his 'Morning Thoughts' and come to all kinds of clever conclusions about them, and would resent them because they hadn't drafted them. Now that is taking a rather low view of the Foreign Office attitude. I think they would also have thought that it was premature – because nobody had considered this really properly – and that he was expressing his own uninformed thoughts rather, and this was not a good thing to do in the hearing of a neutral power like Turkey. That, I imagine, is what they felt.

CHARLTON: But does this accord with your view of what their opposition might have been? We know that, for example, Eden, who also looked upon all this with little enthusiasm, did so for roughly two reasons: that Harry Hopkins, Roosevelt's confidant, had told him that if Europe *did* organise itself along these lines it was likely to lead to isolationism by the Americans, that the Americans would say, 'If they're doing this without us they don't need us'. And secondly, that it would annoy the Russians. Now if this is true Churchill can hardly have been unaware of the consequences of his 'Morning Thoughts'. What defence do you believe he'd make to both those things?

JACOB: I think it's very easy to answer that. His defence on the first point would have been 'But of course the United States is closely bound in'. This 'Council' if it existed would be under a world organisation in which the United States would be one of the leading members and therefore it was *not* just the kind of body which would lead them to take an isolationist point of view. He wouldn't have agreed with that. And as for the Russians, well I don't think he ever would have hesitated to do anything for fear of the Russians. If the Russians didn't like it, they could lump it!

CHARLTON: And so therefore the fundamental point of the Foreign Office opposition is that they were opposed to Churchill's view of the Soviet Union? The Foreign Office hoped that the Soviet Union could be a reliable partner in the post-war settlement but Churchill had deep suspicions about it?

JACOB: Oh yes, absolutely. Because after all, all the contact with the Russians throughout the war had led to no other conclusion. I mean, they were beastly in every way.

CHARLTON: But why did it lead to different conclusions in the Foreign Office in your view?

JACOB: Well, because the Foreign Office had their heads in the sand half the time. Certainly Churchill never thought that the Russians would be a reliable bunch of people after the war. He speaks at some of his meetings and in his post-war speeches – at Fulton I think he speaks about the admiration that we have for the Russian people and the great struggle they'd made, and he talks in glowing terms of the strength and courage of Stalin, but I don't think he for one moment thought that politically they would be anything but extremely awkward people. Certainly this aim made itself quite clear a little later on when the examination was made of the occupation of Germany. The arrangements were produced and put up to the Cabinet and Winston was absolutely horrified at 'letting the Barbarians right into the centre of Europe'. He wanted to keep them as far east as possible, and certainly east of Berlin and Vienna if he could, and only allow them to station anybody further west than that in return for a con- siderable concession.

CHARLTON: Why is Churchill staggered by the post-war plans when they're put to him for Soviet occupation up the Elbe?

JACOB: I think simply because he hadn't studied it – the occupation business. And I may say I was right in on this because they had a small committee which went into all these things and teed them up. It consisted of Sir William Strang of the Foreign Office, Gousev, who was the Russian ambassador, and the American ambassador who was Winant. And the three of them sat constantly and I used to attend their meetings and made all these arrangements, you see. And I don't think Winston paid any attention to it. We all, I must admit, thought that we were really settling just billeting areas, because the whole country was going to be administered on a quadripartite basis. It never occurred to us that the Russians would take over their zone and make it into a country, which is what they did. Winston perhaps was more far-seeing than we were. When he did see this he said, 'Well, we must stay as far east as we can get with our armies until we've talked further'. But the President wouldn't play on that. The President didn't want to annoy Stalin in any way.

CHARLTON: Do you recall anything in particular Churchill said when the post-war plans for Germany were produced?

JACOB: Well, he said just that – that we should never let the 'Barbarians' in the middle of Europe. He regarded the Russians as barbarians. I mean, the way that Stalin treated us was monstrous. Every single telegram, if you were to make a study of the correspondence with Stalin – the way they made everything so difficult. They wouldn't help in any way. They wouldn't allow us to land, to help them, the wretched people fighting in Warsaw . . . they wouldn't allow our crews, they wouldn't help the Russian convoys . . . There was nothing, there was nothing. They were absolutely awful. They didn't provide us with any information as to why they wanted things, what use they'd made of them. Oh no, they were very, very . . . I felt all through the war that we'd taken the wrong attitude towards the Russians. We gave way to them on every point, and they merely got nastier and pushed harder. That's what they're like.

WELL BEFORE CHURCHILL'S suspicions about Russian intentions found readier confirmation in subsequent developments – it was on 21 March 1943, after his visit to Turkey and the composition of 'Morning Thoughts', and his recovery from pneumonia attributable to the rigours of flying in unheated bombers – the Prime Minister delivered what Harold Macmillan, who was listening to it in North Africa, called a famous broadcast. Much of this was devoted by Churchill to his ideas for the reorganisation and reconstitution of

Europe. It was in this speech, broadcast by the BBC on 23 March, that Churchill made public the essence of what he'd been urging in secret upon his Cabinet, upon Eden and upon Roosevelt.

CHURCHILL: One can imagine that under a world institution, embodying or representing the United Nations, and some day all nations, there should come into being a Council of Europe and a Council of Asia. As according to the forecast I am outlining the war against Japan will still be raging, it is upon the creation of the Council of Europe and the settlement of Europe that the first practical task will be centred.

Now this is a stupendous business. In Europe lie most of the causes which have led to these two world wars. In Europe dwell the historic parent races from whom our Western civilisation has been so largely derived. I believe myself to be what is called 'a good European' and I should deem it a noble task to take part in reviving the fertile genius and in restoring the true greatness of Europe ... Anyone can see that this Council, when created, must eventually embrace the whole of Europe, and that all the main branches of the European family must some day be partners in it. What is to happen to the large number of small nations whose rights and interests must be safeguarded?

Here let me ask what would be thought of an army that consisted only of battalions and brigades and which never formed any of the larger and higher organisations like army corps? They would soon get mopped up. It would therefore seem to me at any rate worthy of patient study, that side by side with the great powers there should be a number of groupings of states or confederations which would express themselves through their own chosen representatives, the whole making a Council of Great States or Groups of States. It is my earnest hope – though I can hardly expect to see it fulfilled in my lifetime – that we shall achieve the largest common measure of the integrated life of Europe that is possible, without destroying the individual characteristics and traditions of its many ancient and historic races. All this will, I believe, be found to harmonise with the high permanent interests of Britain, the United States and Russia. It certainly cannot be accomplished without their cordial and concerted agreement and direct participation. Thus and only thus will the glory of Europe rise again.

REMOTE AS ONE feels it probably must have seemed to his British audience, coming as it did in the middle of the war, Churchill dwelt upon this theme. It is apparent that his rallying call for European unity was not wholly due to the sharpening prospect he saw of a Europe dominated by a single great power, Soviet Russia; but that he was moved by those same ideas which were taken up by the Continental Europeans as practical politics in the first years after the war. Sir John Colville was Private Secretary to three Prime Minsters, Chamberlain, Churchill and Attlee, and he served Winston Churchill both during the war and also during his post-war administration.

COLVILLE: I think Churchill considered himself a European as far as Europe was concerned but not necessarily as far as the United Kingdom was concerned. In this connection he wrote a really rather important essay as long ago as 1930, and on this matter he always remained consistent. In that essay he said

that 'the conception of a United States of Europe is right. Every step taken to
that end which appeases the obsolete hatreds and vanished oppressions, which
make easier the traffic and reciprocal services of Europe, which encourages
nations to lay aside their precautionary panoply, is good in itself.' But in this
same essay, when he's talking of Britain's place in this United Europe, he says,
'But we have our own dream and our own task, we are *with* Europe but not *of* it.
We are linked but not compromised.' And I think this remained his thought
throughout. He believed that a United Europe would solve the century-old
rivalry, hatred and war between the French and the Germans, or the German-
speaking peoples. And to him the peace of Europe, which was so important for
the world as a whole, depended on some kind of unity among the Europeans.
And we, of course, I think he thought, would contribute to that in a variety of
ways.

THE ESSAY MENTIONED by Colville was given the title 'The United States of
Europe' by Churchill and was published in the *Saturday Evening Post* in America
in February 1930. In those days Churchill was a backbench MP and was earning
his living by journalism. The article showed Churchill to be more than a
sympathiser with the concepts of a European federation being put forward by
the French statesman Aristide Briand. 'Jock' Colville says that Churchill
'admired Briand enormously'. What became known as the Briand Plan was a
proposal for a United States of Europe initiated in the 1930s and which Britain
was invited to join. The Foreign Office recommended against doing so and,
largely in consequence, the Briand Plan came to nothing.

In the *Saturday Evening Post* essay Churchill asked his readers this. 'What are
the causes which are favouring the New World and hindering the Old? The
demand of the masses in all countries is for higher economic well-being.
Science and organisation stand ready to supply it. Why is the contrast between
American and European conditions so cruel and unequal?' Churchill's prescription in 1930 was a United States of Europe. To emulate the inspiration of
the American model and experience.

It seems understandable enough that confusion about British intentions
should subsequently arise now that, as the Second World War was ending, he
began to circulate and promote the same basic concepts again. After all, what
Churchill had written in 1930 seems almost indistinguishable from the
objectives which men like Jean Monnet and other Continental Europeans
moved to implement after 1945. But Sir John Colville is confident that Churchill
continued to make an all-important qualification in so far as Britain itself was
concerned.

COLVILLE: It didn't alter the fact that our principal role was to be the centre of
the British Empire, closely allied with the other great English-speaking community of the United States.
CHARLTON: He used somewhat later the metaphor of a house – that this
'house of Europe' has to be built and it would have to be built by the English.
Now, did he see it as within the power of Britain to do this and that that was to
be its task?
COLVILLE: I don't quite know when he said that but if, as I suspect, it was
towards the end of the War or just after the end of the war . . .

CHARLTON: It was just before the end of the war.
COLVILLE: Yes. I think what he really meant was that Europe had collapsed, Europe was overrun, Europe was short of food and Europe was occupied. The only so-called European country which was of any size or importance which had not been overrun was Britain, and therefore Britain would have to build the house for the Europeans.

IN 1943, following the writing down of his 'Morning Thoughts', Churchill's concepts still tended to dominate Anglo-American strategic thinking. Then Britain was continuing to make the larger contribution to the war effort. It was not until after the D-Day landings in France in 1944 that the equation changed. Only then did the American weight in the balance of the Alliance become so much greater and, in consequence, the American voice predominant.

The American objections to Churchill's first formulation of the need for a regional organisation in Europe and European unity formed an important part of the arguments deployed by the Foreign Office against the Prime Minister's concepts. Lord Gladwyn gave this as the essence of the American concerns.

GLADWYN: They thought it was a plan, I think, really to reduce the American participation in a world organisation. They were, I think rightly, convinced that if we got that, the danger was that the Americans would organise North America, 'Fortress' America, and leave the others to cope by themselves – to get along as best they could. That was a danger they saw. And therefore they thought that any kind of undue emphasis on *regional* organisation would end in that direction. And we saw their point of view, yes we did.
CHARLTON: Churchill's pretty unrepentant, though. After your being dumb-founded and complaining about his 'Morning Thoughts' from Adana, he broad-cast to the nation here in 1943 publicly. I'd just like to remind you of one or two of the things he said.
GLADWYN: What does he say?
CHARLTON: Well, he says this (remember that he's back from Casablanca and the 'unconditional surrender' meeting), and he talks publicly about this 'instrument of European government' that he wishes to create, and then he says this: 'It must eventually embrace all of Europe and all the main branches of the European family must some day be partners in it. Only through this will the glory of Europe rise again. We must achieve the largest common measure of the integrated life of Europe that is possible.'

You say the great issue was whether Churchill ever thought we should be part of this, but he clearly is using here, isn't he, what is to become the political rhetoric of the post-war years – words like 'integration', 'unity' and 'Europe rising again'?
GLADWYN: Well, I think he was never clear whether he wanted Russia in it, you see. Russia is after all part of Europe. Certainly the Ukraine is and Russia I suppose up to the Urals. Well, he always avoided that issue. Were the Russians going to come in or weren't they? Actually he never really came to a conclusion, never said that we ourselves would be part of this new Europe which would extend from Brest to Kiev or somewhere as far as we could make out. It wasn't clear how we were going to organise it. Wouldn't it be rather a menace to us if we were outside and they were all united, perhaps under the Germans?

CHARLTON: I know that you put your finger on that, saying that it was the flaw in the Churchill argument, but isn't it really apparent that Churchill has suspicions about the Russians as post-war partners which the Foreign Office are not prepared to share, and that he is therefore seeing the *need* for the West to organise itself politically?

GLADWYN: Well, I daresay that's possible. I wouldn't deny that. But from the point of view of trying to get a world organisation going, which we *had* to do, if only in order to get the Americans in, it wasn't a reasonable conception to put forward.

CHARLTON: I wonder why it is, though, that the Foreign Office acquiesces in this American view that Stalin and Russia will be partners with whom agreement is possible in organising the post-war world?

GLADWYN: Well, I must say I never myself thought it extremely likely. I thought it was a thing we had to aim for, but I never had any great hopes that it would actually come to be, myself. Only I thought that we had to do it, we had to go on an assumption and see. We couldn't be certain what would happen in Russia; there might have been a revolution in Russia for all we knew. Anything might have happened. But you had to provide for the possibility that they *would* come in, if only to get the Americans to come along.

CHARLTON: You see, by the end of 1944 we have the record showing Eden (apart from appearing to knock down Churchill's United states of Europe idea!) saying: 'Apart from the consideration that a unified continent might once again fall under the domination of a resurgent Germany, it is clear that the Soviet Union might regard any continental bloc as a threat to its own interests and it is extremely doubtful whether, especially in the post-war period, we would be able to work towards a United States of Europe in the *face of Soviet opposition. . . .*'

GLADWYN: Well, I think that's probably true. I understand that for that moment.

CHARLTON: But why do we take the view that nothing must be done to provoke the Russians?

GLADWYN: Oh, I don't know about that. Provoking the Russians I think probably is false argument. You can't really provoke the Russians. In the climate of opinion in 1943/4, when the Russians were saving us really from disaster, I should have thought that was a thing which would appeal to a good many people in this country for sentimental reasons, that's all.

WINSTON CHURCHILL'S 1943 broadcast was another of those swoops of intuition he had about the future. Europe had been deemed by him to be Britain's 'prime interest' and 'prime care', and he left the question of the relationship Britain itself would have to this new Europe unspecified. But he also asked this fundamental question of Britain itself. It was a question which was lost sight of, and which would not be fundamentally examined for another seventeen years and then by Harold Macmillan as Prime Minister, who was, as we remember, listening 'enthralled' that night in Alexander's camp in North Africa as Churchill spoke about the 'noble task of taking part in reviving the fertile genius and in restoring the true greatness of Europe'.

CHURCHILL: I have said enough I am sure to show you at least the outline, the mystery, the peril and, I will add, the splendour of this vast sphere of practical action into which we shall have to leap once the hideous spell of Nazi tyranny has been broken.

AND THEN there followed this.

CHURCHILL: Coming nearer home we shall have to consider at the same time how the inhabitants of this island are going to get their living at this stage in the world's story. Our foreign investments have been expended in the common cause. The British nation that has now once again saved the freedom of the world has grown great on cheap and abundant food. Had it not been for the free-trade policy of Victorian days our population would never have risen to the level of a great power and we might have gone down the drain with many other minor states to the disaster of the whole world. Abundant food has brought our forty-seven million Britons into the world. Here they are and they must find their living. It is absolutely certain that we shall have to grow a larger proportion of our food at home. . . .

'VICTORY AT ALL COSTS', Churchill had said. In that speech he was warning that the cost would be close to ruin. Albeit glorious ruin. By 1944 Churchill's views had become subordinate to those of Roosevelt in the formulation of strategy. For Britain itself bankruptcy was in sight, and vast debts were being incurred. Those under the unselfish American Act of Lend Lease were eventually waived by the terms of a radical political settlement with the Americans. Britain was committed by Roosevelt to the establishment of a new world order, to the elimination above all else of discrimination in trade and the ending of imperial preference. The latter was the commercial glue of Empire.

Franklin Roosevelt was a radical who was importantly dependent on the votes of the Left in the United States for support. He was someone upon whom the British position in India, in particular, and the British colonial system in general appeared to have much the same effect as the Rhondda had had on the Prince of Wales: 'Something must be done!'

JACOB: We used to think it was very odd; after all, we were allies and it was to their advantage as much as to ours that the British Empire existed and gave us a great deal of support. But they – Roosevelt, in particular, was determined, if he could avoid it, to prevent us going back into it. He would have liked to have stopped ourselves and the Dutch and the French ever getting back into South-East Asia, that sort of thing. I mean, he was quite 'anti' any sort of empire – except the American one.

CHARLTON: What do you remember of Churchill holding forth about this tremendous American challenge to something Churchill believes he is fighting for. 'I have not become the Queen's first minister', as he says some time later, 'in order to preside over the dissolution of the British Empire.'

JACOB: The British Empire. That's quite right and he resented it terribly. He thought that, in time, the Americans would come to realise this. But there is no doubt at all that from about the Teheran Conference onwards, or perhaps a little before, there was a change in the close connection between us and the Americans. It was Roosevelt's doing, of course. He was determined. He foresaw that after the war they would be only two big powers, the Americans and the Russians – and he was not prepared to do anything from then on which would annoy the Russians because he felt he could deal with Stalin and that he and Stalin would be able to settle everything comfortably after the war. This was particularly noticeable at Teheran and on all subsequent discussions and actions about Europe. For example, he wouldn't help the Poles, he gave way on all these things, you see, to the Russians, nor would he discuss things with us before going to meet the Russians. 'We mustn't gang up on the Russians.' Well what a ridiculous phrase! You have combined interests and if you don't do it, invariably the other chap puts a wedge between you and neither of you get what you want. But he was very strange in this way.

CHARLTON: How did you notice that Churchill himself saw the difference in the relationship between himself and Roosevelt from about 1943 onwards.

JACOB: I think the main thing was that it became apparent of course that Roosevelt was not prepared to accept any of our suggestions for the strategy of the war. From there on things like 'Anvil', the code-name for the landing in the south of France, which he thought was a complete waste of time when they ought to be pressing on through Italy and getting into Austria. I mean, he wanted to go on and seize Berlin and Prague and Vienna. He couldn't budge Roosevelt of course. Roosevelt was a dying man by then probably, but he couldn't budge him on the necessity to end the war in such a way that you achieved a certain amount of your political aims. Roosevelt seemed to regard war as something you finished as quickly as you could and then you scuttled away home. That is one of the things that upset Churchill. Things like the Poles were a very good example. I mean, after all here were we doing our utmost to try and save the Polish people and their government over here, and the closer the Russians got the worse it became. Then they finally stopped outside Warsaw and the rising took place in Warsaw and they sat there while the Germans crushed it. All those sort of things, he wouldn't help at all. He wouldn't really fight. At Yalta he was a dying man and it wasn't really worth talking about his actions at that point. I've never seen such a change in a man.

CHARLTON: What stands out for you in the exchanges between Churchill and Roosevelt over Europe?

JACOB: The fact that Churchill couldn't get the slightest response from Roosevelt about any of the problems in Europe.

CHARLTON: And why was that do you feel?

JACOB: Well, I have always thought it was mainly because Roosevelt didn't know anything about Europe.

WHILE THE PASSAGES from Churchill's broadcast in 1943 which have been quoted already hailed the turning of the tide after Montgomery's victory over Rommel in the desert, they also contained sentences full of foreboding about what would be Britain's destiny after the last victory would come, as even then the Prime Minister was emphatic it must. Churchill thought that Britain would very likely be impoverished. 'We have expended our foreign investments in the common cause' and 'coming nearer home we shall have to consider how the inhabitants of this island are to get their living' were forecasts of the end of the pre-war architecture and the days of 'cheap food' – in which, under imperial preference, the exports of British manufactures were exchanged for imports of agricultural produce from the great 'British farms abroad' in places like

Australia and New Zealand.

Sir Ian Jacob has said that it was perhaps a little before the Teheran Conference between Churchill, Roosevelt and Stalin in 1943 – and the Conference itself would leave no doubt at all – 'that there was a change in the close relationship between ourselves and the Americans'. After Teheran Stalin knew that he had found common ground with the American President on issues which divided them from the British. At Teheran Stalin had had confirmed to him by the President no less than this, that Roosevelt's policies involved the destruction of the British Empire.

And so Churchill's emphasis on 'Europe' as Britain's now 'prime interest' and 'prime care' – while it might not have made clear the extent to which Britain itself would be linked or comprised – cannot be divorced from this whole context in which the Prime Minister increasingly urged and pressed it. The record and the recollections of his closest associates leave small room for doubt that Churchill saw not just Europe prostrate but Britain reduced in status and dramatically diminished from her former reach and influence. It is the view of Sir John Colville who, like Sir Ian Jacob, worked in the closest and almost daily intimacy with Churchill in his wartime and his later government of the 1950s, that there was one development in particular which settled Churchill's convictions about Russian intentions and the need for a 'political Europe'.

It came almost at the same time as the Prime Minister was having to contemplate the impact of American prejudices and American policy on the future of the British Empire and the old Commonwealth.

COLVILLE: He believed profoundly in the benevolence of the American government and people, and thought that was something which was part of their natural inheritance and that one didn't need to be worried. I think the first time Churchill really became worried about American policy was when Roosevelt was a dying man and the State Department, with Byrnes and Stettinius and so on, reached the conclusion that the future lay in American friendship with the Soviet Union and not with the British Empire. Then, I think, Churchill did become alarmed. After all, at Yalta the Americans went and talked to the Russians about the future of Hong Kong, a British colony, without even consulting us! Well luckily Churchill didn't know that at the time. He only discovered it afterwards, but I think that atmosphere was one which did begin to worry him. When he (I didn't go to Yalta) but when he came back, I asked him how it was, I remember him saying, shaking his head from side to side broodingly and saying practically nothing, but he did say to me, 'The President is a dying man'. I think those words summed up really what he felt.

I mean, had it not been for the now absurd policy of allowing the Russians to occupy Berlin, Prague, Budapest when we could have got there before them, had it not been for the American refusal to allow Alexander to keep eight divisions [in Italy] which would have enabled us to go through the Ljubljana gap in Yugoslavia and take Vienna from the rear, the Iron Curtain, had it fallen, might have fallen a very, very, very long way further East.

CHARLTON: You say 'through the Ljubljana gap'. Is that what's referred to normally as the 'soft underbelly', Churchill's wish to attack through the Balkans?

COLVILLE: Well, he never talked about a Balkans landing. What he wanted to do was to keep the eight divisions. He had a frightful row with both the

President and General Marshall about it. He wanted to keep these eight crack American divisions which would have given Alexander just enough extra force – I mean he had quite a big army in Italy – but it would have given him the extra force to go through the Gothic Line, I think it was called, take Trieste and go right through the Ljubljana gap, cutting off eighteen German divisions who were fighting Tito's Partisans in Yugoslavia. That in itself would have been a coup, they'd have been cut off from their supplies. Then the idea was there would be a left hook by Alexander's victorious army which would take Vienna in the rear. If that had happened Budapest equally would, I think, have fallen to us. At that stage the war could have ended in the autumn of 1944 and there might well have been no Iron Curtain. You've also got to remember that, right up until Yalta and beyond but almost certainly up to Yalta, we did hope that the Russians were going to play ball over Poland and that there would be a free Polish government. Maybe, looking back, it was silly to think that, but we did believe it. I think Churchill certainly had hoped for it and believed it, and I think the Foreign Office did too.

CHARLTON: How does this square with Churchill's known 'history'? After all, he'd promoted the British intervention after the Revolution in the Soviet Union with the landings at Archangel. From your knowledge of how he thought was he not working for the consolidation of a western bloc against the Russians, no matter what the outcome?

COLVILLE: He began to get alarmed about the Russians. At the beginning, as you know, he said we've got to support the Russians, they're coming in, they're on our side, the one thing to do is to defeat Hitler. He said to me once, 'If Hitler were to invade Hell I'd at least make a favourable reference to the Devil in the House of Commons!' That's how he felt about it in the beginning, but as less and less did the Russians cooperate with us or show any signs of friendship, and as more and more we were getting some kind of indication of their imperialist designs, then I think Churchill became alarmed, and long before the Americans did. But I think the thing that *really* made him feel that the future was fraught with danger was when Stalin deliberately stopped the Russian armies short of Warsaw in order that the Polish Army might be exterminated by the Gestapo before the Russian troops got in. That was something he never forgave or forgot. It was an indication to him that Stalin was prepared to be entirely ruthless and to the extent of letting thousands of people be massacred.

CAN IT BE SAID therefore that the mounting aggregate of unshared opinions between the British and Americans has resulted in public opinion being too little aware, as the formulation of policy over Europe begins to evolve, of the deep differences between the British and the Americans. These differences which were constantly being underpinned by the enormous political figure of Churchill and his insistence that the 'special relationship' must be paramount. Ian Jacob thought not.

JACOB: I don't think they did us all that harm you know. They had to be convinced all the time that we weren't doing something nefarious by asking them to do this, that or the other. But they generally did come round and I think, taking it by and large, it was an extraordinarily happy relationship. I don't know any one which was better on any previous occasion. As the war went on the Americans became, of course, enormously more powerful than we were, culminating in 1944 and 1945, and you can imagine they naturally wanted their own way at that time. They had put out these enormous efforts, they spent vast sums of money and people, and they wanted some return on it naturally. And they weren't terribly interested in the things that we were bothered about, like saving the Poles, or doing something in Europe.

CHARLTON: What about where we were direct competitors and where our interests appear to have directly conflicted? There appears to have been towards the end of the war a rather sharp exchange over oil between Roosevelt and Churchill. Churchill wrote to Roosevelt saying the British were concerned because they'd heard the Americans wished to remove or to alter the British position in the Persian oilfields. Roosevelt wrote back accusing the British of 'trying to horn in' – they were the words he used in Saudi Arabia. And Churchill then responded, rather more in sorrow than in anger the tone seems, when he says to Roosevelt, 'You have the greatest navy, the greatest air force, you will have the greatest trade, you have all the gold. I do not believe Americans will wish to pursue vainglorious ambitions as well after the war.' Now was that a representative view, do you think, of the 'special relationship' towards the end of the war?

JACOB: Oh yes, undoubtedly. I think that as time went on Churchill found it more and more difficult to catch on to something solid. It was becoming rather hollow at times.

IN THOSE RATHER RUEFUL – they are among the last – personal exchanges which Churchill had with Roosevelt lies some of the first painful and practical awareness of a most unpalatable reality – the extent to which, victory notwithstanding, Britain's former freedom of action was now inexorably limited. If, as Sir Ian Jacob commented, the special relationship was becoming 'rather hollow' at times and Churchill was finding it 'more and more difficult to catch on to something solid', how do we know for a fact he now looked at the European dimension?

JACOB: He was also very emotionally tied to France. Why, it's hard to say. He constantly used to go there, of course. He used to paint in the south of France, and he was there a great deal in the First World War, particularly when he was Minister of Munitions. He kept it up between the wars, he was constantly going over there and seeing some of their generals and seeing how they were getting on. He had a great admiration for the French people. So I think that he was strongly torn, well not 'torn', but he was firmly attached to *both* sides of the Atlantic. He would have been very upset if France and Britain had become permanently estranged. He found General de Gaulle difficult, but he certainly wanted us to be *in* on any European organisation that was set up. He would have liked, he always did, he would have liked it to be set up in terms he would approve of.

CHARLTON: Which were?

JACOB: They would have to be terms in which Britain had a proper say, an effective one, and which would bring about the main idea which was to prevent the French and the Germans from ever going at each others' throats again.

CHARLTON: But, as you know, in that essay which he wrote in 1930 when he

first raised the concept of a United States of Europe he said that Britain, while 'with' the continent, was not 'of it'. Britain in other words belonged to no single continent but to them all. Would you say that now was still his view?
JACOB: I think, you know, this is one of the great difficulties we all have, and I feel very much in sympathy with Churchill over this, that on the one hand you feel you're certainly very closely part of Europe, on the other hand you've been all over the world and you've got the Americans and the Empire and the Commonwealth and all the rest of it. You therefore find it very difficult to attach yourself to Europe with the kind of singlemindedness that might be necessary. And I always rather sympathised with de Gaulle when he refused to have us in – do you remember? – because if you read what he said it makes sense. He said, 'You weren't European, you're much more concerned in the outer world and you weren't ready to come in'. I understood that. One always went into the EEC, I think, only with half one's mind. And I think Churchill, whether consciously or unconsciously, was in that same boat.

AS THE END of the war approached, Winston Churchill was ruminating upon the bleak prospect of a shrunken Britain under a staggering load of debts disguised as sterling balances. A burden so large that, merely to mitigate it, British exports would have had to be quadrupled. British policy-makers were also in pursuit, because of disagreements over high strategy in Europe and the commercial and political future of the British Empire, of what seemed to be a vanishing relationship with the Americans.

Churchill's remarkable life had spanned such personal experiences as the sabre charge of the 21st Lancers at Omdurman in 1898, and now in the 1940s he had lived to share the awesome initial decisions over the atomic bomb. The first, as it has been remarked, was a military metaphor which Homer would have recognised, the latter one which nearly all of previous history would have found incomprehensible. The atomic weapon became at once the new and ultimate determinant of the conduct of relations between states. Its significance was grasped by Churchill from the beginning. Therefore, in addition to what was regarded as the 'natural' connection between Britain and the United States – those ties of language, of culture, and of the inheritied institutions of parliamentary democracy – there was added, by the war's end, this overwhelming new factor. It dictated all immediate strategic choices, and was a new lens through which the perhaps growing disposition to think that Britain and Europe shared wholly common problems had now to be viewed.

JACOB: There was always at the back of his mind the bomb; which after all the Americans had manufactured and which we had taken a considerable hand in developing. For reasons of safety and all that it was actually developed in America. He felt that possession of this in some years would be of enormous importance. The British and the Americans in partnership and in conjunction should take advantage of the situation to secure a considerable peaceful future. He felt that this could not be exactly dictated, but he felt that we would be in such a strong position if we were closely allied to the Americans that nobody could stand against it.

In fact I remember hearing him, at a party he gave at Hyde Park Gate for Eisenhower and General Marshall at the time the Foreign Ministers were meeting here towards the end of 1945, saying that the Americans ought to take advantage of the present situation to *demand* certain concessions from Russia, and to say well you've jolly well *got* to make them, otherwise we're going to bomb you. Because, he said, otherwise in a few years' time you'll become the burdened donkey of the Russians. You see, he saw that, naturally, they would develop a bomb. He had no confidence whatever in their methods or objectives and he felt sure that unless the Americans acted firmly and decisively there was a grave risk that the others would get the upper hand.

CHARLTON: Can you remember what responses Eisenhower or Marshall made to that?

JACOB: I think they just smiled. They didn't make any response.

CHARLTON: From what you say he did fully grasp the strategic significance of the atomic bomb?

JACOB: Oh tremendously so. He knew about it all, of course, right from early in the war that we were working away on it. He came out of power just before it was going to be dropped, of course. At Potsdam Stalin had been informed. It appeared that Stalin either didn't realise the significance, or else was a very good actor. But Churchill certainly thought this gave the Allies, or the Americans and *ourselves*, as he was thinking, a tremendous pull in everything that was going to happen in the next two or three years.

AS THE ATOMIC ERA began, 'Lord we know what we are, but we know not what we may be' might be said to summarise some of the distractions and challenges which lay before British policy. It may be useful now to set down the principal, durable assumption and formulation upon which it had, up until this time, been based.

In what is regarded as one of the greatest of Britain's state papers, Sir Eyre Crowe of the Foreign Office had declared this to be the essence of Britain's foreign policy: 'Its general character', he noted in the course of an historic memorandum reviewing Anglo-German relations in 1907, 'is determined by the immutable conditions of her geographical situation on the ocean flank of Europe as an island state, with vast overseas colonies and dependencies, whose existence and survival as an independent community are inseperably bound up with the possession of a preponderant sea power . . . Britain is the neighbour of every country accessible by sea.'

Among the more obvious and remarkable testimonies to that sea power and its commanding reach was the existence, on the other side of the world, of the white population of British stock in Australia and New Zealand. Naval historians have paid great attention to the Battle of Jutland in the First World War as the emerging of the writing on the wall for that 'preponderant sea power'. But in a popular sense the symbolic destruction of British sea power came in 1942 with the fall of the great naval base at Singapore and the sinking of the British battleships *Prince of Wales* and *Repulse*, which had been sent to the Far East as a deterrent to Japanese adventure. Thereafter it was beyond the capacities of Britain as a nation state unilaterally to restore her former command of the seas.

It is surprising how relatively small was the impact of this event, psychologically at least, in Britain, where final victory helped to obscure it, and how great it was in Australia, where sharper and more far-reaching conclusions

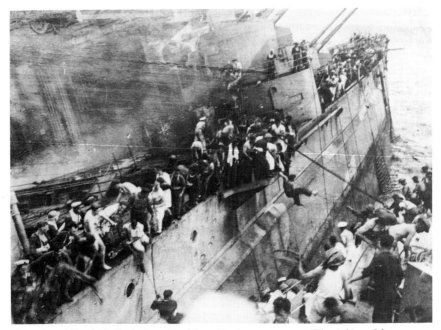

Nineveh and Tyre? Kipling's Recessional from Empire comes to pass. The sinking of the battleship Prince of Wales *(and* Repulse*) precedes the fall of Singapore, December 1941.*

were drawn. The acrimonious contemporary exchanges between Churchill and the Australian Prime Minister, John Curtin, were a portent of what would prove a lasting change.

Curtin went to an unprecedented length in writing a signed newspaper article within three weeks of the loss of Singapore in which he said: 'Without any inhibitions of any kind I make it quite clear that Australia looks to America, free of any pangs as to our traditional links with the United Kingdom. We know the problems the United Kingdom faces, but we know too that Australia can go and Britain can hang on.'

Thereafter Australia sought the long-term guarantees of the United States. It would be accompanied by the rather fast decline of Britain's former privileged commercial position. Overstretched even before the war, a whole political and economic system established by Britain overseas started to fall.

A former head of the diplomatic service, Lord Garner, has written an official history of the Commonwealth Office whose Permanent Under-Secretary he was in the 1960s.

GARNER: I think it was very different from all the other empires one knows in history. The biggest distinction was that the British empire was to a large extent an empire of settlement and not of subjugation. I think another thing that marked it apart was the fact that we'd lost the American colonies. We learned a lesson from that, in fact we never forgot. We applied it quite rapidly in Canada, namely that we didn't expect our colonies, particularly those of settlement, to remain permanently under our jurisdiction. It was for us to lead them on to their own independence and nationhood. I've always regretted myself that Indian independence didn't come about a little bit earlier. I think that but for the war it might well have done. But I do think that the grant of independence to India, to this huge subcontinent, was a major achievement, and the fact that both India and Pakistan wanted then to retain the benefits of the Commonwealth association and showed such extraordinarily friendly feelings towards Britain was, I think, something quite special.

I think both the French and the Dutch empires, to name those two specifically, were very centralised in administration. The British way had never been that. We always devolved a substantial amount of authority. Partnership was the key word we were always using and consultation was the main method of procedure. The fact is that we did have extraordinarily close links through our own high commissioners in Commonwealth countries and theirs in ours, through prime ministers' meetings and finance ministers' meetings. There were quite astonishingly close links permanently maintained which I don't think ever happened on an empire-wide basis in any other empire. I always thought the one big stumbling block between Churchill and Roosevelt was precisely on this question of colonialism. I don't think Americans in general – and I married one so I'm free to say this – understood the British colonial system at all. They equated it with what they thought were the misdeeds of George III.

CHARLTON: Why, if as you say the British felt that they'd learnt the lesson of the American revolution, was it not possible to get this across to the Americans?

GARNER: I don't know why we never got it across. The plain fact was that when I travelled in America I was frequently asked what was the rate of taxation the Canadians, for example, paid to Britain! There is a deep inbuilt prejudice among many Americans and some of the most eminent – John Foster Dulles was another – against the whole colonial system as perpetrated, especially, by the British.

CHARLTON: How then did we see the implications of how the Americans felt for the cohesion of the Commonwealth?

GARNER: I think this is putting too much importance on the Americans. I think we had our thoughts about the cohesion of the Commonwealth. Perhaps I just ought to say this, because I think it is not easy for people in the present day and age to understand this. At the end of the war, and certainly after 1947, we did have a very genuine belief in the Commonwealth as something that was valuable not only to us, not only to other members of the Commonwealth, but we did genuinely regard it as an illustration of how a new form of international relationship could be peacefully carried out.

CHARLTON: But what inferences did we draw from the obvious change in the balance of power. We had been a great strategic sea power – Commonwealth and Empire existed because of the Royal Navy. The sinking of the *Prince of Wales* and *Repulse* and the fall of Singapore signalled the end of British naval supremacy in the global sense and has had a profound political effect throughout Asia. What did we deduce from that change in the balance?

GARNER: I think probably we didn't draw enough inferences. We did still see ourselves in 1945 as a great power. And this I think was an illusion – that we did do so. And I suppose there was some reason for our doing it. After all, we had won the war, were the only country that was in it from beginning to end; we had survived, contrary to all expectation, the Hitler onslaught; and we did see ourselves as a great power, allied, it's true, to the United States. But don't forget, we were one of the three, or one of the two to begin with, nuclear powers in the world. We saw ourselves as entitled to a seat at the top of the table, and we continued to operate as if this were true, and as if we hadn't transferred powers in India. Until 1967 we still maintained our forces in the Middle East and in the Far East and insisted on our world role. It took a very long time for those lessons to sink in.

CHARLTON: But the proposition, trade and the flag? If the flag doesn't fly, could we have the trading position that we had under the Empire?

GARNER: When we did withdraw, of course we argued the reverse. We argued – and I was one of those who did so – that the withdrawal of military presence didn't mean the absence of British presence, and that we could make our contribution in ways other than those of military – by economic aid, by information and by trade.

CHARLTON: But while one can understand a reluctance to draw what would have been such uncomfortable conclusions, it is surely puzzling that above all a *maritime* power saw no need for a fresh analysis or reappraisal of its world position, given that the fall of Singapore and the sinking of the battleships had sounded the death knell for British supremacy at sea.

GARNER: But *we* weren't put at risk. I mean we in London here. We'd had the Hitler bombs and all. We weren't put at risk personally, individually, selfishly by the loss of two battleships. Australia was.

CHARLTON: The British constantly make use, in their subsequent arguments over Europe, that we cannot join these things that you propose in Europe because the Commonwealth wouldn't like it, while the Commonwealth was drawing its own conclusions and moving into new and more diverse patterns of trade and alliance anyway.

GARNER: We didn't think it was in British interests to take the plunge. We may have used Commonwealth arguments as an argument in our negotiations. I don't think it was a real cause at all. That wasn't the cause of our attitude. The basis of our attitude was – in the late 1940s and the 1950s – we didn't want to go in, we didn't see it to our advantage to go in: we didn't really particularly *want* to be associated with this sort of grouping.

CHARLTON: And the Commonwealth argument was used as a prop in support for that, but not the reason?

GARNER: No, I don't think it was the reason. I don't know that it was specially used. We always said we couldn't join a closed bloc. And the sort of alternatives we thought of in the 1950s were a Free Trade Area, which of course would exclude agriculture.

CHARLTON: What had the earlier discussions, near the end of the war and shortly after, with the Commonwealth leaders, with the Dominion Prime Ministers, revealed. After all they meet the British Prime Minister fairly regularly. What had those discussions with the Commonwealth leaders shown us when it came to talking with them and discussing the establishment of a new world order? The Americans, for example, wanted world institutions. Churchill was arguing for regional councils. The Commonwealth appears to have been opposed to that.

GARNER: The Commonwealth were very opposed to regional councils for two very obvious reasons, I think. The first reason they would have objected to was that it might have been held as committing them to some imperial burden they didn't want. None of them really liked the idea of an individual part of the Commonwealth in a particular area accepting the responsibilities for the Commonwealth on that area. None of them wanted that. The second objection, I think, was that – and New Zealand put this very forcibly and I remember Peter Fraser taking this line at one of the Prime Ministers' meetings – this was way back in 1944, I think – that he didn't want to be held down to just a Regional Council. He wanted to have a say in the affairs of the whole world. After all, New Zealand was interested in the whole world. New Zealand had always fought in the Middle East and in Europe, not in the Far East. He objected very strongly to limiting individual countries to their particular area.

AS VICTORY APPROACHED, the changing relationships of Britain with her overseas Empire and Commonwealth had been made disconcertingly apparent. Yet closer to home, in Western Europe, Britain had never been in such a strong position politically. The prestige of Britain under Churchill was very great, he was the figurehead of liberation. Churchill was still sticking to his proposal for a Council of Europe leading to a United States of Europe. Eden and the Foreign Office thought this impractical, specifically because there was no chance of the Russians agreeing to it, since they would see it as restoring power to Germany, and because it might encourage America to go home and return to isolationism. Throughout the war London had been the refuge of all the governments in exile from Hitler's conquests in Europe. King Haakon of Norway recalled being asked by the receptionist in the BBC during the war, 'And which King are you Sir?'

By 1944 that older British constituency (older in historical terms than the newer ones of Empire and Commonwealth), the smaller states of Western Europe, were showing a particular interest in Churchill's ideas. They wished to know the British government's views and the future policy of Great Britain in Europe. The Norwegian, the Dutch and, in particular, the Belgian Foreign Minister, Paul-Henri Spaak, told Eden that their countries had learned a bitter lesson in 1940 and were determined to collaborate in future with the United Kingdom. Spaak's son Fernand, who recently served as the Ambassador for the European Communities in the United States, is our witness for his father's time in London in 1944.

SPAAK: There are a few things one can say about that period, and the first one, perhaps the most important one, is the sense of very deep solidarity that existed between these people and the British. There they were in London, sharing the same dangers, the same hopes. It is, I think, a unique experience for governments to be in such a relationship with another government. Second thing one can say is that they had leisure, they could think about the future, having no immediate responsibility, no day-to-day responsibilities to meet; they could think about the future. And that's what they did. And thirdly, they were under the pressure of vested interests. They were relatively free to look at the future as they thought it should be reorganised. Those three together could have created something quite extraordinary.

CHARLTON: How far, for example, did your father think it would be possible to go in reaching an understanding with Britain? After all, while the British had intervened on the Continent of Europe often in war, in Churchill's words they considered themselves 'with it' but not 'of it', that is detached and apart. Given that long history and the fact, the reality of Commonwealth and Empire, what do you believe your father thought was possible to do with the British?

SPAAK: You know, I think my father, like most European leaders in exile in London, had lost faith in the nation state because it had failed. This is really the main element that explains the appeal of the European Union idea after the Second World War. The fact that Britain was in a different position, that they were winning the war, and finally they won the war, therefore this feeling, shared by most Europeans, was not a British feeling.

CHARLTON: Would you say that beyond the emotional and sentimental feeling of gratitude to Britain as host in wartime and for prosecuting the war against Hitler, there is, too, a reasoned feeling, an agreement among, say, the Belgians and the Dutch, by Norway, that Britain is acceptable and is wanted as a *leader* on the Continent of Europe, that British leadership would have been acceptable?

SPAAK: There is no doubt. We are now in 1943, 1944. The danger is Germany and these countries are looking towards Britain after the war as a protection against resurgent Germany. In those days the motivation 'Germany' was much stronger than the motivation 'Soviet Union', which didn't exist yet.

CHARLTON: Yes, and that doesn't come until the post-war settlement collapses.

SPAAK: Absolutely.

CHARLTON: ... in 1947, and then Stalin becomes in effect a substitute for Hitler in reinforcing the same ideas.

SPAAK: Exactly.

PAUL-HENRI SPAAK, as the record of his talks in London in 1944 with Anthony Eden shows, wanted a western bloc, including Britain. He told Eden that the Belgians and Dutch had determined to form a Customs Union. He told Eden also that he thought the British 'had not yet realised how much all the countries of Western Europe looked to them', although they 'sometimes wished the British would state more clearly their views'.

The essence of Eden's position in late 1944 was contained in a long reply he wrote to a despatch from a most senior and influential diplomat, Duff Cooper, as part of the debate within the Foreign Office over future policy. Duff Cooper was at this time in Algiers as the British representative with the French. His despatch explicitly called for the creation of a Western European grouping as a precautionary measure against a Russian attempt at Continental domination. It was given full consideration and circulated to the War Cabinet. Eden disagreed with it fundamentally. His concern was that it would increase the danger Duff Cooper pointed to, of an expansionist Russia, rather than diminish it. Eden said further he himself was not a supporter of the concept of spheres of influence. 'Were we to do so,' the Foreign Secretary thought, 'we should be throwing away the considerable chances of the USSR pursuing a policy of collaboration after the War. More than that, we should be risking the deployment against us in Europe of Russia's immense capacity for power politics and disruption.'

Eden's private secretary in the Foreign Office at the time of the first discussions with the Belgian Foreign Minister and other European politicians in London about the post-war order was Sir Guy Millard.

The allied governments go back to Europe from exile in London after the war: Paul-Henri Spaak, the Belgian Foreign Minister.

MILLARD: Well, I think you have to remember that our historical experience had been quite different to that of these Governments. They'd been over-run, in some cases defeated, forced into exile, they were a kind of appendage; they had no real support, no real constituency in their own countries. They'd been elected at one time but they were forced into exile and they were no longer in contact with their electorates.

CHARLTON: Do you think, from what you say, that Eden wrote them off – I mean, however nice it was to have them?

MILLARD: No, I don't think he wrote them off at all, but I think it was generally accepted at that time that when these Governments returned from exile they'd naturally have to make contact again with their own people and that there would have to be another electoral process.

CHARLTON: You see, we know that as early as 1941 Spaak had written to a Conservative MP in this country saying this: 'After the war Europe will be glad to unite behind Britain's victorious leadership. If Britain fails to recognise her duty in Europe, if she does not pursue a continental policy which makes her a strong leader in Europe, she must expect to be rapidly deprived of the fruits of her present efforts.' Three years later, in 1944, Spaak comes to Eden and presses him to declare his intentions about Britain's role in Post-War Europe. He wants Britain to lead in Western Europe. How do you remember that Eden thought of, or dealt with this initiative from Spaak, this opportunity, and invitation, for an initiative by the British?

MILLARD: I think that those words of Spaak which you quoted in 1941 were certainly very prophetic words. I haven't the slightest doubt that, had we given this lead in Europe after 1945, Europe could have been organised under our leadership in such a way as to provide a much more satisfactory framework for European unity than the one which we have today.

CHARLTON: At this time, when Eden eventually says no to Spaak – that Britain doesn't see this is the time to form any sort of regional organisation in Western Europe – on what basis does he take that decision? He turns Spaak down flat. I'm just wondering what you remember of that initiative?

MILLARD: Frankly I don't remember anything about it. I think probably at that time it was regarded as looking too far ahead, there were too many day-to-day preoccupations, too many urgent problems about the post-war administration of Germany, the formation of the United Nations, relations with the Soviet Union, all that. I think that it was very difficult at that time for politicians to address themselves to questions which seemed to be so far ahead, even if they weren't really as far ahead as we thought. I think perhaps Spaak was a man of great imagination, and great eloquence. He was also regarded in London as a bit of a visionary. If he was a visionary, well he was right, his vision was very often a true one, but all the same I think at that time, preoccupied as we were with finishing the war successfully and the immediate post-war problems, that it was thought to be looking too far ahead, all these rather vague notions about the future of Europe and so on. People didn't *want* to look ahead as far as that.

No doubt we were wrong. I think we missed a great historical opportunity, of course, but had we given a lead in Europe at that time, with the immense prestige which we then had at the end of the war, then I think that Europe would have organised itself around us and perhaps the shape of European union would have been a more satisfactory one, at least from our point of view, than it is today.

IT IS IMPORTANT, I think, not to quit the wartime arena without recalling that the most dramatic ideas yet formulated about European union had, a little earlier, received a most remarkable exposure and high consideration. Today, forty years have passed since, on 16 June 1940, with Hitler marching down all the roads of France, Churchill offered France *union* with Britain in a last-minute effort to keep her in war against Germany. The essential ingredients of this extraordinary moment were that France and Britain should fight on as one country. There would be a joint cabinet, a joint meeting of the two Parliaments or a single Parliament. But whatever the methods the 'indispensable condition for any hope of victory for the two is the real, complete, immediate, and enduring unity of the two countries acting in all things as one, without regard to separate interests'.

On 16 June Sir Robert Vansittart of the Foreign Office, General de Gaulle, and Jean Monnet sat down in London to draft those words and the declaration of Union. It was sent by de Gaulle to the French Prime Minister Paul Reynaud. But it was too late. The French government collapsed and France surrendered to the German armies. The architect of this proposal, which won the support of Churchill and of the British cabinet, was Jean Monnet. Monnet was in London as chairman of the Anglo-French coordinating committee and, as such, was directly responsible to both Churchill and Reynaud.

It was Monnet's ideas which subsequently were to resonate so effectively in post-war Europe. He succeeded in having them accepted as the path to practical action and they became the principal strand of thinking about unity in Europe in the vital decade of the 1950s when Britain stood aside and the Coal and Steel Community was formed. Those ideas had, as their fundament, the ceding of national sovereignty, and were those which Britain, after the war, tried unsuccessfully to deflect and contain.

In 1940, at the first moment of vaulting departure from convention on the part of ancient nation states, our principal witness for what took place is Sir John Colville.

COLVILLE: Yes, I do remember it very well indeed. It was a 24-hour wonder or a 48-hour wonder. It started, funnily enough, as far as Churchill was concerned with René Pleven (who was Monnet's assistant in London) going to talk to David Margesson, who was the conservative Chief Whip, and putting this idea that possibly the collapse of France might be averted by Union between England and France. It came to Churchill in a roundabout way. Margesson went to see Neville Chamberlain, who was Lord President of the Council in Churchill's government. Chamberlain started by being very sceptical but after a bit was rather impressed by the idea and agreed to go and mention it to Churchill. He went downstairs from No. 11 to No. 10 and told Churchill about it. Churchill was polite but not particularly interested. What he was interested in was saving the French fleet at all costs. However, he paid attention. Then we went off to Chequers, I remember. All sorts of things were going on in London over this idea of unity but it wasn't really brought again into the Prime Minister's thoughts until we came up on the Sunday morning from Chequers. Churchill had asked de Gaulle to luncheon at Chequers, and because of all this sudden excitement all that was cancelled and we all went up to London, and Churchill had lunch with de Gaulle and one or two others at the Carlton Club. And a whole idea was put forward and everybody became wildly enthusiastic, including de Gaulle, because they thought this would stop the otherwise inevit-able drift of the French government towards a separate peace with Germany and towards a take-over by Pétain and Weygand. It was this hope that inspired the interest. So much so that Churchill rang up Reynaud, and so did de Gaulle, and I was one of the people who was going with him, a cruiser was ordered and we got as far as Waterloo to set off and see Reynaud at sea, off Brittany I think it was, in order to put the whole thing on the map. But of course it was turned down flat by Reynaud's government who thought it was a device for turning France into a British Dominion.

It was a very short-term thing. It was a marvellous idea and I have never seen such enthusiasm. I remember one small thing. Just as we were setting off for Waterloo, the Cabinet having unanimously agreed to it, somebody said, 'But my goodness, what about the King? He's suddenly going to find himself King of France as well as King of England, the fleur de lys will have to be put back in the Royal Standard.' So Neville Chamberlain went off to Buckingham Palace to explain to His Majesty what was proposed. The King, I think, was rather sceptical, and quite rightly so as it turned out.

CHARLTON: Did Churchill see this purely as a tactical device for the moment, or was he moved by the rather profound implications of something which was, of course, visited upon this country again as serious politics after the war?

COLVILLE: Well, he said to me at the time, if we can bring this off it will stave off the collapse, and of course it would have meant the French going on fighting for North Africa. It would have meant all the people in Morocco and Algeria fighting on, and it would have been a tremendous coup. I think that is what he was thinking of primarily. But on the other hand the eventual effect was something that was fascinating, and he did say this is going to need a great deal of working out afterwards. And indeed it would have.

CHARLTON: Odd, though, to find de Gaulle an enthusiastic supporter of supra-national ideas when of course he was so vigorously and effectively opposed to them later in post-war Europe?

COLVILLE: Well, of course the interesting thing about that to me is that de Gaulle and Churchill had very comparable ideas about Europe. They both believed quite strongly in L'Europe des Patries. They were neither of them Federalists.

BUT FOR JEAN MONNET, as we shall see, these ideas never lost their validity. On 13 April 1945, the day after Roosevelt died, the State Department in Washington placed on the desk of the new President, Harry Truman, a memorandum headed 'Special information for the President'. It said this: 'The British long for security but are deeply conscious of their decline from a leading position to that of the junior partner of the Big Three and are anxious to buttress their position vis-à-vis the United States both through exerting leadership over the countries of Western Europe and through knitting the Commonwealth more closely together.'

Churchill's thinking was based on the presumption that Europe was already irrevocably divided between East and West. It is clear that in contemplating a United States of Europe the unity he wished to promote called for the inclusion of Germany. But in August 1945 Churchill was deracinated by the result of the General Election. Although he lost any direct political power and had no responsibility for policy, his prestige, and his influence on the new political sentiments which were then stirring in Western Europe, remained very great. In 1946 he made two great speeches which still stand, landmarks of the time. One was the corollary of the other.

In his 'Iron Curtain' speech at Fulton, Missouri, in January 1946 he insisted that Russian ambitions had to be countered and that the division of Europe was a reality which must be faced. The unwillingness to accept this verdict may be gauged from the fact that a motion of censure was put down against him in the House of Commons. Then, in September 1946, he deliberately chose Switzerland, with its long history of reconciliation of different languages and peoples, to raise in his speech at the University of Zurich a more direct and more emotional appeal for a United States of Europe in the West. It was this speech which is credited with doing so much to arouse and promote on the continent the movement towards European unity. It set an objective and it altered a whole climate.

CHURCHILL: I am now going to say something that will astonish you. The first step in the re-creation of the European family must be a partnership between France and Germany. In this way only can France recover the moral and cultural leadership of Europe. There can be no revival of Europe without a

'I am now going to say something which will astonish you.' Churchill chooses Switzerland, which keeps in harmony the fratricidal aptitudes of European nationalities, to deliver his famous call for a United States of Europe, Zurich 1946.

spiritually great Germany ... We must re-create the European family in a regional structure called, it may be, the United States of Europe. And the first practical step would be to form a Council of Europe.

IN ITS REPORT of the Zurich speech, *The Times* noted familiar Churchillian characteristics, that there was 'imagination ready to overleap caution and convention'. That he was 'unafraid to startle the world with new and, as many must find them, outrageous propositions'. Above all, *The Times* thought that British policy 'could not yet afford to despair of avoiding the division of Europe' and believed that France would not tolerate, even from Churchill, the suggestion that the first step in the re-creation of the European family must be a partnership between France and Germany.

The author of those leading articles in *The Times*, as Churchill began to play an unofficial role for Britain for leadership of Europe, would soon resume a diplomatic career in the Foreign Office, and, indeed, many years later would have charge of Britain's negotiations under Edward Heath as Prime Minister to enter the European Community. He was Con O'Neill.

O'NEILL: Well, it so happens that I *was* writing leaders for *The Times* at the time of Churchill's two – I think two – earliest major speeches on this subject: that was his speech in Zurich in September 1946, and his speech here in London at the Albert Hall in May 1947. I've looked up the leaders I then wrote and they're consistent with what I was writing about throughout my period with *The Times*, namely that it was far too early to abandon hope of establishing satisfactorily with the Russians a single world and a single control, as it were, to sort out post-war problems and live in peace and harmony together on a world-wide basis. I was preaching all the time that 'we mustn't prematurely abandon hope of being able to work with the Russians, and we mustn't rush into Western European institutions which would be divisive'. So that was really the main line I took about Churchill's speeches in Zurich and London. But at the same time I did say that this was the road we would have to travel, if the effort to get on with the Russians and agree with the Russians and work together with the Russians were to fail – and, indeed, I thought it might.

I might perhaps quote a passage from the leader I wrote on 15 May 1947: 'Advocates of a United Europe, which in present circumstances can only mean a united *Western* Europe, must acknowledge that Western Europe is not united in sentiment and therefore cannot be united in structure. This doesn't condemn that advocacy. On the contrary, it favours it. Their aim might, in certain circumstances, become prudent; their task is to make it acceptable if those circumstances should ever arise. At present it is not, both because most moderate opinion in Western Europe thinks it premature, and because a great deal of less detached opinion thinks it wrong. Whether the malaise which now divides Western society will prove to be passing or profound, only time can show, but a premature attempt by governments to force union on Europe, before it is wanted, can only make divisions deeper. And such an attempt will remain premature till the Western world is convinced by even more persuasive evidence than Russia over the last two years has been rash enough to offer it, that the One World ideal must be abandoned as impracticable.' You see the style of *The Times* leaders which afflicts everybody who finds himself obliged to write them!

CHARLTON: I just wonder about what seems to be this essential conflict between Churchill and the Foreign Office. Churchill's ideas are often dismissed by the Foreign Office as 'romantic and impractical'; on the other hand, if you look for a voice on the British side in Europe, which is reflecting the stirrings and the sentiments and the passions which lie behind this move towards unity in Western Europe – that Western Europe is a civilisation and an entity which must defend itself – it is Churchill who is echoing those sentiments.

O'NEILL: I entirely agree with you. What he did in those speeches and other speeches and actions was enormously important. But let's not suppose that he was going further than he was. I don't think Churchill thought for a moment that this country, that Britain would be part of his United Europe. It was for the French, it was for the Germans, for the Italians, for the Belgians, the Dutch; but not for us. Equally, I don't think he thought for a moment – whether we were in it or not – that it should be an organisation of constitutional, legal and treaty obligation. That is why what Churchill launched in 1946 led up not to the European Community. It led down quite a different road. It led to the Council of Europe – still in existence, still useful, but no longer since the foundation of the Community right back in 1950 and 1957, no longer enormously important.

SO IT WAS THAT *The Times* and Sir Con O'Neill delivered what was also the sceptical national verdict upon Churchill's European enthusiasms immediately after the war. Not for the first time Winston Churchill was ahead of his time. 'Ideas are born as the sparks fly upward. They die of their own weakness.' This

Churchill seated, Zurich, September 1946.

one did not. His Zurich speech of 1946 lit a fire which would not be put out. As far as Europe was concerned Churchill had all the ideas of the future. Britain had all the hesitations of the present. Later it would be shown that he had some of them too.

With Churchill out of power and office the great cadences and rousing flourishes of the old leader gave way to the more punctilious accents of Clement Attlee and the new government, and Britain itself fell to greater introspection. As we follow the long course of the many and various watersheds for Britain's European policy, we shall see in later chapters why it was that Churchill, when he had the chance in the 1950s, hesitated to include Britain in the new unity developing on the continent which, by his eloquence and advocacy, he had done so much to promote. And why most importantly of all, as today it must be seen, Britain passed up the invitation to reconsider the whole nature of European Union at Messina in 1955 and become a founder member of the Common Market – a story Lord Butler will reveal for the first time. But that Becher's Brook for our diplomacy lies, at this stage, some way off.

With Churchill gone in 1945, it now fell to the other great natural leader that wartime Britain produced to deal with this emerging question of the British and Europe – Ernest Bevin.

2

Bevin at
Victoria Station[1] – 1

IN THE HANDFUL of years which followed the ending of the Second World War the old concept of Europe was almost entirely altered. Half of it entered into captivity. All of it found that a former freedom of action was diminished. In the terrible quiet which follows battle a demoralising new awareness formed. 'The parent continent of modern nations and of civilisation,' as Churchill had described it in his remarkable minute to Anthony Eden in 1942, had succeeded through its latest exhausting war only in summoning into existence on either side of it the new Colossi of East and West – the 'Super' Powers.

The British prepared themselves for the liquidation of their global inheritance. Britain was about to divest herself, and to be divested, of her Empire; and hardly any other empire in history cleared the way so thoroughly for its own eclipse. In that small time measured from Victory to the Schuman Plan for the Coal and Steel Community in 1950 – the beginning of six-power federation – all of Western Europe became, as Churchill predicted in the broadcast he delivered in 1943 about the need for European integration, 'a vast sphere of practical action'.

During this time Britain was invited to assume the leadership of Europe in determining the range and compass of Churchill's rallying cry, 'Europe Unite'. Of critical importance in these years was the fact that the concepts of integration quickly came to enjoy the radical support of the Americans. In Britain the particular emphasis and urgency with which Churchill had invested the idea of united Europe dwindled with the change in power after the general election of 1945. Churchill's personal dream was rooted, although not wholly so, in an assumption to which neither the Foreign Office nor the Americans were yet willing to subscribe – that it wasn't going to be possible to work with the Russians for common objectives, and that the division in Europe was a fait accompli.

Nonetheless it was a wide array of the bleakest prospects which devolved upon the first Labour government to have an overall majority in the House of Commons. Labour had a mandate to implement radical social reform at home – the unfinished business of the 1930s – unfinished because of the downfall of Ramsay Macdonald. Inevitably it was a government of a more inward-looking disposition. It did not intend to be deflected from its task by unprofitable foreign entanglements or preoccupations. The whole tone of voice of Britain changed.

In the field of foreign policy the voice was Ernest Bevin's, down to earth and

[1] 'Diplomats asked me in London what the aim of my foreign policy really was. And I said, to go down to Victoria Station, get a railway ticket and go where the Hell I liked without a passport or anything else!' – Ernest Bevin.

unafraid, conveying in his public utterances a human warmth and a muscular common sense. One public occasion in particular stayed in many memories as Europe began to close down in the first obstructions, intimidations, and constraints of the Cold War.

BEVIN: If you want to help mellow and soften this position between Russia and Great Britain, the greatest enemies to friendship are the Russian supporters in this country and always has (sic) been ... I want to grapple with the whole problem of passports and visas. Diplomats asked me in London what the aim of my foreign policy really was. And I said, to go down to Victoria Station, get a railway ticket and go where the Hell I liked without a passport or anything else. . . .

ERNEST BEVIN'S POPULARITY with the Foreign Office, and the affection in which he was clearly held by its officials, is universally attested. The warmth of their relationship was reinforced, in small part no doubt, because this new partnership returned to the Foreign Office the principal authority over the conduct and directions of foreign policy. It reversed the situation in the Churchill administration where the Prime Minister himself had been the dominant figure. In the new Labour government Bevin's bulk was so large that Attlee never really stood against it.

Because the Foreign Office had been cool, and frequently reached out its hand in restraint of Churchill's enthusiasms for some new organic unity among the Europeans, the relationship between Bevin and his senior advisers is therefore of particular interest when it comes to the formulation of official attitudes over Europe. If Bevin was less inspired than Churchill, more plodding, he was clearly welcomed as being innately more sound and less disposed to incautious adventure.

Lord Gladwyn, then Gladwyn Jebb, had a major role and influence inside the Foreign Office upon early post-war planning. He drafted and worked out with his American counterparts much of the architecture of the post-war settlement and the new 'world' institutions like the United Nations. It was there in the early 1950s that he became something of a 'world' personality in his own right during his almost daily adversarial confrontations and skirmishes with the Soviet Union's representatives at the onset of the Cold War.

This is how Lord Gladwyn, who went to Eton and Magdalen, recalled, just after Bevin had become Foreign Secretary with the change of government, that the great trade unionist who had been raised in rural poverty sent for him.

GLADWYN: I was in Potsdam at the moment when the changeover came. I didn't see Uncle Ernie at first, saw him at a distance, that's all. I knew Attlee as a matter of fact before. I'd worked with him and he was a friend of mine, so he asked me to dinner the first night he arrived. He didn't know anybody. He was a charming man, Attlee, you know, and incidentally I discovered that his favourite work was Sorel's *Réflexions sur la Violence* – he was philosophically inclined.

Then, I came back and was labouring away in Church House, because I was the Secretary General of the Preparatory Commission of the United Nations and the first Assembly was going to meet the following January. When Uncle Ernie came into the Foreign Office, after coming back from Potsdam, he'd heard that a young man from the Foreign Office, whom he'd never heard any-

Ernest Bevin. Revered in the Foreign Office, compared there with Cardinal Wolsey as 'one of our greatest foreign secretaries'. (Standing behind Bevin, as the organisation to administer the Marshall Plan is created, is third from the left, Sir Frank Roberts).

thing about, was organising this very important work, you see, and he was very suspicious! He summoned me to come along and not unnaturally I did. I arrived in this huge room at the Foreign Office and he sort of glowered at me and said, 'Sit down', and I sat down. He didn't say anything for a moment and then he said, 'Must be kind of queer for a chap like you to see a chap like me sitting in a chair like this?' I had the sense to say nothing, I sort of smiled amiably and let him go on. He was rather nettled by this and he said, 'Ain't never 'appened before in history'. So I said, 'I'm sorry to contradict you, Secretary of State, in the first words I utter in your presence, but you are wrong.' He said, ''Ow do you mean that?' 'Well', I said, 'it was a long time ago, about 400 years or more, that there was a young fellow and he was of just as humble an origin as you were. I think he was a butcher's boy actually at Ipswich, and he became one of the greatest of our Foreign Secretaries; in the end he became a Cardinal, too. His name was Tom Wolsey. And furthermore I see that, yes, he looked rather like you', I said. And Uncle Ernie said, 'My God, I never thought of that!' And after that I could do no wrong with Uncle Ernie. He appointed me as adviser for the Peace Treaty and I became, in a sense, his principal political adviser.

CHARLTON: I've seen Bevin's writing on Foreign Office papers, making comments and initialling things in the margins. His handwriting seems not just almost unintelligible but practically illiterate?

GLADWYN: Well, he could hardly write and so he *couldn't* write anything very much. But he was an extremely astute man, frightfully intelligent naturally. He was a great realist and he knew also whom to trust and who was talking nonsense and who was not. His method of work was to summon people up to his room and go around them. People said one thing or another, and then he used to get a conclusion from that and sum up, and that was a very good way of doing it, in fact. Uncle Ernie was a very, very clever man. Of course he was the 'Dockers' QC' and that kind of thing. He could speak beautifully and he could marshal his thoughts. He was very, very able. But he couldn't write. He could read, but not write, yes.

CHARLTON: So I think this whole relationship between the Foreign Office and Bevin is an interesting one. You all obviously formed a deep affection for 'Uncle Ernie', and a more cynical age of course is likely, I think, to suggest. . .

GLADWYN: That we nobbled him?

CHARLTON: Yes. That you nobbled him.

GLADWYN: Well, I don't think I nobbled Uncle Ernie because I think he had very good views. He gradually got more fed up with the Russians and I thought he was quite right. And he got other advice. No, I don't think we nobbled him at all. He was a very powerful figure. He had all kinds of awful prejudices. As you know, he was not exactly pro-Jewish and he had strange sorts of feelings about things. I remember once he took me to a TUC conference, very odd for a Foreign Office official to come to a TUC conference, at Southport. We went up in the train with 'Flo' – Flo was his wife, you know. We went up there in a first-class, corridored carriage, and it was very full. People went up and down the corridor and there was a Catholic priest who went up and down in a cassock. Whenever the Catholic priest came by Uncle Ernie sort of crossed his fingers. Aunt Flo looked daggers and said 'Black Crows', you know, as if they were sort of bad luck. He was a very, very superstitious man! But he was an extraordinarily powerful figure. He was such a powerful figure that he couldn't be ignored. With him you could not be overruled at No. 10, and therefore he had complete command of a situation. He could do what he liked. Attlee was sometimes rather nervous about his policies but he could not intervene. No. 10 had no role when Uncle Ernie was there. Foreign policy was entirely run by him really.

IN 1945, WHILE he was still Foreign Secretary, Anthony Eden had declared, 'Our foreign policy is a wreck'. The probability, he noted in his diary, 'is that we may well have to cast about afresh.'

The appointment of Bevin, who made Britain's early post-war choices in foreign policy, was the result only of a last-minute switch in intentions by Attlee. Bevin had been intended for the Exchequer and Hugh Dalton for the Foreign Office. The change was immediate evidence of the particular difficulty the Labour government and party would have in agreeing, within its ranks, a European policy which would cast the Soviet Union in the role of potential aggressors rather than as allies. The Russians were, by this time, rapidly obtaining a position from which they could have dictated the outcome in Europe, when influential representations were made that Ernest Bevin should go to the Foreign Office.

One of Bevin's biographers, and his principal private secretary at the Foreign Office, was Sir Roderick Barclay.

Bevin and Attlee in Downing Street with Schuman and Pleven, December 1950.

BARCLAY: Some years later Attlee, I think, claimed that it was entirely his own idea to switch the two appointments. But there is a certain amount of evidence to show that perhaps the King, and perhaps the Cabinet Secretary, Sir Edward Bridges, and maybe the King's private secretary, Alan Lascelles, might all have said to Attlee, you know, 'Bevin would be a very good Foreign Secretary'. There was no doubt at all that he himself was expecting to be Chancellor. He used to like to tell the story of how he'd planned a little holiday in the south of England and he rang up Mrs Bevin and said, 'It's not Devon for me tomorrow, it's Potsdam.' To which she replied, 'Potsdam, where on earth's that?'

THE UNADORNED PROBABILITY would seem to be that Dalton was regarded as being too far to the left, and likely to prove of insufficient weight and resolution in dealing with this sharply emerging reality, that as the Americans were demobilising their armies, pulling out and going home, Britain would be left alone in a prostrate Europe with Stalin's Russia as the dominant power.

BARCLAY: I think that, whereas the Americans, of course, had rosy ideas about the possibilities of future collaboration with the Russians, Ernie Bevin from a pretty early stage came to the conclusion that it was not going to be possible. The Russian behaviour at the various post-war conferences, the various conferences of Foreign Ministers which succeeded one another in 1945, 1946 and 1947, made it clear to him that the Russians were just not out to collaborate. And I think that Eden probably reached the same conclusion, although of course he was no longer in the government, and Winston of course reached it earlier at the time of the Fulton speech in 1946. So I think probably all three of them, having had just slight expectations of the possibility of post-war collaboration, pretty soon reached the conclusion it was going to be extremely difficult, and therefore you've got to look to the building up of Western Europe.

CHARLTON: There must have been something of an upheaval inside the Foreign Office with the collapse of a policy of collaboration with the Soviet Union in which we had invested so much? Just how much was clear, I thought, when a lot of this came out very much later with the publication of books, like Tolstoy's book, about our policy of repatriation of refugees to Russia. Can you expand on this time when Bevin comes to the Foreign Office and the old policy lies in ruins?

BARCLAY: Of course the relationship began half-way through the Potsdam Conference, and from the outset I think the Foreign Office officials found that he was a surprisingly effective defender of the British interests. I think that there was a very rapid change in the outlook of his senior officials and they found themselves in full agreement that you had to switch your policies. It may be that there were a few officials who were late in coming to that conclusion, but on the whole I think that he and his officials really had the same approach and drew the same conclusions.

WITH EUROPE DIVIDED, there loomed ahead the heart of the problem, Germany. 'Building up Western Europe' meant the rehabilitation of Germany in the community and the councils of the West, and was something for which public opinion was almost wholly unprepared. By 1947 Bevin had had two years to ponder upon Eden's diagnosis that 'our foreign policy is a wreck'. Another of Bevin's private secretaries, Sir Frank Roberts, had met Bevin for the first time at the beginning of 1947 while serving in the Moscow embassy, when Bevin had gone there for the conference of the foreign ministers of the victorious powers. By then the Russians had already torn up the Declaration of Liberated Europe. This was the promise of free elections and self-determination in Eastern Europe, to which they'd agreed at Yalta and after which the Western Allies had withdrawn their own armies from their line of farthest advance East back to the Elbe. At the United Nations the West was met with veto after veto from the Russians. The post-war 'settlement' was breaking down.

ROBERTS: I think by then Ernie had decided that the post-war hopes of a new world order based on the cooperation of the three victorious powers just wasn't on. That famous phrase, you know, 'if only you'd treated Stalin like a member of the club and indeed behaved like one', well, of course, Ernie was one of the very few British ministers who'd read Karl Marx and who knew about Communism. He at least knew that the kind of club Stalin wanted to be a member of was not that kind of club! The essence of Ernie's views, I think, was really two things. First of all, Europe was in a very sad state. When you think, the three strongest armies in Europe at that time were probably the Swiss, the Swedes and the Yugoslavs. France had not recovered, Germany didn't exist as a country, the Americans had withdrawn their troops across the Atlantic, and we'd taken a lot of forces out. The Russians had, of course, in their way disarmed. There was the atom bomb which was the basis of a sort of western security at that time. Ernie felt two things were needed. You had to get the Americans back into

Europe as military security, and secondly you had to go even more quickly into reviving the European economy and bringing Western Germany in as an essential element of that Western economy, not just as a defeated enemy whose population had somehow to be fed, which had been the situation in 1945 and 1946. I think he went on hoping against hope that, in Germany, we'd manage to keep some sort of agreement with the Russians, but it became more and more difficult, with the Russians taking reparations out of their Zone when we were pouring aid and food into the other three zones. He'd obviously given up the idea by the time we had the conference with the Russians, the Americans and the French in Moscow in 1947.

CHARLTON: But even in 1947 does he still look upon Western Europe as the least important leg of the tripod on which the country has traditionally stood – the Anglo-American relationship, Commonwealth and Empire, and Europe? Does Europe still come last for him?

ROBERTS: I don't think he would himself have said that there is a stronger leg and a weaker leg. He said, here is the stool and there are three legs. But of course the American leg was basic; it would be from there that the strength would come, both economic and military. The Commonwealth leg was not, I think, in his view any more important that the European, if indeed it was as important. But on the other hand it was a priority because it was our responsibility and we had to do something about it. We couldn't just say, 'Well, Commonwealth, you stay there, while we get on with Europe for the time being'. So I think that, to me anyway, explains the lack of, if you like, urgent priority which we gave at the time, not to Europe as such, but to the construction of a more united European political system.

BY 1947 THE SOVIET occupation of Eastern Europe was assuming a character which the previously indulgent opinion of the middle ground in the western democracies found profoundly disturbing. The Soviet techniques which had been pioneered in Poland were being applied to Rumania, to Bulgaria and to Hungary. The moderate political parties in these countries, not just the right-wing elements, were being coerced into impotence and oblivion. When the Russians attempted to extend these Eastern European footholds down to the Mediterranean and exploit there the strategic void left by the eclipse of both France and Italy as effective powers, Stalin's design seemed confirmed as both predatory and expansionist. It led Bevin to continue the support both Churchill and Eden had given to the Greeks. Bevin backed the right-wing government in Athens against the indigenous communist bid there for power, and against a good deal of criticism from the Labour Party.

All this time there had been no clear indication of American policy. There hung above Europe a premonitory cloud of conflict. Bevin, looking over his shoulder at the Americans, took some first steps nearer to home.

ROBERTS: First of all, he was very keen to get France strong again. It was Ernie, I think, as much as anyone else in the government of the day anyway, who insisted with the Americans and with Stalin that France should have an equal voice in Germany. The Russians weren't the least bit keen on France getting a zone or a sector in Berlin, and it was the British who fought for that because we realised we could not do it alone. We needed another strong

European ally. He was a bit slower, I think, in feeling that the Germans should come in as partners. From the days of the First World War he was not exactly pro-German. He came round to regarding Germany as a necessary partner.

BEVIN'S HESITANCY OVER Germany was one significant shift in emphasis in British policy towards Continental Europe brought about by the change in government. Churchill had argued a good deal earlier than this and publicly it will be remembered in his famous Zurich speech in 1946, for bringing Germany quickly into a Western European political system.

Churchill had, incidentally, revealed his thinking about the German problem after the war at what was surely a most remarkable moment. It was during the course of a conversation in 1940, in wartime Britain, which Churchill had with General de Gaulle. Churchill's private secretary, Sir John Colville, was present and made the notes of it at the time.

COLVILLE: It was at Chequers in August 1940 during the middle of the Battle of Britain. I remember de Gaulle had come down for the day. He had been saying that the Germans had really got to be put down, as it were, because we'd had the trouble with the Hohenzollerns and now it was the same thing all over again with Hitler; and Churchill was saying that he didn't agree at all. He thought – and I remember the expression, the phrase he used was 'Germany existed before the Gestapo', only he didn't ever pronounce it 'Gestapo', he used to call it the 'Jesterpo' – he would never listen to any suggestion that the German people as such were guilty. He then went on to talk about what we were going to do in the future, and that was remarkable because, at that particular moment, the middle of August 1940, the rest of the world thought we were beaten, thought the war was over and that we were done. De Gaulle, I remember, was very impressed by that.

BY THE SAVAGE WINTER of 1947 the whole of the projected post-war settlement in Europe had collapsed. Eastern Europe was being sealed off from the West, and Roosevelt himself, before he died, had acknowledged that Stalin had reneged on the spirit of the promises he'd given at Yalta. Churchill's 'iron curtain' had descended, as he said in his historic Fulton speech, from Stettin in the Baltic to Trieste in the Adriatic.

The Americans at this time were not committed in any way to Europe or to Britain in the post-war world. As Ernest Bevin undertook the huge task of innovation and of organisation which these new circumstances required, Britain was making a start on that role of leadership which some of the exiled governments of Europe during their time in London in the war had foreseen and wished for. Britain herself was in a weak position to give such a lead, contemplating her reserves running out and, at home, a lower food ration than during the war itself. The prospect in Europe was a good deal worse and hardly one to invite intimate involvement. Ten thousand bridges were down in France alone. In Germany the shivering mass of its inhabitants were living in rubble. The miracle of the Marshall Plan had yet to be performed.

A consistent strand of concern is visible in the Foreign Office documents available on this period which shows that, allied with Britain's historical policies of detachment rather than close involvement with the continent, the possibility

that an impoverished Britain might be chaining itself to a corpse was a thought
which, if it was unspoken, was present in the minds of its policy-makers. Sir
Roderick Barclay was with Bevin at the time.

BARCLAY: One has to remember what a terrible state Western Europe was in
in those days. This country had emerged with great prestige, we'd fought all
through the war, we'd emerged victorious but we were exhausted. Everybody
was thinking about having a quiet life and perhaps a welfare state. Nobody
wanted foreign adventures. The countries of Western Europe were, to begin
with, in an even worse state, their industries destroyed. They'd been occupied,
there were all the problems of those who'd been for the Resistance and those
who'd been against. The whole of Western Europe was a pretty good shambles.
Ernie Bevin often used to say, when I was with him, used to wonder whether we
would be able to do more than 'preserve the outer crust of Europe', by which I
think he meant that there was a grave risk that Italy would go communist and
France might possibly go communist. He hoped the Benelux countries would
be all right and the Scandinavians, but he foresaw very great difficulties in the
centre of Europe. Of course Germany was in a state where all her industry had
been destroyed and was being further dismantled, particularly by the Russians,
so that the whole thing was really a shambles. In that situation the first step was
really to build up the Anglo-French relationship and that, I think, everyone in
the Foreign Office accepted. And so you have first of all the Treaty of Dunkirk
and then followed quite soon by the Brussels Treaty, which brought in the
three Benelux powers. That was quite a step forward but it wasn't enough. I
think both Ernie and his advisers quite soon accepted that, if the West was
going to be able to withstand Russian pressure, it was essential to bring in the
power of North America.

THE METAPHORS 'preserving the outer crust' and later 'keeping the rim of the
world', which Roderick Barclay and Frank Roberts among his advisers quote
Bevin as using at this early post-war period, were themselves in keeping with,
and therefore no departure from, Britain's traditional thinking as a maritime
power, involved and dealing with the 'periphery', throwing her weight now in
this scale and now in that, but in Europe not going beyond a position from
which it would be possible to withdraw.

The early initiatives by Bevin and the Foreign Office, like the Brussels
Treaty, in the days before Marshall Aid and when the Americans had gone
home, were the beginnings of unification in Western Europe. But so far they
were, in British eyes, carried out as immediate objectives, directly aimed at and
achieved. A wider consideration of policy, and in particular what was meant by
the generalised ideal of 'unity', was yet to be made. Because the pace at which
British policy responded or adapted to the political ambitions of the Europeans
after the war has come under such a rueful scrutiny, it must be said that to have
travelled even thus far was a measure of Bevin's forcefulness within the governing party and the decisiveness of his choice as Foreign Secretary.

At this time, in 1947, Bevin's Minister of State at the Foreign Office was
Hector MacNeil. MacNeil commissioned a long report which was an attempt to
draw up some conclusions and to define the basis for an approach the Labour
Party should take to Europe generally, and the Marshall Plan in particular. He

gave this task in 1947 to a young man who was then the secretary of the Labour Party's international department, Denis Healey.

HEALEY: I think that it's now easy to forget that 1947, when Marshall made his speech, was only two years after we'd been allied with the Soviet Union and fighting the Germans, and the very concept of a Western Europe from which really the Communist powers had excluded themselves, and a Western Europe which was supported by the United States – for which the Labour movement in Britain had never had very close sympathy politically – was a very difficult concept to get over. Of course all this argument about economic cooperation with Europe was being carried on at the same time as the Soviet military pressure on Western Europe was becoming more apparent. We'd had the civil war in Greece and we had the crisis over Czechoslovakia in March 1948, and I think for the Labour movement at that time it was a very, very traumatic period. A lot of my friends and colleagues in the Labour movement found it very difficult to accept that the Soviet Union was as hostile to Britain as a social democratic country as, in fact, she was. But, of course, the Russians at that time under Stalin saw the socialists as their main enemy, because they were the main obstacle to communist control of the working class, to use their jargon.
CHARLTON: One *sees* that it was still a very delicate matter, this change, for the Labour Party, in something you were saying even a little earlier in a 1947 pamphlet called 'Cards on the Table', taken I imagine from the words Bevin addressed to Molotov at one of the conferences, 'Why don't you put your cards on the table?'
HEALEY: Yes.
CHARLTON: And you say this: 'No Labour man blames Aneurin Bevan for the housing shortage yet many seem to think that Ernest Bevin is personally responsible for the apparent deterioration in relations between the Big Three since 1945.'
HEALEY: Well, there was that feeling. You see, you've got to remember that before the war I would say the strongest single current in the Labour Party in foreign affairs was pacifism, represented by George Lansbury, who was the biggest figure in the Labour movement until just before the beginning of the war. Beyond that it was a form of collective security which was curiously ill defined. The Labour movement in Britain, particularly the Trade Union movement, had always had particularly close relations with the Soviet Trade Union movement, much more so than most of the Continental Labour and Socialist movements. And so, recognising that the Russians were taking over Eastern Europe, destroying the Socialist parties there, forcing Socialist leaders into exile, putting them in prison and so on, although it was happening in front of their own eyes they found it very difficult to accept. I wrote a pamphlet called 'The Curtain Falls' about the Socialists in Eastern Europe for which Aneurin Bevan wrote a preface, but as I say it was very difficult to get this accepted at the time.

That, I think, was the party side of the problem. The other side of the problem was to do with the government and, if you like, Britain as a state. I think what is very difficult for people now to recall is the thing which dominated government thinking in Britain at that time. It was that we had been enormously weakened by the Second World War and our main concern was to find new sources of power and influence rather than new sources of responsibility. The Americans, on the other hand, always had the feeling that, somehow or other, it was Britain's job to organise European unity so that they could relax into normalcy. You remember they committed themselves to permanent neutrality in 1937 by the Neutrality Act, and they really wanted to get back to it. We faced a need to turn the colonial Empire into a Commonwealth of free nations, and we had this very difficult problem – on the one hand, of persuading the Labour movement that Britain herself could not survive without close cooperation with Europe and support from the United States; on the other hand, of persuading the Americans that we couldn't assume a vast range of new responsibilities in Europe at a time when we were having to get rid of old responsibilites outside Europe.

However, by July 1947 the more diffuse and pessimistic residual objective of 'saving the outer crust' or 'keeping the rim of the world' had, perforce, become more precisely focused. The refusal of the Soviet Union to take part in the Marshall Plan, and Molotov's announcement to Bevin that acceptance of American aid for recovery would be 'bad for Britain and France, but particularly France', marked the virtual declaration of the Cold War. The Russians had threatened Bevin directly that they would try to disrupt the European recovery programme in the West. 'I do not object to them coming to that conclusion,' Bevin said, 'but I do not see why I should be a party to keeping Europe in chaos and starvation.' When the great political strikes occurred throughout France following the Marshall Plan's announcement, Bevin added, 'Who can doubt that the Cominform and the Russians are behind them?' By 1947 the unifying threat of Hitler's Germany, having been removed, was about to be replaced by the unifying challenge of Stalin's Soviet Union.

On 22 January 1948, in the House of Commons, Bevin announced a new policy. It was called Western Union. 'The time for consolidation of Western Europe is ripe,' he said. As to British policy in Europe, he believed, he said, 'that the old-fashioned concept of the balance of power should be discontinued'. He announced that Britain was taking a lead in drawing the countries of Western Europe closer together: 'We are now thinking of Western Europe as a unity,' he went on. 'We shall do all we can to advance the spirit and machinery of cooperation.' The junior Foreign Office minister when Bevin made this speech was Christopher Mayhew.

MAYHEW: This was the great speech which started off the whole process, starting with the Brussels Treaty which united us with the continent of Europe in a defence agreement, and led on indeed to NATO. I do have a personal memory here because, I remember, I was brought in on Ernest's first draft of this speech. This was to be a major foreign affairs debate and Ernest's prestige was not good with Parliament. He often made long and rambling 'tours de reason', as he called them, which bored everybody. And this, when I saw it, was the 'tour de reason' to end all 'tours de reason'. So, I thought, as Parliamentary Under-Secretary I really must try and assert myself and do something about it. And I had a very good idea. I recalled that, only a week or two before Bevin had got through the cabinet a paper written by Gladwyn [Jebb] on the future of Britain and Europe and America. Now this was a paper drafted in the Foreign

Office – precise, clear, interesting and bold – looking forward to everything that happened, NATO and everything else. It suddenly occurred to me that this had gone through the cabinet and it was Bevin's paper. Why not say it? Why not put it in the speech? So I spent a hectic hour or two putting the whole of this cabinet paper into Ernie's ghastly 'tour de reason'. I then rushed along to him, because it was the day of the speech, and I sold it to him. I remember, he read it, and of course these things, these phrases and sentences which in a cabinet paper look one thing, were tremendous statements if said in the House of Commons by the Foreign Secretary! There was a long pause, and then he said, 'You've done me a good job here, Chris, this is a big thing'. And he said it all, in the House.

Then the fat was in the fire, because the Foreign Office had made no preparation for this great oration, and every Foreign Office in the world was ringing them up and asking them for details and asking what did it mean, what did this or that sentence mean? I remember Gladwyn coming round to me and saying, 'I say, this is terrible! What do we say to all these people? We've made no preparations, you see, and everyone's asking us for explanations.' But the thing was launched. It was very important and a very good speech.

CHARLTON: I'm glad you mentioned it because it certainly did seem to strike a chord among the Europeans. Paul-Henri Spaak, the Belgian Foreign Minister and one of the progenitors of this whole drive for European unity, mentions it in his memoirs. He says, 'I have never understood why Bevin changed his view as he did. In that speech he put forward the idea of organising the Atlantic powers and proclaimed his desire for European unity. Never again was he to show up in this light. On the contrary, he seemed surprised and even worried when he saw the ideas, which he himself had pioneered, being put into practice.'

MAYHEW: How extraordinary. I never knew Spaak said that. I used to meet Spaak. I wish I'd explained to him the little story, because that is the explanation.

THE BEVIN CABINET PAPER, or papers, to which Christopher Mayhew referred were probably those dated 4 and 5 January 1948, and marked, as was customary, Top Secret. They were drafted by Gladwyn Jebb and have been included as extracts in an appendix. They contained in one paragraph this interesting aspiration suggesting in one respect an alignment of views about the objectives of 'unity' with those of the continental Europeans. 'Provided we can organise a Western European system such as I have outlined above, backed by the power and resources of the Commonwealth and the Americas, it should be possible to develop our own power and influence to equal that of the United States of America and the USSR . . . By giving a spiritual lead now we should be able to carry out our task in a way which will show clearly that we are not subservient to the United States or the Soviet Union. I have already broached the conception of what I called a spiritual union of the West tentatively to Mr Marshall and M. Bidault, both of whom seemed to react favourably without, of course, committing themselves. I now propose, if my colleagues agree, to ventilate the idea in public in my speech in the forthcoming Foreign Affairs debate, and thereafter to pursue it, as occasion demands, with the governments concerned.'

So it was that, before the Americans became deeply involved in the recovery and defence of Western Europe in 1948 and 1949, Britain and Bevin took the first practical lead in uniting the West. The coup by which the Communists seized power in Prague in 1948 was probably decisive in precipitating France's agreement to join Bevin in the completion of the Brussels Treaty, which combined in a common organisation Britain, France and the three Benelux countries, Holland, Belgium and Luxembourg.

This now became the first time that Britain's policy-makers were dealing in the field of practical action with the Continental politicians who had returned from their exile in wartime London impelled, as we have seen, by the same motives and excited by the same hopes of European unity. These were the ideas to which Churchill was giving such prominent support. They were ideas which were most vigorously represented by the 'Federalists'. They were sentiments which were to prove such a durable challenge to British policy and possessed a strength which Britain, it may now be seen, so consistently misconstrued.

The Brussels Treaty, while it was a first and successful British accomplishment of a drawing together in Western Europe, uncovered fundamental differences about the nature of unity. At this obviously important conjuncture, confusion arose about the basic intentions of British policy, when Ernest Bevin and Winston Churchill appeared to be arrayed on opposite sides of the fundamental argument about what constituted 'unity'.

Lord Gladwyn, whose drafting in the Foreign Office of major policy positions has been compared with some of the finest of Britain's state papers, was employed by Ernest Bevin to negotiate the essentials of the Brussels Treaty. It showed that the Foreign Office was fully aware of the existence, if not the strength, of the new ideas burgeoning on the continent.

GLADWYN: It was a new concept as a Treaty, I think. In negotiating it we had consciously borrowed some of the ideas of the Federalists certainly: that there should be a Parliament, for instance, and that it should cope with all kinds of social and economic matters which would not normally be in a Treaty – like, for example, the Franco-British treaty after the war, the Treaty of Dunkirk. I think we had consciously taken over some of the ideas of the Federalists short of accepting their actual supranational element which we thought, and I think everybody thought at that time, was not acceptable to Great Britain. The Foreign Office, I think rightly, thought that immediately after the war we couldn't come into any supranational organisation of Europe because it wouldn't have gone through Parliament.

CHARLTON: But you've said elsewhere that perhaps a chance was lost here, that in order to avoid this split over European unity which is going to bedevil our policy for years to come, perhaps we should have gone further to meet the wishes of the Federalists?

GLADWYN: We might have said to them, and we did not say to them, 'We must build up on Western Union, and the Treaty of Brussels'. We merely said we could not go as far as they wanted in their efforts after the Congress of the Hague, and they were very annoyed by that. If we had made more efforts to bring them in, and said, 'Look, this is as far as we can go now but we may go further in this direction if you come along with us' . . . I blame myself for not having done that very much.

CHARLTON: Somehow you appear convinced that European unity, with British participation in it, sadly miscarried at this time?

Bevin takes the lead in Western unity with the Brussels Pact, 1948. He is accompanied by his senior Foreign Office advisers (standing, first from left, Sir Roderick Barclay, fourth from left, Sir Frank Roberts, and seated with Bevin, fourth from left, Gladwyn Jebb).

GLADWYN: I didn't realise at the time so much, I think, but in the light of hindsight, yes, I did think so. If we'd gone to the Europeans more and to the Federalists, and said, 'Look, this is as far as we can go now, certainly in Britain. Public opinion won't go further than this. Nevertheless, if you come in with this and with your own ideas and build up on that Parliament, you see, even though it won't have many supranational powers, *it could have more* as time goes on', then I think we might conceivably have got them to come along with us rather than in the parallel channel of building up the Council of Europe. This, in the event, proved to have no supranational elements at all actually, much to their disgust and to France's disgust. Spaak resigned as President of its first Assembly as you know. Some of the American planners, like Phil Jessup, came and said, 'Look, why don't you go further in this direction?' and I think we should have. I blame myself that we didn't go further, that we didn't build up more on the economic and the social side of the Brussels Treaty organisation.

But you see, by that time the Federalists had got hold particularly of Churchill, who was in Opposition, and organised a sort of counter show called the Congress of Europe at the Hague, which eventually resulted in the Council of Europe. That was a mistake really. I think we ought to have somehow or other manoeuvred or got them on to our side, and not to have had two organisations.

I believe, always have believed, that Churchill decided to have it both ways; that he was not really, as it proved when he came into power a second time, in favour of joining anything like a supranational Europe. I'm quite certain he wasn't really, but he maintained he was in a general way. That was where the Federalists on the continent were so deluded. I think it was a great mistake on his part to take up this ambiguous attitude, if I may say so. I always have thought it. I think it was all very deplorable and tragic. The more convinced Europeans of course were mostly Federalists, like Spaak and Monnet. There was much more support for the federal conception on the continent of Europe than there was in England. There were some English who were Federalists and some who pretended to be, but they were many fewer than on the continent and that is the first thing. Therefore it was very difficult to get support, in Parliament at any rate, for a genuinely federalist conception. However, if we'd gone on entirely building up on the Brussels Treaty organisation with its Parliament, we could have inserted gradually more federalist conceptions into that as time went on.

The tragedy was that the Federalists, despairing of the British government joining some kind of federal Europe, organised their own and got Churchill actually to lead the great Congress at the Hague, which met to form a real European entity and unity. And after that tremendous confabulation of all the Federalists, led by Churchill, there emerged a movement for something more extensive than the Brussels Treaty organisation. If we'd got all their enthusiasm behind the latter, then I think we could have made a real advance. We could have got much more into the idea of an eventual European army by degrees, the idea which was turned down in 1954. As it was, Western Union, WEU, was quite soon merged into NATO and faded out as a representative of European Union. If we had gone in the direction I've mentioned, I think there would have been more of a chance of gradually getting even the British to admit to some kind of supranational conception than would otherwise have been the case. On reflection I think this is a fact.

CHARLTON: Yes, but the consistent drive and the thrust of our policy is to dilute quite deliberately the supranational idea in Europe.

GLADWYN: Yes, it was.

CHARLTON: To which we cannot belong?

GLADWYN: Well, it was the case that we could not accept at that time any, or very few, supranational obligations.

CHARLTON: Why is it, though, that we misjudge the intensity of this movement towards European unity at such an early stage? After all, well before we get as far as the Hague Congress in 1948, Spaak has kept Eden informed of the intention to form a customs union within the Benelux countries, there has been a lot of talk about a European customs union, and the Foreign Office plainly does not wish this movement to prosper. We delay, we make no commitment, and this begins to cause some hostile reactions among the Europeans. Are we 'with them or against them'?

GLADWYN: I think that was a mistake. I do, yes. I am to some extent to blame myself, no doubt. I was more in favour of going in that direction than some of my colleagues were, I think. A lot of them thought that this was a lot of non-sense anyhow and that we ought to concentrate chiefly on our relations with America and that was the only thing which really mattered; and if the others wanted to get together then, as I think Churchill fundamentally thought, if they really wanted to get together in a supranational organisation, well, let them, you see. But that is where things went wrong, I think. That's true.

WHILE LORD GLADWYN is convinced that it was a 'great mistake' for Churchill to take up an 'ambiguous attitude which deluded the European

Federalists', it would also seem clear that Churchill was concerned at the slow development of British policy over European unity and had chosen to ally himself with the more dynamic forces in search of it. However, what also seems apparent is that the new emphasis and priority for European unity, upon which Churchill was becoming more insistent, did not mean that he had surrendered a fundamental premise. It was one in which, at this particular time, he instructed Oliver Franks who was then the British Ambassador in Washington. Franks would prove to be a pivotal figure in the conduct of the whole Anglo-American relationship. Lord Franks, as he is today, was about to take over at the critical apex of Anglo-American relations in organising responses to the Marshall Plan for European recovery when Churchill, from the lowlier summits of Opposition, handed down these tablets of British foreign policy.

FRANKS: Mr Churchill as he then was once gave me a lecture on the three intersecting circles – those represented by the United States, by the Commonwealth and by Europe – and he said to me, 'Young man, never let Great Britain escape from any of them'. Now, if you come to the question of priorities, that is more difficult. If you are thinking in strategic and military terms there is no question that our relationship with the United States was the priority. On the other hand, in terms of tradition, emotion and affection, the Commonwealth came first; and in terms of our neighbours without whom we were literally not safe or secure, then Europe came very much into the picture. So I think that in many ways what Winston Churchill said to me, and this would be in early 1948, represented the way a great many people in Britain thought and felt at the time. I think that he hoped it would be possible for Britain to have a foreign policy, both political and economic, of a kind which permitted Britain to live in all three circles satisfactorily.

CHURCHILL'S FORMULATION of the three intersecting circles, to which Bevin also subscribed, was a straddle which, it later became so painfully obvious, misrepresented Britain's real strength. But from the outset in post-war Europe the Foreign Office fought a rearguard action to preserve the freedom of action which this self-defined orbit demanded. This reinforced a certain attitude of mind and action. Each time Britain was urged by either the Americans or the Europeans to 'go a little further', Britain felt it was, in consequence, likely to give up too much.

A most powerful figure, by all accounts, at this period in the formulation of policy over Europe was Sir Roger Makins, Deputy Under-Secretary of State at the Foreign Office. Some of his former colleagues place him in the ranks of those who were inclined to dismiss the prevalent aspirations about European unity as either nonsense or unlikely to succeed, and that the fundamental concern of the British should be with the Atlantic partnership and the Americans. Lord Sherfield, as he is today, came from a military family and is a Fellow of All Souls'. He is a huge man of impressive physical bearing and clearly a personality of some force. His influence with Bevin, some have suggested, was such that it made him almost a quasi-minister. When speaking of the growth in both European and American pressures for Britain to go further with 'integration' after the war, he told me this: 'We knew we were fighting a rearguard action – but we were determined to fight it!'

One overriding concern in the mind of the Foreign Office, according to Lord Sherfield, was fear of the endemic American disposition to isolationism.

SHERFIELD: We had a shock, in a sense, at the reversals of American policy immediately after the war, the sudden cutting off of Lend-Lease and so on. We certainly had a fear, I think, that the Americans might want to pull back, to pull out of Europe. I think we felt that, if we became involved in the purely European grouping, they were more *likely* to pull out. So the whole of the policy was designed, I mean that was Ernie Bevin's concept, gradually to build up a Western European organisation in which the Americans were fully involved.

I'm sure the record shows that a great many people in the United States, and influential people, wanted to see us, and regarded us, as a purely European power. They were not sympathetic to our colonial obligations; they wanted to get us out of our colonies, and pushed us far too hard, I think, in that respect. They never understood the sterling area and regarded that as an impediment to the free world economy which they wanted to achieve. We were under constant pressure from the American representatives in Europe, Lew Douglas in London, Jack McCloy in Germany, later on David Bruce in Paris, Paul Hoffman, Averell Harriman, Douglas Dillon, continual pressure on us to go into Europe and then '*we*', the Americans, shall have a much easier time.

CHARLTON: But why are we so antipathetic to the idea that the Americans consider us a European power, that our imperial mission is over. Why are we so antipathetic to that when there is recognition in the Foreign Office, quite plainly, that things with the Commonwealth are going to be much more difficult in the years ahead, that Britain just hasn't got the capital goods for the Commonwealth, that we can't digest all their raw materials, that the old imperial relationship is changing very quickly. Why are we so hostile to that?

SHERFIELD: At the time we're talking about they were assets, no question about it. They were not only assets, they were obligations, and what we were being asked to do was to liquidate, have a forced liquidation of our assets and a false repudiation of our obligations. Clearly our position had changed substantially, particularly on the economic front. For example, we'd been cut off almost completely from our side of American trade which was an enormous loss. On the other hand the Commonwealth, the colonial Empire, even the sterling area outlook – that was more or less intact. The independence of India and Pakistan had made a tremendous difference in the strategic sense which was not immediately apparent, but apart from that the Commonwealth structure was more or less intact.

The American attitude and doctrines tended to be too doctrinaire in terms of international economic policy, and their attitude to our colonial connections was fundamentally unfavourable to us. One of the difficulties, I think, was that they wanted to go too fast. It was all going to happen very quickly. And of course you can't suddenly go at a jump from the very low level which Europe had reached economically into convertibility and free trade.

CHARLTON: Why do you say that? Because it would have undermined the whole sterling area?

SHERFIELD: Well, it did in a sense. We were obliged as a condition of the American loan to jump into convertibility of sterling in 1947, and it lasted six weeks!

CHARLTON: But we considered American insistence on convertibility was
something to undermine the sterling bloc?
SHERFIELD: Yes.

THE ABRUPT TERMINATION, without consultation, of Lend-Lease had left
Britain incapable of sustaining her economy at home or overseas. It had
enabled Britain, still paying off debts incurred in the First World War, let alone
the Second, to overspend her income to the tune of some £2 billion a year at
'1945 prices'. Without such aid there was no hope of maintaining an equilibrium
in the balance of payments. The terms of the subsequent huge American loan,
which Churchill considered to be harsh, meant acceptance, as Lord Sherfield
pointed out, of 'unfavourable' policies and constraints. Not least of the shocks
administered by the United States to Britain concerned those, by now, supreme
instruments of national sovereignty and power, the nuclear weapons. The
United States suspended the exchange with Britain of technical information,
and with it the intimate collaboration of wartime which had jointly developed
and made possible the atomic bomb.
    This conglomerate of things did not turn the Foreign Office in the direction
of Europe, however. Rather, it led to redoubled efforts by British diplomacy to
catch up with the American coat-tails and to arrest the continued falling away
from the 'finest hour', by resecuring what appeared now to be hardly even a
junior partnership but a vanishing relationship with the Americans.
    During this period of radical political reconstruction in Europe, British foreign
policy was constantly being undermined by the country's economic performance.
Christopher Mayhew recalls that Bevin was preoccupied by it.

MAYHEW: He bewailed it constantly. He was always complaining about Hugh
Dalton, as Chancellor of the Exchequer, that he undermined everything he was
trying to do, as he couldn't keep the pound strong, or that he couldn't get
enough coal for export. Ernest was always complaining about Britain's
economic weakness undermining his foreign policy. I think that's the reason he
had to ask for things all the time. And of course, if you have to ask for things the
whole time, you can't initiate, you can't have a positive foreign policy.

THE BIG POST-WAR LOAN to Britain, after Lend-Lease had been ended,
evaporated without measurable effect. The terms of that loan, the early convertibility of sterling – an early dose of monetary disciplines, was rejected by the
British government as unacceptable in terms of probable unemployment, and
inappropriate for victors who had fought alone and thereby saved freedom for
all in the West. By 1949 Britain was forced into a first and major devaluation of
sterling. Bevin set out for the United States to get the essential American support to back the British currency.
    Dean Acheson, the American Secretary of State, chose a title for a chapter in
his memoirs dealing with this episode which invoked the memory of Paul
Revere's ride during the war of American independence from George III's
England. He called it 'The British are Coming'! On receipt of the news that the
British, in the persons of Ernest Bevin, Stafford Cripps and the Treasury, were
indeed coming, the American Treasury secretary, John Snyder, literally left
town to evade the early diplomatic exchanges.

Paul Nitze, who was head of Policy Planning in the American State Department, took the notes of the eventual meeting which Snyder did finally have with
Bevin.

NITZE: Bevin came over and we had a meeting in the State Department with
Mr Snyder, and I guess Acheson and I were the two on the State Department
side. I being the junior member present was delegated to keep the minutes of
the meeting. At one point Secretary Snyder made some very – well, remarks
which I thought were wholly undiplomatic and rude and showed his irritation
and lack of concern for the UK problem. That so irritated Ernie Bevin that he
held forth for about five minutes in defence of the United Kingdom and a
description of why Snyder was wrong. I was trying to keep minutes. There were
just words, no sentences of any kind. It was impossible to reduce it to sentence
structure, but when Ernie Bevin had finished I looked up at Secretary Snyder
and there were tears in his eyes. Honest to goodness, I couldn't believe what I
saw. And that wholly converted Secretary Snyder!
CHARLTON: Can you remember what the uncomplimentary remarks were? At
what were they directed?
NITZE: My recollection is that the general sense of them was why didn't the
UK get a hold of itself, and why didn't its people do some work for a change,
and why don't you cure these productivity problems in the United Kingdom
and why don't you get off your butt . . . I think that was the general sense of his
remarks!
CHARLTON: And what did Bevin say that brought tears to Snyder's eyes?
NITZE: As I say, it was impossible to make any sentences out of it. But one was
left with a realisation of the tremendous contribution to world history that
England had made by its standing alone against the Hitler threat, and the
sacrifices England had made on its own behalf but also the impact of that upon
the rest of the world. The degree of honour and respect to which England was
entitled by virtue of that tremendous contribution.

THE DETERMINATION TO FIGHT a rearguard action, and sustain a world role
– which after all was still a reality – could, of course, point to successes. Certainly they were at first sufficient to moderate a sense of urgency about the need
for a more radical reappraisal of policy.
     At the very time when Bevin was under pressure to take Britain into forms of
closer cooperation and integration in Europe there was the huge event of Indian
Independence in 1947. The outcome was interpreted in Britain as holding out
the prospect of a successful evolution and continuity of traditional relationships,
and a riposte to the American-inspired reformation and renunciation of
Empire. Lord Garner was later head of the Commonwealth Relations Office
and wrote an official post-war history of this department of State.

GARNER: Certainly after 1947 we did have a very genuine belief in the
Commonwealth as something that was valuable, we did genuinely regard it as
an illustration of how a new form of international relationship could, peacefully,
be carried out. After all, at the very least it assured peace and stability to no less
than a quarter of the whole globe at that time. And we felt very satisfied,
particularly after Indian independence, and the friendliness with which it came

about. We could see it leading, as indeed it did although we didn't see the time-table at that stage, to the independence of various other territories.

CHARLTON: Had India decided to quit the Commonwealth rather than to stay with it, do you feel that we may have judged the whole situation rather differently? We found rather to our surprise that India had reinforced the whole 'Commonwealth idea'.

GARNER: I must make this clear. I think – this is my own recollection of the situation at the time – while we were, if you like, euphoric about the Commonwealth and its possiblities and significance for us, we were most pessimistic about Europe. Of course, we recognised our closeness to Europe and how important it was for us, but not very much so in the trade sense at the time you are talking about, in 1948. What is more, we were highly sceptical about Europe. Europe was a collection of aliens and foreigners – I am putting this in extreme terms rather, but I'm trying to recreate the atmosphere of the time – who were erratic. They were unreliable. Some of them had let us down. Some of them had fought against us. All of them were seen, in 1948, to be liable to communist subversion and they were, quite frankly, not the sort of area that we – in contrast to the Commonwealth and all its glittering prospects as we saw it – wanted to tie ourselves down to.

ONE IS INCLINED, against this large and many-faceted background, to over-look just how early it was that the essential arguments for and against Britain joining a common market in Europe had their first rehearsal in Whitehall, and how early the basic mould of policy became set – as early indeed as 1947.

While Bevin was taking the first steps for Western Union in the field of military and political cooperation, as with the Brussels Treaty, the pressures on Britain for integration of a closer kind in Europe quickly became focused on the economic front. The landslide in the balance of power meant that huge trade surpluses were building up in the United States. Europe and Britain were being drained of their gold and their dollar reserves. It seemed clear that this in-exorable process would bankrupt the world unless something radical were done.

The record shows us that Sir Edmund Hall-Patch, who was Bevin's economic adviser in the Foreign Office, told the Foreign Secretary that America was, in consequence of the outcome of World War II, in the same position Britain had found herself in after the Napoleonic wars. In a paper to Bevin he wrote that, as Britain had done then, so America now would have to lend the greater part of her formidable surplus, without hope of repayment for a number of years, in order to stop world trade freezing up.

As one design for economic advance and recovery, as we have already noted, the Benelux countries had determined to achieve a Customs Union, to push back their own restrictive small frontiers into a common market. France wished to perform an imaginative act to catch the attention of the American Congress in order to get dollars. Both these new departures conformed to the basic and insistent objective of American policy, that freer trade exchanges were to become the foundation of new rejuvenated post-war order, and to which Churchill had been committed by Roosevelt.

In 1947 and 1948 Britain was one of sixteen nations with study groups of officials meeting in Brussels to examine the feasibility of a Customs Union in

Western Europe. The American Under Secretary of State, Will Clayton, gave this concept the powerful support of the United States. Clayton came to Europe in 1947 and was the real progenitor of the Marshall Plan. He was acting at this time on a report prepared for him by Paul Nitze, then assistant head of Policy Planning in the State Department.

NITZE: Mr Clayton took this seriously. He also took seriously the reports that he got from Europe that there was a breakdown in the exchange of food for manufactured goods, for instance in France, and that this was resulting in a decline of both French agriculture and the rest of industry, that the French economic situation was in terrible shape and would get worse, and that this was also true in Italy – that it was, indeed, a general phenomenon. So he went over to Europe and looked at this entire situation and came to the conclusion that a large and continuing aid programme to Europe was necessary. But if the United States *were* to do this, then really the Europeans should do everything that *they could* in order to make their recovery more feasible and easier. His conclusion was that it would be much easier if there were a Customs Union in Europe and there were not artificial barriers to trade within Europe.

A CONCOMITANT AIM of the American promotion of the Customs Union concept was the destruction of preferential systems. This issue of the Customs Union in Europe was the first litmus test of British attitudes to real, functional integration with the European countries.

The record reveals that, as early as 1947, the Foreign Office made a seminal judgement to oppose this concept, particularly if it were to include the United Kingdom. The documents also show that it was the British view that the Customs Union was unlikely to succeed without British participation. 'It would imply a closer degree of association in the social and political field,' one of Lord Sherfield's Foreign Office papers in August 1947 says, 'which would require very careful thought.' It was felt that this sort of integration could only be at the expense of links with the Commonwealth which, if they were weakened beyond a certain point, 'would lead to the disintegration of the sterling area and spell the end of Britain as a world power'.

The tactics of British diplomacy, basing itself on the formulation of the 'three intersecting circles' and in line with its traditional posture of balance of power politics on the continent, was to delay while appearing to be constructive. Another of Lord Sherfield's Foreign Office memoranda notes that it was 'the general decision of British Ministers to go slow on the whole matter'. As a result the sixteen-nation talks, and the study groups at work for more than a year, got nowhere as far as the Customs Union was concerned.

Lord Sherfield (then the Deputy Under-Secretary in the Foreign Office with responsibility for economic affairs in Europe) has already reviewed the working relationship between the British and the Americans over Europe at this time. He mentioned Ambassador Lew Douglas as among the influential Americans who were applying a 'constant pressure on the UK to go into Europe'. Indeed Douglas, like McCloy in Germany and Bruce in Paris and London, was one of those American 'proconsuls' in post-war Europe who had wide discretionary powers in not just the implementation, but the design of American policy.

The Foreign Office archives for August 1947 record Lord Sherfield's reactions to a conversation with Douglas over the Customs Union which the Foreign Office regarded as little short of 'blackmail'. Douglas had said he thought it 'would be most unfortunate if the impression got abroad that the United Kingdom was blocking an advance of this kind'. The Americans wanted tariffs reduced in Europe progressively and at regular intervals. If there were to be study groups for a year or so he was afraid 'the moment would be lost and it would be too late'. While he 'understood the difficulties over the Commonwealth, it was *very important for the launching of the Marshall Plan* that the Customs Union went ahead'. Lord Sherfield's assessment for Bevin of this conversation was that it was the 'first step in a campaign of pressure. It was quite clear that the French thought the Customs Union was necessary in order to get the dollars. They were also aware that Scandinavia and the Benelux countries would not join unless the United Kingdom gave the lead.' The French had made it clear that they believed Britain was the only obstacle to the Customs Union being formed and it was up to the Americans to put pressure on Britain. Noting that it was quite clear that the French 'had had some success with Clayton and Douglas', Lord Sherfield concluded to Bevin that 'from now on the pressure will increase. It will be harder for us to resist as our own financial difficulties increase.'

But resistance to the Customs Union became an important priority within that general 'rearguard action' which, as Lord Sherfield has said, 'Britain was determined to fight'. Two figures centrally concerned in these manoeuvrings were Oliver Franks and Paul Nitze. Nitze was acquainted by Franks with 'the rub', as far as Britain was concerned.

NITZE: I arrived in Paris and every day I would have breakfast with Oliver Franks and we discussed this at great length. Finally he came to the conclusion, yes, that he was persuaded this was something that he would recommend to his government. So he went back one weekend to London and met with his Foreign Minister, Ernie Bevin. Then there was a cabinet meeting, I believe, and the decision was against the proposal. The decision was that the UK's relationship with the Continent should not be inconsistent with the Commonwealth relationship.

A Customs Union with the European members of the Marshall Plan would in fact be inconsistent with all the arrangements which had been worked out with other members of the Commonwealth, particularly Australia and New Zealand with respect to wool and tariffs and God knows what not. But there was a fundamental issue as to which came first, the Commonwealth relationship, or the European relationship, and the decision was made that the Commonwealth relationship came first.

CHARLTON: How did you Americans view that?

NITZE: Well, we viewed it with regret. But I don't think anybody on the US side felt that this was necessarily a permanent decision on the part of the United Kingdom. As things evolved it would be possible to work out a reconciliation between the UK's relationship with the Commonwealth and a closer relationship with the Continent.

THE LAST MONTHS of the Customs Union affair had been marked by increasing restlessness among the Europeans, and the Americans in the later stages, with the progress being made. There were signs of impatience at the failure of the British to declare their position. Britain was finding it harder to avoid taking a more definite line.

Just before the Cabinet decision, the British delegation to the study groups in Brussels was minuting back to the Foreign Office that 'an adverse decision would have to be on carefully chosen ground if it were not to create some disturbance in our relationship with our neighbours'. A special report written for the British Cabinet by the delegation in Brussels in March of 1948 recommended that 'we would want to show that, if we decide to break, we were acting as good Europeans rather than self-regarding islanders'.

Those words, written so soon after the end of the Second World War, foreshadowed the long, slow-moving, tactical battle which would be fought between Britain and the continent over the nature of unity in Europe – a battle which would occupy the next twenty years and more, and which would halt only, and then perhaps not entirely, with Britain's eventual entry into the Customs Union called the Common Market.

The emotional, post-war, creative ambition of European unity had been endorsed and promoted by Churchill. Now British policy under Ernest Bevin had blocked progress towards one, ultimately successful, method of bringing it about. Reassured, as they must have been, by the developing American interest in and support for the Customs Union concept, the Europeans had begun to canvass 'going it alone' without Britain. There are the manifest beginnings of disenchantment with that prospect, declared and wished for at the war's end, of British leadership of European 'unity'.

While it was not said before the world, British diplomacy was now looking for 'carefully chosen ground' upon which to break and thereby kill the Customs Union idea as being inimical to Britain's Commonwealth interests and inconsistent with her occupation of the 'three intersecting circles' – her world role. An alibi would be needed which would demonstrate that the Customs Union approach was unnessary and impracticable. The opportunity for Britain to deflect down a different path, as she now did, these earliest efforts to achieve closer integration in Europe came in the wake of America's famous act of creative generosity towards European recovery and reconstruction announced in June of 1947. It was the single, most effective programme of economic cooperation the world has yet known. The Marshall Plan.

The years immediately in front of us now are those in which Churchill's vision and enthusiasm manifestly outran what Bevin and the Foreign Office considered desirable or practical politics. Churchill and Bevin continued ranged on opposite sides of an argument which, in the end, altered British history. Churchill continued to mount, in effect, a powerful 'unofficial' British foreign policy. Out of the founding of the European Movement at the Hague Congress, to which he had lent his immense prestige and support, emerged in 1949 Europe's first official institution – the Council of Europe. The Marshall Plan would inspire and demand radical innovation in methods of cooperation in Europe. The year 1949 also included an encounter and an exploration of which almost nothing has been known, but which may, in retrospect, be seen to have thrown a very long shadow indeed across the ambivalent path of Britain's European policy.

3
Bevin at
Victoria Station – 2

WHEN NAPOLEON WAS LANGUISHING on the island of St Helena it is recorded he maintained to his captors that, a hundred years after his death, Europe would be either Americanised or Cossack. This perception which, it would later become apparent, so animated General de Gaulle must have seemed unnervingly delphic in the Europe of the late 1940s. Soviet hegemony over all of Europe was an acknowledged possibility, more particularly so after Stalin's coup in Czechoslovakia in 1948. The large Communist parties of Italy and France were poised in the ascendant. Behind the new Diocletian Line, Churchill's 'Iron Curtain', the Soviet Union had tightened its grip on all that lay east of the river Elbe, and Stalin was continuing to assist this process by the arrest, or murder and coercion, of those in the political parties who declared their sympathies with the West.

Ernest Bevin had this assessment put down on paper for his colleagues in the Cabinet. 'The Russians think they can intimidate or wreck Western Europe by political upsets, economic chaos and revolutionary methods.' That this proved not to be the experience was Bevin's lasting contribution to the survival of the West. The political and military organisation of Western Europe under the embryo Brussels pact by Ernest Bevin was that necessary evidence of a will to self-help which secured the essential American twin commitment which super-seded the Brussels Treaty – the Atlantic Alliance and the Marshall Plan.

At the outset the Marshall Plan was on offer to all of Europe, not only to the West. It was rejected by Molotov, the Soviet Foreign Minister, as being an infringement of sovereign rights. This dictated Europe's future as its division into rival and competitive economic and political systems.

Now that the full involvement of the Americans was in prospect or accom-plished, Bevin confided a retrospective satisfaction to Christopher Mayhew, who was then the junior minister at the Foreign Office.

MAYHEW: I think above all that he felt he'd helped to see off Stalin and Molotov. 'They're evil men, Chris,' he said, and at a time when not everyone was saying it, you see. There were a whole lot of Stalinist illusions, especially in the Labour Party, right up to, well, 1949 and 1950. Ernie did see through that. He hated the Bolsheviks.

NOT UNTIL THE MARSHALL PLAN and this now renewed commitment to Europe by the United States, following their departure from it at the end of the war, did Bevin feel it prudent to make a limited entry into the Continent on Britain's behalf. His often-quoted remark, which has provided the title for this chapter, in which he defined the aim of his foreign policy as being able 'to go down to Victoria Station and go where the hell he liked without a passport', disguised no grand design and hinted at no new revelation about Britain's relationship to Europe in the future. The general view accords with Christopher Mayhew's.

MAYHEW: Frankly it didn't seem to me to relate to anything he had in mind particularly about passports or about freedom of communication. I saw it rather as a hangover from the kind of old Labour party 'Brotherhood of Man' orations that he made before the war. That's all I think it was, frankly.

HOWEVER, THE OFFER by the Americans of economic aid on a vast scale for reconstruction and recovery presented all the governments of Western Europe with the need to define a common goal. It also required common responses and joint results.

The Marshall Plan was originally an emergency programme to prevent that subversion of Western Europe which Bevin had described to his cabinet colleagues, and to which the longer-range implications of unification were subordinate. It proved to be a forcing ground for what became a consuming debate about European unity. This process disclosed, more openly, major differences of opinion, between Britain and the Americans in support of the Europeans, about the progress to be made in the direction of integration. The board outlines of this argument, as we have noted, first appeared in the Customs Union affair.

By 1949 we find that the Permanent Under-Secretary, of the Foreign Office, Sir William Strang, was writing a memorandum in these crisp and ruffled terms to the Washington Embassy:

> 'Ministers here have a growing sense of irritation, amounting at times to resentment, at the lack of consideration and understanding by United States authorities in their dealings with us and other European countries; and at the implicit assumption that the European Recovery Programme is giving American agents the right to press for changes in internal policy, and that when Congress says no matter what European governments must toe the line.'

This particular minute was written to the British Ambassador, Oliver Franks, who had become the chairman of an acronym around which the economic life of Europe would revolve for the next fifteen years, OEEC, the Organisation for European Economic Cooperation, set up to administer the funds available under Marshall Aid, which had given Europe its first common goal.

FRANKS: Yes, it began with the Marshall Plan and it began with the initiative of the Americans who, you will remember, insisted that while they wished to do everything they could to enable Europe to reconstruct itself and to recover, insisted that any programme that was to be drawn up had to be drawn up by the Europeans themselves, that it had to be a joint programme. The first notion of the unity of Europe came from the United States. It was there in the planning of George Kennan, when he was Chief of the Policy Planning Staff for General Marshall. What he advocated and what General Marshall accepted was that, through the Marshall Plan, Western Europe must become a less fragmented economy, that it must come to have a wider market, that the people must be more – in these economic ways – at unity with each other. That was where the first impulse came from. Then when I went to Paris in July of 1947, and became chairman of what became the OEEC, the Organisation for European Economic Cooperation, there, I think, these American impulses began to take root in European soil and we found ourselves debating about the ways in which that kind of unity could be achieved.

Then there was a major debate between the British and the French about what form the OEEC should take. The French really wanted to institutionalise it. They wanted to have a strong central secretariat, they wanted the Secretary General to have the power of initiative in policy. They wanted him to be able to take the initiative with member countries. The British did not take that view. The British wanted a conference of close intergovernmental cooperation *without* a strong institution at the centre. And on the whole at that time the British view won. What was set up as the OEEC was an intergovernmental conference with a Secretariat, but without the powers which the French had desired. And, I think, by the irony of history what happened was not what was intended. An institution grew up which was powerful, more powerful than the British ever intended, nearly as powerful as the French had hoped. It grew because the delegations from the sixteen countries were in permanent session. As they worked together they became a force which worked back on their governments, and they became, as it were, a separate and an influential power. It is true that they limited the sovereignty of their States.

THE MINUTE WRITTEN BY Sir William Strang to Lord Franks which has already been quoted (p. 67) was circulated in December 1949, at the end of a summer in which some of the American officials closely connected with the huge aid programme had become convinced that Europe's economic problems were much more fundamental and intractable than had been supposed. They had come to feel that aid was insufficient in itself to overcome the 'grave psychological and institutional weaknesses of continental society'. It was felt that the methods chosen to bring about liberalisation of trade in Western Europe by mutual consent – those upon which Britain had successfully insisted – had proved thus far to be 'quite inadequate'. These feelings found their fullest expression in a speech made by the American administrator of the Marshall Plan Fund in Europe, Paul Hoffman, in October of 1949, and they mark the moment when American pressure for economic integration in Europe became overt.

Lincoln Gordon, Professor of Government at Harvard, was Director of the Programme Division of the US Marshall Plan Agency in Europe and economic adviser to Hoffman and Averell Harriman.

GORDON: What was called European economic integration was only very vaguely referred to at the beginning of the Marshall Plan. You don't really find in Marshall's speech in 1947, or in the Marshall Plan legislation, a more than glancing reference to integration. The real initiation of that particular stream came with a famous speech by Paul Hoffman on 1 October 1949. I remember the occasion vividly. It happened also to be the day on which Germany entered the OEEC as a full member for the first time, the first international organisation into which West Germany had been admitted after the war. It was a very important occasion. That was when Hoffman made his famous plea. I remember it vividly partly because I worked over the draft of the speech during the previous two days. The draft with which I was first presented in my opinion went too far. My recollection is that the key noun was not 'integration' then, but was something like union or unity or something.

CHARLTON: Unification.

GORDON: Yes, unification, that was the key word. I was hotly opposed to this because, first I thought it was unrealistic, and secondly I thought that with that word there would be no chance basically of having British participation. You must realise that I probably had the kind of professional deformation that comes from having been a Rhodes Scholar! I was something of an Anglophile!

THE ESSENTIAL CORE of Hoffman's speech when it was delivered, purged of the word 'unification', contained these sentences reflecting the official American belief that Western Europe's economic ills could not be cured, until the narrow national economies were combined into 'a single market within which goods, money, and people could freely move and within which all barriers to trade and payments could be swept away'. Lincoln Gordon remembers this as being the British reaction to Hoffman's major intervention.

GORDON: The British response was very chilly indeed. I remember having lunch with Edwin Plowden [Lord Plowden, in charge of British economic planning under the Chancellor, Sir Stafford Cripps], and he was cross-examining me rather intensely on what did we really mean by integration. Many of the speeches being made by the Americans at that time, including Paul Hoffman's, pointed to the United States. I mean, the model always was 'what did *we* do in 1781 and 1787 when they wrote the Constitution', and obviously any European and any Briton looking at that, and taking the analogy seriously, must have assumed that what was being talked about was indeed a pooling of sovereignty; and the general feeling at that time was of course among the British that it was simply unacceptable.

I think that Hoffman's own conception of what he was after was rather simplistic. Essentially the notion was that you would get productivity by enlarging markets and by opening things up to competition. That was the great secret of American productivity and its standard of living – the continental-wide market. It should be reproduced as nearly as could be in Europe and would be the key to long-term European recovery and prosperity. I believe that it was a view almost devoid of what I would call 'high' politics. I think it was probably fairly innocent on the kinds of higher political considerations which would clearly worry London, including pooling of sovereignty, longer-term relationships with a Continent of dubious political stability – as then seen from London.

Acheson was keenly aware of these higher political considerations. I think both in terms of realism and of wanting to make sure that nothing was done in a sense to push the British out, he felt that the Hoffman language had to be tempered. The implication of the Hoffman view was that, not only in his own view, but in the view of the majority of the United States Congress, the continuation of Marshall Aid beyond its second year, which it was then in, would be contingent upon progress towards European economic, as he would have preferred, 'unification', and, as the words came out, 'integration'.

As LORD FRANKS HAS SAID, 'On the whole at that time the British view won'. That tactical victory was the British insistence that European recovery and the use of the Marshall Plan money was to be pursued and administered by 'loose' but 'close' intergovernmental cooperation. It was a victory gained against what was quickly developing as the most dynamic of political sentiments on the Continent – those in favour of using the opportunities afforded by the Marshall Plan to forge a new and comprehensive post-war 'unity'. It was something of a pyrrhic victory. From this moment onwards the early disappointments with the British attitudes to European unity, now that the Americans had shown themselves overtly sympathetic to that ambition, were kindling into something less disposed to compromise 'next time', a more watchful determination to see the ambitions for 'unity' more positively explored.

Lord Franks gave these as the essential reasons for Britain's opposition to the Customs Union formula in Europe were it to include Britain, a design for recovery which had just received a powerful reinvigoration from Hoffman. The Customs Union was a concept upon which the American economy itself was constructed, and it was the concept to which the Europeans now aspired.

FRANKS: I think essentially because we did not see how we could both preserve the sterling area and be full members of a European Customs Union. At that time in the post-war period's early years the sterling area was, we believed, (a) a source of strength to us, and (b) a lifeline. It was the channel through which a very great part of our trade flowed back and forth: manufactures *to* the countries of the Commonwealth, raw materials *from* them. And we did not see how we could do ourselves anything but harm if we put ourselves in a position in which *that* position could be damaged. There was a strong belief in the Bank of England at that time that sterling as a reserve currency, and running the sterling area, was an important source of strength for Britain itself. But I think that everybody knew that what it mediated, by the use of this same currency, was trade. It was like a great Free Trade Area, and this was very important to Britain. People did not foresee then that the sterling area would one day break up; that the countries of the Commonwealth wouldn't all want to hold their reserves in sterling. None of this was foreseen at that time. This is, I think, what really constituted the barrier to our full membership of a hypothetical European Customs Union.

CHARLTON: At this time would you say British policy-makers rejected the idea that the post-war world was going to be, other than temporarily, a vastly different place for this country?

FRANKS: Yes, I would agree with that. I think the realisation that the world had changed came slowly home to the consciousness of the British people, and it was not finally made clear until the lightning flash of Suez in 1956.

CHARLTON: I wonder, therefore, if you'll forgive me if, perhaps unfairly, I quote to you from a paper written in August 1947 to the Foreign Secretary [Bevin] by Sir Edmund Hall-Patch, who was Deputy Under-Secretary of State and Bevin's economic adviser in the Foreign Office? Hall-Patch wrote:

'There is a well-established prejudice in Whitehall against a European Customs Union. It goes back a long way and is rooted in the old days of Free Trade. It is a relic of a world which has disappeared, probably never to return. The Board of Trade is overstating the case against it. One of their most potent arguments is that we have to *choose* between a European Customs Union and the Commonwealth. However that may be, the Board of Trade have successfully blocked for two years our efforts to look at these proposals objectively. As a result of Marshall's proposals (i.e. OEEC) European imaginations have been fired. It may be possible to integrate in some measure comparable with the vast industrial integration and potential of the United States, which the Russians are trying to emulate. If some such integration does *not* take place Europe will gradually decline in the face of pressure from the United States on the one hand and the USSR on the other.'

And Hall-Patch adds right at the end, 'I have discussed these issues with Oliver Franks exhaustively'.

FRANKS: Indeed, that is quite true. Edmund Hall-Patch was a friend of mine. He was, as it were, my opposite number in the Foreign Office while a lot of this was going on: and he was a very prescient man. But I still think that what I said was true both for ministers, politicians of the time, and for the mass of the British people, and no doubt it was true for the Board of Trade, which remained Gladstonian for as long as it has ever existed. Now Hall-Patch had these opinions and, if you look at them over a longer period of time, fifteen or twenty years, of course he was seeing ahead with very considerable accuracy. But if you're asking yourself, as I am trying to do now, what we thought and what the possibilities seemed to be in, say, the five years after the war, then I don't think the views which he puts forward so lucidly there carried as much weight as he would have liked them to.

CHARLTON: The interesting thing to me is that they were there at the very centre of British policy-making but appear to have had little or no impact upon that. Now, accepting that the British voter may not have been educated to accept this, is that the reason they weren't put forward? Or was Hall-Patch a voice in the wilderness at that time?

FRANKS: No, he was not a voice in the wilderness. But he was not a typical member of the Foreign Office. He'd spent a great deal of his time abroad, as a representative of the Treasury and in places like Bangkok. He was a widely experienced man. In early life he'd earned his living as a musician in the streets of Paris! He was not a typical Treasury mandarin. But I don't think that's why his views didn't gain universal and immediate acceptance. I think it is because the structure of thinking in government departments and among ministers – and more generally – was more as I have been describing it. Therefore, while he was listened to, I don't think people went his way.

CHARLTON: But we're coming to a time when it's clear that we are creating hostility on the European continent because of our 'stand off' attitude, our refusal to take part. Also, presumably, we're incurring the hostility of the Americans, because within twelve months or so the final text of the Foreign Assistance Act [the Marshall Plan] for the approval of Congress has a sentence which was not in the Administration's original draft bill in 1947 for Marshall Aid. That said, 'It is further declared to be the policy of the United States that the continuity of assistance provided by the United States should at all times be dependent on the continuity of *cooperation* among countries taking part in the programme'. That was the original wording, but the word 'unification' replaces 'cooperation' in the 1949 and 1950 enactments in Congress as the only way Europe is to get its money. Therefore it seems that the Americans are making

their money to Europe dependent upon this process of 'unification'. Now, if we wouldn't have the Customs Union because it implied 'unification' – and we'd successfully opted for 'cooperation' in OEEC – how did we get away with that?
FRANKS: I think because, and here my recollection might be at fault, it's because Paul Hoffman, who was the director of the ECA, the American 'European Cooperation Agency', was pleading before Congress to get his money and he knew that Congress wanted to see more unity in Europe. He was perfectly willing to substitute the word 'unification' for 'cooperation'. And he had a meaning for it too. This wasn't merely words, but what he wanted were the two great measures which *did* happen in OEEC, which were the measures for the abolition of quantitative restrictions on trade, quotas and all that, and the abolition of exchange controls. These were unifying Europe. They were unifying the flow of money and the flow of trade, and this is what Paul Hoffman wanted and what he got. He would have said, had he been questioned by a Committee of the Congress about that word 'unification' and what had happened in Europe, 'they've done it, they're unifying themselves'. He never thought, or at least he never thought in terms of a practical objective that he himself could pursue and go for, of either a wider nor a more intense form of unification than that. It's very easy to read into the word 'unification' a federal government, like the United States. It wasn't in Paul Hoffman's mind.

THE BATTLE WHICH Britain 'won' over how Marshall Aid was to be administered reflected the British disapproval of strong and independent organisations – independent, that is, of sovereign governments. There was an obvious suspicion that they might be captured by those who wished to further federalist designs or sympathies. But there was, according to Lord Franks, an extra dimension to this opposition – something inherently different in the British approach which distanced Britain from the continental politicans who hitherto had earnestly canvassed for British leadership in Europe – and at a time when the material assistance from the Americans, together with the Russian threat, had plainly made it possible for the very first time seriously to entertain the idea of European unity.

FRANKS: One answer would be that the British very rarely, when they are innovating, think in terms of new Institutions. The Americans always do. The French are apt to. The things you were telling me, and I accept it, that the British objected to, were *all* institutions of one kind and another. And you will remember that it took us until 1975 to accept European institutions – and then we had to have a referendum. Now, I think that the real question is not about the reality of cooperation, the genuineness of the desire to cooperate, it is about why we didn't like being tied up with *institutions* of cooperation. This is why we jibbed at the Customs Union, and this is why we jibbed at the Coal and Steel Community.
CHARLTON: But if we could have had a part in shaping them and forming them, does that argument still stand?
FRANKS: I think that the ordinary British opinion of the actual decades I'm talking about would be that of course it makes a difference. The point is that, if you are part of, and subject to, an institution which in some degree has a life of its own, initiative, spontaneity, ability to formulate policy, then you are no

longer as free as you were before. And this is the point. Now, even though you can help mould the institution, the facts about the institution remain even when you've had your influence. The problem has been that we have been very reluctant to submit ourselves, if you like, to the rulings of an institution.

AT THIS TIME, in 1948 and 1949, the vast American aid received under the Marshall Plan was allied in the American mind to the undefined concept of a European community of which Britain would become a member and which the Americans would help to stand upon its own feet. It is also clear that British policy was hostile to, and was arousing hostility in return, going any further than the more detached forms of cooperation expressed so far in OEEC. A prominent skirmish took place in 1948 between Britain and the Americans, whose impatience with convention, combined with the largely unfamiliar opportunities for constructive 'statecraft', inclined them to side for the most part with the Continental Europeans. The central figure in this developing tactical battle was a staunch admirer of Britain who, as we have already seen, had been almost the first earnestly and persistently to seek British leadership of post-war Europe – the Belgian Foreign Minister, Paul-Henri Spaak. Spaak was an ardent proponent of European union and the issue was his nomination to the Chairmanship of the Organisation for European Economic Cooperation (OEEC). Ernest Bevin and the Foreign Office successfully vetoed his appointment. In his own memoirs Spaak strikes a wry, if not sour, note about this incident, saying that when he went to America in 1948 as the prospective Chairman of OEEC, both President Truman and John Snyder, the Head of the Treasury, had told him 'everything was at my disposal'. Then, Spaak goes on, 'I returned to Europe with great prospects in this task, but I had not reckoned with British obstinacy and influence'.

Spaak's memoirs also quote an extract from a personal letter he received from Bevin which sounds rather like Henry V's sentiments about France. The King's friendship for France having been questioned, he replied that he 'loved it so dearly', he 'would not part with a village of it'! Spaak was told by Bevin that he was 'playing a major role as Belgian Prime Minister and Foreign Minister in the renaissance of the West and, I fear, you may not be able to exercise the same influence and authority in OEEC'. Spaak noted he had every reason to believe that this advice was meant sincerely. 'However, Bevin's feelings were undoubtedly influenced in part by his wish to prevent the OEEC from being led by a man whose ideas about the organisation of Europe differed from those of the British government.' There seems little reason to doubt that the Foreign Office considered that a personality of Spaak's force and vigour could not but enhance the centrifugal pull of the OEEC upon the European governments towards the politicisation of 'unity' in Europe. The most powerful and influential voice among Ernest Bevin's Foreign Office advisers upon the European policy of this period belonged to Roger Makins, now Lord Sherfield.

SHERFIELD: The issue came up specifically in 1948 when there were discussions about the organisation of the OEEC in Paris. The Americans were very anxious that there should be a kind of Director General of the OEEC, in the person of Spaak, who would be in a sense independent of governments. He would be a kind of what the French called 'haute personnalité compétente'.

Marshall Aid gives Europe its first common goal and leads to a fundamental split about the nature of unity. Bevin signs for Britain, July 1948. (Seated with him are Sir Stafford Cripps and, on his left, Lew Douglas, the American Ambassador. Standing behind Cripps is Harold Wilson, President of the Board of Trade, and third from left Sir Roger Makins (Lord Sherfield), perhaps the most influential of Bevin's policy advisers about Europe.)

Now, we resisted that because we felt that there should not be an individual of that kind standing between the governments. We wanted an *intergovernmental* body, which was eventually agreed. We had absolutely nothing against Spaak who we regarded as being an absolutely first-rate fellow.

CHARLTON: And a great friend of Britain?

SHERFIELD: That's right. But it was more a matter of principle. And of course it did show a tendency which really ran throughout that period in American policy, of picking a man in whom they put all their confidence, with whom they wanted to deal rather than backing the government. Rather than going for the dynamics of the situation they went for the personality. The Americans wanted to stand back a bit and deal with Europe through the individual, the personality, rather than having to negotiate with the governments. We did not want that. We wanted the whole thing to be on an intergovernmental basis.

CHARLTON: But surely they were dealing with a personality like Spaak because they wanted brought about the political result that Spaak stood for, which was integration in Europe?

SHERFIELD: That's right.

THE INCIDENT INVOLVING SPAAK, although perhaps it qualifies for the French category of an 'affair', was a powerful indicator that British policy had moved from detachment or apathy about closer integration in Europe to one of outright opposition, in this instance, to the perceived 'federal' implications in the Spaak appointment. By succeeding in blocking his advance to take control of OEEC, Britain therefore still held the initiative over political developments on the Continent as far as defining what was meant, or desirable to achieve, in the form of 'unity'.

That was 1948. The year 1949 saw and foreshadowed major developments in this argument. In that year Winston Churchill saw the birth of his Council of Europe – that 'instrument of European government' which at the very earliest moment when it was possible to foresee with conviction ultimate victory – at the time of Alamein and Stalingrad in 1942 – he had told Anthony Eden Britain should seek to establish. Vigorous and restless in opposition Churchill had founded the United Europe movement at home after a big rally at the Albert Hall in 1947. A principal part in the launching of this movement was played by his son-in-law, Duncan Sandys. In terms of the history of Britain and Europe to come, the most notable appointment made by Churchill was of Harold Macmillan to head the London Committee of what became, at the Congress of Europe at the Hague in 1948, the 'European Movement'.

At this seminal meeting, amid great enthusiasms, Churchill delivered anew his call for European Unity. Almost a thousand delegates, eight former Prime Ministers, twenty-seven Foreign Ministers and all political parties except the Communists took part. The main outcome – the lead was taken by Churchill himself – was for a new European institution to be created, a Parliamentary Assembly at Strasbourg.

Reinforced by the official views of the Foreign Office, which seemed still to draw upon its dismissive reception given to Churchill's original suggestion in 1942, Bevin was uneasy and reluctant about involvement in this new proposal. It was clearly his intention to restrict its scope as much as possible. Sir Roderick Barclay was Bevin's Private Secretary at the Foreign Office and one of his most clearly informed biographers.

BARCLAY: Admittedly he had slightly ambivalent views about the Council of Europe. He was once heard to say, 'If you open that Pandora's box, you never know what Trojan horses will jump out', and that represented to some extent his doubts about the future of the Council of Europe. He was much more confident about OEEC and NATO.
CHARLTON: About that happily mixed metaphor, Pandora's box and Trojan horses, what informed him? What led him to make that judgement, a very damning one, really?
BARCLAY: I think that at the outset he saw it as one of the ways of bringing the French and the Germans together, and there is no doubt he appreciated very clearly the need to bring France and Germany into a state of mutual understanding and cooperation. You had to avoid the dangers of the past and the Council of Europe might help. And then, when the negotiations developed beyond a certain point, he had a slight fear that the Parliament might take too much upon itself, that they would get out of hand, and the Council of Ministers of the Council of Europe would not be able to keep the Parliamentarians in check. I think that he feared it might become a nuisance.

BEVIN'S 'SLIGHTLY AMBIVALENT VIEWS' were seen by the more ardent 'Europeans' only as evidence that the British were deliberately dragging their

Churchill's renewed call for European Unity at the Hague, 1948, results in a new European institution, the Parliamentary Assembly at Strasbourg.

feet in terms of the spirit of innovation and experiment which underpinned the widening support for European unity on the continent. Bevin's insistence upon an Assembly which was to be only consultative and stripped of all but debating powers would soon prove to be manifestly insufficient for the mood developing in Western Europe. We enter a period which may now be seen as beginning a gradual but more visible and significant loss of the initiative by British diplomacy in Europe. Christopher Mayhew, the Parliamentary Under-Secretary for Foreign Affairs, remembers the following exchanges with Bevin and the context in which the Foreign Secretary considered the growing support for 'unification' which led to the establishment of the first new European institution, the Council of Europe.

MAYHEW: The United States had this incredible egotistical feeling that Europe should do what they had done. It was quite clear that the Americans thought Europe should federate, and of course Bevin was wholly against this. I mean, you couldn't mention it. I remember very dashingly mentioning the word 'federation' to him once and he bit my head off! I never mentioned it again.

CHARLTON: Can you elaborate a bit more on Bevin's outburst to you over 'federation'. How did it come up?

MAYHEW: It was not that he was anti-European. I think I can frankly say that he was being pressed all the time by Churchill and the Tories to take a strong lead, and sometimes of course by the soft centre of the Labour Party, the Crossmans and so on. They had this concept that we didn't belong with America and we should have a third force of Western European countries and the idea of an independent Western Europe. There were times when this was quite a happy thing to say to the Labour Party because it was, so to speak, anti defence arrangements

The birth of the European Movement: Churchill at the Hague Congress in 1948.

with America. With these two pressures against him Bevin was absolutely stoutly opposed. Occasionally he had to yield something. I remember after the Hague Conference, where Churchill made a great song and dance about our future in Europe, I remember Bevin saying, 'Well, you know, Chris, we've got to give them something and I think we'll give them this talking shop in Strasbourg, the Council of Europe, we'll give them this talking shop'.

CHARLTON: Did Bevin take the view, do you remember, that by refusing to take part, to the extent that the Europeans wished, in all this that Britain did have a more or less effective veto over continental union? That our abstention, or our reluctance, was tantamount at least to a brake upon progress in this direction?

MAYHEW: I don't recall that Bevin actually wished a veto, but certainly as far as Britain was concerned he was determined that we shouldn't go into any kind of federal thing.

THERE ARE ADDITIONAL INCREMENTS in Bevin's overall judgements of British interests at this time which deserve attention. Mayhew hints at what is confirmed by others, that Bevin was somewhat nettled by the clamour over Europe and Churchill's role in promoting it. The public display of Churchill's European enthusiasms was not confined by him to the customary forums of Parliament and evangelistic assemblies like the great Congress of the Hague in 1948 where he placed himself at the head of the commitment to European unity made by so many political parties and leaders. Churchill carried that banner through the streets of London, too. Harold Macmillan recalls in his diaries how, upon returning from the Hague, Churchill led Macmillan and others in solemn procession from his rooms in Westminster up Whitehall, waving his cigar and giving his victory sign to gathering crowds before turning down Downing Street. There, upon reaching No. 10, he deployed the case to Bevin and to Attlee (who 'received this deputation with gravity') that they should be taking the initiative in constituting a European Assembly, as Churchill put it to them, 'on as wide a basis as practicable'.

A participant in this 'deed' of Churchill's was Kenneth Lindsay, the Member of Parliament for the Combined Universities. He told me that, when assembled in Churchill's rooms before they set out, the old leader had looked around the assembled company and, with that ubiquitous sense of adventure which he could on such occasions still command and communicate, had rumbled with infectious enthusiasm, 'Have we a flag?', and then with mock solemnity, 'Let us march on Downing Street!'

That the great figure of Churchill should choose to lay siege to No. 10 in so public a manner carried the weighty implications of rebuke for the incumbents, and the lack of creative imagination being shown by them over the emergent European issue. What then did Bevin think of Churchill's interventions at this time in Europe? Sir Roderick Barclay's recollection is that, in these highest considerations of policy, the more worldly human emotions and frailties played their part.

BARCLAY: I think that he had a slightly – I don't say that he was jealous of Churchill's position in Europe, but he had a slight feeling that Churchill was using his enormous prestige in all the liberated countries to weigh in on Foreign Affairs issues which, Ernie thought, were really his responsibility. And I don't think Churchill consulted him before making any of these speeches. I think that Bevin probably thought he was taking advantage of his reputation to push ideas which hadn't perhaps been fully worked out, and on which he, Ernie, would have had some suggestions to make.
CHARLTON: What would they have been?
BARCLAY: I think he would have approved the Fulton Speech entirely. I'm not sure about the European integration speeches, because I think he would probably have said to Churchill, 'Well, do you think that we could go along ourselves in an integrated Europe?' He was – there was a certain jealousy, I think. I remember the first trip I made with him to Washington. Churchill was over in America at the time, and there was a suggestion that he might be staying at the British embassy in Washington just when we arrived for the arrangements preceding the signing of the Atlantic Pact. Ernie got very excited and said that, if Churchill was going to be staying at the Embassy, he would have to stay somewhere else. He had a slight feeling that Churchill would steal his thunder, that he was such a glamorous character, and that it was a bit annoying to have him there just when Ernie wanted to be in the limelight and to make the great speeches and to be the chief British representative. There was this irritation at Churchill's interventions in the field of Foreign Affairs.
CHARLTON: Later on, David Maxwell Fyfe [Lord Kilmuir], the Conservative Lord Chancellor, wrote that, despite all Bevin's talk of a world without frontiers, of a world without passports, in which it would be possible to travel freely, Bevin was at heart a Little Englander.
BARCLAY: No, I don't accept that. He travelled a lot in the world. Before the war he'd been to North America, he'd been to Australia, he'd seen quite a lot of

the world. He enjoyed foreign travel, and on the whole enjoyed meeting foreigners. I don't think it's fair to say he was a Little Englander.

CHARLTON: Or that he meekly accepted the official scepticism about the movement towards continental unity?

BARCLAY: There was nothing ever meek about Ernie, and he certainly never accepted any official view without going into it very thoroughly. He was the Minister and he made up his own mind. And he always talked about 'my' policy, my policy this, or my policy would be to do this or that. It was really he who took the decisions and, on the papers which used to go up to him, you quite often had a tremendous 'NO' written against some recommendation.

CHARLTON: On the other hand, if you'll forgive me, I've seen a couple of Foreign Office files in which that rather proprietorial air – the instance I'm thinking of was a paper about Western Union in which he'd said something to the effect 'When I foresaw the need for Western Union' – was greeted by some anonymous, but no doubt very high-ranking, official with tremendous exclamation marks in the margin! It would seem the Foreign Office at least had reservations about who was the real author of that?

BARCLAY: Well, it's quite true that sometimes he persuaded himself that he had been the first person to think of this or that. There were obviously occasions when some new suggestion was put up which he rather liked the look of, and then adopted, and probably persuaded himself that he really thought of it in the first place. He was open to suggestion, he would openly receive recommendations, but it was in effect his policy.

AT THIS TIME, in 1949, the head of the Western Department of the Foreign Office was Evelyn Shuckburgh, later to become the principal Foreign Office aide to Anthony Eden. Sir Evelyn kept a diary which is an invaluable source of authentic contemporary reactions to events – most obviously of importance during the Eden years, but also more generally. As the prospect of the Council of Europe advanced, Bevin's personal deprecation of Churchill's interventions (which were, to a large extent, responsible for its emergence) had strong Foreign Office support. The division between Bevin, who thought of it as a 'talking shop', and those in Europe who wished it to become a more literal interpretation of Churchill's long-expressed desire for an 'instrument of European government' was an acute and unwelcome irritant to Whitehall. Shuckburgh's diary records a mutual confession of earnest desires that the developing implications of Churchill's stand could be averted.

SHUCKBURGH: Now this is February 1949. I see from my diary that I was present at an interview between Hector MacNeil, who was the Under-Secretary in the Foreign Office in the Labour government, and Rab Butler. They were really, in effect, sharing their concern together about the activities of Winston Churchill on the European scene and thinking it was going to be a great embarrassment to either, whether it was going to be a Labour or a Conservative government. And they were quite frank on the subject and let their hair down a bit about it. Hector MacNeil thought he would do damage to the Council of Europe by his activities. He used the phrase, 'We ought to have twentieth-century minds on both sides of the House in this matter'.

CHARLTON: What do you think they meant by that? The implication might be

that MacNeil and Butler supported the European 'idea', whereas in fact we
know they did not. It was Churchill who was calling for a political authority, a
Council of Europe?
SHUCKBURGH: I think that they were both thinking that the Council of
Europe would be ruined by Churchill's overenthusiastic espousal of
Federation.

ON 10 AUGUST 1949 the new Consultative Assembly of parliamentarians from
the European nations met in Strasbourg. There was some suspicion that those
who were most uneasy about this new institutional adventure in Europe, like
Ernest Bevin, thought its very remoteness from the national capitals would
inhibit any undue authority accruing to it.

   Churchill was still forcing the pace of British and European policy from the
foothills of opposition. It was at Strasbourg that he revealed the inner core of
his design and broached openly the cardinal question for the immediate future.
Looking around the Assembly he asked, 'Where are the Germans?' and went
on to press for an immediate invitation to the new German government to
attend. Harold Macmillan, who was there, thought that Churchill was at that
time in 1949 – four years after VE day – the only politician in Europe who could
have made such a speech. Later, in the lovely central square in Strasbourg, the
Place Kléber, with every part of it and every window overlooking it filled (the
only one not being so was Ernest Bevin's) Churchill spoke in French from a
balcony to enthusiastic crowds.

   By 1949 the noise of the infectious tumult in Strasbourg was making it clearer
that, while British policy had secured the principal flank it sought to safeguard
– the full participation of the Americans in the defence as well as the recovery of
Western Europe, this accelerating participation of the Americans, allied with
the regenerative idealism of the Europeans, was leaving Britain odd man out on
the issue of integration and defining the scope and structure of European unity.

   The year 1949 also marked the more forceful impact upon European affairs
of Jean Monnet who, above all others, orchestrated the beginnings of European
union in its practical forms and, with their advent, what became the routine of
powerful nations. By then Monnet had established an unassailable position in
the Fourth Republic as head of Le Plan – the French Plan for economic and all
other recovery. He had control of Marshall Aid funds and was protected in his
role as 'haute personnalité compétente', to use Lord Sherfield's job description,
from the frequent falls of government.

   Jean Monnet was, in reality, more than a Minister. He had been a British civil
servant on the Joint Purchasing Commission during two world wars and had
always worked closely with the Americans, with Roosevelt in particular in wartime. And, a fact of the greatest importance, the American support for the concept of 'integration' owed a good deal to the force and the clarity with which
Monnet was heard in Washington.

   Monnet's ideas grew out of the experience of World War I. He considered
that the outcome was so long in the balance then because the Allies 'had fought
side by side and not as a single organised force'. That to him was a self-evident
truth. It shaped and influenced all his thinking thereafter. And for Monnet to
demonstrate a truth as self-evident was, or ought to be, sufficient to have it
politically accepted.

Churchill in the Place Kleber, Strasbourg, 1949, four years after VE day. 'Where are the Germans?'

It was Monnet who was the real author of the dramatic offer of 'common citizenship' which Churchill had sponsored in London in 1940 as a last effort to try and keep France from surrendering, and in the war against Hitler. While Churchill did not conceal from his cabinet colleagues in 1940 his own doubts and objections to this proposal, he had said to Monnet as he came out of the cabinet room, 'At a time like this it shall not be said that we lack imagination'. The words of that Declaration were as follows (the occasion itself has been dealt with in more detail in the first chapter) and bear repeating as we come to reflect upon the personal influence now about to be freshly, and more widely and successfully, exercised by Monnet:

'At this fateful moment in the history of the modern world, the governments of the United Kingdom and the French Republic make this declaration of indissoluble union, the two governments declare that France and Great Britain shall no longer be two nations but one Franco-British union.'

For Jean Monnet this spectacular declaration was not an opportunist appeal at a moment of critical tactical importance or a merely formal text. It was an act which could have changed the course of events for the good of Europe. He died in 1979 heartily believing that still to be the case. Here is a characteristic judgement of his on Britain's ultimately undefined vision of European Unity, which Monnet himself gave to me in a BBC interview in 1975, some years before his death. I recalled that he would have nothing to do with the Council of Europe in the form in which, at British insistence, it finally emerged.

MONNET: Because it was nothing. Because it was a meeting of men of good-will, but with no power, no authority. It was a gathering of people, expressing general views and going home. But that is not *acting*, not taking decisions, which is the case in the Common Market; and for one reason you must understand, and I think we had better talk about that. The reason is that the Council of Europe was just a continuation of the cooperation of nations as we'd known it for years past. What we are trying to do is to create between the nations of Europe *a common interest*. And it can be achieved, we think, by a gradual transfer of sovereignty. Because the problems today transcend any nation. Look at the oil question. You think you can settle your oil question by the oil in the North Sea. You will find, I think, as things develop that something more is needed. It is common action. And what is needed today towards the Arab is common action. Because the problems are not national any more.

IT WAS IN 1949 that Monnet drew up his own blueprint for United Europe, the genesis of his own post-war thinking, based on the concepts of 1940. Monnet's opposite number, handling the planning of the British economy under Stafford Cripps, the Chancellor, was someone Monnet knew well, Edwin Plowden. Monnet considered Lord Plowden to be an essential channel and link in any closer-integrated relationship between France and Britain.

An unsuspected but major defeat for Britain's European policy lay in wait just twelve months ahead. This was the unfolding in 1950, at Monnet's direct inspiration, of the Schuman Plan for an integrated pool of strategic commodities, the Coal and Steel Community. This was the beginning of the practical implementation of Six-Power Federation in Europe. It addressed itself to the fundamental question of how Germany was to be safely reinstated, and within the Western Community. What is *not* so well known is that Monnet came first to the British before he, in the end, turned to the Germans for the building of this 'nucleus' of what became the European Community. In March and April of 1949 he held meetings with Edwin Plowden and Robert Hall (now Lord Roberthall) of the Treasury which, in retrospect, must be seen to have had great importance and significance. At those meetings Monnet was exploring afresh whether Britain and France would once more consider their joint problems as one nation. At the first meeting with Monnet, in March 1949, the Chancellor of the Exchequer, Sir Stafford Cripps, was also present together with Lord Plowden.

PLOWDEN: I must confess that my memories of that particular meeting are rather hazy. But Stafford Cripps of course was in many ways romantic, and he was interested, or beguiled, by Monnet's persuasion that great economic developments could come about through much closer association or unification of the British and French economies. I don't think that Stafford really ever thought in terms of the surrender of sovereignty to a joint nation or whatever the ultimate was, but he did see – he was conscious of – the economies of scale, and he was conscious of the need for change. He'd been very much influenced by his experience as Minister of Aircraft Production during the war when we *did* plan an enormous part of the British economy in detail. So therefore he saw this as something that might be extremely interesting. From that meeting there arose the meeting that Monnet and I held in April of 1949.

ARISING OUT OF THIS first discussion in March 1949 with Monnet, Plowden wrote to the Foreign Office for official policy guidance. Monnet had urged that Britain and France could not continue to treat forty million Germans as though they did not exist. He had made it clear that he thought Britain and France should act as one country. Plowden wished to know therefore from the Foreign Office how much importance Britain attached to relations with France.

PLOWDEN: My recollection is that they made it quite clear that France was extremely important to the United Kingdom, but that pre-eminently our relationship with the United States was the most important thing in our foreign policy.
CHARLTON: And how did you respond yourself, and how did the Foreign Office respond, to what you reported Monnet as saying – 'Here lies Western Europe between Communism in the East and the dynamic forces of American capitalism'? The unspoken thought is what are *we* jointly going to do about it. Monnet says that he 'did not think American capitalism could be transplanted to Europe in its American form, but would merely become what the Europeans thought the Americans would like to *see* in Europe', and that therefore 'it would have no dynamic force of its own'.
PLOWDEN: Well, this of course was a very typical Jean Monnet view. I'm afraid I was used to his rather higher flights of this kind and I didn't pay a great deal of attention to that analysis.
CHARLTON: But when Sir Roger Makins [Lord Sherfield], who has broad control of these large economic issues in Europe when it comes to policy, reports your meetings to Sir William Strang, the Permanent Under-Secretary, the record shows that he says this: 'For some time there has been a French desire for some special Franco-British discussions ... and Sir Edwin Plowden's solid realism and good sense should be helpful in expounding the United Kingdom view. He is going over there in April with Robert Hall of the Treasury and subordinates of sound sense.' Would I be right to suggest to you that there is a whiff there from the Foreign Office side, from Sir Roger Makins, of intent, perhaps even determination, not to get involved with any of this Monnet, 'Cartesian' philosophy – these rather highfalutin schemes. The words are mine, but was that the feeling?
PLOWDEN: You mean that he personally didn't want to get involved? Or do you mean that he didn't want the country to get involved?
CHARLTON: Either or.

PLOWDEN: The Foreign Office view was that we must pre-eminently hang on to the relationship with the United States and that nothing – no matter how important France was to us and Europe was to us – should stand in the way of that.

CHARLTON: But when the time comes for you to go to Monnet the following month – in April – and you are taking with you 'treasury officials and sub-ordinates of sound sense' as the Foreign Office has it – you have had your guidelines given to you. We are *not* going to get too closely involved in this sort of thing. Is it fair to say that?

PLOWDEN: I think that is so. But I think in fairness I can say we did look at the thing objectively. And again, to be fair, I don't think that those of us who went, and it was myself and Robert Hall and Alan Hitchman, just the three of us – and we discussed for a week in Monnet's country house outside Paris with him and Pierre Uri and Etienne Hirsch the possibilities of some closer association – I don't think that we three ever thought in terms of going as far as Monnet obviously did towards something so close that it meant the surrender of sover-eignty. We were quite prepared to think of very close relationships, but between two quite separate economies and quite separate countries.

I think you have got to put against it something broader in UK thinking. First of all, one's got to realise that we'd just won a war. We were still the centre of an Empire, not a Commonwealth, an Empire. There were lots and lots of colonies. We thought of ourselves still as one of the great world powers. Then there was a basic thing which entered into the thinking of a great many people. If you moved towards the surrender of sovereignty towards Europe, the Americans would go away. There is no doubt at all in my mind, and this is very clear in my recollections, that there were a lot of Americans who thought, well, if we can get the British into Europe and get them all tied up together into some nice federal or confederal system, then *we* can go *home*! And that all of us who had been associated with the wartime policies were very conscious would have been a disastrous thing. Maybe we took much too short a view, but I think that was a great influence at all discussions about closer unity with France and surrender of sovereignty.

AS LORD PLOWDEN MENTIONED, another participant on the British side during this fateful exploration in 1949 of the possibilities of unifying British and French policy objectives was an Australian-born Rhodes Scholar, Robert Hall of the Treasury. He was subsequently ennobled, without that frequent penalty involved in assuming a title of loss of a former public identity, as Lord Roberthall.

ROBERTHALL: It had been proposed to ministers, and as far as I was con-cerned to Cripps, the Chancellor of the Exchequer, that there should be talks on the official level about a closer economic relationship – in the first instance, between Britain and France. Monnet really wanted a *political pact* and, as one often hears it said nowadays, we could do it if there were the 'political will' present. Certainly I had not been accustomed to thinking in those terms, having been a civil servant from 1939. We felt that it was up to ministers to tell us what their 'political will' was, and then we could operate within that framework.

CHARLTON: Did Monnet discuss that difference with both of you? Because he was working outside the machinery of the government as Head of the French 'Plan' and it would seem that he may have seen in Plowden, who was heading the 'Plan' for Cripps in Britain, a kindred spirit. Did he talk to you about that? ROBERTHALL: I expect he thought that if there were this sort of agreement, Plowden and his organisation in London, and Monnet and his organisation in Paris, would work out the details. But he didn't seem to be at all ready with suggestions about how the details were going to be worked out. His idea was that we should, as it were, marry first. Then, with that commitment, we'd be under pressure to make it work.

ON THE FRENCH SIDE with Monnet at his Paris home during this week of talks was Pierre Uri, who later drafted for Monnet the essential precepts of the Treaty of Rome in 1956 and 1957, and also another of Monnet's closest confidants, Etienne Hirsch. What was it that Monnet believed to be possible to achieve with the British?

HIRSCH: Monnet realised that we had quite a number of difficulties in France and that you had other kinds of difficulties in England. And, according to what he had done in the First War and during the Second War, he felt that, in merging our problems, it would make everything easier. I think that was his main approach to the situation.
CHARLTON: But do you think that he was confident that he would find a sympathetic voice in Britain? That *we* should see things as *he* saw them?
HIRSCH: When Monnet started anything it was always with confidence. He was very optimistic and he would not have started if he had no confidence at all.
CHARLTON: Why did he choose the English?
HIRSCH: Because he had done in 1914 and in 1940. It was quite natural.
CHARLTON: Do you say that Monnet thought, at this time, that the British *were* the natural partners?
HIRSCH: Certainly!
CHARLTON: But why did he think that?
HIRSCH: Well, I just told you; because he had done that twice – to work for England and France going along together, solving their problems, and so it was quite natural for him to try that again. When we had our discussions together, I think we arrived at a certain number of constructive proposals. It was therefore a shock to Monnet and Uri and myself when we got the answer from Plowden that the government was not interested. We really thought that something could be done, because we had arrived at some constructive proposals.
CHARLTON: And what were they?
HIRSCH: The most apparent was that you had, in the UK, great problems for food, and we had in France great problems for coal. You had coal, we could produce the food, and that it would be of mutual benefit to do something together.
CHARLTON: What impression did you gain from your talks with Plowden?
HIRSCH: I had the impression that he was sympathetic, but that he had not the authority or position that Monnet had in France; that he had not the same kind of influence on his government as Monnet had upon the French government.
CHARLTON: Yes, economically it made good sense? But the political case was . . .

HIRSCH: Not even economically. My impression was that he had no real influence on the decision-making process.

CHARLTON: Monnet says in his subsequent memoirs that he found it very difficult, at this meeting, to steer the discussion around to those 'broader issues' for which, in his view, 'the discussions themselves were merely the point of departure'.

HIRSCH: I agree. I had the impression of some 'shyness' on the part of our British counterpart.

A SHYNESS ACCOUNTED FOR, to some extent no doubt, by the instructions, or guidance, Lord Plowden had received from the Foreign Office that Britain was *not* to become too closely involved in this mutual journey to an unknown destination which Monnet was suggesting. Within these restraints the exchanges were probably, of necessity, rather 'elliptical'. Can it be said that Lord Plowden, for his part, had the impression by the end of this week-long meeting in April 1949 that the French side had put forward a clearly defined idea of what they wished to do?

PLOWDEN: I don't think we appreciated that Monnet wanted to go as far as he obviously showed that he did want to go.

CHARLTON: But that week-long meeting had certainly clarified ideas as between the two countries rather deeply?

PLOWDEN: It brought out that he wanted to do things which, we actually said during the discussions, we did not think were possible. I mean much closer unity of the economies. And we came back with a limited number of proposals which, when we did put them through Stafford Cripps to Ernie Bevin, died the death because Bevin felt that *this* would go too far in the surrender of sovereignty. Even the limited proposals. I don't want to pretend that any of us really, who were dealing with these things, had anything like the vision that Monnet had towards a 'Western European power' or whatever you like to call it. We still were thinking in terms of Britain, and of standing between the United States and Western Europe and Russia, and so on; as being an independent great power.

CHARLTON: Monnet agreed, as you've just said, that you'd make it clear to him there was no place in your philosophy – Sir Edwin Plowden's philosophy – for delegating any of Britain's national sovereignty. But Monnet wondered, in his memoirs, whether you, Lord Plowden, had been too little prepared to grasp the point, or had he, Jean Monnet, been insufficiently explicit?

PLOWDEN: I think probably the latter is true. I don't think we realised how far he wanted to go. Now that doesn't mean it would have come to any different result. I think it might have frightened us even more! I don't think he did make it clear at the time how far he wanted to go.

CHARLTON: He quoted a letter that you wrote to him at the end of this year, 1949, after Robert Hall of the Treasury had been talking to Monnet again, and in the letter you said, 'Robert Hall has mentioned to me his recent conversation in which you [Jean Monnet] reverted to the idea of exchanging United Kingdom coal for French foodstuffs, in a manner which would make plain to the world the reality of Anglo-French cooperation.' Then, Lord Plowden, you said this: 'Without challenging your underlying idea, I think we must take account of the facts as they exist, which suggest that there is, at present, little basis for an arrangement of the kind you suggest outside the ordinary commercial exchanges.' Do you remember this letter?

PLOWDEN: Yes, I do remember now.

CHARLTON: Monnet proceeds in his memoirs to add this: 'It could not have been more clearly or authoritatively stated that the British Government had no desire to commit itself, however loosely, to a relationship which might lead to a closer one with France. And therefore' – and this to me is the most important point – 'the attempt to create a nucleus around which a European Community might be formed had met with no response from the one great power in Europe which was then in a position to take on such a responsibility, the United Kingdom.' Now, that rather apocalyptic verdict – was that apparent to you, do you believe, at the time that you had these talks with Monnet in March and April of 1949?

PLOWDEN: I don't think, you see, that we really believed in the vision he had of forming a nucleus around which a new Europe could be built. After all, for I don't know how many hundreds of years Britain had kept out of Europe. And suddenly to ask it to change, to give up its external, its worldwide, role in order to join with a Europe which was *down and out* at the time, required a vision which I'm quite sure I hadn't got, and I doubt whether very many people in the United Kingdom had. Some may now *think* they had, but I don't think they *did*!

CHARLTON: If I may just quote to you again that last phrase of Monnet's: 'Therefore the attempt to create a nucleus around which a European Community might be formed had met with no response from the one great power in Europe which was then in a position to take on such a responsibility.' Is that not the answer to a British doubt, often expressed then and since, that Monnet wanted us in Europe?

PLOWDEN: Oh, I have no doubt that he did want us in Europe. No doubt at all. He did hope, although I don't think he really *expected* that we would join and form the nucleus. But he felt it was necessary to make the first approach to us. And then he hoped, as I think he says in his memoirs somewhere, certainly he said it to me on many occasions, 'When it is a working thing, *then* you'll want to join.' He was quite right. We did.

CHARLTON: Let us be quite clear, because we are a few months away now from the 'shock' of the unfolding of the Schuman Plan to us in the summer of the following year, 1950, can Monnet have been under any illusion about what our attitude would be? And could we have been, legitimately, under any illusion about what he intended to do?

PLOWDEN: He hoped, I think, up until December – certainly Etienne Hirsch told me only the other day – they hoped up until December 1949 that something might come between England and France. And then, by then, he became completely convinced that we were not going to do anything. It was then that he turned towards trying to form the Schuman Plan, the Coal and Steel Community.

AND IN THE FOLLOWING retrospective verdict from the French side as to whether the British and the French, in the persons of Plowden and Monnet, had fully understood one another, Etienne Hirsch spoke for Monnet:

HIRSCH: I believe that Monnet could get something through the French government, and apparently that was not the case for Plowden.

CHARLTON: Yes. So Plowden wrote to Monnet, didn't he, after these meetings, and Monnet seizes upon the Plowden letter which says it is impossible to push these forms of cooperation beyond a certain point – and Monnet takes that as evidence that the British had made a decision – this is never publicly declared – but that they had made a decision that they would not link themselves so closely in any relationship with France. Can you remember his reactions when he got that letter?

HIRSCH: Monnet expected something more positive. It was certainly a deceit, do you say that?

CHARLTON: A deceit? That sounds a bit harsh. He was deceived, do you think?

HIRSCH: He was deceived, very disappointed, by this letter. He really thought that we had arrived at some positive conclusions and that something would come of it. He didn't know exactly what, but something.

CHARLTON: Now that is interesting. There was a difference between the tone of the talks and the subsequent formal reply, was there?

HIRSCH: Certainly. The talks started slowly, but living four days together – it changes the atmosphere. At the end the atmosphere was really very cordial and constructive.

CHARLTON: Then comes the letter throwing cold water on the whole thing?

HIRSCH: Yes, exactly.

CHARLTON: And what did Monnet think had happened?

HIRSCH: He thought that Plowden did not get the ear of the government.

CHARLTON: How important, in retrospect, is that meeting between Plowden and Monnet when it comes to future developments? Because within a few months we are going to see the birth, in embryo at least, of the Schuman Plan.

HIRSCH: Yes, I think that if an agreement had been reached between France and England it would have been the stepping stone for the further developments with Germany and the other countries. So Monnet had to find *another* way then to get things moving.

CHARLTON: Yes, but that's the point. In other words, it is only when he got a rebuff from Britain that he turned to Adenauer and to Germany? Is that what you say?

HIRSCH: Exactly.

THE MEETINGS IN Jean Monnet's house in Paris in 1949 would seem to be a hardly known reconnaissance, even a rehearsal, for the events of 1950. Foremost among these was the bombshell, as it was received officially in Whitehall and by public opinion, of the Schuman Plan. And with it the beginnings of six-power 'federation' on the Continent. Its advent produced a major row between Britain on the one hand and the Americans and Europeans on the other. It marks the first most obvious and public moment when British diplomacy 'lost the initiative' it had held over the nature and form of the political reconstruction of Western Europe after the war.

4
The Schuman Plan
– Losing the Initiative

So IT WAS THAT, five years after the end of the Second World War, just when Ernest Bevin and the Foreign Office could look back with deep satisfaction upon Bevin's decisive contribution in securing the full involvement of the United States in both the defence and the economic recovery of Western Europe – when they could therefore hope that an adequate, stable place had been found for Britain in a world that was greatly changed – British diplomacy in Europe was suddenly outmatched. The immediate cause was the startling innovation and challenge of the Schuman Plan. The decision made by the British government in 1950 not to take part in the negotiations which put the Plan into effect and which led to the setting up of the first European 'community', the Coal and Steel pool, altered the further course of European politics.

As a consequence of the immediate and continuing favourable responses the Europeans and the Americans made to the Schuman proposals, Britain lost the more or less controlling influence it had managed to exercise until then over the evolving character and extent of European unity. Until the Schuman Plan, Britain and the United States with France had travelled together, albeit at times out of step, but together, in the exploration of common approaches to the use of American aid for survival and the looming question of including Germany within the community of the western nations. At the crossroads of the Schuman Plan they parted company. France got the decisive endorsement of the United States to go in a direction to which Britain had been opposed at almost every step, the closer, practical integration of Europe.

It was not just the far-reaching implications of the Schuman Plan – which was the beginning of a distinctively European economic system – that came as a surprise to Whitehall. The real shock was the calculated detachment of the United States, implicit in their support of the Plan, from that privileged and more exclusive embrace, the Anglo-American 'Special Relationship' which it had been the most dedicated task of British policy to cement and reinforce.

Jean Monnet, at his meetings with the British Treasury representatives Edwin Plowden and Robert Hall beginning in April of 1949, had explored his general proposition that Britain and France should act together as one nation to deal above all with the imminent problem posed by the growing independence and recovery of Germany. Monnet wanted an economic union between Britain and France which would form the foundation block of a future European community. The British side in those talks had negative instructions from the Foreign Office about encouraging support for Monnet's concepts. By

December of 1949 the talks had failed. Britain would not cooperate in the manner suggested.

Lord Sherfield, to whom Lord Plowden had referred Monnet's overtures in 1949 for official Foreign Office guidance as to Britain's reply, corroborates that it was only at this juncture, having been turned down by Britain, that Monnet took the course he did.

SHERFIELD: I think he can't have been under any illusion, or if he was Plowden would certainly have disabused him of it, that we would enter a federal grouping. And I think that was the reason that he persuaded Schuman to go ahead with the Schuman Plan without us and without consultation with us.

ONLY FIVE MONTHS LATER, the Schuman plan designed by Jean Monnet was announced. It was published, without prior consultation, on 9 May 1950. It was also revealed to Dean Acheson, the American Secretary of State, in Paris the day before Britain and Ernest Bevin got to hear of it.

The Schuman Plan was a reversal of the traditional French policy towards Germany. It marked the departure from Britain's side, and in a direction the British were known to oppose, of the Americans. Sir Roderick Barclay, who was Bevin's principal Private Secretary at the Foreign Office, believed this was the situation in which the British Foreign Secretary found himself suddenly out-flanked by the diplomatic coup of the Schuman Plan.

BARCLAY: I think that he felt things were beginning to move the right way for us. He had got his Atlantic Treaty. You had the beginnings of coordinated European defence, and he was entirely in favour of that. You had got a fairly well-developed system of cooperation in economic affairs, and he was all in favour of that. All these were, to some extent, working towards European unity, and at the same time they were not impinging on our relationship with the United States – or apparently not – and equally our trade with the Common-wealth (which then, of course, was far more important than our trade with Europe) was unaffected. So that was all good and in accordance with his ideas.

Then you have this new concept which seemed to him, and I think to a lot of us in this country, to be something which was alien to our way of thought. It involved a certain, well, surrender of sovereignty if you like, which was some-thing which didn't appeal to us and it didn't seem to us to be necessary. There were other good ways to collaborate without having all this.

CHARLTON: Were you with Bevin when he actually learnt about it, the Schuman Plan?

BARCLAY: Yes. And of course what made it worse was the feeling that it was suddenly sprung on him, and that there had obviously been a lot of discussion about it before, and from which he had been kept in ignorance. Then he dis-covered that Acheson knew all about it. That was another sore point, that the Americans had been told and he had not. After all, this affected the policy of the three governments towards Germany, and we were as much involved as they were; and he certainly ought to have known about it. That immediately started it off in an unfavourable light as far as he was concerned.

PASTEURISED THOUGH MEMORY may be by the proprieties of diplomacy and

The Schuman Plan, 1950. Europe does not wait for Britain. The French Foreign Minister, Robert Schuman, with Bevin in the Foreign Office (Sir Roderick Barclay in the background).

the passage of the years, it is not in dispute that Ernest Bevin had two sulphurous rows in the second week of May 1950. One with the Americans and one with the French.

BARCLAY: He could be fairly rough, particularly with people who could talk English. Of course, with Schuman it all had to be translated, which made it slightly more difficult. But I think he made it pretty clear that he felt that he should have been consulted at an early stage and that he wasn't at all sure that he liked this idea at all! I remember him looking absolutely like death. His face was very expressive and, if something had gone wrong, he looked absolutely like a thundercloud. What made it worse, perhaps, was that he'd just come out of hospital a few days before. He probably wasn't in very good shape physically. And, of course, his health was one of the problems all through this period. That was probably an additional factor in his response to the Schuman Plan.

I think the immediate cause of his fury was the manner of its presentation, this going behind his back as he saw it. But then, the more he looked at it, the more he saw the objections from his point of view and the less he liked the whole thing, the whole idea. There were two stages: there was the immediate response; and then there was the more considered response which was really equally unfavourable.

BEFORE EXAMINING THE REASONS why the British cabinet said 'No' to the
Schuman Plan, we should recall the wider context in which this revolutionary
proposal saw the light of day. In May of 1950, the American, British and French
foreign ministers were due to meet in London to discuss the future of
Germany. Preparatory talks among the top British and American foreign-policy
officials for this meeting were held in London in April. The State Department
archives, which are now available, show that the Americans, for their part, had
come to London prepared to make a searching examination of the whole
question of Britain's relationship to Europe and to the United States. In summary, these American records of the discussions with their Foreign Office
counterparts reveal that it was the American view that Britain could and should
be doing more, short of 'federation', both to lead and to participate in an integrated economic system in Western Europe.

The British officials (principally Lord Sherfield and Lord Gladwyn)
countered that to do so would lead down the path to 'federation', to which
Britain was flatly opposed. A key American intervention in these talks came
from an influential roving ambassador, Charles 'Chip' Bohlen. Bohlen said that
the United Kingdom 'was now indicating a substantial change in its position'.
That while in 1947, with American aid under the Marshall Plan, 'the idea was
born of a European community of which the United Kingdom would be a
member, and which the United States would help to become a self-sustaining
entity, an idea still held by the American Congress and the American public', it
appeared that Britain 'was now saying that such a community was not attainable
with Britain in it'. The Americans added that there was little chance the French
would agree to a continental union without the British in it because 'they were
scared of the Germans'.

The State Department minutes show that Lord Gladwyn, then Gladwyn
Jebb, responded for the British side to Bohlen's assertion. He replied that the
'United Kingdom was concerned that the Americans wanted to push Britain
into steps leading to economic or political union of Western Europe'.

In addition to being challenged with the exercise of 'undue caution', the
British side were further charged at this meeting in London with 'not exercising
the required leadership at times'. The Americans appeared to concede that
while this may have been attributable in part to uncertainty about what the
United States really meant by integration and whether the United States was
pushing Britain into full union with the Continent, the British attitudes
stemmed in part from 'an unwillingness to subject the domestic economy of the
United Kingdom to the impact which would result from greater freedom of
movement in goods, capital and labour within the area of Western Europe
generally'.

The American summary of these talks, prepared for Acheson for his forthcoming visit, said that the American side had continued to insist that 'the
pressures of a substantially free market' would lead to the most efficient use of
resources in Western Europe. They believed that the United Kingdom could
stand the competition and that they must, the other countries of Western
Europe having done so, if they were to make 'the necessary adjustments'.
Acheson was also told that it was the British view that 'the maintainence of high
and stable levels of employment throughout the Western democracies limits the
pace at which progress could be made in this direction'.

Philip Jessup, one of Acheson's senior advisers and Ambassador at large, told the British representatives towards the end of the discussions that 'what the United States wanted was a healthy Europe', and that 'the situation facing us is such that the United Kingdom's position should be looked at again'. Lord Sherfield (then Sir Roger Makins) rejoined that he 'understood that the United Kingdom was not being asked to enter any institutional adventures' in Western Europe. The Americans demurred about 'adventures' and said only that 'the UK could go further'.

The flavour which emerges from these important exchanges in April 1950 is that, overall, the British seemed confident that, in their determination *not* to go any further in forms of cooperation with Europe than they had done already, they had in effect checkmated the developing American support, particularly in the State Department, for commitment to more positive forms of 'integration'. In consequence, the British believed that the United States would have to sail the tack which Britain advocated, of a wider and looser but, above all, Atlantic community, to include the Americans as well as the Germans. It was this feeling which was no doubt why, as Sir Roderick Barclay has recalled, Ernest Bevin by April 1950 thought 'things were moving Britain's way'.

It was into this month of Anglo-American stalemate over the most desirable directions to be pursued in Europe for sustained recovery, and on the American side a reawakening of their latent frustration and impatience with what they considered to be Britain's undue caution and lack of leadership in achieving a European 'community', that Jean Monnet now stepped adroitly with his radical and comprehensive alternative, the Schuman Plan.

The principal architect and influence among Foreign Office officials of the European policy at this time was Lord Sherfield, who agrees that the Schuman Plan could not have succeeded without the vital American endorsement.

SHERFIELD: Oh, undoubtedly. Well, in a way the Schuman Plan let them off the hook.
CHARLTON: Let who off the hook?
SHERFIELD: The Americans. Because immediately before, or in the period before, the announcement of the Schuman Plan the Americans, or some Americans certainly, were coming around much more to the British view of the *Atlantic community* development, including of course Europe in this wider grouping. They were coming around to that and there were certain Americans who certainly understood the British view and had some sympathy with it. George Kennan was certainly one of them, Julius Holmes, their Minister in London, was one, and there were others who certainly had some sympathy with the British point of view. They certainly understood it much better, I think, than the Hoffmans [Paul Hoffman, the American administrator of the Marshall Plan funds in Europe], the Harrimans [Averell Harriman] and certainly David Bruce [then the American ambassador in Paris], who were moving strongly on the other tack.

LORD SHERFIELD'S OPINION that the Schuman Plan 'got the Americans off the hook' would seem well justified, to judge by the evidence available in the State Department archives in Washington. Just three weeks before the Coal and Steel community proposed by the Schuman Plan was announced, David

Bruce had written to Dean Acheson, the American Secretary of State. As already suggested, Bruce, like Jack McCloy in Germany and Lewis Douglas in London, was a powerful figure in the writing of American policy, not just carrying it into effect. All three of these American diplomats were enthusiastic supporters of political and economic integration as the way to a healthier and self-sustaining Europe which would diminish, in the long term, the cost to the Americans of their present obligations and commitment. In his letter to Acheson David Bruce said that he 'could well understand why our most dependable and powerful ally, the United Kingdom, might claim "special status" from us. However, it is almost impossible for us to acknowledge this without, at the same time, prejudicing our hopes of coordinating the efforts of the free peoples of the Occident for a common purpose.' Bruce went on:

> 'I think we should face this problem of the United Kingdom cold bloodedly. First there will be no real integration without the wholehearted cooperation of the United Kingdom. The United Kingdom will *not* wholeheartedly participate in a purely European integration. Ergo, there will *be* no purely European integration. Consequently the United States must probably cease to press for integration in the full sense in which it has been advocated to date.'

Armed with this pragmatic, if perhaps doleful, advice from Bruce in Paris, Dean Acheson set out for London and the Foreign Ministers meeting between Bevin, himself and Robert Schuman of France. Travelling with him throughout this journey was his special assistant, Lucius D. 'Luke' Battle. Battle was rather more than an 'assistant'. He was also Acheson's trusted and intimate confidant throughout these years. We have his word for it that British attitudes were much on the Secretary of State's mind.

BATTLE: I would have said that there was a sense that the British were in greater trouble than we'd realised. We had hoped that they could be saved, if there were leadership, that both the Commonwealth relationship and a new relationship to Europe could be projected and protected. But I don't think there was a clear view as to precisely what ought to happen, and there was no one stepping out in front saying, 'Let's do it this way'. There was also the very prevalent attitude that marked the Marshall Plan thing, which was that the Europeans *had* to get together to determine their own cooperative arrangements and we would help them in an Alliance. This, I think, was the fundamental thing.
CHARLTON: But as far as Britain and Europe are concerned, indeed Britain and the United States, does Acheson have at the back of his mind a feeling that perhaps the whole question of Britain has to be re-examined in some way?
BATTLE: Yes, I think he would have said it had to be re-examined. But I think he would not wish, in the process, to pull up the crops and see how the roots were getting along! I don't think he set out in any way for a major upheaval.
CHARLTON: To what extent did he share the British view about how European cooperation should develop? The British believe that this should be largely an Anglo-American partnership expressed in the Organisation for European Economic Cooperation (OEEC); other Americans and other Europeans think quite differently, that this is not enough, and insufficient to ensure progress towards a real European community. What side does he come down on?

BATTLE: Acheson would, I think, have felt always that there was a special arrangement between ourselves and the British. He would have felt, and did always, that like an affair with a lady it's fine if you don't get caught! But as to what the future role of the British was to be, as I said, as we moved into that four-year period of 1949 to 1953 it became increasingly apparent that the British Empire was on the decline. And I think he believed, as that became more and more apparent, that a need to involve and to have Europe integrated in some respect – I hesitate to say politically, he would never have argued for One Parliament or whatever – but he, I think, saw this, and he increasingly felt that the British had to be a part of it.

WITH THOSE BROAD REFLECTIONS firmly in mind, and what Luke Battle makes plain was a determination to be 'even handed' and not to become impaled on the fence which Britain wished to place around the 'special relationship', Dean Acheson made an ostentatious and fatefully important prior stop on the way to London, in Paris. Luke Battle travelled with him.

BATTLE: We had come to Paris, somewhat concerned, because the French felt that we were paying more attention to the British at that moment than we were to them. We had come there for no particular reason that I can recall except for a bit of 'handholding'. It had the appearance of our having had some involvement in the creation of the Schuman Plan, which was absolutely untrue. We drove in, David Bruce came to the plane to meet us. We were both staying at the Residence. The Achesons and I and the Bruces were all fond of each other and we stayed there frequently, and for long periods of time. On the way in, in the car, David Bruce said to Mr Acheson that the French Foreign Minister wanted to come and see him as soon as possible, and wanted to call on him that afternoon. It was urgent. I don't think Mr Schuman brought anyone with him as I remember. I did not go to that meeting. I wasn't told to. I wanted to, but I wasn't invited. So I went upstairs, sorting out papers or something . . .
CHARLTON: Any significance in the fact that you were not invited? You seem to have been present at everything else?
BATTLE: Oh, I was at everything else. But you must realise that my constant presence, like so many things, evolved. It didn't start out that way. I was very young, and in the beginning I hadn't known Mr Acheson well enough to move in without a clear indication that I was wanted. Later, it didn't bother me at all! But at that point I was still being a little reticent and I did not automatically go. The meeting occurred and lasted an hour or more, and right after that Dean came up to my room. It was the Lindbergh room, the room where Charles Lindbergh had stayed when he first came to Paris and he was an early hero of mine! Dean walked in to me in the Lindbergh room – he had an adjoining room – and he said, 'I have just had a most startling statement made to me.'
He told me that Mr Schuman had offered this proposal [i.e. the Schuman Plan]. Dean's initial reaction was one of shock. He saw it, immediately, as a return to a giant cartel. His immediate reaction was that it would present all kinds of political problems in the United States and the United Kingdom, and that the world would be distrustful. But by the end of the day – I don't recall what we did that evening – my recollection is that we had dinner with the Bruces and there was conversation with Bruce and we talked at some length

about it. By the end of the day he was beginning to see it as a very progressive step, and a very constructive one.

CHARLTON: Largely because Bruce had been explaining it to him?

BATTLE: Well, it – historically, contrary to some speculations, Mr Acheson had absolutely no knowledge of that. And there had been, for once, no leak out of the French Foreign Office. And they leaked everything immediately, as you know. They were the leakiest in Europe; much worse even than Washington, which was bad enough! And we were terribly worried about the Quai d'Orsay, the French Foreign Office, at that point. There were numerous rumours that the Soviet Union was being told everything. At any rate, Mr Schuman himself distrusted the Quai d'Orsay.

CHARLTON: Yes, it is said that Schuman was so dependent on Acheson that absolutely crucial messages to the Americans from Schuman were being routed though the American Embassy!

BATTLE: That happened on numerous occasions.

CHARLTON: I just wonder whether some of the British suspicion that all this might not have been *quite* as innocent as it appeared is, perhaps, justified historically? Is it possible for you to say so now? If one accepts that Acheson himself knew nothing about it, can one really believe that David Bruce, the powerful ambassador, almost a minister, a known supporter and enthusiast for Monnet's ideas, didn't know and really present this to Acheson and make him a convert?

BATTLE: Well, it's an interesting idea. I hadn't thought of it quite that way. The period, looking back on it, the period was enormously exciting. There were so many new concepts and new directions that were moving in Europe. And the United States was more involved in international affairs than it had been for years – ever really. All these things were happening. It would seem abnormal to me had there been *no* discussions of ways of coping with things like the Coal and Steel Community. I suppose and suspect that was the case. But to have it advanced as a Schuman Plan for a Coal and Steel Community was a step beyond. We had not heard of it at all.

THE POINT HAS BEEN made already, or suggested, that British diplomacy, in dismissing the ideas of Jean Monnet as visionary or impractical 'adventures', underestimated the influence this gentle, but enormously tenacious and persuasive, personality exercised upon the Americans – and at the highest levels. American support for integration in Europe owed a great deal to the force of Monnet's advocacy, which he brought to bear at the most direct and influential levels of effectiveness. One such characteristically important link forged by Monnet was with Tommy Tomlinson, a young American adviser on the staff of David Bruce in the American embassy in Paris. Tomlinson bombarded the State Department with papers about Monnet's ideas, generating a reciprocal interest there.

Lincoln Gordon, the Harvard professor who had been in charge of Marshall Aid programmes in Europe in 1949, was economic adviser to Averell Harriman, the special assistant to the President in 1950–1. Gordon adds this personal recollection of Bruce's Paris embassy and the role it played in the genesis of the Schuman Plan, and above all in that on-the-spot conversion of Acheson which secured American support for this form of 'integration'.

GORDON: I think it's fair to say that the initiative in this field came mainly from American diplomats abroad, from David Bruce in Paris, and from Jack McCloy, our High Commissioner in Germany. They in turn were enormously influenced by two respective aides, Tommy Tomlinson, a relatively young, but brilliant, Treasury attaché in Paris, who I think clearly was the most influential staff member of that Embassy in relation to David Bruce, and, with somewhat lesser intensity, Robert Bowie who was an assistant to McCloy. Tomlinson became a complete convert to the most intensive version of Monnet's ideas about integration. That is a belief that European political unity was something which could be achieved within a generation, perhaps even less – within a decade or two. Tomlinson really thought he was participating in the making of a new political structure in Europe. In my view he became almost intoxicated by this thought.

CHARLTON: What was Tomlinson's influence on David Bruce over this?

GORDON: Bruce, I think, being a much older man with a variety of life experiences and some scepticism about things, probably never was converted to the sort of mystic faith in the early prospects of European unity. But he did believe very strongly that some special kind of Franco-German rapport would make a vast difference to the way in which Germany would fit into the future.

CHARLTON: Can one believe that, in the famous episode of the unveiling of the Schuman Plan to Acheson before it had been revealed to the French government, certainly before it had been revealed to the British government, Acheson was as innocent as, then and subsequently, maintained?

GORDON: Whether Acheson endorsed the Schuman Plan so enthusiastically immediately after it was revealed to him – which is what the public prints say – whether he had some kind of advance notice of it, I simply don't know. I was then working for Harriman in Paris. I remember talking with Harriman very soon after and my surmise is that he probably had some advance inkling of it. But in any event the basic reason for the endorsement was the political reason, that he saw this as the basis for a permanent Franco-German rapprochement.

THE TWENTY-FOUR HOURS which Dean Acheson spent with Bruce in Paris and being visited by Schuman in effect swayed the whole future balance of British politics, and fundamentally altered those of Western Europe. The American endorsement of the Coal and Steel Community plan was indispensable to its implementation and success. We have Luke Battle's word for it that among Acheson's first thoughts on hearing 'this most startling statement', made to him by Schuman in Paris, was his anticipation of the displeasure it would occasion Bevin. The British had regarded Acheson as a highly desirable and satisfactory agnostic in this matter of integration in Europe, and towards what Lord Sherfield had referred to, in the preparatory meetings with the Americans for Acheson's visit to London, as 'institutional adventures'. The Foreign Office believed that Acheson broadly was disposed to take their side in such things. But this weekend in Paris in May 1950 had changed Acheson, and vastly more also, as he flew to London with Luke Battle for the Foreign Ministers' meeting.

BATTLE: I don't think his conversion was either that total or that apparent. He had no position really from his own government. He sent off the telegram to the

President about it. The President initially was not in Washington, so the telegram, if I remember, didn't go for a few days, when I guess it went from London. But he had no position backed by his own government. Mr Acheson could not, and would not, have been able to say any more than 'I will take this up with our President, our cabinet. We will see . . .' There were consultations necessary with our Congress.

CHARLTON: I can see that. But from his first reaction to the Schuman proposal of 'good heavens, here's a cartel', and 'there are going to be difficulties with the British', he very quickly seems to grasp, or somebody enlarges his thinking about it?

BATTLE: Well, I helped it along a little bit. My immediate reaction was entirely favourable. And I remember what I said to him. I said, 'Don't dismiss this; this is a revolutionary concept.' I was responding too quickly, but immediately, I thought it was a sweeping and very constructive new direction.

CHARLTON: And so did David Bruce?

BATTLE: And so did David Bruce. By the time we left Paris there was no doubt that we were all quite excited about it.

CHARLTON: And in London?

BATTLE: As I remember it, going over there, Acheson was talking at great length about it. He was concerned about Mr Bevin. He was worried that somehow Mr Bevin would think that we'd been involved with it and that we'd known about it. Mr Bevin was quite upset when they met. And was quite irritated. I wasn't present, but he was very cross apparently. It's hearsay of the worst sort when I start reconstructing things of thirty years ago at which I wasn't present, but Acheson told me that Ernie, Mr Bevin, had been *extremely* upset. It was not considered that this was permanent damage. It caused a degree of distrust. I'm sure that the British Foreign Office, for obvious reasons, wanted very much to make it appear that we had in fact known and that we were, just exactly as we feared, 'guilty as charged'. We weren't.

IT HAD BEEN ONLY three weeks before these transactions in Paris that, as we have seen, David Bruce, the American ambassador in Paris, had concluded reluctantly in his letter to Acheson that the British had an effective veto over further integration in Europe, and that the United States should therefore stop pressing for it. Bruce had now moved adroitly and swiftly to exploit the new lease of life which Monnet and Schuman, with their innovation, had given to the whole concept. In those few hours, as Luke Battle suggests, Acheson's enthusiasms had been enlisted. 'We were all quite excited by it,' Battle recalled as he and Acheson flew to London.

The text of the Schuman Plan received by Bevin from René Massigli, the French ambassador in London, following its disclosure to Acheson, declared its intentions to be these:

> 'To place the French and German production of Coal and Steel as a whole under a common "Higher Authority", within the framework of an organisation open to the participation of the other countries of Europe . . . by pooling basic production and by instituting a new Higher Authority whose decisions will bind France, Germany and other member countries. This proposal will lead to the realisation of the first concrete foundations of a European federation . . .'

As will be apparent, France and Germany were the only countries mentioned by name. However the French Foreign Minister, Robert Schuman, at once made clear at the first press conference held after the Plan was publicly unfurled that 'in particular, Britain, Italy and the Benelux countries' were invited to join.

The man who had inspired the Schuman Plan was Monnet. He flew to London to be made aware of the British reactions and to give more detailed explanations of its implications. Waiting for him was the man in charge, day to day, of the management of Britain's European policy in the Foreign Office, Lord Sherfield.

SHERFIELD: I do remember very well the sequence of events following the announcement of the Schuman Plan, which was made without consultation with us. Maybe we should have known it was coming. I don't know about that. But anyway we did not. The next day Monnet got in touch with Edwin Plowden and myself and said that he was coming over to London to talk about this – which we had heard about the day before – that he would like to see us and talk about it, and would we meet him at the Hyde Park Hotel the morning after his arrival. So we go around to the Hyde Park Hotel and there is Monnet. And we say to Jean Monnet, you know, what's all this about? And he said: 'Oh, it's all in here, you read it.' It was quite a short piece of paper and it contained the essence of the Plan. It said that a condition precedent for participating in this project would be that we would accept the principle of a Federal Europe. We said to him, 'Now, look, does this mean that if we are not prepared to accept the principle of a Federal Europe that we're not in, we're not wanted?' Monnet said, 'Yes, that is the position.'
CHARLTON: But was it a 'Federal Europe', or ceding sovereignty to a supranational authority?
SHERFIELD: I don't remember the exact words, but there was, at that time, not very much difference.

As LORD SHERFIELD'S ACCOUNT of his meeting with Monnet makes plain, the British chose to cleave to the sticking point, as far as they were concerned, of the principle of pooling sovereignty, the supranational character of the Schuman Plan. And in particular whether to accept this principle in advance of the negotiations over the Plan and not as the subject of them.

Leaving on one side the basic and sceptical British disinterest in any such closer involvement with Europe, the sovereignty issue was essentially the one which had ensured the failure of the exploratory talks Monnet had had with Plowden and Hall only a few months before in 1949. The concept had been implicit in that joint exploration during the four days of meetings at Monnet's Paris home with Edwin Plowden, in charge of the British 'Plan' under Stafford Cripps, and Robert Hall of the Treasury, the government's economic adviser. There Monnet's idea that Britain and France should 'act together' was examined at length. Now, immediately after the announcement of the Schuman Plan in which *Germany* and France were 'acting together', Monnet had come to London, where, in addition to Lord Sherfield, he saw Lord Plowden also.

PLOWDEN: I can't remember the general atmosphere, but I know that those of us who had been concerned with discussions with Monnet – when it came about, we felt that we should, in some way, be associated with it, but not in the sort of surrender of sovereignty which he wanted. Speaking for myself, we were disappointed that we did not work more closely with it. I can't remember the reasons, but it didn't come about. I'm not saying by that that I think we should have joined it at that time. I was not feeling like that.

CHARLTON: But was the thing a surprise to *you*, when you were presumably called in hurriedly and consulted about the Schuman proposals as they were handed to the government finally?

PLOWDEN: I think probably it was a surprise that it was so comprehensive, but not that something was going to happen.

CHARLTON: Monnet does say that in his memoirs: 'Plowden had the idea of inviting the Permanent Under-Secretaries of the relevant ministries to dine with us', once the Schuman Plan had been revealed. (There have been by this time the rows between the British and the Americans and the British and the French.) And 'at the end of the evening one of the Permanent Under-Secretaries sighed, "Blessed were our forefathers for they knew what to do in all circumstances".' Do you remember this?

PLOWDEN: I can remember the dinner. I can't remember the actual remark.

CHARLTON: Monnet seized upon this, and he says it was typically British nostalgia. After the dinner, Monnet tells us, he met Schuman and Massigli, the Ambassador, and 'then I said, the British will not find their future role by themselves: only outside pressure will force them to change'.

PLOWDEN: Well, Monnet always thought that. He always thought that we would only join in anything when it existed and when we felt the pressure on us was so strong that it was in our interest to join something.

ON THIS SAME DAY in May 1950 that he talked to Edwin Plowden, Monnet also met Cripps the Chancellor of the Exchequer. Cripps asked him whether, if the British did not take part in the Schuman Plan, France would go ahead without her. Monnet apparently repeated to Cripps more or less what he'd said to Plowden, that 'with her traditional realism, Britain would adjust to the facts once she saw that the enterprise was a success'. He insisted that France wanted Britain in, and used the analogy of Hitler's march into the Rhineland in 1936, saying that Britain had not been willing to act then and had, in consequence, paid, as he put it, 'a bitter price for it'.

A participating witness of these exchanges between Cripps and Monnet was one who had been present with Monnet throughout the 1949 meetings with the British in Monnet's Paris home, his principal assistant, Etienne Hirsch.

HIRSCH: Monnet was always optimistic. When he tries something he thinks he will get the result. His reaction was, well, 'you are not ready now but when you see that we succeed then you will join'. It took a few days until the British gave their definite answer. The explanation was, you see, 'You in Europe have been defeated, you have been occupied; that is not *our* situation. We can have our word in world affairs, while you cannot any more by yourselves. The situation is completely different. Why should we join?'

CHARLTON: Yet Monnet wrote afterwards he could see at once the British were shocked by this [the Schuman Plan]. The phrase he used was: 'The first cracks had begun to show in the majestic ramparts of British self-confidence.'

Jean Monnet (right), the 'father of Europe', created the Schuman Plan. Robert Schuman gave it his name.

HIRSCH: It was certainly a shock to them. They were not prepared for that. They had a historical habit of having a *divided* Europe on the other side of the Channel. This was something new to them, that is quite certain.
CHARLTON: Up to this time their general stance appears to have been, 'Well, we can't participate in this but by all means if you wish to go ahead and form . . . a customs union at one stage, or the Schuman Plan, by all means go ahead and do it.' Although one suspects . . .
HIRSCH: Although that was *not* their attitude. Their attitude was, 'We do not agree. We do not participate and you will *not* go ahead.'
CHARLTON: That question was put specifically, wasn't it, by Cripps to Monnet? If we refuse will you go ahead without us?
HIRSCH: They thought that we would not make the decision to go on without Britain.

ETIENNE HIRSCH'S FIRST-HAND RECOLLECTIONS resurrect in sharp relief that official British scepticism as to whether the continental Europeans could bring off the kind of cooperation to which they aspired. As we have had occasion to remark of earlier post-war British reactions, it was a consistent theme in previous decisions. And it would prove to be among the foremost miscalculations in British foreign policy.

There are questions about the Schuman Plan which have been of lasting historical interest, but which belong, historically speaking, to that invalid category of 'what might have been'. Did Britain, for example, really have a

The Treaty creating the Coal and Steel Community is signed in Paris, April 1951.

choice in acting as she did? And how far was the country, or indeed the Cabinet, aware of all the implications of the decision not to take part in the negotiations which led to the founding of the first European community with the Schuman Plan.' Inside the Foreign Office the principal personal influence exercised upon these considerations was Lord Sherfield's.

SHERFIELD: Now, of course it is said, has been said since by a number of people, that we were rather naive about this. That what we ought to have done was to have said, 'Oh yes, in principle we'll accept this, we'll come and talk to you about it', knowing perfectly well that we would not in effect adopt any form of agreement which involved a federal solution.

British governments don't behave like that. It would have been a completely misleading thing to do. Speaking for myself, I was not in favour of getting involved in the European Federation at that time. So the advice that I gave was what I believed. But supposing that we had been convinced by Monnet; that we *had* gone to the government and said, 'We think the time has come when we ought to join a Federal Europe'. Well, we would no doubt have been applauded by present-day historians. But in fact, of course, we would have been thrown out! Because there was not the faintest chance of the Attlee government accepting the principle of a Federal Europe. Attlee, Bevin, they would not have agreed to it. Bevin himself was not in favour of it. So that we would have been knocking our heads against a brick wall. And, as I say, we would no doubt get the plaudits of future historians, but the policy would not have been changed in the slightest degree.

CHARLTON: Your insistence that, at the time of the Schuman Plan, it meant a 'Federal' Europe – unequivocally a 'Federal' Europe – why is it that you insist on this word 'federal' as being the *only* implication? Surely it would have been, had we agreed to negotiate, it would have emerged as what was negotiated with us?

SHERFIELD: Well, I'm only stating this because it was in the document and it was not only in the document but it was made perfectly clear.

CHARLTON: I just wonder because, after all, it emerged as something rather different in its final form, the Schuman Plan – the proposition for the Coal and Steel Community. It wasn't confined to the 'supranational High Authority', this divinity of technocrats which excited almost automatic rejection by us. It came into being with its own Assembly and its own Parliament as a brake upon it. Would you agree that it didn't quite turn out to be in the end what you feared in the beginning and the basis upon which you rejected it?

SHERFIELD: It was not, obviously, the pure milk of Federalism. On the other hand, it was made quite clear that that *was* the objective. That this was only the first step, followed by Euratom, and it was only the first step on the way. What you say supports the argument that we ought to have ignored all that and said, 'Oh well, we'll go in and talk anyway, on the basis that we're not going to accept a supranational organisation, but we will go in and talk all the same.'

FROM THE OUTSET of this new situation, created by the birth of the Schuman Plan, it was clear that the British thought of possible 'Association' not 'Membership'. Lord Plowden has said that 'when it came about we felt that we should in some way be associated with it, but not in the sort of surrender of sovereignty which he wanted'. And, Lord Plowden added, 'speaking for myself, we were disappointed that we did not work more closely with it'. The 'we', in this instance, I understood to mean himself and Robert Hall, those who had been involved in the 1949 discussions with Monnet.

From May 1950 onwards therefore, British diplomacy headed down this new path of 'Association' into subtly closer forms of collaboration with Europe than hitherto. Like Plowden, another who was very closely concerned with the formulation of official attitudes at this time was Robert Hall.

ROBERTHALL: I think we rejected it on grounds that we didn't want to be as closely knit as Schuman wanted us to be. The Plan involved coal and steel, and the Ministry of Fuel and Power, or whatever it was called then, did not think it was in their interests to join because we had more and better coal than they did; and the steel people thought that it would be useful to have a relationship with them. As far as I can remember, the recommendation from the Treasury, representing the economic side, was that we did not want to join the whole Plan, but we would like to establish 'close relations' with the Iron and Steel people – which we did, of course. We had a strong team sitting with them all the time.

CHARLTON: And that was later, in 1952 when we had a Treaty of Association with them. But do you regard the Cabinet's decision over the Schuman Plan, not to take part, as in effect a deeply considered national decision?

ROBERTHALL: I think 'deeply considered' is the word that is giving me difficulty. I do not think they were thinking in terms which would entitle one to say 'deeply considered'. After all, they were still thinking that we and the Americans had mainly won the war and that Britain was a large independent power. It was a very strong feeling. You remember a long while afterwards Gaitskell said that we'd be turning our backs on a 'thousand years of history'.

CHARLTON: He said that in 1962.

ROBERTHALL: Yes, of course. He presumably felt that even more strongly at this time. It might have been a sort of gut reaction.

THE PEREMPTORY APPEARANCE and the character of the Schuman proposals, with their lack of previous consultation, was a factor in the British response. It caused offence and annoyance in London. Monnet was convinced that Britain would do everything she could to prevent the realisation of the Plan if she took part without acknowledging its principle – the derogation of sovereignty in a limited area – in advance. A particular confidant of Jean Monnet's over many years, and at this time, was someone who would come to play a most important part himself in Britain's European considerations. This was the American who would, ten years later, become President Kennedy's Under-Secretary of State, George Ball. Indeed, in this European dimension Ball is to be ranked with Monnet himself as a forceful and effective influence at particular junctures.

George Ball gives his own explanation of why Monnet thought Britain could not be allowed to take part in the *creation* of the new facts with which he'd presented the government of Mr Attlee in London.

BALL: Because he was convinced that, on the basis of all the discussions he'd had with the British – and there was quite a long history of discussions with them – that the British would only agree on their own terms; which would mean that nothing would be evolved other than something very loose and, from his point of view, quite useless. But that if he did go ahead the British would recognise that this was a good thing once it was done, and they would ultimately come along.

I do not think the British really understood the full significance of it, and I think that only a few people did in the United States. I think Acheson did, but I don't think there was any general comprehension of what the full meaning was.

CHARLTON: Why do you think the British misjudged, as I suggest they did, the influence of Monnet on American thinking?

BALL: Well, I think to some extent because of the special relationship. They felt that they had a kind of inside track. They had firm friendships in the United States, and they really did not conceive of a foreigner, a Frenchman, being able to exercise anything like the influence that Jean exercised. Even though, you may recall, Jean had worked for the British government after the fall of France in the British Supply Council. He always felt very close to the British and was extremely fond of the British. He had a great admiration for the British always. This may not have been fully understood but it was, in fact, the case. And he always had a feeling that, at some time, the British would come along, but that he could not *begin* anything with the British. He felt that he had to get something started – create a kind of political fact – and that, once that was done, the British would come along.

GEORGE BALL'S BELIEF that the British 'had not understood the full significance' of the Schuman Plan, that London had made a superficial, and perhaps emotional, judgement about the presentation and relevance of this new concept for Britain – and, in addition, that a sort of 'anti-intellectual' feeling about it was abroad in official circles in the United Kingdom, is not alone. The leader writer of *The Times*, whose magisterial editorials had reflected the sceptical national verdict about Churchill's calls for a United States of Europe in 1946, 1947 and 1948, had just at this time resumed an interrupted career in the Foreign Office. As the Schuman Plan was unveiled he was serving in Germany. This was Sir Con O'Neill. Twenty years later he would be placed in charge of the official Foreign Office negotiations of Edward Heath's successful bid for entry to the Common Market.

O'NEILL: I don't think we thought the Coal and Steel Community was a very significant development at that time. We were wrong, but we did not realise its significance. Funnily enough, I myself got involved in this accidentally in Germany at that time. As you know, the initiative was taken very independently by the French and they made a communication to London, long after they had fixed up everything with the Germans, and some others. The French, since they shared sovereignty over the Federal Republic with us and with the Americans, felt obliged – as they were proposing to bring the Germans in on the ground floor with the Coal and Steel Community – to mention the matter to their two colleagues in the High Commission, the British and the Americans.

It was communicated to me on the day it surfaced. I am ashamed to say that I did not realise its enormous importance. I realised it was very important for Germany, but I did not realise just *how* important it was even for Germany. I remember, years later, I was talking to Professor Blankenhorn [one of the German Chancellor Konrad Adenauer's principal advisers and confidants], reminiscing about this time. Blankenhorn told me – it was no surprise in a way and yet it was rather more than I had thought at the time – how it was that, immediately after either Schuman himself, or perhaps it was François-Poncet, had been to see Adenauer and explained to him the proposal for the Coal and Steel Community, Adenauer had called Blankenhorn into the room and said, 'Look here, this has just come. Das ist unser Durchbruch – this is our breakthrough, this is our beginning'. Adenauer had said that in 1950.
CHARLTON: The beginning of what?
O'NEILL: The beginning of an independent German existence, an independent German role, and the recovery of some authority for Germany from the total collapse of defeat. The beginning of an independent sovereignty and statehood.
CHARLTON: But also a quite new and historical departure from traditional German policy? Rather than looking East, her commitment to the West?
O'NEILL: Yes, indeed. Indeed. And a departure enormously welcome to Adenauer personally, who was always – long before the Schuman Plan – a man of the West, a man of Europe.
CHARLTON: But what was the intrinsic significance of the Schuman Plan,

which you say, disarmingly, you failed to grasp and which the British failed to grasp? The Germans as late as 1962, the record shows, in the person of Hallstein, Adenauer's foremost adviser on foreign policy, are accusing the British, to the Americans, of 'total insensitivity' to the political implications of these economic developments. That these economic groupings, like Coal and Steel, fundamentally have political objectives in mind?

O'NEILL: Of course. It is that which we failed to grasp. We failed partly because of our own tradition and our political system. The fundamental novelty of the Monnet concept and the European Community as an international organisation is its basis in Treaty, and Law, and legal obligation – something to which we in this country unfortunately, I think, are exceptionally averse and allergic. Because we do not have a written Constitution. Because the notion that there are certain imperatives which cannot be overridden by Parliament, for instance, is something which we do not have, and are not accustomed to. Therefore the idea that there should be a body with real authority over the decisions of national governments – admittedly in a small and perhaps unimportant field, but *real* authority – was something we felt was grotesque and absurd at that time. We still had such self-confidence as late as 1962, which was the date you mentioned. We have lost it now; but we had it then and we were not prepared to stoop to this, as we saw it, rather superfluous, rather fancy arrangement that the European constitutional theorists were indulging in.

CHARLTON: But did we not also see it as a bit breath-taking that Germany, this defeated, prostrate power in Europe, and the French, who had suffered only a slightly less humiliating defeat, had jointly taken an initiative without us, the British?

O'NEILL: Well, I think we did. I think we thought it rather offensive, rather bad form. But I'm sorry to say we probably also thought that it was not fundamentally important.

SIR CON O'NEILL'S MEMORY of his service in Germany in 1950 invites us to pursue, at first hand, how the Germans themselves perceived the opportunities extended to them by Schuman and Monnet's design. The recollections which follow, from two of Adenauer's most intimate lieutenants of that time, highlight the fundamentally new direction and new thinking for Germany which integration in the West portended, and the eagerness with which, upon due reflection, Adenauer cultivated it.

The new Federal Republic had come into being on 23 May 1949. Adenauer had thereby agreed to the postponement of reunification, and integration in the western camp and the new anti-communist alliance of NATO to take up Stalin's challenge of the Cold War. A powerful figure in the development of an independent German foreign policy was the man Adenauer entrusted in particular with the fundamentally important new alignment with the Americans. He was one of 'Der Alte's' most trusted advisers, the German ambassador in Washington, Wilhelm Grewe.

GREWE: Without any doubt Adenauer was a German politician leaning to the West and who had strong affinities to France. He was from the very beginning decided to lead the new Republic into a close relationship with the West of which he never had any doubt. Also he was never in any doubt that it was impossible for Germany, in the future, to have some kind of intermediate position *between* East and West. He hated this idea. He always felt that a neutralised, reunified Germany would be a catastrophe; and that we would be again driven into the same dilemma of the pre-war time – to choose between East and West. From the very beginning he was for a strong and close western relationship of the new State.

CHARLTON: That seems to make him almost a unique figure in German tradition, doesn't it? The fact that he is so unequivocal a 'westerner', rather than a political leader of a central European power whose traditional opening is to the East?

GREWE: Yes, I think that's correct. At least, among the prominent figures of German history there are no comparable people with such a leaning.

EVEN SO, while Adenauer made a choice for Germany, by which he meant to predispose or prejudice all future choices, there can be no doubt that he had considered all the options when, four years after the war, the Germans were still wandering around amid the residual rubble of junk cities.

Walter Hallstein, who made perhaps the most forceful and comprehensive contribution overall to German foreign policy, as Adenauer's State Secretary in the new German Foreign Office, was another of 'Der Alte's' close confidants. Hallstein remembers this seminal occasion with Adenauer, at Lucerne in Switzerland, just before the restoration of a qualified sovereignty to the Germans with the founding of the new state in 1949. It took place above those umbrageous avenues of chestnuts which overlook the lake. During it Adenauer solicited opinions which foreshadowed Germany's future and Germany's choices.

HALLSTEIN: Adenauer's ideas were rather vague at the moment we started building. He had got me to come, in order to look me over, whether I could be his first aide or not; and it was a conversation I'll never forget. It was in Switzerland, on the Bürgenstock in the morning, and we made the trip together and alone. He put me on trial, put to me a test case. 'Is it not time that we must speak with the Russians?' And then he looked at me. I had come back from America, and you may know that I had spent a year as a guest professor at Georgetown University in Washington. And I had been a prisoner of war in America. I had been the adjutant of an artillery regiment in Normandy. I had looked very closely at the Americans, at what phenomenon this was, because my interest was political. And what I told Adenauer was, 'Of course we must speak with the Russians, but in no circumstances *alone*. That's the reason why we must build up Germany in stages. We have first to take the people who are willing to work with us.' I understood the Americans and I was convinced that they would be good allies, and I was not mistaken.

DURING THIS RECORDED CONVERSATION with Walter Hallstein, I was impressed by the powerful revelation to him of his wartime experience in Normandy. There he had watched, he agreed, 'overwhelmed' by the scale and dimension of that flood tide of material, as it poured out of the bridgehead and swept over Germany. There was no mistaking, I believe, the inferences Hallstein had drawn from that. He had reflected upon the scale and nature of the political and economic organisation which had marshalled such apparently limitless resources. He had come to an analogous conclusion with the Monnetists – those who, like Jean Monnet, considered that any hope of Western European civilisation resuming a former status now lost, and wielding any effective political power in future, was inseparable from this question of 'resources' and, above all, with the answers being given to that question by the theories of the large internal market pursued in their different manner by both the Soviet Union and the United States.

HALLSTEIN: Adenauer was a realist. He looked for an ally who could help him to add something for the well-being of Germany. And there was not the shadow of a chance that he could find this help in the East, but there was more than a shadow of a chance in the West – this was clear. Take the case of Schuman, Robert Schuman. In his personal life he had studied in Bonn. He spoke German as we speak it. And he was a French statesman.

CHARLTON: He'd fought in fact on the German side in the First World War?

HALLSTEIN: Ja. Ja! In the East there was nothing comparable with it, and this, of course, made the Russian question something which had to be looked at later. Adenauer was, like myself, a West German, a man from the Rhine, and we in the west have always been very close to France and the French people. It was a part of our history, parts of Germany in this region have been under French government for decades, so this was a basic understanding. But the Schuman Plan, what did it bring? What was Adenauer's hope when the Schuman Plan came? We were no state any more. We were occupied zones governed by foreign military powers. And here was a chance, with the Schuman Plan, of establishing a first, rather mighty force which included Germany, composed out of the free forces, or free forces of the market as Erhard would have said! This, of course, he saw, we *all* saw, as the chance of emerging from the absolutely unnatural situation in which we were, creating at least something like a state, to prepare the re-establishing, the rebuilding of a state.

AS IT WAS ORGINALLY presented, the Schuman Plan contained a clause which would have imposed less than equal status for the Germans. But, as Hallstein reveals, he made it clear to Monnet, at the very outset, that Germany's objective was not just integration but the restoration of sovereignty also.

HALLSTEIN: I remember the first time I saw Jean Monnet in his beautiful country house, I told him quite frankly, 'Cher ami, I will never sign a draft Treaty which contains this clause. Either you make what you have in mind – and this is a great idea and you know how strongly I am for it – or we do another thing. But this cannot be combined.' It was, categorically, a contradiction of the basic idea of the Schuman Plan.

CHARLTON: Which was?

HALLSTEIN: Community. Community and equality.

CHARLTON: I think that is very revealing, because what you and Adenauer have agreed between you as a strategy for Germany is – would I be right to say this? – that, if Germany is to opt for the West and choose the West, then the West must give Germany equal treatment?

HALLSTEIN: Ja.

CHARLTON: So when we talk of Adenauer's support for integration and for

European unity, should we think that he saw it above all as stage-by-stage acceptability for Germany?

HALLSTEIN: Surely this was one of his motives. But I think in his mind the idea of securing peace was stronger even than that. He was convinced that that is what the people wanted and that they were ready to do it.

IT IS THE EVIDENCE both of Sir Con O'Neill and of the American George Ball that the real significance of the Schuman proposals – the creation in one sector, coal and steel, of a path to economic and political unity in Western Europe – was not fully comprehended in London. Certainly, when it came before the Attlee Cabinet for formal decision, it would seem to have received only cursory attention. Among those who sat at the Cabinet table in 10 Downing Street, when Great Britain made her decision to stay out of the Schuman Plan and not to take part in the negotiations which led to the formation of this, the first European community, was the President of the Board of Trade in Clement Attlee's government – and destined later to be Prime Minister himself – Sir Harold Wilson.

WILSON: I think in the first place there were still in both parties in the House of Commons a very strongly pro-Commonwealth group and sentiment, and I shared that myself. I think also that, although the Schuman Plan was highly imaginative – and I was under almost weekly pressure from Jean Monnet on this because I had been on his staff for a short period at the beginning of the war – nevertheless, if it had gone a lot wider, I think, than just the coal and steel industry, if it had been a rather looser arrangement than that, covering a lot more industries, I think there would have been a lot more interest in it in this country. In the Labour Party, and certainly as far as I myself am concerned, it was because it was narrowed to coal and steel.

CHARLTON: Would you say that it was a carefully and deeply considered national decision that we made, or was the whole thing, as some have suggested, too hastily dismissed?

WILSON: I think – I do not remember the line Bevin took at the time – but I think he was having one of his rare fights with the Foreign Office at that time. I think Bevin was pressing Attlee, and Attlee was of course very crisp about these European things because he thought that they were 'talking shops'. The only real difference between us and the Conservatives – and Churchill made a superb speech in the House – was that Churchill thought we should be *in* the negotiations and be perfectly free to say, 'We're not having it' or 'We're not going to join it', whereas Attlee and Bevin said, 'No, let them have the negotiations and we'll look and see what they produce at the end of the day, and *then* we'll decide and see whether there is any relationship we can have with it.' And it was interesting that Harold Macmillan, for example, whose influence I think was growing very rapidly at that time, took a very strong *anti*-Schuman line. He said he was not having anyone in Europe telling him which pits to close down. He said our people will not hand over to any supranational authority the right to close down our pits or our steel works. We will not allow any supranational authority to put large numbers of our people out of work in Durham, in the Midlands, in South Wales or in Scotland. I think that he meant that; I think a lot of his people had taken the same view. But on a question of *behaviour*,

Churchill said, 'Let's go and talk, and say why we don't like it, or see if we can improve it to the point where we *can* go in. Don't let's just sulk on the sidelines.' That was the difference and it was a procedural one.

CHARLTON: Yes, but it's an absolutely vital difference, isn't it? Churchill is asking you why not *be* there to give the answer: all right, we don't know how this will turn out and it is perhaps unacceptable, but why not *be* there?'

WILSON: Yes.

CHARLTON: Now what in the Cabinet, because you were a member of the Cabinet which took that decision, what is the answer to that proposition?

WILSON: I think the answer would have been – Ernie and Clem are not here to tell us or to refresh my memory – that, once they actually got into the talks, we would then have the onus for breaking it up and stopping other people getting on with the idea. I think that was probably what was on their minds. In fact, we got the onus and the blame anyway for not showing up at the talks!

Churchill's speech, I think, on that occasion was not only one of his best from the point of view of vision, but also for its forensic qualities, for its debating qualities. How far he had had help in preparing it I don't know, because I know he used to, he liked to, prepare his own speeches. But he was devastating on the question of 'Why not be there', and when you get there tell them to go to Hell if you like.

CHARLTON: We know that the Foreign Office is credited with having a very strong influence at the time over decisions involving these sorts of developments in Europe, but can you remember, at the actual Cabinet, how much time was devoted to this?

WILSON: As I recall it – I have not looked at the Cabinet papers before this interview – it was a pretty long meeting. It had come up once or twice, we'd been warned of it by Ernie Bevin at the Thursday meeting. It was usual after Parliament – after considering parliamentary business, and who speaks next week, what line they'll take – we always had a short discussion of Foreign Affairs, even if there were no papers from the Foreign Office and the Foreign Secretary. My recollection is that we'd been warned of this and we decided to spend a pretty full meeting on it.

CHARLTON: But the decision is then taken without Attlee being there. Bevin has been ill in hospital, Cripps is not there – both Attlee and Cripps are away on holiday in France – and it is deduced from *that* that the thing is not really taken seriously.

WILSON: And that was a point very strongly made in the House by the Conservatives. Looking back on it, it is extraordinary. I had forgotten this until I came to look through the parliamentary debates. Either Attlee should have flown back – there are many occasions when Prime Ministers flew back from holidays – either he should have flown back, or he should have postponed the meeting. Or, perhaps, if he could have seen how things were going to go, he might have had the meeting before he went away.

CHARLTON: Is it therefore fair to say, as some historians have said, that the Schuman Plan just wasn't taken seriously?

WILSON: I think Attlee and Bevin had decided against it, and were pretty confident the Cabinet would do so. And yes, I think it is fair to say it was not taken very seriously at all.

APART FROM MONNET'S VISIT to London in the middle of May 1950, immediately after the announcement of the Schuman Plan, and a single meeting then between Bevin, who was ill, and Schuman, there was no ministerial contact between London and Paris. A volley of 'notes' was exchanged between the Foreign Office and their counterparts in the Quai d'Orsay, which went on for about a fortnight, the British, for their part, declaring in these official intimations that they were interested in taking part in the negotiations, but refusing to accept the French condition of a previous commitment to the concept of the Coal and Steel Community. Explorations did not proceed beyond this point.

On 1 June 1950 the French Foreign Minister, Robert Schuman, handed to the British ambassador in Paris a virtual ultimatum, asking for a Yes or No from Britain by 7 pm London time the next day. This was the peevish context in which the Schuman Plan proposal went to the Cabinet for formal decision. The circumstances were peculiar. The full Cabinet did not meet; the governments of the Commonwealth were not consulted. And with Bevin ill, and Attlee and Cripps both on tour or on their holiday in France, it hardly suggests that the Government was putting its foremost endeavours into reaching some sort of agreement or accommodation with the French. Britain's decision not to become a member at the foundation of the first European 'Community' was taken, as we have seen, by a rump cabinet.

Another of the Cabinet Ministers who was present then was Patrick Gordon Walker. Lord Gordon-Walker was, at this time, the Secretary of State for Commonwealth Relations. A rump cabinet?

GORDON-WALKER: Morrison [Herbert Morrison] was in charge. Yes, that's true enough. I remember that wretched rump Cabinet had all sorts of difficult decisions like Nye Bevan's resignation, to deal with. The thing we were arguing about was the proposal which had been put to us with the supernatural thing in it.
CHARLTON: Supranational not super . . . *laughter.*
GORDON-WALKER: Supranational.
CHARLTON: It may have *appeared* supernatural!
GORDON-WALKER: Well, it *was* supernatural, too, I think probably! But we were discussing this, and we were preparing an answer saying that we could not accept this ahead, as they had asked us – we could not commit ourselves *before* we had talked – but that we would, *when* talking with them, we would consider this proposal. Then, suddenly, we were summoned in the afternoon, because Schuman had said you must give us an answer by seven o'clock tonight. A real ultimatum, with a date, and a very *short* ultimatum. Then we simply said we can't do this – I mean, we can't be pushed about like this. And so it was rejected.

But I think that it would have been rejected anyway. A couple of weeks later Bevin made a speech in the House of Commons saying that we could not abandon our centuries-old, our age-old, whatever it was, sovereignty. So I think that even if the ultimatum had not come we would have rejected the Schuman Plan. Nonetheless, it made me think at the time that Schuman did not *want* us in. I mean, you don't do that to a proud country. We would never have sent an ultimatum to France in those circumstances. To send an *ultimatum* with a date on it, and a very early date, made me think at the time that Schuman did not want us in anyway. So why should we worry too much?

CHARLTON: But how was it presented to the Cabinet as an issue for decision?

GORDON-WALKER: The proposal which reached us first was that we should accept the supranational thing *before* we met; that there should be a sort of pre-condition. This we turned down. And we were actually discussing this matter of allowing it to be on the Agenda, and to discuss it, when the ultimatum arrived. And this made us just simply say, well, we cannot have *anything* to do with this. I mean, you just don't give way to ultimata!

CHARLTON: And feeling was high, was it, about the manner in which it was presented.

GORDON-WALKER: Feeling was terribly high about the manner in which it was done. And the general conclusion was that we were not wanted in by the French. Schuman was the one who dealt with us, and I was convinced that he did not want us in, and that he thought that this would be one way, one easy way, of stopping us. But he could have done it, in fact, much more comfortably, because I don't think we would have come in anyway. But that gave us a good excuse by the way.

CHARLTON: For what?

GORDON-WALKER: For rejecting it. To have an ultimatum presented to you is something you cannot really accept.

CHARLTON: But what am I meant to understand by that – that you welcomed the excuse?

GORDON-WALKER: No. I was against going in to the Schuman Plan at that time. What I mean is that it is hard to blame the British government for reject-ing an ultimatum. Although this has been very largely forgotten.

CHARLTON: Trying to think back, as neutrally as you possibly can, are you saying that the central issue on which it was rejected by the Cabinet was that we saw it as an unacceptable ultimatum? We dismissed it in those terms? Or was it a more widely, deeply considered decision?

GORDON-WALKER: It would have been a more widely and deeply considered decision had we not had this ultimatum thrown at us. But I am quite sure that we would not have gone in at that time. I don't think any, well there may have been one or two people in the Cabinet who wanted it, but practically no one, and we were in fact *absolved* from making a decision by the ultimatum. We simply said – I think we did not reply at all by seven o'clock – that is how we settled it.

CHARLTON: On the question of the ultimatum, it is said that for a time in between the unveiling of the Plan on 9/10 May and the ultimatum, call it what you will, that the French issued on 1 June that Schuman himself was prepared to yield on this point. Did that come through to the Cabinet? Was it continually being discussed?

GORDON-WALKER: Yes, I think we thought we might get our way, and there were some reasons to think that Schuman would play. But then something came to stiffen him, maybe the whole French cabinet; then he hardened and produced this ultimatum. When I said I wasn't sure Schuman wanted us to join, I really meant the French government. I think Schuman did really want us to join and was prepared to make concessions.

CHARLTON: And Monnet?

GORDON-WALKER: Monnet was more rigid, I think, than Schuman.

CHARLTON: I'm wondering whether, at the time you took this decision, the Cabinet itself was fully aware of the nature and importance of the overtures that Monnet had made to this country in 1949, the year before, when he had wished to explore with us the possibility of a very intimate collaboration between Britain and France: that it should be the basis of post-war Europe. And that it is only when we said 'No' to *that* that the Coal and Steel plan comes up. Were you conscious of that?

GORDON-WALKER: I don't believe that. He was a subtle man. He may have said that, but I don't believe it was the way it happened. The way the thing happened was that it was a Franco-German proposal which we were invited to join as a founder member. I'm sure it wasn't because we rejected him that he went to Germany; the basic idea was to tie France and Germany together. After all, it was over a hundred years since we'd fought a war with France!

CHARLTON: Monnet appears to have been genuinely convinced the year before that the British just did not attach, or see the priority of, the German question as the French saw it.

GORDON-WALKER: That is undoubtedly true, and that remained so for a long, long time, right up to the full Community itself. That's perfectly true. The German problem was never so grave for us.

CHARLTON: So in view of what you've just said, do you therefore acquit Monnet and Schuman of a clear design to weaken this country?

GORDON-WALKER: I think they came to the conclusion, on quite a lot of evidence, that we were not going to come in and therefore they might as well shut it off with an ultimatum and get on with Germany.

CHARLTON: That would confirm what Monnet said, that the risk of alienating Britain was a risk worth taking, a better risk than making no progress at all over the German question. Do you accept this?

GORDON-WALKER: I think that is right. I think the ultimatum came really – it was a horrible thing to do to an allied country – but it wasn't really intended to be such a rebuff. It was intended just to put a full stop to discussions which were going on and over which he became convinced, quite rightly, that we were not going to come in.

CHARLTON: Can you say whether the course of accepting the principle, which Monnet insisted we do, and as the Dutch then did – accept the principle but make a reservation about their commitment if it didn't turn out to be to their liking; that they could withdraw from it later had they wished – was that course seriously discussed in the Cabinet?

GORDON-WALKER: Some people said, I think it was probably Morrison, you must not worry too much about 'decisions in principle', because on the Continent this does not mean you accept the thing. But *we* said that we can't behave in this way. If we accept a principle we accept it. It is perfectly true the words 'in principle' have a different meaning in French and in English. In English it means that you have burnt your boats. In France it means that you have just opened an argument! Maybe this misunderstanding of language was part of the trouble. What we were prepared to do really was discuss it when we met. Well, the French would have been perfectly happy for us to discuss it when we met as long as we'd use the word 'en principe'. It's a fundamental difference between the two, the way the two countries approach problems of this kind. Maybe now we know more about it. Now we are perfectly prepared to join the Common

Market and argue like billy-o *after* we are in it. I mean, we accept it in principle, in the way the French accept things 'in principle'. Maybe nowadays, when we know these things better, we would have said 'in principle' and then started arguing! But in those days we rather thought that the British way of doing things was the best way, and the British use of words was the best use, and things like that. And we thought that all these Continentals, Europeans, were sort of 'closed in' in Europe; whereas we were out in the World, East of Suez and in Singapore and so on, and that we really were not, so to speak, swimming in the same ocean.

CHARLTON: Can you comment on this? Kenneth Younger, the junior Foreign Office Minister to Bevin, writing in later years before his death, thought that the decision made was inevitable, but he agreed it was a rather perfunctory sort of decision. And he said this, that 'senior Ministers were sick or tired, and the vitality of the Labour Cabinet was beginning to ebb away'?

GORDON-WALKER: Yes, I think there is something in that, though it's a little bit of hindsight, looking at it afterwards. At the time I cannot remember thinking of my colleagues as worn-out old crocks at all. They all seemed full of life and vigour. But, looking back, you can see that they had been in office through the war, some of them, and after the war had had a terrible time. Maybe in hindsight one could say that. He did not say it at the time.

CHARLTON: Do you feel able to give us a portrait of Attlee's views? What did he think about such an involvement?

GORDON-WALKER: Attlee was a very nice conservative gentleman, whose pre-war experiences in the East End had thrown him into an action as an active reformer. He then joined the Labour Party, and gradually, through the accidents of Lansbury resigning, and Morrison not being elected, he became Leader.

CHARLTON: But, if you put the essential question to Attlee, whether Britain is about to return, as a consequence of the outcome of the Second World War, to a European destiny, what would he have said? What did he say?

GORDON-WALKER: No, no. He would not have accepted that. He was, first of all, enormously influenced by Bevin. He never really disagreed with Bevin as far as I can remember. Certainly not on great matters like this. He simply took the view that we were all taking, that he did not want to have anything to do with the Schuman Plan at all. He had a certain, almost 'Jay-like' contempt for foreigners.

CHARLTON: A Douglas Jay-like contempt for foreigners?

GORDON-WALKER: That's what I meant to say, yes. He thought the English were far better than anybody else. He even thought the Indians, whom he helped enormously, were a dilatory, delaying lot whom you *had* to present with an ultimatum to get them to move at all! He had all those views really. He'd been a major in the First World War, and he'd remained a major in a sense, but one who was, who had been, pushed into radicalism.

CHARLTON: And Cripps, the Chancellor of the Exchequer? One might have supposed that the element of planning which was implicit in Monnet's ideas, but on a European scale and basis, might have appealed to him?

GORDON-WALKER: No, I think not. I think he believed you had to plan within your national boundaries where you had sovereignty, and that to get away from that would make planning more difficult. A lot of our people thought that to plan you needed a national border with sovereignty over it. It was one of the reasons why, later on, a lot of people didn't want to go into the Community, the Common Market.

CHARLTON: Is there, in view of what you've said, for example, about Douglas Jay and the distrust of foreigners by Britain, is there a comparison to be made between the post-war Labour governments and, perhaps, Rosebery's 'Liberal Imperialism' at the end of the last century?

GORDON-WALKER: Yes. Our glorious isolation, or splendid isolation, or whatever we called it. Yes, undoubtedly. It was very generally felt, as long as we had a position overseas – as we did with Rosebery, of course. But later on this could not be said any more. Isolation, glorious or inglorious, could not be maintained any more.

LORD GORDON-WALKER'S first-hand account of how the British Cabinet dealt with the Schuman Plan decision (he was Commonwealth Secretary at the time, and fourteen years later was appointed Foreign Secretary in Harold Wilson's first administration), supports, in an all-important respect, another of the first-hand memories of what happened. Sir Harold Wilson himself has told us, of both the proposal and the decision, 'It was not taken very seriously at all'.

Because of Bevin's illness (he was consulted in hospital), the Foreign Office at the time was led by Kenneth Younger, the youthful Minister of State. Younger wrote subsequently of his own conclusion that the Schuman proposals were 'handled in a curiously off-hand way' in London, and 'largely by officials' in the absence of the relevant ministers. Only Younger himself was, politically, in charge of the Foreign Office at a crucial period. And there the principal figure who dealt with the formulation of official policy over this and other economic and political questions concerning Europe was Lord Sherfield. His advice, and his formidable experience and authority, were a key influence overall in the way the British reacted and the eventual decision was reached. Lord Sherfield was not prepared to agree that the Schuman Plan got only, in Younger's words, 'curiously off-hand' treatment, or that it was not taken very seriously at all.

SHERFIELD: I would think it *was* taken seriously. I think Bevin was somewhat upset that he had not been consulted [i.e., at the outset on 9 May 1950 when the French had revealed it to Acheson before letting the British know] and rushed into it by Schuman. I think he was upset by that. But I think that the answer to your question is that the whole policy towards Europe had been under *constant* review and discussion. It was a highly important matter and the views of the senior ministers involved were extremely well known. It was not as if this was something *new* - our relationship with Europe. It was under constant discussion, and the views of the Prime Minister, of Bevin, Cripps and Dalton, were all well established. And, all right, supposing as an implication that this was pushed through at a low level, or a bureaucratic level, you would have thought that if the senior ministers had any reservations about it, *when they came back*, there would have been an investigation and a lot of displeasure. In fact a fuss about it. There was not any!

CHARLTON: What did they do, pat you on the back?

SHERFIELD: The decision was taken in accordance with their views. Let me say again, if we had advised differently, there would have been no change in the decision. You say that it was only junior ministers who took the decision, but they were perfectly well aware of the view of the Cabinet on this matter. It was not the first time that these issues had been ventilated. The thinking was perfectly well known. I was expressing what I thought, but I also knew perfectly well that I was expressing the thought of, well, I could say the entire Cabinet.

CHARLTON: Your point is that this *was* a deeply considered decision, if not at this particular time – because there were important absentees from the vital Cabinet meeting – but over a period? It was not a rush to judgement?

SHERFIELD: Absolutely not. It was implicit in the whole of our dealings with the Americans over Europe throughout the period.

CHARLTON: Can I ask you to comment on something Harold Macmillan says in his memoirs? 'I had been shocked', he wrote, 'by the Foreign Office view that complete union of the Schuman Plan countries would not be harmful to the United Kingdom in the short term, and only ultimately dangerous if Germany emerged as the dominant partner. A degree of myopia', he says, 'which a mole might envy.' Now, what do you think about that?

SHERFIELD: Well, it is strong language. I'm not quite sure what he means by saying that we regarded the Schuman Plan as a threat.

CHARLTON: No, he is saying the opposite: that the Foreign Office was taking the view that, while we could not take part – at least this is my interpretation – that *if* they went ahead without us it would not be harmful to us in the short term. Macmillan is plainly suggesting that here in embryo *was* a threat, and of course historically that proved to be the case, didn't it? It was something we were ultimately forced to join, this idea of European integration?

SHERFIELD: Yes, but in very different circumstances, because in between the Schuman and Euratom concept, and the time of our first application to join the Common Market, de Gaulle had intervened. De Gaulle was, I would say, largely responsible for reducing to a very small group of people the concept of a Federal Europe. He was against it. He was for Europe des Patries. At the time we came to apply to join the Common Market the 'federal' implications had been very much diminished.

CHARLTON: Do you remember those as being the views of Macmillan at the time? When he talks about 'what follies we committed in these years', or 'the hostility of the Foreign Office', 'the isolationism of Bevin', these are his words . . .

SHERFIELD: I don't recollect talking to him about this in those days. I was, I suppose, totally absorbed in what I was doing in the Foreign Office, and he was trying to build 300,000 houses in a year. [Harold Macmillan was Minister for Housing from 1951 to 1954.]

CHARLTON: What does that mean? That as Housing Minister he can't have known too much about it?

SHERFIELD: No, it doesn't. It just means that he was in one box and I was in another box.

CHARLTON: But what about what he says – 'the hostility of the Foreign Office', 'the isolationism of Bevin'?

SHERFIELD: I think that is exaggerated. The Foreign Office was hostile to what?

CHARLTON: European integration.

SHERFIELD: Yes, to European integration as thought of at the time.

CHARLTON: Well, I am using integration, rather than cooperation, the word you preferred.

SHERFIELD: Yes. We were not in favour of joining a small European grouping at that time. I think I felt that the situation would develop, and that there would probably be other moments in which we could, if we felt it was in our interests, join with Europe.

CHARLTON: That was the essence of your advice, was it? Don't join now but wait and see? Is that fair?

SHERFIELD: Well, don't join now, yes, wait and see. Two things we were not to foresee. The first was de Gaulle and what that meant in terms of European defence, European political organisation, and so on; and the second thing, which I certainly never foresaw and would not, I think, perhaps have credited at the time we are talking about – 1950 – was the economic and industrial failure of the United Kingdom in the 1960s. It was perhaps to be foreseen, but I certainly did not foresee it.

LORD SHERFIELD WAS Under-Secretary of State at the Foreign Office as Britain and Europe were presented with what Monnet called 'the bold constructive act' of the Schuman Plan, and was the man in charge, at the official level, of Britain's European policy. It seems to me important to add to his frank and emphatic recollection of why Britain acted as she did only this: the one foundation for the official belief that Britain could afford to 'wait and see' was the British disbelief that the Continental Europeans could or would succeed and carry the Coal and Steel pool into full effect. The decision not to sit at the table with 'the Six' in the ensuing negotiations meant that on 20 June 1950 they began between France, Germany, Italy and the Benelux countries – and without Britain.

While Monnet claimed subsequently that he had detected the first cracks 'in the majestic ramparts of British self-confidence', from this time onwards British responses to the gravitational pull the new collaboration at once began to exercise were improvisations. They were improvised within the constraints of a Cabinet decision which, in practice, seems to have been interpreted as having a 'once and for all' or rather dismissive ring to it.

A special assistant had been appointed in the Foreign Office, to concentrate on the Schuman Plan developments. This was Michael Cullis. Since joining the Foreign Office in 1945, Cullis had had responsibility for Austrian affairs, and notably the protracted negotiations for the Austrian State Treaty. While these led eventually to the withdrawal of the Soviet Union from her occupation of Austria, the talks had in the summer of 1950 come to a full stop, coincidentally with the launching of the Schuman Plan. This became Cullis' brief.

CULLIS: I was attached for that purpose to the Department headed by Duncan Wilson, the German Economic Department. This was thought to be the most appropriate, or the least inappropriate, for the subject. This is interesting, I think, because it was seen very largely, on the official level at any rate, as part of the German problem, of the problem of the Ruhr and the Saar. I do not think there was any different view in the Foreign Office than there was in the country as a whole about our place in the world. But there was on the official level – lower down – I think a much more constructive view of the possibilities that an initiative like Schuman's offered in relation to such problems as the Ruhr. I remember that Sir Roger Stevens and Sir Duncan Wilson himself were interested in the perspectives which it offered from that point of view.

But the overriding decision had been taken at the outset, governmentally but without much cavil. We were reminded from time to time by higher authority in the Foreign Office that this was so. Our working party on the Schuman Plan, for example, whenever it began discussing possible amendments which might make it more acceptable to us, was rather sharply called to order. We were told that we had no such remit.

CHARLTON: By whom?

CULLIS: Well, I think that Roger Makins [Lord Sherfield] was the most influential official at that time. He had a very strong position as the Economic Deputy Under-Secretary. I believe he attended even Cabinet committees in that role. He was, whether reflecting his own views or what he knew to be the Government attitude, fairly firm on that subject. I can certainly remember being told that the working party had no business to concern itself with possible amendments to Schuman. I think there was a feeling of frustration and that we would have liked more leeway and rather more scope. But it was all decided, as I say, very quickly. Ours was very much a *status quo* policy. Internationally, or *vis-à-vis* Europe, we were not in the mood for any new, imaginative departure such as the Schuman Plan.

I cannot honestly claim to have been in strong disagreement with official policy in this matter. My sympathies were with those in the Foreign Office, certainly like Kenneth Younger himself and Duncan Wilson, who would have liked to see us take a more positive approach. It was not an issue on which I felt, at that time, that any very different decision could have been taken. What I did feel, strongly, was that we should have realised that this was a potentially very important new development – and a very salutary one. One which, even if we could not associate ourselves with then, we should have remained in close touch with and been prepared to develop and amend our views about. I think the whole thing was mishandled technically on both sides. I remember Massigli, the French ambassador in London, who was closely involved in all this, saying that to me. He was almost in tears once; he said that he thought the stupidity of people on *both* sides had been a tragedy.

SO, WHILE BRITAIN HAD her small interdepartmental 'working party' within Whitehall to keep an eye on the Schuman Plan negotiations, it was an eye which, according to Michael Cullis, was firmly deflected from any disposition to stray or to rove in the direction of change or amendment of the existing policy which had led to the British refusal. And meanwhile the Six of Europe began their remarkable task.

Lord Sherfield recounted how, in the meeting at the Hyde Park Hotel with Jean Monnet in May 1950, Monnet, in response to Sherfield's 'What's all this about'? had pulled a single sheet of paper from his pocket and said, 'It's all in here!' 'It' was the essence of the Coal and Steel Community. Just as Miss Jane Austen's 'two inches of ivory' on which she 'worked with so fine a brush' could hardly deceive her readers – she was a whale for length, her novels running to 400 pages and more – so was it with Monnet's 'quite small piece of paper'! He had set the participants in the Schuman Plan a gargantuan task to make it a reality.

In this task they became absorbed, and into it the enthusiasms and energies of the continental Europeans were flung. It was the brief of the Whitehall working party to contemplate and consider the likely fruits of these endeavours and suggest ways and means for Britain to take account of them.

As disclosed already, this working party came under the German Economic Department of the Foreign Office, headed by Sir Duncan Wilson. Sir Duncan was, therefore, a particularly informed observer of the diplomatic gavotte which now ensued – the stately measures Britain began to tread while trying to keep closely informed and at the same time appearing to keep her distance from the negotiations under way in Europe.

WILSON: The formation of the working party was, in itself, a sign that we had cooled down a bit and were going to look at the whole thing afresh, and from a stricter view of our own material interests. Our remit was a strict and simple one – to see whether it was worth our joining it as it stood. I think that a draft Treaty emerged round about the beginning of 1951, which was a rather fuller version of the sketch plans we had had before. We had to consider this very carefully, but again in the same terms. I do remember that we were told to find out what the text of one or two of the crucial articles meant, but to show no interest in doing so! So that I found myself going to Paris with one or two other extremely powerful colleagues, including Humphrey Trevelyan, and I remember being told in casual conversation with the French, you know, to 'find out what Article 51/2 on exports to the community really means'! Well, this was not a very easy remit, going cold into the subject, so to speak! Going up to Monnet or any of his officials and saying by the way, 'It's a fine day and what does Article 51/2 really mean?'

I do remember I was made to act as spokesman of this powerful group of officials because they felt that they were Foreign Office instructions and very silly ones. The way I did it, right or not, was to say something like 'By the way, Article 51/2 – extremely interesting and our interpretation of it has been as follows', dead stop! I think Etienne Hirsch appreciated exactly the situation. I remember him smiling broadly and saying, 'Exposition assez méritoire!', then proceeding to point out where it was wrong in detail! But this was the degree of distance which we were required to keep at this time. It did seem to me absurd, when we'd reached the point which I described, of talking in Paris, and then trying not to show any real interest in the thing at all!

CHARLTON: What was the verdict the working party reached, broadly?

WILSON: The working party really reached an absolutely neutral verdict, in my memory, on the commercial advantages and disadvantages. Coal and Steel in Britain both said there are potential gains and losses – essentially it is a political decision.

CHARLTON: Did you have any political guidance?

WILSON: Well, to a certain extent, yes. I do remember Roger Stevens [Sir Roger Stevens, the Assistant Under-Secretary of State at the Foreign Office] saying, 'Well, thank you for the report and your bits of drafting at the beginning of it, but the question of *political* decision and, when it comes, to *recommendations*, I know your views, I know Roger Makins' and my own – *our* – views' – he didn't add 'which are much weightier and opposed to yours', but anyhow he did say very kindly, 'I think that I'll do the drafting of the recommendations'!

CHARLTON: Did you have a view yourself of what those recommendations should have been?

WILSON: I had the feeling that a sort of political decision had really been taken in advance – unless Industry were able to come forward with enormously powerful reasons for going ahead. I would have been in favour of a bit more exploration, and of going as far as we could towards a political arrangement. As it was, I felt that we were certainly going to stick to the 'three interlocking circles' and the 'special relationship' and all that. There was a strong climate *against* associating more closely with Europe. In that climate I think it would have needed an enormously powerful *economic* argument to make us change course towards Europe.

THERE IS NO SERIOUS DISPUTE that the Foreign Office's advice and the British government's decision, precipitate or not, to stay out of the Schuman Plan reflected basic British attitudes and national self-perceptions of the time. Nor that these feelings were reinforced by the fact that Britain had elected a Labour government to power, in its own right, for the first time. In the creation of the Welfare State and the accompanying social 'revolution' at home, the United Kingdom had opted for a less adventurous and aggressive role for Britain.

Denis Healey, who well before he became a Member of Parliament drew up, in 1947, a special report for Hector MacNeil and the Foreign Office about Labour Party attitudes to Europe, made this assessment of the contribution to the British refusal of the Schuman Plan due to Britain having a Socialist government with its hands on power for the first time.

HEALEY: There was an important factor there, because I think there was a great deal of suspicion – and some of it justified – that certain types of cooperation with governments which were at that time mainly Conservative, Christian Democrat in Germany and in France and Italy, would inhibit the pursuit of Socialist policies in Britain, if we'd gone for the Federal type of structure. This was a major factor in dissuading us from joining the Coal and Steel Community. My personal opinion is that, as the French say, people who don't go to something are always in the wrong – 'Les absents ont toujours tort!'

I think that we would have done better in fact to *go* to the discussion on setting up the Coal and Steel Community, and to go to Messina, because I think then we would have established a European Community which was not condemned to the sort of sterile constitutional arguments which the European Community, in its present form, has been suffering from for the last ten years.

CHARLTON: But the question still has to be answered, I suppose, why a Labour government did not find it possible to take these initiatives when it had the opportunity?

HEALEY: Well, because we had no one to cooperate with on the Continent to share our views. You see, the German government was run by Adenauer, the French government was run, in the critical years, by Schuman, the Italian government was run by de Gasperi – and all of them were following economic policies very different from ours. Their political and their religious views were very different from ours. Don't forget that they were all Catholic parties and at that time the Catholic Church had a very ambiguous attitude to Labourism.

The Dutch Social Democratic Party had completely reconstructed itself after the war and turned itself into a Labour Party with no Marxist dogma at all. Yet, in the first election after the war in Holland, the Dutch Catholic hierarchy excommunicated people who voted Labour. Now you have got to remember that the world we were living in then was very different from the world we are living in now.

CHARLTON: But does that apply to people like Spaak? Labour politicians themselves?

HEALEY: No. No. Spaak himself was very keen, as you know; but then Spaak belonged to a very small country, and the small countries in Europe, particularly the Dutch and the Belgians, saw a European federation as a means of giving the Small countries more influence over the Big than they would ever have in a Europe of States. This is still the case, of course; on the whole the smaller European countries are more keen on the supranational attributes of the European Community than France, or Germany or Italy or Britain.

BUT, WERE THERE IN THAT SUMMER of 1950 other, less articulate, concerns at the root of the British refusal? Monnet himself thought so. Many years later he quoted, in his memoirs, this extract from a letter written to him about the British decision by Félix Gaillard, his chef de cabinet.

> 'Members of the Labour Party are opposed to the Schuman Plan because they are defeatist about continental Europe, which they have deliberately written off in case of war – something they regard as inevitable, and very near at hand . . . the Conservatives are more or less of the same opinion.'

In June 1950 the Cold War gripped the heart of Europe and the Korean War had broken out in Asia. A pervasive uncertainty and fear had produced, or helped to reinforce, contrasting reactions. Monnet defined them for himself as 'unity on the Continent and isolation in Britain'.

When, on 3 June 1950, the Six in Europe had published their joint communiqué proclaiming the beginnings of Six-Power Federation, following closely Monnet's prescription of ceding to this new 'community' limited functions but real powers, the British ambassador in Paris, Sir Oliver Harvey, was quoted by Monnet as reacting thus: 'There are precedents of international organisations set up with fanfares of trumpets which encounter only difficulties and disappointments when the time comes to put them into practice.' Such British confidence soon faded; the penumbra of doubt began to expand.

The debate in Britain, however, had shown how the British saw themselves in Europe five years after the end of the Second World War. That Clement Attlee himself may have needed reassurance, in the early aftermath of the Cabinet decision, or that he viewed this point of departure with something more than unease, could perhaps be inferred from a request he made to the Foreign Office to provide him with a summary and a clarification of the British stance.

The Prime Minister's wish clearly called for a very important minute. With it we might suitably end this account of the Schuman Plan. The paper which resulted was the official British reflection then of the new situation – with Britain forced to self-examination while the major Continental states plunged, without her, into their new activity. The minute was written for Attlee by Lord

Sherfield, undoubtedly the most authoritative of the government's Foreign Office advisers on Europe throughout this particular period. In quoting from this paper Lord Sherfield thus provides us with his own instructive, historical appendix to the many recollections of this first great watershed in Britain's post-war European odyssey.

SHERFIELD: I came across by chance the other day a minute that I wrote. You see, the Americans thought that our reluctance to join the Schuman Plan was due, first of all, because we were jealous of the French and French leadership and all that – which was absolutely untrue; and also because we were opposed to accepting any arrangement which would inhibit the Socialist government from carrying out economic policy, and anything they wanted to carry out – there was certainly a truth in that.

But here we are: 'Sir Roger Makins, a Deputy Under-Secretary of State of the Foreign Office, wrote a memorandum to Attlee making clear the reasons for British doubts over the Schuman Plan.' I am recorded as 'denying that British refusal to take part in the preliminary talks implied a lack of concern for European affairs'. I argued that 'Britain favoured increasingly close Association with Europe in every field, political, economic and cultural'; and specified the OEEC, the Brussels Treaty and the Atlantic pact as all being 'infringements of sovereignty which will lead to the growth of international organisation, a development which we had continuously encouraged.' I appeared to have argued that 'following the collapse of Four-Power cooperation we had acted to consolidate the Western democracies politically in establishing the OEEC and the Brussels Treaty,' but our policy had always been, and I quote, that 'Western Europe with the United Kingdom *was not strong enough to stand alone.* A wider grouping, a larger unity was essential if the Western democracies were to be secured. Western Union was never synonymous with Western *European* Union, hence the negotiation of an *Atlantic Community*'. 'We had', I go on, 'we had in fact to consider, while developing foreign policy, our responsibilities not only to Europe, but to the Commonwealth and the rest of the World' – and I seem to have said, 'in particular in the Middle East and South-East Asia; in all respects bearing in mind the essential importance of our relationship with the USA.' 'Protection of the Sterling Area was essential since it was inseparable from the Commonwealth. The cohesion', I said, 'of this system is a vital element in the maintenance and restoration of economic health to the free world.' And then I go on to say that 'Anglo-American cooperation was also essential not only for European defence but for the security of South-East Asia and the Middle East from communist penetration.'

So that seems to have been my view, as expressed to the Prime Minister; and whatever I think about it *now*, those are the words on paper!

WHILE THE BRITISH GOVERNMENT chose to reject participation in the Schuman Plan on the constitutional issue – refusal to devolve sovereignty upon any European institution – a more powerful reason lies closer surely to something Etienne Hirsch remembered that both he and Monnet were told by the British at the Hyde Park Hotel at that strained meeting in May of 1950, and, in Hirsch's recollection, by Lord Sherfield: 'We are not ready; and you will not succeed.' But, as subsequent events were, in the end, to prove, Britain had made the first major misjudgement of how Europe was going to 'evolve' and would pay a heavy price for standing back in 1950.

By the end of that year Labour's large parliamentary majority was evaporating. Ernest Bevin, exhausted by his prodigious efforts in the war and vast contribution over the Marshall Plan and the defence of the West, had entered his final, and fatal, illness. Cripps' life too was ending. Attlee, in the unsentimental view of one observer, had 'shrunk into a Sphinx, without a riddle'. The life of the Labour government itself, physically and creatively worn out, was drawing to a close.

The Conservatives, under Winston Churchill, won the General Election of 1951. We have Harold Macmillan's word for it that Churchill's return was 'hailed throughout Europe as likely to mark a wholly new approach towards the question of European Unity'; and he added this – that 'if what followed was to prove a sad disillusionment, almost a betrayal . . . it is right to consider some of the difficulties'.

5

A Sludgy Amalgam

THAT ONLY SIX YEARS after the end of the war words like 'sad disillusionment' and 'almost a betrayal' could be uttered in the same breath as the name of
Winston Churchill, the national hero, and that they should be written as retrospective comment by one of his greatest admirers and his loyal lieutenant,
Harold Macmillan, is some measure of the confusion and controversy which
surrounds the actions of the second Churchill Government when its turn came
to address – this time in office – the question of Britain and Europe.

In the autumn of 1951 the Conservatives had won the General Election, but
with an insubstantial majority of seventeen seats. Overall, some 200,000 more
people had voted for Labour than for them. Rejected at the polls in 1945, even
in the glow of Victory – 'I have therefore laid down the charge which was placed
upon me in darker times,' he had said then in his last broadcast – Winston
Churchill was back as Prime Minister, and anointed in that office, for the first
time, by the popular vote – perhaps the crowning ambition for him. The old lion
was seventy-seven and in the political winter of his life. With him, and once
again as Foreign Secretary, came Anthony Eden who had had the Foreign
Office during their victorious wartime partnership. Eden was fifty-three – the
Rose and Expectancy of the Fair State, the heir apparent.

Winston Churchill's prestige, great throughout Europe at the end of the war,
was unimpaired, and had even been enhanced during the years out of power. In
that time he had given his still considerable energies and his contagious
enthusiasm to the concept of unity in Europe. He had been the figurehead of
the European Movement, pointing the way. His support of it was astonishingly
active. At the Hague Congress in 1948, he was the dominating public figure and
appeared to be leading a crusade.

By 1949 the pressures which this unofficial organisation was able to mount
had ensured the establishment of that official body desired by Churchill as early
as 1943. This was the first 'European' institution, the Council of Europe,
divided into its constituent parts, the Council of Ministers and the Consultative
Assembly. Ernest Bevin had agreed to it only with reluctance – 'Let's give them
a talking shop,' he had said to Christopher Mayhew, and to Sir Roderick
Barclay of the Foreign Office, even more memorably, 'Open that Pandora's box
and you'll never know what Trojan horses will jump out!'

From the ramparts of Opposition Churchill had continued to chase the
Labour Party around the walls of Troy, chiding Attlee and Bevin for their Little
Englandism and lack of creative imagination over Europe. It was Churchill who
had taken the lead, daringly ahead of all others, calling for the admission of
Federal Germany to full membership of the Council of Europe at Strasbourg.

With that first step Germany was on the way to sovereignty, rehabilitation and independence within the Western Community. Still, today, in the halls of their party conferences, the German Christian Democrats, for example, have displayed huge photographs of Churchill, giving him equal prominence with Adenauer, the first Chancellor of the post-war German State.

Sir Harold Wilson has reminded us that Churchill's assault on Bevin and Attlee for their refusal to take part in the Schuman Plan negotiations had been 'devastating'. But by 1950 Churchill's broad generalisations about Unity and his view that it could be brought about by acts of concerted good will, as Monnet put it, had proved insufficient for those who, like the author of the Schuman Plan, were determined to go beyond all past practice and embark, step by step, on the real, functional integration of Europe. Yet it had been Churchill, surely, who by his great speeches and the significance of his own presence upon 'European' occasions had largely formed the whole climate in which it was possible for Monnet and the Federalists, and the Americans too, to make the new concept of the Coal and Steel pool a matter of practical politics.

When he led the attack in the House of Commons on the Labour Government's refusal to entertain Monnet's prior conditions for the new 'Community', Churchill had turned to Stafford Cripps and said that if he, Churchill, was asked, 'Would you agree to a supranational authority which has the power to tell Great Britain not to cut any more coal, to make any more steel, but to grow tomatoes instead?' he would say, without hesitation, the answer was No. But *'Why not be there to give the answer?'*

In taking this line Churchill, while himself rejecting the 'federal' prescription, was suggesting that the Schuman Plan in its final form must have emerged in a different and possibly more acceptable mould if Britain had gone in, and taken part as a foundation member in the drafting of the proposals. On the specific ground on which the British Cabinet had said No, the constitutional issue of 'Sovereignty', Churchill had said this in the House: 'The Conservative and Liberal Parties say, without hesitation, that we are prepared to consider and, if convinced, to accept the abrogation of national sovereignty, provided we are satisfied with the conditions and the safeguards.' Thus it was that Winston Churchill was thought of as an almost uniquely good and desirable 'European', if an uncertain and indifferent 'federalist'.

However there was, by now, less freedom for manoeuvre. The challenge of the Schuman Plan to British foreign policy no longer lay in its novelty, but the fact that it was policy and reality. Six countries in Western Europe were engrossed in making the new, precedent-shattering idea work, as they set about devolving limited functions but real powers upon an embryo economic and political community constructed around the strategic resources of coal and steel. From this process Britain had excluded herself, and by so doing of course had helped to make a bed in Europe which many years later she would find it decidedly uncomfortable to lie on.

The particular and the general context was rapidly changing. In 1950, with the outbreak of the Korean War, the emphasis had switched from the economic recovery of Western Europe – which had been the dominant consideration essential to combat subversion from within – to rearmament, believed indispensable in order to face a growing external threat and test of will. As the tone of the exchanges between the Americans and the Russians grew ever sharper, events seemed to be dragged in a fatalistic slip towards the brink of another war. In the volley and thunder of accusation between East and West, the voice of Europe itself was almost a whisper.

Then, once more, it was Churchill who had called upon his own deep feelings and aroused, in doing so, those of others. The lightning flash in Korea had created new facts and new possibilities. Speaking to the Assembly of the Council of Europe meeting in Strasbourg on 11 August 1950, he had successfully moved a resolution which gave the first concrete expression to the radical notion of a European Army. The ensuing development of this issue – the means of safely incorporating and rearming Germany itself – was to confuse and baffle European diplomacy for the next four years. 'La recherche de la paternité' is invariably a delicate issue, but Winston Churchill was, henceforth, regarded as the 'Father' of the concept of a European Army. This is what he said:

CHURCHILL: We ought to make our united convictions known. We should send today a message of confidence and courage from the House of Europe to the whole world. Not only should we reaffirm, as we have been asked to do, our allegiance to the United Nations, but *we should make a gesture of practical and constructive guidance by declaring ourselves in favour of the immediate creation of a European Army under a unified command, and in which we should all bear a worthy and honourable part.* Therefore I propose to you the following Resolution:

'The Assembly, in order to express its devotion to the maintainence of peace and its resolve to sustain the action of the United Nations in defence of peaceful peoples against aggression, calls for the immediate creation of a European Army subject to proper European democratic control and acting in full co-operation with the United States and Canada.'

CHURCHILL'S MOTION was duly carried, amid scenes of enthusiasm, in Strasbourg by eighty-nine votes to five.

It is the reason, no doubt – together, of course, with all that he had spoken and written before on the grand theme of 'Europe Revived' – that Harold Macmillan had subsequently written, in his own memoirs, of the hopes raised by Churchill's return to power with his well-known independence of mind and spirit. It was, according to Macmillan, 'hailed throughout Europe and America as likely to mark a wholly new approach towards the question of European unity'. Macmillan had gone on: 'If what happened was to prove a sad disillusionment, almost a betrayal, it is right to recall some of the difficulties.'

The fact is that, when Churchill did return to power, he and Anthony Eden made no important changes to the fundamental stand taken by their predecessors, Attlee and Bevin, on the political, economic and military projects afoot on the Continent of Europe. The President of the Board of Trade in Churchill's Cabinet was Peter Thorneycroft, now Lord Thorneycroft.

THORNEYCROFT: There was a moment when, just after the war, Winston could have gone in and led it. You remember the Hague Conference? His position was unassailable then – but he was tired. He had forces deployed against him including, I think, the Foreign Office, who were never very keen on it. Then, I think, he didn't want to fight the battle in the Cabinet (it was just before I was playing any major part in it). And so we did not take the lead. But

The Parliamentary Assembly in Strasbourg: Churchill in power again.

still, in 1951 and 1952 we had a very strong position, we could have gone in as equals, and this was our proposal, but we could have negotiated, of course, terms far more satisfactory than exist today.'

CHARLTON: By the time you went to the Board of Trade in 1951, the Schuman Plan was an established fact, but not yet ratified. What can you tell us about how the Conservatives, when they came to power in 1951, reconsidered, and then decided to reject, British participation in the Coal and Steel Community?

THORNEYCROFT: Yes, I think the decision was probably the wrong one – that's the first thing to be said, though it would have been swept up in the larger concept of a Free Trade Area if that had ever taken place. I can remember co-operating very closely with them; I can remember going over there, attending its meetings, and really representing, for all practical purposes, this country as a full member. I think that those concerned with Coal and Steel in this country probably thought of themselves as full members – I mean they were inter-nationally minded. Steel, particularly, was an international commodity. Our role should have been in it – that is the answer.

CHARLTON: The Labour government, your predecessors, rejected partici-pation on the constitutional grounds that it would have involved a prior commit-ment to ceding sovereignty to the collective authority of member states, the pooling of sovereignty. Are you saying that we should have participated and then dealt with the question of sovereignty later?

THORNEYCROFT: All forms of co-operation involve some erosion of sovereignty. Every treaty does – NATO does – and that was just the classic argument, or one of the classic arguments, for doing nothing. I think on balance we would have done better to do something. We ought to have taken it as part and parcel, not of itself, but as part and parcel of a total move forward into Europe.

CHARLTON: Why then, when the Conservatives were in power and there was still an opportunity to reconsider this proposition, did you take the same view, apparently, that Attlee and Bevin had taken?

THORNEYCROFT: Because at that moment the Conservative government, indeed the Conservative party, had not made up its mind on the strategy. This was tactics really – iron and steel and coal. The strategic decision was, were we ready to move forward and be part of Europe or not? We delayed that decision – perhaps fatally. One must understand the problems that faced the Cabinet at that time. They're not so easy to visualise today. At that time you must remember, there was the whole Commonwealth position. One had to carry Commonwealth leaders who still, although the system of imperial preference was going, had large advantages in *this* market. There was the whole agricultural lobby; it would be a revolution for them to think of new approaches in this field. So one must not be too harsh, or make too harsh a judgement about the delay. But there is no doubt that this Cabinet, at that time, delayed and, I think, rather tragically delayed what could have been a dominating move by the British in Europe.

CHARLTON: Well, having passed up, on those grounds, the opportunity to participate in the Coal and Steel Community, in what frame of mind would you say you were, in the Conservative Cabinet, should such an opportunity present itself again, another opportunity?

THORNEYCROFT: We were divided. You must understand, in governments a lot depends on the personalities involved and a lot depends on the attitude of the ministries involved. The old Board of Trade, as it then was – a sort of combination of the Department of Industry and the Department of Trade today, was I think essentially 'Free Trade' in its spirit. It believed in world trade. Pushed on by that, and perhaps because it had a President, like myself, who was also a very keen European and wanted to go in anyway – for *political* reasons as well as *trade* ones – we were pushing for our corner. We were certainly the first, and for a long time the *only* Ministry arguing for participation in Europe. The Foreign Office, at the other extreme, were opposed to it – under Eden to start with and for quite a long time afterwards they were opposed to it again – for almost historical reasons. After all, foreign policy was the balance of power, it was the division of the world, of balancing groups against groups. It was deeply based on a special relationship with the United States of America. *All* these deeply ingrained concepts in the Foreign Office were challenged by the proposal of this upstart Board of Trade, saying that we ought to alter the whole thing and move in, as a partner, in a new European venture. Nevertheless we were arguing in my time from the Board of Trade that we should *change* this and we should work out a European co-operation.

CHARLTON: You said that we were divided. Eden is Foreign Secretary, and on our relationship with Europe Maxwell Fyfe, the Home Secretary, had this to say afterwards: 'We were bound by Eden's hostile approach to a matter in which he was nominally opposed by Macmillan and myself at least.' He also couples you with that, Lord Thorneycroft, but what was the difference between Eden and Churchill over this European issue?

THORNEYCROFT: Churchill was a European. He had it in his mind – in his heart, at any rate – that he would have liked to bring a great group of nations together. Do you remember early in the war when he offered common, equal

citizenship to France? I mean, Churchill *thought* in those terms about Europe. I was at the Hague Conference after the war, and the reception he got! He was a god-like figure in Europe. Here was the man who, at that time, really was the saviour of Europe, and the Europeans would have gone almost anywhere he asked them to go. This was the Churchill attitude. Anthony [Eden] did not feel *any* of that at all. He was really opposed to it. He and the Foreign Office believed that we should maintain a special relationship with the United States.
CHARLTON: But you must have argued this with Eden, yourself? What is the difference between you? Why does Eden have no belief that this can be made to work in Europe, and even if it can that it is not for us?
THORNEYCROFT: Why did he believe it? I think it is a question of history as much as modern-day politics. The whole basis of the Foreign Office approach had been something utterly different to what we were seeking in Europe.

PETER THORNEYCROFT GIVES, as major reasons why Churchill's characteristically independent European idealism lost the name of action in office, the Prime Minister's age – 'he was tired' – and the 'forces deployed against him'. It would have meant a major battle in the Party and the Cabinet and with Whitehall – the Foreign Office under Eden in particular – which he, by then, lacked the necessary concentration and energy to fight.

By this time, in 1951, the Americans had made it clear, with their endorsement of the Schuman Plan, that such fresh points of departure in Europe had their own blessing, and support for integration had now become a basic formulation of their own policy. Can it be said with certain knowledge, therefore, where Winston Churchill's thinking about Europe lay, as he returned to power in 1951? One who speaks with a particular authority about Churchill was his Principal Private Secretary, Sir John ('Jock') Colville.

COLVILLE: Frankly, to my certain knowledge, nowhere! That is to say, he did not talk about the great message he'd given at Strasbourg, Luxembourg and so on, at all during those first few months. It wasn't until the European Army situation developed that he began to talk about the future of Europe. I don't think that in the first six or nine months of his 1951 government any thought of European unity really entered his head. He was thinking of two things: one was reasserting and re-creating the special union with America, the special alliance; the other was – he put it in so many words to me – he said, 'My policy is simple, it's houses, and meat, and not getting scuppered!'
CHARLTON: What did he mean by that?
COLVILLE: Not getting scuppered? He meant making sure that we were strong enough to stand up for ourselves in the world. Houses, because of the great housing shortage, and of course the Conservative government had a tremendously triumphant, 300,000 houses programme, which Macmillan brought to fruition. And meat? He meant he was going to get rid of rationing as soon as he could. Churchill thought it was a total disgrace that, six years after the end of the war, there should still be heavy rationing in this country and *not* in any European countries.
CHARLTON: But on the specific question of Britain's European policy, and the place it occupied at the time, did he give all that to Eden as Foreign Secretary? Was he, in your own words, preoccupied with the Anglo-American relationship?

Churchill's return to office. With President Truman, Secretary of State Dean Acheson and Anthony Eden on board the presidential yacht, Williamsburg, January 1952.

COLVILLE: I don't think Eden was at all preoccupied with the European policy. I don't think that anybody was. I don't think the government as a whole were, I don't think the House of Commons was, and I don't think that the country was. There were, of course, a few very keen Europeans but they were a tiny minority. They were people like Duncan Sandys, far-sighted, who really thought that our future was with Europe. But they were a tiny minority. This is where I think history is sometimes slightly distorted. People now talk as if there were great opportunities missed. I doubt that there were those opportunities. Nobody wanted that particular solution. Certainly during the Churchill government of 1951–5, and also I think for the next three or four years, the mere suggestion of our becoming part of an integrated Europe would have been totally unacceptable to the House of Commons and the country, and no British government would have considered it. I mean, even those tremendous Europeans, and the man who did as much as anybody else to bring us in – Harold Macmillan! I find in my diary in May 1952 that, having seen him at the Turf Club for luncheon, he said to me he thought the development of the *Empire* into an economic unit as powerful as the USA and the USSR was the only possibility! Now that, I think, represented a view held by not merely Harold Macmillan, but certainly by Churchill, and very strongly I am sure by Anthony Eden. And, I think, by the whole government.

CHARLTON: And that's a year *after* the founding of the Schuman Plan for Coal and Steel.

COLVILLE: Yes, and I think for any British government to go to the House of Commons in those days and say, 'Look! We've got a marvellous idea! We're going to join Europe and help them to build a United Europe and become part of it . . .' I think there would have been howls of wrath and anger!

CHARLTON: But was Churchill exercised by that? To what extent was policy dictated by the climate of public opinion?

COLVILLE: Oh yes, he was very conscious of the climate of public opinion. In this particular case I think it coincided with his own ideas – that we should consider ourselves indeed a *part* of Europe but not *comprised* in Europe, and that the overriding importance was the Empire and our special relationship with the United States.

CHARLTON: So that is the essential answer as to why Churchill does nothing about the United States of Europe when he had the chance? That he just doesn't see Britain as part of this endeavour? After all, he had summoned the country to a war against Hitler by his own courage, personal authority and leadership; one assumes he could have summoned the British to a role inside Europe if he had wanted . . .

COLVILLE: I think if he'd felt as strongly about the future of a European Federation as he'd felt about stopping Hitler dominating Europe, he might have. But I don't think he did. I think he *was* perfectly conscious of what the general climate of opinion was in those days – which was *not* pro-European.

CHARLTON: But in the famous speeches he makes after the war, Zurich, Fulton and Strasbourg, where he stirs these sentiments for European unity? He leads the European movement, he creates the emotions out of which it is born, and he gives his own authority to it. Why does he do that? Is he just striking out for a policy? Why does he believe it necessary then?

COLVILLE: I think he thought it was absolutely vital then, as he had thought for many years before, to make sure that there was no future European war, that the Europeans got together, that they became united so there was no more struggle between France and Germany and I think he thought the British should become involved in some way or another; I don't think he was entirely specific as to how. But I don't think that he was merely, as it were, *lecturing* them and saying we will stand back! I'm not suggesting that. I hope I didn't give that impression. I think he *did* feel that we ought to take part over the European Army. I think he thought that we should send a contingent, but not just put the whole army into the European Army! In the same way, I think he thought the British should no doubt take a part in a United Europe, but *not* to the extent of sinking everything, their Parliament, their law, their weights and measures, the lot, into the European system.

CHARLTON: But does he deliberately create these ambiguities, or are they just unsolved in his own mind? You see, about the European Army, which after all is not finally decided, or doesn't finally collapse until much later, he says this in August 1950 at Strasbourg: 'We should send a message . . . from this House of Europe to the whole world . . . We should make a gesture of practical and constructive guidance by declaring ourselves in favour of the immediate creation of a European Army under a unified command, and in which we should all bear a worthy and honourable part.'

COLVILLE: I do not think that is at all contrary to what I said. I don't think it crossed Churchill's mind that we should become part of a Federal Europe. As I've said before, he believed in 'L'Europe des Patries'. He thought that close union with Europe was very important, but I do not think he ever saw within, shall we say, living experience the end of the nation state.

CHARLTON: So what then did he think of the European federalists at this time, people like Monnet, Spaak, who were very active?

COLVILLE: I think he was very impressed by a lot of their arguments. He would not have objected perhaps, I don't know, but he would not have objected to a European federation with which we would have had some kind of *association*. But I think it is really rather wrong for people to suggest that Churchill ever believed Britain would sink everything in Europe. I think that perhaps he wanted to have the best of all worlds. He wanted to make sure that the Empire prospered. He wanted to have the closest possible relationship with the United States, in whose benevolence he entirely trusted, but at the same time he wanted to play a part in uniting Europe. I don't think it is a contradiction to say that he was, as it were, teaching the Europeans their own business while saying we should take no part. I think he intended we should, certainly, in the European Army. I say again, he intended we should send a contingent.

'JOCK' COLVILLE IS A remarkable figure in his own right. He has been private secretary to no less than three Prime Ministers – Chamberlain, Churchill and Attlee – and also to the Queen when she was Princess Elizabeth. He was by Churchill's side during the war, leaving it only to go off and fly the high-performance fighter aircraft, the Mustang, in operational missions over Europe during his service with the RAF in the volunteer reserve! He is a cultivated exemplar of the virtues of the man of action, for whom Churchill had a special affection and liked to gather close around him. Colville accompanied Churchill's return to office in 1951, as his joint principal private secretary – a daily and intimate observer and adviser.

We are left, then, to set beside Harold Macmillan's own choice of words – 'sad disillusionment', 'almost a betrayal' – Sir John Colville's emphatic recollection that there had been no fundamental advance in Churchill's thinking about Britain's place in Europe at the time of his second Government. Furthermore, that what he had written so many years before, in the 1930s, calling for a United States of Europe – and which has been discussed in the first chapter – remained the broad framework of his thinking. Britain was, as Churchill had said then, 'with Europe but not of it, linked but not comprised'.

To hold the scales impartially in the matter of diary entries concerning Harold Macmillan – while Sir John Colville's for May 1952 records a conversation with Macmillan and the latter's declaration to him that 'he thought the development of the Empire into an economic unit as powerful as the USA and the USSR was the only possibility', I must record that both Lord Plowden and Lord Roberthall remember a dinner with Harold Macmillan at which he canvassed their views whether he should resign from Churchill's cabinet because of its failure to take up in office the challenge it had so recently led over Europe in opposition!

Churchill's 'devastating attack', as Sir Harold Wilson considered it, on the Attlee government for its handling of the Schuman Plan – during the debate in the House of Commons he had accused the Labour leaders of piling their own prejudices upon French pedantry – included this additional comment on the issue of sovereignty: 'It is not inviolable. It may be resolutely diminished, for the sake of all the men, in all the lands, finding their way home together.' Was there not there, in the deep feeling and sentimentality of Churchill, the poet/ statesman, something close to the core of Jean Monnet's and the Federalists' beliefs?

COLVILLE: I don't think it represented Churchill's deepest thoughts. He had a great benevolence towards and feeling for Europe, but I mean he was such a patriot! I can't see him ever saying the British individuality, or the separate existence of this country, should be sunk in anything else. I don't believe it was at all in his thoughts. There has been a great deal of confusion.

CHARLTON: This is a time when his son-in-law, Duncan Sandys, has enlisted Churchill as the patron of the European movement.

COLVILLE: I think he had a lot of influence on Churchill over Europe, in fact I am sure he did.

CHARLTON: Are those Sandys' words, do you suggest, rather than Churchill's – this talk of a possible need for our sovereignty to be 'resolutely diminished' in a greater cause?

COLVILLE: I was back in the Foreign Office and I wasn't party to it, but I'm perfectly sure that Duncan Sandys, with his very great enthusiasm, had an enormous effect on Churchill. And Churchill, I'm sure, was very impressed by what Duncan Sandys proposed. Whether he ever got as far as thinking we should sink our own identity in that, I would personally doubt.

CHARLTON: There was a quotation which has been used about him, not unkindly I think – I am not sure you haven't used it yourself – about Asquith saying that, whereas Lloyd George had no principles, Winston Churchill had no convictions. Would you say that applied to his thoughts about Europe?

COLVILLE: Asquith said that to my own grandfather who told it to me, so I was the original, the only source of the quotation! I think – whether it's true of Lloyd George I would hesitate to say – because it might upset a lot of Welshmen – but as far as Churchill is concerned I think it is totally untrue. Although Asquith liked Churchill, I think he found that, you know, he wavered from side to side on certain other issues. But I don't think it is true. I think Churchill was remarkably consistent. I said that in those quotations from the article he wrote in 1930 he really expressed the views he felt in the 1950s. But above all, I think, that he was totally convinced that the country as such was not ready for any such experiment, and the climate of opinion was opposed to it, which indeed it was!

AND THIS LAST MUST no doubt have weighed heavily with Churchill, a politician to his fingertips. In the Cabinet itself 'we were divided', Lord Thorneycroft has told us.

In the new situation created by the successful establishment of the Coal and Steel Community, and faced with the issues created by German rearmament, it would become apparent that Churchill did not hold sufficiently forward views on Britain and Europe to satisfy Harold Macmillan and those who, like him, had been in at the founding of the European Movement. Despite the generosity of his European feelings, Churchill now hesitated and appears to have had his

own misgivings. Very probably Anthony Eden gave them powerful reinforce-
ment. The combination of Churchill losing energy and vitality, and his now-
qualified enthusiasm for a United States of Europe if it meant British
participation in the organic forms of integration under way on the continent,
means that from 1951 onwards, the differences within the Conservative
hierarchy over Europe must be seen more as a conflict between Macmillan and
Eden, rather than Eden and Churchill. They are differences which seem
inseparable, to an extent now, of course, very difficult to determine, from the
question of the succession to Churchill himself. They were, however, differences which would grow in importance.

Christopher Soames, who married Winston Churchill's daughter Mary,
became, in his late twenties, the Prime Minister's Parliamentary Private
Secretary on his return to Downing Street in 1951. Lord Soames had this to say
about 'sad disillusionment' and 'almost a betrayal', to which Macmillan added
that 'it was right to consider the difficulties internal and external' with which
Churchill was faced.

SOAMES: Well, this is true. Perhaps Europe came ten years too soon. I think
that, looking back historically, it could be seen whichever way you choose to put
it. Either the British public realised ten years too late that we were no longer
going to draw our greatness from being at the heart of an Empire which did our
bidding, or that Europe came ten years too soon for us. This was just after the
war and the feeling towards the Commonwealth, the Australians and all those
who'd fought with us – it took a long time for the people to realise where our
destiny did lie. In hard terms there's no doubt where it lay, but in sentimental
terms it was different.

I remember his [Churchill] saying, in one of his great speeches on this subject in the post-war years, that 'France must take Germany by the hand' and
lead her back into the community of nations. I mean his vision was of creating a
degree of European unity which was going to make it impossible to have
another war. Now that was his basic thought. As to the part we would play in it,
he used to draw, you remember, these three concentric circles, one of Europe,
the other of the Commonwealth, the other of the English-speaking world, and
the only common factor in all three of them was Britain. This is really how he
saw it. He was a man of Empire essentially. He was born in the latter half of the
last century and he'd been through India and Kipling's days and all that. He
was a man of Empire, and he found it hard to envisage – after all, he was a man
of nearly eighty in 1951 – he found it difficult to envisage Britain, I think, as a
part of Europe, interwoven inextricably with Europe; as General de Gaulle
found it difficult to think of France being also. The basis of de Gaulle's thought
was one of nationalism, of the Generals. And of Churchill's it was the basis of
Empire, and of the English-speaking peoples, and the feeling towards America
– but that we *had* to play our part in the uniting of Europe.

Now, as to what that part should be, in the late 1940s, when he was launching
it, it was that we should give a lead to others. They were very early days and
nobody thought then about the European Community as we know it today.
Gradually it evolved. Then when he got into power, in 1951, you must remember
the Foreign Office was then very much against it. Anthony Eden was Foreign
Secretary and he did not like it, he thought it was wrong. He thought it was fine

Anthony Eden arrives at Downing Street as Prime Minister, April 1955, and departs after his breakdown over Suez, January 1957. The single most important factor governing Britain's European policy becomes the personality and convictions of Anthony Eden.

for Europe to unite, but not for us with it. There was a great stirring in Winston's breast for the kith and kin argument, for instance. He realised that, politically, we were not ready for a total immersion, as it were, in Europe; to the degree of exclusion of the rest of the world other than America – which other Continental powers *could* achieve, and do, politically. Public opinion was not ready for it.

Now over and above that there was Anthony Eden. Churchill felt he'd rather, you know – he had a bit of a conscience, that he perhaps should not have taken the Premiership in 1951 – if only because he was holding Anthony Eden out. Eden had been waiting in the wings as his deputy for a long time. I think he did feel this sometimes – that he had been hard on Eden – and that was a limit that he felt, although Winston dominated the Cabinet, and neither the Cabinet nor the Party in Parliament or in the country could lift a little finger against him because of his immense popularity with the nation as a whole. He realised that Anthony Eden was a very experienced politician in foreign affairs. He therefore did not push beyond a certain point. There were a number of areas that I saw of foreign policy where he thought that he would have liked to have gone farther or faster, but he did not push it if Eden said, 'So far and no further'.

CHARLTON: He is a much older man now – he's nearly eighty – and he has surrendered more authority, would you not say, over the field of foreign affairs to Eden than had been the case in wartime?

SOAMES: Yes, certainly, certainly. That's right.

CHARLTON: But the evidence is clear, isn't it, that the Foreign Office and Eden think Winston Churchill is a romantic – that these ideas he has are not always practicable – and they're placing, would you agree, a restraining hand upon his shoulder all the time?

SOAMES: Oh, very definitely, undoubtedly. The Foreign Office thought – I am not just talking now about Eden, because I'm sure the Foreign Office had a considerable impact on Eden's thinking – but the Foreign Office thought at that time that our destiny did *not* lie bound up with Europe to the degree they now think it should be. They changed. They changed, probably soon after the Treaty of Rome, I think in the late 1950s.

CHARLTON: But to be fair to Eden, you would not suggest that Eden talked Churchill *out* of going further in 1950/1/2 when in office? Rather that he received no *encouragement* from Eden to go further in this European business?

SOAMES: Oh no, not so. Eden was definitely hostile to it – *hostile* to it – and so was the Foreign Office! That's a lot for a Prime Minister to carry. I mean, it would be such a big departure. It was not something he felt he could do, and also he had his misgivings as to the extent we should be in. He had his own feelings.

CHARLTON: Did they go as far as any suggestion that maybe he was beginning to rethink it – was withdrawing from the whole idea?

SOAMES: No, certainly not, under no circumstances. Of course the formation of a European Community did not come about until after he'd left, but Europe was pointing in that direction; and he liked what he saw about the movement towards European unity.

CHARLTON: Can I ask you a specific thing, the row over the European Army, between two parts of the Conservative Party, between that part of it represented by Eden and his attitudes over Europe and that part represented by Macmillan and Maxwell Fyfe who thought Britain should be doing more. Macmillan tells us that he and his colleagues tried to get Churchill to intervene in this argument but that Churchill was unwilling to press it 'against the hostility of the Foreign Office'.

SOAMES: Against the hostility of *Eden* and the Foreign Office. It's the same story we are talking of. The Foreign Office plus Eden.

CHARLTON: And the other charge – that there is a struggle going on for Churchill really, that in a sense he was being manipulated at times by people like Duncan Sandys and Macmillan over this European issue? Saying more than he meant in fact?

SOAMES: No, I don't think so. Look at his speeches. I think he meant every word that he said, and he felt it passionately. They were marvellous speeches. You don't make speeches like that if you don't feel it. Certainly he didn't. The Zurich speech is a marvellous speech, so was the speech at the Hague. Those who were close to him, and who fervently believed in Britain being a part of Europe and in creating a 'United Europe', nobody quite knew what it meant in those days, or where they were going – but they knew that something *must* be done to prevent another holocaust happening. Winston was of course an extremely valuable ally for them, because what he said carried great weight. It was much better that *he* should say it at Zurich than Macmillan or Sandys or any of the others who were close to him at that time. Indeed, it did a lot to concentrate the minds of many Europeans, and it clearly fitted in with the thinking of Monnet and Schuman and others. And away it went – a Great Adventure, the adventure of trying to pull together the interests of what are now [1981] nine countries, all with their own histories, all with their own paths, their own prides and, God knows, with our own prejudices!

CHARLTON: You know, deep down I'd like to put to you something about this country. He is its national hero, and he is one of its great historical figures, and yet somehow it is that very thing, that sense of adventure, which was distrusted. The British don't warm to adventures. I wonder if that's not, at heart, the reason – that he is never quite forgiven for having all the ideas of the future? He was right about the Germans, and the Foreign Office was wrong, before the war. He had all the ideas, he was right about post-war Europe. Did he see it like that himself in your view?

SOAMES: Well, he knew more than anyone else perhaps of the difficulties of democracies, that you have to carry people. It takes so long! But by God he meant it! You can't accuse a man who played the part he did in not one, but two, world wars and then say that his efforts to ensure that there was not a third were just catchphrases or trying to capture votes. He really felt it deeply. But he was not unequivocal, and he did not see exactly where Britain would fit in this. He did not.

IT IS TIME TO RETURN to the twin issues of the Coal and Steel Community and the European Army, which provided a frequent and embarrassing litmus test of British intentions – embarrassing because (we have Lord Thorneycroft's word for it) the Cabinet 'fatally delayed' coming to a strategic decision over Europe. Churchill's speech in Strasbourg in August 1950 calling for the immediate creation of a European Army, under unified command, was subsequently criticised publicly by Eden in his own memoirs as having given rise to many misunderstandings. Not the least of them within the party itself.

An informed witness of the almost daily exacting challenges with which the European policy in the Churchill government was in the end presented was Sir Anthony Nutting, Eden's political protégé at the Foreign Office and, as the junior minister, the one who had particular responsibilities for Europe.

NUTTING: I think Churchill was trying to develop a somewhat emotional, as well as a very grand strategic, plan for Europe. I remember tackling him on this at the time when I was trying to push Eden into some gesture towards Europe, in early 1952. I remember tackling Winston about this and saying, 'But *you*, Prime Minister, made this speech yourself and spoke of the "European Army in which we would play an honourable and active part". What did you mean by that?' And he said, 'Well, I really meant it for them and not for us.' So I said, 'Well, your words do not bear that interpretation.' And of course I couldn't get any further, he wouldn't develop the answer any further.

When I spoke to the Prime Minister on a different occasion he had another explanation. This was that he did not want to go any further into Europe for fear of, I think the way he put it was, 'embarrassing Anthony when he succeeds me as Prime Minister'. He said, 'I hoped that by the time we got into office there would be some British participation in a European community, political community or defence community or economic community of some kind, and that it would have developed before Anthony actually took office as Prime

Minister. But as things worked out he didn't do so, therefore I didn't want to push us into Europe any more closely and any further than Anthony would him-self have liked to go.'

ALMOST FROM THE BEGINNING of Churchill's second government in 1951 the weight of evidence suggests that the single most important factor governing Britain's European policy was the personality and convictions of the Foreign Secretary, Anthony Eden.

Before examining his position we should perhaps look quickly at the one immediate, practical consequence of the 'No change' policy of the Conservatives over Europe. The Schuman Plan question was *not* reopened. Having rejected 'full participation', Britain was embarked upon a new line of approach which we might call 'close association'. This was seen as 'keeping in touch' with the new developments.

As the formal expression of 'close association', which was a careful detach-ment from any obligations, in fact, and evidence that Britain continued to think of Monnet's concepts in economic rather than political terms, a Glasgow industrialist, Sir Cecil Weir, was appointed to the Coal and Steel Community headquarters in Luxembourg. He had been head of the economic department of the British Control Commission in Germany for many years. This is how he became well known to Sir Con O'Neill, who was appointed by the Foreign Office to Bonn in the early fifties and who offers this memory of 'close associ-ation' in practice.

O'NEILL: After the Coal and Steel Community was set up we entered into an Association Agreement with it. A part of that agreement was that we should establish a permanent commission in Luxembourg with the high authority of the Coal and Steel pool, under Monnet as it was then. Cecil Weir became the first head of this Commission. He was a delightful, able man and he very soon became a tremendous enthusiast for the idea of an economically integrated Europe. He and his staff, which included, by the way, Derek Ezra who is now [1981] Chairman of the Coal Board, all became very enthusiastic, and Cecil perhaps played his hand not terribly well. Instead of arguing the case coolly and rationally on paper with the people in London, he was always dashing back brimming with enthusiasm, rushing around the corridors of the Foreign Office, the Treasury and the Board of Trade – and he rather got on people's nerves by singing the praises of an organisation which they all regarded as totally in-significant. I'm afraid they were bored by it. I probably should have been myself had I been there!

IT WOULD ALSO APPEAR to be demonstrable early proof that the dismissive attitude of Bevin to the Schuman Plan had been carried over in the Foreign Office under Eden. Weir's enthusiastic reporting on the possibilities evinced in Eden no aroused interest.

From Winston Churchill's post-war journeyings to the Continent and his exhortations there in the cause of European unity, Anthony Eden had been a notable absentee. He had been silent and apart. He had deliberately not gone to Strasbourg where Churchill, Macmillan and Sandys had conducted, as has been suggested, almost an unofficial foreign policy. Harold Macmillan when he wrote his own memoirs – indispensable for an understanding of British attitudes to Europe – said that he 'never understood why Eden held himself aloof'. Others suggest that the reason is clear enough. Eden, for reasons of temperament, belief and policy, questioned the directions, and resented the influence on foreign policy being urged by those close to Churchill who, like Macmillan and Sandys, had a presumptive interest in the succession. Some who were close to Anthony Eden agree that this feeling and his lack, because he did not see for himself, of first-hand experience of the enthusiasms generated in Strasbourg were a root cause of his questioning of the forces in favour of European integration, and his doubts about their likely consistency or durability.

Eden's Parliamentary Private Secretary was Robert Carr, who is now Lord Carr of Hadley. This was his comment in the first place upon that lesser, baser motive of either 'jealousy' or 'vanity', often attributed to Eden by those critical of him, as an important factor circumscribing his judgement about the relevance to Britain of the new 'community' spirit in Europe.

CARR: Human nature is such that that, I'm sure, is an element in the overall equation. Personally I would not rate it too highly. There was undoubtedly a different approach, in temperamental approach, between Eden, on the one hand, and Macmillan and those close to Macmillan in this matter, Julian Amery, Duncan Sandys and David Kilmuir [Maxwell Fyfe], and Bob Boothby on the back benches, who really did take up Europe with a passion which Anthony found somehow out of tune, not altogether British. I don't know quite how to put it, but there was an element of distaste, in Eden, for this whole *emotional* approach towards it, I think.

THIS WOULD SEEM TO BE rather more than an 'important' factor, but perhaps a governing one in future policy. For the evidence is surely abundant that it was emotions and deep feelings which lay at the heart of the whole 'European' enterprise. It was this which Churchill had, from the beginning, intuitively understood and appealed to. But this was the 'romantic' view of history which Eden, according to Robert Carr, found unappealing, or 'distasteful'. Lord Carr believes Eden addressed the European issue, in his own mind, in these essential terms.

CARR: I think Eden was always sceptical in the first place about the practical possibilities of these separate nationalistic countries in Europe ever forming a cohesive, organic union. I think this was one of the main motivating thoughts in his attitude. He simply did not believe that it could come about, and was convinced that it would be very bad for Britain were she to become associated with an attempt of this kind which failed. Because he saw the need for Britain, if it *did* fail – particularly in view of Britain's standing in Europe in the first decade after the war, and particularly also with Britain's remaining position as a world power – for Britain, if it did fail, to have been independent of it, and to be able to play a part in putting something different in its place.

SO, WITH ANTHONY EDEN at the Foreign Office the pervasive British scepticism was sustained. Among the first of the new government's basic presumptions was that the early success demonstrated by Monnet with 'The Six' was unlikely to be consolidated or developed. This accorded, of course, with the positive themes in Eden's philosophy and the bedrock presumption of British policy after the war, that a move into Europe would mean a move *away* from the United States and with it the loss of those coequal opportunities of a distinct and separate role and, in the case of the special relationship, playing, as it were, Greece to America's Rome.

The Under-Secretary of State for Foreign Affairs when Anthony Eden was Foreign Secretary was Anthony Nutting.

NUTTING: Eden was, essentially, an Atlanticist rather than a European, certainly during the latter two periods when he was Foreign Secretary – in the Second World War and between 1951 and 1955. This, I think, largely sprang from the fact that he never got over Neville Chamberlain turning down Roosevelt's offer to intervene in the European conflict with Hitler in late 1937. And he thought that America *must* be involved, and that we and the Americans must go hand in hand, must proceed step by step; and he did not want to get *out* of step with America; and he did not want to get into Europe if America was not prepared to come with him. I think that is why he was always so much more detached from the European scene than, for instance, other leaders of the Tory party. It was also partly because he did not want to upset the apple cart with the Russians. He wanted to try and preserve what he could. He was, after all, in 1951 particularly, the first practitioner of what we would call now 'détente'. He did not want to upset the Russians by forming too close a European Alliance over and above the NATO Alliance, which might have made relations more difficult than they were with the Soviet Union.

There was also the element of personal rivalry involved. Macmillan, Sandys, other Tory leaders of the time, apart from Churchill himself, were very much in the forefront of the European movement. Eden rather resented the fact that they, as it were, were taking Tory foreign policy out of his hands. So he just held back. He wouldn't have anything to do with their efforts in Strasbourg and the Hague. Throughout his whole life, particularly his life as Foreign Secretary, he liked to have foreign policy in his hands. He resented any interference. After all, he resigned from Chamberlain's government in 1938 not so much because of Chamberlain appeasing the Dictators, appeasing Mussolini in particular, but because Chamberlain was trying to run foreign policy from Downing Street while Eden was Foreign Secretary on the other side of Downing Street. He equally resented, of course, some of Churchill's interventions in the fields of foreign affairs. Eden thought *he* should be the maker of Tory foreign policy.

There is also the fact that, when he got into office in 1951, there was a considerable prejudice inside the Foreign Office against the European Movement; against the idea of hitching our waggon to these struggling countries that were bankrupt and had been completely destroyed in the war. There was a fear that, to change the metaphor, if we tried to save the Europeans from drowning and went in with them, we would be dragged under ourselves.

THE BROAD COROLLARY of this compendium of views held by Eden was, according to Anthony Nutting, this.

NUTTING: He did not see the importance of Europe, either in economic terms or political terms, I think largely because Eden was essentially a tactician in politics, in foreign policy. He was not a strategist. He did not see the broad picture, of a Europe revived such as exists today; of Western Europe with Germany as a great industrial and economic giant as it is today. He could not see this. Germany was more or less flat on the floor in 1951, only six years after the war ended. He could not see it in those broad terms. And so he clung to the Atlantic Alliance, and of course, as was so often the reason given in those days, he gave the Commonwealth as the reason why we could not go into Europe any more closely.

WE HAVE ALREADY HAD CAUSE to note that a persistent concern shaping British policy attitudes was that American support for integration in Europe, implicitly to include the United Kingdom, was a possible prelude to some future comfortable withdrawal by the United States into the more traditional American stance of 'isolation'. It was an American disposition which the British diagnosed as endemic. This concern was allied, no doubt, with the resentment that Britain, which had stood alone and been bankrupted for a cause from which all free men had profited, should be asked now somehow to forfeit that particular status and be – the phrase appears in some Foreign Office papers – 'bundled away inside Europe'.

It is worth recalling Lord Sherfield's remark following the American endorsement of the Schuman Plan (see page 93) that 'it let the Americans off the hook' – 'the hook' being the British determination to secure their long-term involvement in Europe, and specifically, if possible, to enshrine the 'special relationship' in the form of a formal, mutually acknowledged, text. The British had actually got this on to the agenda for a meeting with Dean Acheson, the American Secretary of State, in May 1950, when the whole intention was trumped by the ace of the Schuman Plan which Acheson had privately endorsed after his stopover in Paris on the way to London to see Bevin.

This British alternative design, largely drawn up by Lord Sherfield, was the cause of a furious row between Acheson and the Foreign Office in particular. The American Secretary of State was successful in forcing the withdrawal from the agenda of this text, which apparently put the 'special relationship' down in writing, with the intention of having it adopted as official policy. The incident is dealt with at some length by Acheson in his memoirs. He used it to mount an immediate counterattack in the face of Bevin's, and the Foreign Office's, extreme displeasure at the way the Americans had 'got off the hook' with their endorsement of the Schuman proposals. The offending document was apparently consigned to some Orwellian limbo. It was, it seems, literally torn up and became an 'un-document'! Acheson's principal aide on this 1950 visit was Lucius D. ('Luke') Battle.

BATTLE: The existence of the special relationship was, I think, something that most of us accepted. I still believe it exists even today. But it was something that one did *not* write down nor discuss publicly. The idea had floated around for several years in the post-war period in the State Department of putting out a paper making the special relationship an official policy. It was dropped as an unwise thing to do which, if it became publicly known, would destroy the very things it was trying to give life to. In the context in which it happened this time

[May 1950] it was more important. It was not an abstract thing; it was directly related to the United States position with respect to Western Europe and the Continent, as opposed to the United Kingdom. Both were in effect wooing us! We did not want to be put in the position of having to make a choice!

When this Paper was popped in and the item added to the agenda I don't really know. The lines of what was to be discussed had been talked about in Washington before the working party went over, so the general line of what was to be discussed was known. But then, there it was before us in black and white when we arrived. There was this Paper and, in the light of the very delicate situation that we had, resulting from the Schuman Plan, it really became quite serious. The existence of the Paper, or worst of all the concern over any leak of the Paper itself, became very, very serious indeed. And Dean [Acheson] absolutely hit the ceiling when he saw this.

CHARLTON: What did he say?

BATTLE: Well, I think you can't even carry it on the BBC! I mean, it was just – pretty devastating. Fortunately I hadn't written the Paper, so I wasn't the one who got it in that particular baring of the back for lashes! But there were quite a few lashes thrown around. He could be quite outrageous; when he lost his temper, he lost it! So we decided the best thing to do was to take it off the agenda and recall the Paper. I felt it probably ran the risk of drawing greater attention to it, but we did at any rate pull it back.

CHARLTON: Acheson's former secretary, Barbara Evans, told me she remembers you coming out of the room in London in a state of high excitement and demanding that all copies of this be delivered to you, and you personally tearing one up?

BATTLE: Well, that could easily have been. I did that kind of thing on other occasions and it may well be that I did it. I don't really remember, vividly.

CHARLTON: But they were all destroyed?

BATTLE: They were destroyed. That I have no doubt. I know that it was destroyed. I know that the idea of putting out a Paper, and adopting an agenda with it on it – I am trying to be honest about this – the leakiness of a Foreign Office in *any* country, the US, UK, France – the chances of a leak depend heavily on who has a stake in it. At that particular time there were a number of people around in the British Foreign Office who would have liked nothing better than to have it known that there had been a secret arrangement – that there was a 'special relationship' between the United States and the United Kingdom, and that it had been officially adopted. That would have pleased them no end and it would have helped in calming down pressures from other sources to engage more deeply in continental matters.

LORD SHERFIELD, for his part, could not remember this 'affair' in any detail, but added this:

SHERFIELD: I know the passage in Dean Acheson's book, of course, where he says he was 'horrified' and 'shocked' by it. I suppose it was the use of the words 'special relationship'; but I don't think the sentiments in it had any novelty at all. They simply expressed the policy I thought we should be pursuing at the time, which certainly did not differ from any other minutes, memoranda and so on which I wrote at that time. We were poles apart on that particular issue at that particular time. But it didn't affect the fundamental joint interest which we had in preserving Western security, as subsequent events showed. The fundamental relationship with United States governments continued, on the basis of some disagreement, far beyond that date. It really continued up to Suez, and indeed was very much strengthened in certain respects – particularly in the field of defence cooperation, atomic energy, Korean War and rearmament. There were plenty of ups and downs, but I ceased to talk about the special relationship after a time because it became almost a term of abuse!

CHARLTON: Particularly after Acheson tore up your paper on it?

SHERFIELD: I don't know whether that was the reason, because after all it's clear enough. The United States has special relationships with all sorts of countries. With France and Lafayette and all that it has a special relationship. It's had a very important special relationship with China.

CHARLTON: Can I put to you a more personal question? I think some of your critics say that they considered you to be then – and they thought that you might acknowledge – that you were very pro-American in your views; that you had strong family and personal connections with America, and that your advice to Attlee and Churchill governments, your views of policy over Europe, were deeply influenced by this. Is that a fair assessment?

SHERFIELD: It's perfectly true that I spent a lot of time in America and I therefore was presumed to know a good deal about the United States, and to understand it. Whether it had any subconscious influence on my thought I am not in a position to say. I do not think it affected my judgement of the issues. Now, that my judgement may have been wrong, that is one thing. But that it was consciously bias, or personal feelings, is, I think, nonsense, I found it as irritating to negotiate on some matters with the Americans as the next man, and I did in fact have a very long, and aggravated, and irritating, negotiation with them over atomic energy which lasted from 1945 until 1955. It was only at the end of those ten years that we were able to get back to the position of collaboration in the atomic energy field which we had in 1945.

CHARLTON: Not everybody, I'm sure, would wish to reproach you for it at all – historically, who knows, you may turn out to be correct. But I wonder whether you feel comfortable in this category at this time; that you were among those in Britain who thought Europe was a mess, and could not be relied upon. That all we had to show for our involvement there was the dead of two world wars upon its battlefields and America, for Britain, was the hope of the future . . .

SHERFIELD: Well, I certainly felt, and I have even found one or two bits of writing of mine which makes it quite clear that I thought that without the United States' involvement the future was not very bright, and that a United States involvement in European issues was vital.

CHARLTON: And that disputed any other conclusions, particularly the notion that Britain had essentially, after Empire, a European destiny?

SHERFIELD: In terms of an exclusive European destiny, yes. It was something I think we would have wanted to avoid. Here I find myself saying that 'the British Government would hardly be willing to face the risk to be involved in such concessions, in the end of trade controls, and full convertibility of sterling in the 1950s, unless some means were found whereby the United States, the United Kingdom, Western Europe and the Commonwealth *could be tied together more closely*.' That's a fairly general statement, but I think that what I

just said, that's what I *thought* – rather than what I *think* I thought!
CHARLTON: It emphasises, I think, your feeling the high risk, as you saw it, of America bundling Britain away inside Europe and forgetting about it?
SHERFIELD: Yes. I think that's right. I would agree with that.

IN BEING ASKED to hark back to the Acheson 'incident' over the special relationship in May 1950, and then subsequently reading extracts from contemporary papers of his official 'advice' to the Churchill/Eden government Lord Sherfield, the Under-Secretary of State at the Foreign Office, has conveyed, I think, the priority which the Foreign Office gave to the Atlantic dimension, and which, it consistently advised, precluded a move into Europe by the British unless the Americans came in with them.

For their part the Americans refused to make the overt or secret choice the British wished for of the special relationship, as Luke Battle substantiates. And the Americans, who had set out in a fundamental new direction by their support of the Schuman Plan, continued to maintain it. Such differences as there were in the Conservative Cabinet over Europe turned, to an important extent, upon whether a move into Europe would indeed damage the relationship with the Americans, as the Foreign Office thought. Lord Thorneycroft has mentioned already that 'the whole basis of the Foreign Office approach had been utterly different to what we were seeking in Europe'. 'We', in this instance, must be taken as the 'Europeans' in the Cabinet. He followed with this.

THORNEYCROFT: Immediately it depended enormously on the support of the United States. It's true – as *we* said – that you *won't* lose it, because the United States on the whole, and immensely to their credit, were themselves really in favour of an European association, and even thought that it might damage them in the short term from a trading point of view.
CHARLTON: They wanted a political result.
THORNEYCROFT: They wanted a political result. But Anthony Eden and the Foreign Office really felt it would damage our relationships with America if we went into a Free Trade Area or a Common Market, or call it what you will, at that time.
CHARLTON: But that won't wash will it? How can they maintain that when it is known that the Americans take the opposite view?
THORNEYCROFT: Nevertheless I can assure you, when you talk to anybody who at that time had any experience of it, they will say Eden opposed it. It was also, I think, deeper than him. It was deep-rooted in Foreign Office thinking. All their top brass felt the same. They had been brought up on a tradition of the balance of power, the division of Europe, not its unity; balancing one group against another. This was the whole background; and what you were asking us to do then was to ask them to play an entirely new game, a game they did not know the rules of, they'd never seen performed – and they didn't like!
CHARLTON: So their attitude was one of hostility? You'd agree with Maxwell Fyfe's verdict? It wasn't just caution or a proper or a thorough investigation of the prospects?
THORNEYCROFT: They were *wholeheartedly* against it.

BECAUSE OF THE UNCERTAINTIES and confusion in its ranks – division is too emphatic a word for what were really differing opinions and rivalries expressed over European policy – and also the particular issue which became the first really practical test of the Churchill government's European thinking, the Cabinet delayed, 'perhaps fatally delayed' according to Thorneycroft, making any fundamental reappraisal.

The particular issue which turned rivalry into open disagreement among the Tory leaders was the European Defence Community. The war in Korea, which broke out in 1950, led to a final breakdown in confidence – not that there was much left after Stalin's coup to install communist power in Czechoslovakia in 1948 – between East and West. The West, which had demobilised after the war, was called upon by the Americans, as leaders of the Western Alliance, to rearm urgently. The Americans, who were to assume the major obligation for the defence of Europe, demanded a bigger contribution to their suddenly augmented burden from the Europeans themselves.

France had a large expeditionary army in Indo-China and was unwilling to make a large contribution. Britain, in the throes of an economic crisis again – the benefits of devaluation in 1949 had been swept aside in increased defence expenditures – was trying to lighten her imposts, not add to them. The new divisions which Europe required could not be filled without German soldiers.

For France above all, the prospect – and the proximity – of a rearmed Germany posed, as Jean Monnet formulated it, this brutal question: 'Who would recruit the first German soldiers, if not a national War Ministry in Germany? Who would give them orders, if not a German General Staff?' In the prospect of the 1950s this was so unacceptable a vision in France that it encouraged the Federalists, like Monnet, to try to extend the supranational ideas of the Coal and Steel Community into the field of Defence. And into, of course, much more intimate areas of national sovereignty than those of coal and steel.

The Pleven Plan (named after René Pleven, the Minister of Defence, who had been Monnet's assistant in wartime London) was put forward by France as a solution to the problem of German rearmament, incorporating what France considered to be the essential safeguards. Its basic principle was that the first German soldier recruited should be 'a European, in European uniform, under European command'. Unlike the Coal and Steel Community which had deliberately circumvented Britain, the Defence Community was announced in the more wholehearted hope of British participation. Pleven claimed that the Plan was directly inspired by the prosposal for a common 'European Army' which had been adopted at Strasbourg on Winston Churchill's motion in 1950.

But now, when Churchill and Eden themselves accepted without change the decision taken in the last months of Attlee's Labour government that Britain could *not* participate in such a proposal, there was a major European and domestic political furore.

In the autumn of 1951 David Maxwell Fyfe, the Home Secretary and a passionate enthusiast for a British move into Europe, set out for a meeting of the Consultative Assembly of the Council of Europe in Strasbourg. He had been entrusted there with the task of giving the new Conservative government's views about the European Army and the Pleven Plan. The draft of his statement had been carefully worded and was the outcome of protracted and difficult argument in the Cabinet. It was meant to hold out the promise to the Europeans, in the opinion of Maxwell Fyfe, that British attitudes would in future be more forthcoming. The critical passage in the statement was this: 'I cannot promise our full and unconditional participation, but I can assure you of our determination that no genuine method shall fail through lack of thorough examination . . . There is no refusal on the part of Britain . . .' In Maxwell Fyfe's view, coming as it did from a senior Cabinet minister acting on the authority of the Cabinet, this was meant to convey that Britain 'had agreed to the principle of joining a European Army'.

The particular words singled out by Maxwell Fyfe hardly seem to be a resounding affirmation. He agreed, as he wrote subsequently, that 'the final version of this draft . . . was not as definite as some of us would have liked'. However, a few hours after he had delivered this statement in Strasbourg, a statement to which Anthony Eden had been a party in the Cabinet, Eden himself, at a Press Conference in Rome where he had been attending a NATO meeting, was categorical: Britain would *not* participate in a European Army on any terms.

Back in Strasbourg, the European delegations were coming up to the British with reproachful cries of 'betrayal'. The Parliamentary Under-Secretary of State, and the minister in the Foreign Office, responsible for European Affairs at this time, was Sir Anthony Nutting.

NUTTING: I knew the way that Eden's mind was working. I'd seen enough of him in opposition, before we actually got together as partners in the Foreign Office, to know that it was highly unlikely that *he* would go into Europe. But, of course, there was great expectancy in Europe, and the first meeting of the Council of Europe became a shambles. At that meeting David Maxwell Fyfe, as the British representative, held out considerable hope to the Europeans that there would be a new British foreign policy, and that it would show a much greater desire to associate Britain with Europe, all of which was completely knocked on the head by a statement made by Eden in Rome, at the meeting of NATO ministers which happened, unfortunately, to coincide with the Council of Europe.

CHARLTON: In retrospect, when you read what Maxwell Fyfe actually said, it doesn't seem to me to be a very advanced speech. It's full of hedges and complications, that he cannot *promise* this or that. But it does seem to be a very important row, this between Maxwell Fyfe and Eden, because Maxwell Fyfe's position is that what he's advancing at Strasbourg has been agreed in the Cabinet. Are you saying that Eden departed from that agreement with what he said in Rome?

NUTTING: No, I do not think you can accuse Eden of departing from any agreement, because equally, as you've just said, Maxwell Fyfe didn't promise anything. But of course, by saying, 'I don't promise this', you rather imply that 'I am hoping we may get it! That I may be able to, or somebody else may be able to, announce something more forthcoming in the future'. He was keeping the options open.

CHARLTON: Whereas Eden was knocking them on the head?

NUTTING: Whereas Eden was knocking them on the head. I was not a member of the Cabinet at that time – but as far as I can relate from reading Cabinet papers and Cabinet minutes, there was no actual agreement in the Cabinet that Eden should make the statement he made in Rome. But make it he did; and this, of course, precipitated a fearful row, not only with Maxwell Fyfe, but a row which led, you remember, to the resignation of Paul-Henri Spaak as the President of the Council of Europe.

CHARLTON: In response to what?

NUTTING: In desperation that, after all the breathless expectancy that had greeted the return of Churchill's government, they were told by the Foreign Secretary himself – and after all he must speak for Britain – that there could be no question of our joining in any of these Associations.

CHARLTON: Yes, and that's when Belgium – part of Britain's age-old historical 'constituency' of the Low Countries in Europe – defects. Spaak throws in his lot – not with the British, whom he's been waiting for once again to take a lead in Europe, but from this moment on with the Federalists. So the 'federal' idea picks up momentum from this stage?

NUTTING: Oh indeed, indeed. Spaak then turns to people like Adenauer – as well as to his previous associates, Robert Schuman and Jean Monnet – and he says, 'Well, in that case we will have to make Europe without them, the British'. But, to be fair, immediately following upon this row – because I was the Minister for European Affairs, as it were, in the Foreign Office – I did go to Eden and say, 'Look, we are in the most terrible mess, and we have got to make some sort of gesture'. And we did make a gesture. It was a fearfully complicated arrangement, hedged around with all sorts of reservations. The effect of it was that, while we maintained we could not actually *join* the European institutions which had been formed and were in contemplation – the Coal and Steel Community and the Defence Community – there is still a *political* community, which would have been the sort of federal government for Europe. What we would do would be to associate ourselves through the machinery of Strasbourg – by putting all the institutions in the Strasbourg framework – we would be associating, as sort of country members as it were, of the Club! It was a gesture; it didn't really *mean* very much because it did not involve us in any great commitment, but it was a gesture, and it was, I think, a wholehearted effort by Anthony himself, because he led the delegation to repair the damage.

I think he was very shaken by Spaak's resignation from the Council of Europe, because he had a great admiration for Spaak. The Eden Plan, as it was called, for 'country membership' was in fact adopted by the Council of Europe, both by the parliamentarians and the ministers. For a time, until we all moved on a stage further into the European Economic Community, this was the position of Great Britain. The French were not exactly enthusiastic about it, but at least they saw it as an attempt to come closer to them. At long last we were not saying just a flat no to everything. Schuman was slightly mollified by this gesture because he saw British 'association' in a slightly different light to Monnet. Monnet saw it as something which had to be part of a federal system or not at all. Schuman – along with, I think, the majority of French political opinion at the time – wanted the support of England against the possibility of a revived Germany. This is something you can't dismiss from the thinking of the time. Although Germany was still in a state of pretty good economic trauma, nevertheless she was picking herself up. There was a very real danger to the French in this rearming of Germany, this association which we were asking the French, and which they were asking themselves, to undertake with Germany. I remember this was very well put by Hervé Alphand, attending the Berlin Con-

ference in 1954. Then, I think, the Under-Secretary of NATO, he said, 'If you
British want us to get into bed with the Germans, then you British must be the
bolster!' So any gesture of association by Britain was welcome, even though
they would have liked it to have been much closer.

IF IT WAS TRUE that Anthony Eden's deliberate detachment from Winston
Churchill's earlier crusading interventions in post-war Europe was at the cost
of a personal, first-hand awareness by him of the emotional determination
which sustained the 'Europeans', then one might presume that Sir Anthony
Nutting's recollection that Eden was 'very shaken' by the resignation of an
Anglophile like Spaak from what was, after all, Churchill's brainchild, the
Council of Europe, served to warn him henceforward of this intensity of feeling
and commitment in striking fashion.

Referring to Eden's disavowal in Rome of British participation in a 'European Army under unified command', Maxwell Fyfe was at his most trenchant,
saying that his 'personal humiliation, while it hurt at the time, was unimportant
compared to the effect of these two contradictory announcements within a few
hours of one another'. In Strasbourg he had said that Britain was 'not closing
the door' on the proposed European Army; in Rome Eden had said, categorically, that 'no British military formations would be made available' to the Pleven
European Army (now referred to officially as the European Defence Community).

Maxwell Fyfe wrote subsequently that 'this, more than any other single act,
destroyed Britain's good name on the Continent'. He and the other pro-
Europeans among the British at Strasbourg, including Boothby, had sent a
telegram to Churchill protesting and asking him to intervene. There was no
reply. The Home Secretary added his published retrospective verdict that
Churchill 'hesitantly but inevitably' supported Eden, and 'other senior
ministers like Salisbury' opposed. But the terms of the British Cabinet-
approved draft which Maxwell Fyfe had taken to Strasbourg – balanced and
very cautious – allowed only small differences of emphasis, and Maxwell Fyfe
might insist that Britain was 'not closing the door', but Eden spoke for the
reality – no fundamental change in the British position of 'close association'.
The European policy was under 'jury-rig'.

Following his resignation from the Presidency of the Assembly, Spaak
devoted his considerable influence and energies to leading the campaign for
'little Europe', the political and economic federation of the Six *without* Great
Britain. Out of this 'left ear' there issued, eventually, 'Gargantua rampageous' in
the form of the Common Market. Eden's principal Foreign Office aide at this
time, who was with him in Rome when he made his statement, was Sir Evelyn
Shuckburgh.

SHUCKBURGH: Well, this is the great controversial one on which I have always
been unwilling to express an opinion. But I will only say I am sure Eden was not
conscious that he was doing something like that in that speech in Rome. My
recollections, and from the notes I have of that visit to Rome, I'm perfectly sure
that he did not think he was sabotaging a Cabinet decision in favour of Europe.
I think that is a great distortion by Maxwell Fyfe. It *must* be a distortion by
Maxwell Fyfe of what Eden did then. Apart from that I really have never gone

into the thing. But I know that is what worried Eden to the end of his life – that he was accused of being anti-European on the basis of that speech.'

CHARLTON: Maxwell Fyfe said that 'more than any other single act it destroyed Britain's good name on the Continent'. What is your view?

SHUCKBURGH: Well, I certainly think that is a great overstatement. Certainly at the time in Rome I was not conscious – later I was conscious that Eden had made a particularly unhelpful statement about Europe in Rome. He was, I think, from his own subsequent explanations, he seems to admit that he was against putting British troops into the Pleven Plan. That may be. But I have always been a little bit surprised at the huge furore there's been on this subject, that there were two British Cabinet ministers saying diametrically opposite things in two foreign capitals. He was very anxious that EDC should not fail. There was a great problem about whether the French would possibly ratify it, and there were many discussions, I remember, about what could be done to help the French government.

CHARLTON: But why is EDC good for the French and Germans and not for us?

SHUCKBURGH: Are you asking me that question, or are you asking what Eden thought about that question?

CHARLTON: Well, I cannot ask him, but what do you remember him saying?

SHUCKBURGH: Eden wanted the success of a European Defence Community but he was, I think, reflecting the British public's general attitude in being very chary about accepting derogations to our sovereign control over our troops.

It is very nice to have been right in hindsight, but Maxwell Fyfe and Duncan Sandys didn't carry the nation with them, did they? It was easy to take positions that were of a logical, idealistic nature. I think perhaps we did not quite appreciate the political implications of it. I think we probably looked at it more pragmatically and saw the practical objections. Personally, I think it's all a great tragedy. I quite agree we missed all sorts of buses and it is tragic. We should have been in on all these things much earlier and we could perhaps have avoided many of the things which were so difficult when we did eventually come into the Common Market. What I am really saying is that I don't think it's a tragedy which can be attributed to individual statesmen. I think it's a tragedy arising from the position and attitudes of the British people after the war.

I'd like to tell you another thing. Many years later I was the Ambassador to NATO, and there was the similar great question, 'How, with the new generation of nuclear weapons, are we to let the Germans play their part?' The multilateral nuclear force, submarines multi-manned, with a captain of one nationality and officers of all sorts of different nationalities, was put forward as a great, brave, new, far-seeing, imaginative solution to Western Defence, giving the Germans their part but not letting them have a finger on the trigger, as it was called. And we were being pilloried by European-minded people for not being too keen on that. I know this, because a lot of our own people thought it was a nonsense technically. The Chiefs of Staff were dead against it and said it was 'a bloody nonsense' or something – Mountbatten said. I should think that most people now agree it was. But I was being pilloried for having to represent caution on this – by the Europeans who said, 'You British are once again letting down the European concept' – and the Americans were pushing us to agree to it. What I'm saying is that we very often took objection to something of that nature. I daresay the Pleven Plan, and some aspects of the European Defence Community, had the same connotation for us; we were opposed to it on those sorts of grounds, not because we were hostile to the concept of political unity in Europe. By the time I was at NATO I was mad keen on European unity. I had nothing I wanted to do more than encourage the strengthening of Western Europe and the Alliance. It was absolutely my life! But I was not able to support, and I would not have *wanted* the support of, a submarine full of officers of different nationalities, because I didn't think, and nor did anybody who really thought about it think, that it makes much difference *what* the composition of the crew of a submarine is, as regards shooting missiles at the Russians!

Certainly I don't think we were wrong to be leery about the Multilateral Nuclear Force. In a sense, like the European Defence Community, it was a gimmick for solving two very difficult, incompatible concepts. One was having the Germans defend Europe, and the other was not letting them have any power. It is not necessarily easy to find the answer to solving a dichotomy of that kind, is it? The idea that, if we put a division into Pleven's Army, all would have been fine and Europe would have been different, is not any more true, I think, than to say that if we'd gone in for those seventeen nuclear submarines, with the German second officer in them, it would have solved the nuclear problem.

CHARLTON: Can I put to you something which arose in a public exchange of fire years later between Eden and his critics over the collapse of the EDC. Anthony Eden said that he tried 'by every method to associate Britain effectively with the proposed European Army'; but we have it on the experience of Anthony Nutting that Eden reacted to his own suggestion, and that of Lord Gladwyn, our Ambassador in Paris, that we should leave a number of divisions on the Continent for the duration of the proposed Treaty 'like a kicking mule'?

SHUCKBURGH: You see, these phrases are invented by people who have got a very simple task, haven't they? It is easy to say that the Foreign Secretary 'reacted like a kicking mule' to your bright idea, if he did not agree with it at once. I think that is rather typical of the kind of attack which was made on Eden subsequently by advocates – the extreme advocates – of 'Europe'. I think it is quite unfair. He regarded it as a tremendous objective to get European defence going, and European harmony and unity.

CHARLTON: But at the heart of Churchill's idea – and also the Pleven Plan – is some long-term British commitment and guarantee to keep our forces on the Continent. It is *that* which they say, Nutting and Gladwyn, that Eden objected to.

SHUCKBURGH: Well, maybe he did feel doubts about that. It was a principle which *all* British governments have felt very, very great doubt about for a hundred years, isn't it? It's always been a great thing: first of all we don't have a standing army, and secondly it does not want to sit on the Continent – and the fact that it's been sitting in Germany all these years is not bad, is it? But what Eden *would* have reacted like a kicking mule against was, say, putting a British division under a French general or anything like that. I think Eden, who had a very strong political nose, felt it would not go in this country. I'm sure that's it. He felt it wouldn't go. It hadn't gone for hundreds of years – and it wouldn't go now!

HOWEVER, THE DAMAGE DONE to perceptions of Britain in Europe, the 'disillusionment' which Macmillan acknowledged, was considerable. The suspicions and mistrust aroused had a resonance, variously estimated, which lasted into the seventies. It had given the impression of a deliberate distancing by Britain from Europe at a critical moment.

Although he had been the first to raise the concept of a European Army, Churchill's own support gave way when confronted with the supranational aspects of the Pleven Plan, with its closely-woven, integrated 'pedantry' drafted by Jean Monnet. Yet this 'pedantry' owed something at least, in the over-elaborate nature of the safeguards it sought to incorporate in the proposed Defence Community, to uncertainty over the strength and nature of Britain's military commitment to the Continent.

The trace of Winston Churchill's own thinking about the European Army, following his launching of the idea while in Opposition in August 1950, is there-after remarkably faint. However, Lord Sherfield recounted this story of an occasion with Churchill in Paris when the European Defence Community was discussed with the Prime Minister.

SHERFIELD: When it came down to the point of actually having to decide whether we should join the European Defence Community, he was against it. He was against it because he did not believe in a mixed Army. I can remember we were in Paris, and it must have been in 1951 or 1952 – it was early 1952 – and he was going to make a speech. We were all gathered together in the British Embassy in Paris, about seven or eight people in the room, writing or helping to write this speech. Writing Sir Winston Churchill's speeches was quite an undertaking and it was a collective operation! It took a long time and, page by page, it was gradually worked out, and he would talk a lot about it. I can remember him saying, 'European Army, European Army,' he said, 'it won't be an army, it'll be a *sludgy amalgam!* What soldiers want to sing,' he said, 'is their own marching songs!' And then he burst into song, the Sambre et Meuse, or whatever it might be.

So, it was an almost instinctive reaction. You get the romantic view of Europe, and the realistic view of a national army singing its own battle songs. Now, you can bring those two things together on a sort of *romantic* level, but when it gets down to writing a *treaty* it's a different matter.

The interesting thing to me is that, when Churchill himself came into office in 1951, his attitude to the actual, practical problems of the situation didn't differ in essence from the attitude of, say, Mr Bevin. I think he regarded it in a sort of romantic way, this romantic vision of a United Europe, but when it came down to it with the Defence Community he was against it. That's the only direct con-nection that I remember having with him about it – I mean, actually being there, writing a speech. And it was quite clear that, although he had, of course, these romantic views which he expressed about the unity of Europe and 'the great stretch of European history' and all that, when it came to translating it into action that's where the problem arose.

LORD SHERFIELD, then Under-Secretary of State, in using the favourite word of the Foreign Office hierarchy for Churchill in the matter of Europe, 'romantic', puts a pragmatic finger on what the Foreign Office insistently, and consistently, thought was the flaw in his approach.

In trying to unravel these threads of British policy towards continental Europe it is all too easy to convey the impression that it was the central preoccupation of the Foreign Office. It was not, of course. Britain was still at the centre of a vast and complicated pattern of international relationships of several centuries' standing, consistent with her position at the heart of Empire and Commonwealth. It was a pattern which, as decolonisation went ahead, became more and more fragmented but which increased the exacting demands upon British diplomats and diplomacy. But, as had been the case with the big guns of Singapore in 1942 – they could be trained only seawards and could not be brought to bear on that quarter from which the decisive challenge came – so too did British diplomacy prefer to look outwards to the wider world and upon its more traditional perspectives.

Sir Evelyn Shuckburgh, who was Anthony Eden's principal Foreign Office aide, kept a diary of his years with the Foreign Secretary. He says that an inspection of these almost daily entries will reveal that the European theme played very little part in Eden's day-to-day concerns.

Immediately after Eden's abrupt dismissal of participation by Britain in the European Defence Community, he and Churchill set out for the United States. Their purpose was to win American support for the maintenance by Britain of a world role and, as Sir John Colville put it earlier, 'the re-creation and the re-assertion of the special union of Britain and the United States'. Both Churchill and Eden considered that this had been allowed to fall into some disrepair by Attlee and Bevin.

Sir Evelyn Shuckburgh, who made this voyage with Churchill and the Foreign Secretary, read from his diary this entry he made at the time.

SHUCKBURGH: 29 December 1951. Off to America. I arrived at Waterloo with Anthony rather late – the detectives having sworn that the Prime Minister would be even later – to find a whole lot of floodlights and cameramen and Winston sitting in the special coach with Mrs Churchill, Lord Ismay, Lord Cherwell and Lord Moran. I could not see any of my official colleagues and got stuck in this coach for about ten minutes, being called 'Makins' by the Prime Minister from time to time. . . . Having arrived [on the ship] very late at night, we went straight to bed and didn't look around us until morning. We were due to sail at noon and I was with Anthony and a few others in the Prime Minister's bedroom, the Old Man looking cherubic in bed, when the Captain and local representatives of the Cunard Company came in looking shamefaced and evidently expecting an explosion, to say that the anchor was stuck and that we could not sail for twenty-four hours! Winston was in a great hurry to get to America and this was bad news. But he saw it immediately in terms of the telegram he would send to Truman, 'THE ANCHOR IS FOULED: WE CANNOT PROCEED', which he sent! He at once thought, 'What fun it would be to sail to the Isle of Wight'! The afternoon was too choppy and so he stayed in bed instead. . . .

We were there on the evening of New Year's Eve and we had some rough weather. The most amusing thing was to see Winston, in a very short silk dressing-gown with white knobbly legs sticking out below, a large beetroot head above, toddling down the passage to Anthony's stateroom for a morning talk. He invited us all in to see the New Year in with him and gave us champagne.

December 1951: The second Churchill government. Anthony Eden and Sir Evelyn Shuckburgh of the Foreign Office set sail on the Queen Mary *for the United States.*

After hearing Big Ben strike and the BBC announcer wish us all a Happy New Year, we turned the machine off and looked to Winston. He had risen with his champagne glass in hand and was swaying gently with the swell. Everyone thought he was going to make a speech, but he simply said, 'God Save the King' – and we all drank his health.

HAVING UNFOULED THE ANCHOR and successfully crossed the Atlantic in the *Queen Elizabeth* the party arrived at the White House. Sir Evelyn's diary recorded this note of the first formal meeting with the American President, Harry Truman.

SHUCKBURGH: Mr Truman performed an act of continuous hearty efficiency, romping through the Agenda with a loud, gay voice. He was quite abrupt on one or two occasions with poor old Winston and had a tendency, after one of the Old Man's powerful but emotional declarations of faith in Anglo-American cooperation, to cut it off with a 'Thank you, Prime Minister. We might pass that on to be worked out by our advisers.' A little wounding! It was impossible not to realise that we were playing second fiddle.

SIR EVELYN SHUCKBURGH, in that contemporary passage from his own Diary, was recording also the 'failure of a mission'. There could be no 're-creation or reassertion' of the special union between the British and the

Americans in the form in which it had existed most obviously in war. The diary of this distinguished British diplomat seemed acutely tuned to the new reality and the new American mood of self-confident mastery which the President was reflecting. That was no doubt backed by the knowledge that, with the success of the Schuman Plan, American statecraft in Europe seemed to be well founded. One has the palpable feeling in that diary entry of Sir Evelyn's that events have not just moved on, but that they are passing Britain by.

The American Secretary of State, Eden's opposite number as it were, was Dean Acheson. Acheson's principal aide, who was also present at all the talks Churchill and Eden had with the President and the Secretary of State, was 'Luke' Battle.

BATTLE: The first impression we had was that they had been out of touch for a long time. The fundamental thing we were seeking at that time was the re-armament of Germany. The situation in Korea was putting an enormous burden on us, and the pressures that were going to be created for Europe to increase its armament programme to handle what seemed to be an increased threat, all these argued very persuasively, we felt, for getting Germany into the structure. Those were the initial issues.

Now Mr Churchill, he was a wonderful man, whose initial reaction to every-thing was to get on the plane, or the ship, and come over here and say, 'We will straighten this thing out in a few minutes,' you know. It would be done in a very broad brush and I used to love his marvellous phrases which were so very descriptive of things. But we felt they were a little bit out of touch in the begin-ning.

CHARLTON: But Acheson is supporting the European Defence Community, the Pleven Plan. Churchill and Eden are pouring scorn upon it. How did Acheson view that?

BATTLE: I think he always had doubt about the political realities of EDC. As he saw it, it was essential to accomplish what he was seeking to do, and yet he always felt that there were political difficulties, even in Europe, and as you know that became apparent.

CHARLTON: But that is no more than the British attitude.

BATTLE: True, but there was a difference. His conclusion was that it had a chance of working. His position was never an overwhelming 'It *has* to be the EDC', but he had moved. He felt that he had no alternative. The 'community' Europeans were supporting it; the French were moving in that direction; Eisenhower, the NATO commander, was all for it. Most of his own advisers in Europe felt this was a superb thing – there was no other direction in which he could have gone at that time.

CHARLTON: But why did it seem to you, the Americans, that the British – with Churchill and Eden back in power – were not prepared to say or do those things about Europe they had spoken of in Opposition?

BATTLE: Well, that is a problem *all* political parties have. We certainly have it here! But it did seem to me at the time – and it does even more acutely now – that there was a feeling on the part of Mr Churchill and Mr Eden when they came back that, somehow, they could regress – back to an earlier time – and that they looked to a sort of return to Empire. The loss of Empire was always an appalling thing to Mr Churchill. He detested it. I can remember hearing him just a few times on various subjects. Once, with respect to Iran, he said, 'If those fellows are not careful they will feel the splutter of musketry!', which I thought was a lovely way to say, 'We may start shooting!' But this was the kind of attitude he had. He returned to Empire. He did *not* see the position of the UK as essentially and fundamentally tied to Western Europe. He saw it in a broader context. He thought that, somehow, we and the British could, sort of, split up this little world and 'you take a part, we'll take a part, and together we'll make the thing go!'

But that was no longer possible. I doubt that it was possible at any time after World War Two. But it had moved faster than he'd realised, and certainly faster than he had predicted. The situation had changed. So the notion that somehow you could *delay* these events in Europe, that you could bring the UK into it, in some form or other, and still preserve for another period the grandeur that was England – I think he thought that was right. But it was not. And all the things that had happened in the years since he'd been in office had made it impossible. And *we* were moving in *that* direction.

CHARLTON: One can see that Churchill is untouchable really, his prestige and reputation are enormous, but I notice that one of Acheson's biographers, Professor David McLellan, says of this visit that Acheson and Truman 'bore down hard on poor Eden'.

BATTLE: Well, it was difficult to have this kind of conversation with Churchill. In the first place, he respected Acheson and they got along very well. But Acheson and *everyone* was in such total awe of him; and our President – I admired him very greatly – was not up to having an argument with Sir Winston Churchill! Acheson and Eden had no particular problem arguing! They were rather good at it – both of them! There was still, at that time, a wee bit of animosity between them, which came out when they got into arguments and debates with each other. And neither of them wanted it. Eventually it was over-come totally. In the later years, after they both left office, they became very close friends and corresponded over a very long period of time. They used to stay with each other. But at that time there was no hesitation on either part to having this argument – which was fundamental. It really concerned the total direction of British power and relationships with the whole world in the post-war period.

TO THAT FUNDAMENTAL QUESTION Acheson and Eden returned different answers. It is surely revealing that the Americans felt it was not an argument which could be conducted in Churchill's own presence. This was not just because there was no unanimous clarity of view on the American side about the British role – the State Department being inclined to see Britain's natural destiny as a return to Europe, and the defence policy-makers attracted by the still orderly architecture of the British network of stable relationships east of Suez – but also because American sensitivities to the feelings of the Old Leader they deeply respected, and of whom they were 'in awe', precluded it. The broadly consistent American concern that the British *did* need to make some sort of fundamental reappraisal could not yet be openly stated.

Acheson felt that in turning down the Schuman Plan Britain had made the 'first wrong choice' in the post-war world. However, it was this implicit relegation of Britain, as he saw it, which Eden was determined to resist and challenge. A most revealing guide to Eden's own thinking was given by him the

year before his return to office, when he had made a tour of the United States
with his Parliamentary Private Secretary, Robert Carr.

CARR: I remember most clearly the key speech, which was the one he gave at
Denver on the interdependence of nations – at least that was the theme of it. It
was based around the 'Three Circles' of power and the need for interdependence, but seen as a very much *larger* theme, and on a much larger scale than that
of 'Europe'. It was apparent in his talks, which I remember him having with
General Marshall [Acheson's predecessor as American Secretary of State], in
which he was really afraid of Europe becoming too 'inward looking' and us all
forgetting, in our concern with Europe, the importance of our role in the rest of
the world.

I remember one of the main drives of his private conversations during that
tour, and particularly in these conversations with General Marshall I was sitting
in on, that he was trying to stress the point that, unless Britain and the United
States worked together as actively in the Middle East and South-East Asia as in
Europe, then we were heading for very serious world trouble; if not disaster.
The main thing which obsessed him at the time was, I recall, the need to get the
Americans as active and as cooperative with Britain in the Middle East and
South-East Asia as in Europe. There was his alarm at the rather uneven degree
of American interest and the lack of unity between Britain and the United
States – almost a suspicion between them – in Middle Eastern Affairs and
South-East Asian affairs.

CHARLTON: What comes through to me in those speeches that he makes is
that he is challenging all the assumptions the Americans have made – and
indeed some people in this country have made – that Empire and Commonwealth are things of the past, or a purely transitional phase towards Britain's
eventual close involvement in Europe. It is *that* which, it seems to me, Eden is
positively rejecting. He is saying to the Americans, 'We are *not* finished, we still
have a world role to play'. Would you agree?

CARR: Oh absolutely, you're quite right about that. Anthony had this very
strong feeling – I think a rather unreal feeling, alas – about the potential role of
the Commonwealth in the post-war world. I forget the exact details, but I think
I am right in feeling that one of the very formative experiences in Anthony
Eden's career was when he went to a Commonwealth press conference in
Australia. When he saw editors and journalists from all parts of the Commonwealth coming together, together with others invited – statesmen like himself
from the Commonwealth countries – I think that he did get this feeling of this
Commonwealth link throughout the world, and also the belief that it *could* be
made a lasting feature of the post-war world.

One of the blockages in Anthony Eden's mind about Europe was the feeling,
which of course was held very strongly a few years later by the opponents of the
EEC within the Conservative Party, that if you chose Europe you were being
anti-Commonwealth. I'm sure Anthony would never have put it as starkly as
that, but he did have this feeling, I think, that if you got too close to Europe you
were going to separate yourself from the Commonwealth and destroy this hope
of a Commonwealth 'link throughout the world'.

CHARLTON: But when he comes to power himself, when he is Foreign
Secretary and, subsequently, Prime Minister, he can be under no illusion that

the Americans are committed to supporting six-power 'federation', and appear
to see Britain as a member of an integrated European political and economic
community? Everything he does is to be taken in the light of that, yet he
challenges it, doesn't he? Does he genuinely believe it was not the right way
forward, that it was probably going to be a dead-end road – from which one
would then have to back away and find another road?
CARR: Yes. What would be quite wrong would be for the idea to get into anybody's head, a feeling, that Anthony Eden was anti-European. He just had a
totally different concept of what a United Europe should be about. He did not
have any faith in the achievement, or the desirability, of a closely – certainly not
a *Federal* European Community, if it could be brought about. He felt it would
separate Europe from the rest of the world and make us, as one of its members,
inward-looking when we ought to be outward-looking. In other words, he
shared some of the views that people still hold about the dangers of the European Community. I felt that he was wrong about this. But it was not anti-
European. He was very *pro*-European, but in a rather old-fashioned way.

THE PRINCIPAL INFORMED WITNESS for Eden's official views while in the
Foreign Office is Evelyn Shuckburgh, who was in almost daily communion with
him as his principal Foreign Office adviser.

SHUCKBURGH: I think Eden was very much against insularity in Britain. And
so were his advisers – certainly I was. I always thought that it was one of our
besetting sins. But at that time the opposite of insularity was not necessarily
Europe – and I would say that to Eden. The opposite of insularity was all the
relationships we had everywhere else. He was very aware of our influence with
the Indians, the Chinese and the Commonwealth – especially the 'new'
Commonwealth. He was frightfully keen on all that, and I think he would not
have said that we must put all our cards into Europe. But I don't think that
should be described as being anti-European or the European Movement.

I remember him saying to me, 'What you've got to remember is that, if you
looked at the postbag of any English village and examined the letters coming in
from abroad to the whole population, ninety per cent of them would come from
way beyond Europe' – where troops have been stationed, or people have
cousins and relatives and all that sort of thing. Ten per cent only would come
from Europe. Well, Eden was very conscious of that as a public attitude here,
although he himself regarded Europe from the cultural point of view as being
our historic roots.

I remember very, very clearly how *astonished* I was, and really almost unable
to believe it, when I found, later on, that Mr Macmillan and Mr Heath actually
did want us to go into Europe and do things which would be contrary to
'sovereignty' and so on. I mean, you know, a good civil servant reflecting what I
think my masters wanted, I had always assumed, really without question, that *no*
British Government would be willing to give up *any* element of 'sovereignty'.
We want to cooperate, yes, and give a lead and coordinate and all that sort of
thing, but *not* to put British troops under foreign command, or subordinate our
decision-making to foreigners of any kind. And then, when we find Heath
there, it gradually sinks in that that is no longer the case. So perhaps that does
answer your question a bit as to Eden's view of the world and Britain's position

in it. I think under Eden it was a pretty conventional national-sovereignty line, though he was pro-European and very keen on his languages and his talking with Europeans.

CHARLTON: When this proposition is put to Acheson, however, that the Americans should 'help us in the Middle East', agree with our position there if we help them in the Far East, Acheson says that such a relationship would be 'like two lovers locked in a tight embrace going over Niagara Falls in a rowing boat', so the record shows us. Do you recollect that rather vivid metaphor?

SHUCKBURGH: I think I've heard it quoted! There's no doubt that Eden was very dissatisfied with Acheson's attitude on these matters on the Middle East, and American policy towards the Middle East. Dulles [John Foster Dulles, the US Secretary of State under Eisenhower] has always been said to be the great bugbear of the British, but I think it was just as bad with Acheson – probably worse with Acheson. Acheson was very cool and offhand about us and would not support us on any of our things, in Persia or the Gulf. He really was pretty rough with us. It was kind of, really, an 'anti-British imperialism' feeling. After all, we still talked about putting troops in oases and driving people out; putting a sheikh in here or a ruler in there. The Americans did not like this. They ought to have been more understanding of their *own* interests in my opinion.

CHARLTON: There was the great row between us, the crisis over the Anglo-Persian Oil Company and Dr Mossadegh at the time?

SHUCKBURGH: Yes, there was that, and later on there was the row with Saudi Arabia. On all these things they were very unsympathetic to us. I think that built up quite a deep resentment.

CHARLTON: And a determination by Eden to resist American pressure in all dimensions, would you say?

SHUCKBURGH: Well, I think it became really almost a personal thing with some of our ministers. They simply thought that they were being pushed around by the Americans, and then they stopped listening to one another, the British to the Americans.

THIS MAKES IT more readily understandable why it was, as Sir Evelyn Shuckburgh told me, that there should have been 'great excitement' in London when Eisenhower was elected in 1952 as President of the United States. There were plainly hopes that with 'Ike', the spirit of the warmer, more exclusive Anglo-American partnership of the wartime years might be resumed. That partnership, with Eisenhower personally, had been tried, tested and found enjoyable by the British. If the atmosphere of it could be 're-created' it might help to ease the sustained American pressures for closer British involvement with the Continent.

But having marched up to this new milestone in Anglo-American relations, the Foreign Office found that there was cold comfort awaiting here, too. Eisenhower himself, while in Europe as Supreme Commander of the North Atlantic Treaty Organisation, had become convinced of the merits and necessity of European integration. He had made a speech in the Guildhall to that effect in 1951, saying that Churchill's support for the concept of United Europe might 'prove to be the crowning achievement in a career crowned by achievement'. There is every reason to suppose that important elements of Eisenhower's speech had been suggested and incorporated in his address at the urging of Jean Monnet – yet another piece of testimony which demonstrates the pervasive influence of the Frenchman upon ranking American policy-makers. Monnet was, in addition, a close friend of the new Secretary of State in the Eisenhower Administration, John Foster Dulles. Dulles had become himself a wholehearted and determined supporter of Monnet's ideas about Western Europe.

Today, we know from Eisenhower's subsequently published diary that, while he often declares his admiration and affection for Churchill and his past accomplishments, Eisenhower had come to form much the same sort of view that, according to Luke Battle, Truman and Acheson held. He thought the new government in Britain 'was living in the past'. In December 1951 he wrote in his diary of Churchill: 'He simply will not think in terms of today. My regretful opinion is that he no longer absorbs new ideas.'

The head of policy planning at the State Department in the Eisenhower Administration was someone who had been closely involved in the developments over the Schuman Plan in Europe while on the staff of John McCloy, the American High Commissioner in Germany; and who had now returned to Washington as the principal official State Department adviser to John Foster Dulles. This was a Harvard academic, Professor Robert Bowie.

BOWIE: I think the warmth of admiration and respect for Churchill was very great indeed, as a result of his wartime service and the result, in particular, of the close association of Eisenhower with Churchill. But I think also there was definitely a feeling that he was not really in tune with the needs and the actual situation of Britain. What you quoted from 'Ike', President Eisenhower, probably summarised the way he felt about him. During the period I can recall he came to the White House at least once. He was warmly received and treated with great affection, but I don't think that Eisenhower expected to get new perceptions, new insights about the situation from the conversations with him. Similarly there was a meeting which he attended in Bermuda, and there again he was revered and respected as a sort of elder statesman, but again, I think, he was not seen as a source of new initiatives and new ideas.

THE AMERICAN PRESIDENT was plainly suggesting that it was time for Churchill to go. The pressure mounted on Eden. As an accompaniment to his robust reassertion to the Americans of Britain's intention to continue to play a wider role in the world, and that role's value to the alliance of the West, Anthony Eden chose an audience at Columbia University in 1952 to advance this view with a more than usually categorical firmness.

EDEN: The American and British peoples should each understand the strong points in the other's national character. . . . If you drive a nation to adopt processes which run counter to its instincts you weaken, and may destroy, the motive force of its action.

I am speaking of the frequent suggestions that the United Kingdom should join a federation on the Continent of Europe. This is something we know in our bones we cannot do.

THIS METAPHOR, which became extended in the course of Eden's speech, and

Anthony Eden, with the Vice-President of Columbia University, after making a key speech in 1952.

spoke of an 'unalterable marrow' of British life, was I believe prompted by Sir Evelyn Shuckburgh, who drafted Sir Anthony's speech.

SHUCKBURGH: I think we *did* feel, perhaps 'know' is now thought to be the wrong word – we *thought* in our bones that we had this wider role which we ought to keep ourselves free to play. That we were not the sort of people who could give over control of armed forces, or political decisions, to other people. That's what he meant by 'We know in our bones that we cannot do it'.

THESE UNCOMPROMISINGLY DISMISSIVE WORDS of Eden's, his announced determination to remain engaged world-wide, and the persistent use of the word 'Federation' instead of the rather more shadowy acceptance of a degree of supranationality in the defence area, had the effect of arousing a deeper suspicion in the United States and on the Continent that Britain was turning away from Europe. This was considered to be a major factor which in part accounted for the protracted delay by the French Parliament in ratifying the European Defence Community. The urgent issue of satisfying the French that it was 'safe' to rearm Germany remained unsolved. This was for the Americans the first priority.

Warts and all, the EDC appeared to the Americans, as Dean Acheson had confided to Luke Battle, to be 'the only game in town' when it came to rearming Germany. The 'only game' because Churchill and Eden offered no rescuing alternative. Britain continued to withhold her agreement to any permanent stationing of her forces on the Continent, at least any permanence enshrined in Treaty obligations. Although of course Britain did now have, seven years after the war, a standing army in Europe – something almost unprecedented and for the first time since the Plantagenets – it remained the basic axiom of British policy to go no further into Europe than the Americans themselves were willing to go. For their part, both Acheson and his successor in the Eisenhower Administration, Dulles, had told Eden that for the United States to keep troops in Europe depended on the European Defence Community becoming effective!

A trial of will, which became at times a bitter personal conflict, began between Dulles and Eden. In these rival perceptions and analyses of Britain's task and mission one can see clearly lying exposed, I believe, the stones which paved the path to Suez in 1956. Robert Bowie, who was at Dulles' side throughout the developing crisis over the European Defence Community, speaks for the American Secretary of State.

BOWIE: You remember that Pleven put forward the proposal for a European Defence Community, which was an application of the ideas of the European Community to the effort to create a common defence structure, and that, as with the Schuman Plan, Britain indicated that it was not prepared to join in the effort to create such a community. I think there was a feeling that the negative attitude of Britain, at some of these points, was something of an obstacle to solving some of the problems. So that, in that sense, from time to time there was a certain amount of frustration or exasperation at what was seen as the lack of British support and cooperation.

CHARLTON: From your knowledge of the personalities involved, is there any support for the view that Eden believed somehow he might be able to separate Dulles from Eisenhower?

BOWIE: I don't know he thought he could separate Eisenhower and Dulles. As you know, Eden and Dulles were not terribly congenial! I think Eden was not comfortable with Dulles, and Dulles did not like Eden. This was personality in part, but it was also heightened, later, by the difference of view they had at the time of the Geneva Conference on Indo-China in 1954.

CHARLTON: But also at this and an even earlier period, you see, there seems to be something of an animus in Foreign Office circles. Lord Gladwyn says in his Memoirs, and I take it to be rather deprecating although I hope I am not being unfair to him, he says that 'the views of Mr John Foster Dulles at this time were freely quoted'.

BOWIE: I think that there was a very major difference in temperament between Eden and Dulles – with the result that, to Eden, Dulles I think seemed doctrinaire or rigid and legalistic. Eden had known Ike during the war and I think he found him a much warmer kind of person and therefore more congenial. I also think he believed that Dulles was much more in charge *on his own* than I believe to be the case. He assumed, in other words, that if only Eisenhower had taken charge more, then perhaps things would have gone in a way that Eden would have found more agreeable.

As for the Pleven Plan, there was some disappointment because Churchill had so strongly urged the very thing which was, or so it seemed, proposed by Pleven. Then, when the actual proposals were put forward, it was quite clear that the British were not prepared to participate in trying to work out any such scheme. But even beyond that, they were very reluctant to make very firm commitments, even of British forces on the Continent. Yet later on, when the alternate plan was developed – after the defeat of the EDC – the British went further in making firm commitments of their forces than they had been willing to do in the support of the Defence Community.

CHARLTON: How did Dulles interpret that?

BOWIE: Well, I think there was some feeling that the British were not really being as helpful as they might have been, because obviously it might have made a difference in the French attitude if the British had, even if not participating in the European Army and the European Defence Community, been firmly *on* the Continent, with commitments to stay there. It might have made the French a little more comfortable about the grouping of their forces with the Germans. I do not know. But in any event the reluctance of the British to do even as much as they could have done, even accepting their unwillingness to participate in the European Army, was the source of some frustration.

NO LEAD CAME FROM Eden or from Winston Churchill. For the next three years France was left to stew in the juice of the Pleven Plan's complexities. The French maintained, as has been quoted earlier in the reported remark of Hervé Alphand (see pages 147–8), that 'if it was British policy to make France get into bed with the Germans, then Britain should be the bolster!' Britain stayed adamant about this ménage à trois! The active commitment to the continent that the Europeans and the Americans were trying to extract from the United Kingdom was at every invitation withheld.

In this standing aside from the European Defence Community and the public position of rejecting the invasion of national sovereignty the Pleven Plan would have meant, one soon uncovers that tap-root of British policy – to force a commitment out of the Americans. Throughout this period no one prophesied with confidence that there would be a single American soldier in Europe within five or ten years.

In the absence of that additional glue of reassurance which British participation would have provided, the proposed safeguards against German rearmament proved insufficient for French opinion and policy. The elaborate edifice Pleven envisaged – of re-creating the German army, but at once making it do the vanishing trick in the anonymity of European uniforms, and then applying the idealistic principle to the French army too, while at the same time the Germans were to be limited to the formation of units of the smallest possible size – all this fell to the ground.

In 1954, after three years of argument about national sovereignty, the French Parliament refused to ratify France's own proposal. It was deemed the greatest internal debate in France since the Dreyfus affair. While the supporters of European integration had taken the hurdle of the Coal and Steel Community in a single astonishing bound, the European Defence Community was their Becher's Brook. A negative British diplomacy, allied with the eventual incoherence in the French Parliament, killed the EDC. The cock robins of the federal concept of European unity had been brought low by the pragmatic bowmen of the Foreign Office in London.

Churchill's own verdict on the Pleven Plan – a 'sludgy amalgam' – found irreverent echoes elsewhere in the Diplomatic Service according to Sir Con O'Neill, who in the 1970s had charge of Britain's official negotiations to enter the Common Market.

O'NEILL: I think it was a mistaken concept, a mistaken project and it wasted a good deal of time. I know that it was taken up by Monnet and by the enthusiasts for an integrated Europe, but it was no more than a device to reconcile the French to the rearmament of the Germans. I was in Bonn at the time and I remember how strongly this stood out there. I remember a lot of people in the British element of the Control Commission in Germany used to sing a song about the European Defence Community. It was rather a silly song, but it encapsulated the truth of the matter I think. It was sung to the tune of Good King Wenceslas or Hark, The Herald Angels Sing, and it went something like this:

> 'Just in case the Bundesmensch
> Should turn around and fight the French,
> We shall keep your Units small,
> So they'll be no use at all!'

And that of course was really the secret of the European Defence Community. It was an effort to reconcile the French to German rearmament by putting German rearmament in a framework where it would have been meaningless and useless. I shed no tears when the European Defence Community failed.

ANTHONY EDEN SEEMED CONVINCED of the probability that the EDC would fail, and the further probability must be – we will not know for a while yet under the thirty-year rule applying to official documents – that he felt that Britain, given the opposition to it inside France from elements led by General de Gaulle, had some Caesarian power of life or death over the Pleven Plan and the concepts of 'federation' which spawned it. This must await another judgement.

Certainly in the more arcane pigeon-holes inside the Foreign Office there was an alternative plan. With this Eden proceeded to rescue the Western Alliance and NATO – Dulles having threatened all the Europeans with an 'agonising reappraisal' by the Americans of their involvement in post-war Europe unless something were done.

Eden now proceeded to do so, but on his own terms – to the mortification and anger of Dulles. Eden has said that he thought of this plan in his bath, but its original authors were Christopher Steel and Sir Frank Roberts of the Foreign Office. Sir Frank was summoned by the Foreign Secretary.

ROBERTS: I still remember being rung up at home, I think it was on a Sunday, by Anthony Eden who said, 'Frank, we've got to do something. We just can't let this thing fester. We've got to do it very quickly and we've got to take an initiative.'

Anthony's great strength, of course, as a Foreign Minister was a sense of timing. He was more rapid in deciding when and what particular thing should be done. I, of course, as a good official said, 'Well, okay, but what do we do? We just can't say we're going to do something, we must have a plan.' Then he said, 'Well, there is that thing I've never wanted you to talk about, but haven't you got it somewhere in your pigeon-hole? Couldn't we bring it out and dust it off and see whether that would work?'

WHAT EDEN HAD WISHED Roberts 'never to talk about' was a plan to rearm Germany, but to add the essential counterweight, to satisfy the fears of France, of a British commitment to maintain a standing British Army and a significant fraction of the Royal Air Force on the Continent. This was the 'guarantee' which France had been asking the United Kingdom for, for decades. Both before and after the Second World War it had been refused.

However, if the introduction of this Plan, by an acknowledged master of the diplomatic arts, at the eleventh hour upon the collapse of EDC was a deeply premeditated intention of Eden's, then he was an arch dissembler! But it saved the then chaotic and apparently disintegrating unity of the West.

The British Ambassador in Paris then was Lord Gladwyn, who now corroborates what we have partly heard from Anthony Nutting earlier. Lord Gladwyn suggested that Eden's rescue operation was a last-minute improvisation.

GLADWYN: He fought like a tiger until almost the last minute against the one thing which got the thing through [German rearmament], namely our guarantee that we should maintain our forces in Germany and would not reduce them. I remember in Paris, when he was going his rounds after the EDC collapse, you know, he came into the Paris Embassy. And he was adamant on that – that is pushing the idea that the one thing for us to do was to agree to this solution – he was violently against it. Indeed, he was very rude to me and others in the Library, I remember!

I was rather in despair then. I got a telegram from the Foreign Office saying that I must on *no* account push this so-called 'shop-soiled' idea, that we should guarantee our presence in Germany. I was told I must go and tell Mendès-France that he was to stop pressing for it, and must not be so stupid. Well, all that faded out in the event. And of course, when the Conference eventually met in London, Eden produced at the rather critical moment this as his own idea out of a hat – amid universal applause! But he only accepted the idea a few days previously.

HOWEVER, IN AGREEING to station her forces on the Continent beyond the end of the present century – until 2025 – by Treaty, and with the provision that they could be withdrawn only by agreement of her European partners, Britain had gone a bridge further into Europe than she had ever gone before.

There was a sticky moment with the Cabinet, as Sir Frank Roberts makes plain when, in this remarkable switch of position, the Foreign Secretary was juggling the new British commitment with the corollary to it he believed was indispensable – namely that the Americans must come too! In this respect he got most, if not all, he had hoped, in the view of Sir Frank.

ROBERTS: What he wanted to do, in making our commitment, which Anthony was always prepared to do – of course the Cabinet had not been consulted, and were not consulted in fact until the key moment in the London negotiations – but what he wanted before we gave *our* commitment was to get an American commitment. This we got, not as far-reaching a commitment as ours, but it was a definite commitment and it was part of the London Agreements.
CHARLTON: Satisfying our basic fear that the Americans were one day going to withdraw?

ROBERTS: Yes, it wasn't only that we were frightened by Dulles; it was that we did not want to fail to commit the Americans as far as it was possible to commit them!

CHARLTON: But do you mean that Eden's decision to surrender sovereignty over the British forces to collective decision by our European partners, in the matter of withdrawal, was something in your plan from the very beginning?

ROBERTS: Oh yes. We felt that we *had* to give a commitment on having troops in Europe. Exactly at what point we thought up this thing, I forget. There was weighted voting in the seven countries. There we did have a safeguarding clause – that, if the financial burden became too great, etc, etc, then we could ask for the whole thing to be reviewed. We had to do that pretty quickly, in fact within two and a half years! I was back at NATO, and was responsible for this at NATO, where I had to defend our first request before the NATO council for a cut in our forces on the plea that our economic situation required it!

CHARLTON: But you wouldn't disguise, would you, the fact that this is a very major change in terms of British policy? Both political parties have opposed *any* surrender of sovereignty in post-war Europe, and as a result of the collapse of EDC we are *forced* to do so?

ROBERTS: Oh yes, absolutely. It was a major thing. And of course you know how it was done? Neither Anthony nor Winston was ready to put it to the Cabinet; and it was only when we were in the throes of the negotiation in London – and it looked as if it was going to be all right – that it was put to a small group of Ministers, and thrashed out, I think, late at night! This is how it happened. And then, of course, the Cabinet accepted it! But it was known to be a *very* difficult one to get through the Cabinet; and *only acceptable as part of the whole set-up*, with the Americans in. No, it was a major thing.

THE DRAMATIC NATURE OF Eden's triumph with this plan for what became known as Western European Union – a successful design for German rearmament which had eluded the searchings of French and American policy for three long, wearing – and, it must be said, souring and debilitating years – restored an understandable feeling of some confidence in the Foreign Office that the directions of British policy were well founded. There was a feeling of some optimism that those pedantic concepts of 'federation' and 'the functional integration of Europe' had been dealt a blow from which they could not hope to recover fully. That they had perhaps fallen like Lucifer, never to rise again! There was the hope that after this arid search along the lines of the European Defence Community for unity, political events on the Continent might now return to those wider but looser forms of cooperation which Britain found more congenial to her. The evidence suggests that, in the Foreign Office, there was a feeling that 'we had got it made'.

We had not! What is, arguably, the most important of all the post-war events which dictated Britain's destiny lay, unsuspected, just ahead. This was a meeting which took place at Messina, in Sicily, in the summer of 1955.

As Calais would be found, in her own celebrated lament, lying in Queen Mary Tudor's heart, so too might we venture that when, one day, the Foreign Office is opened, this name Messina will be found embedded there in its innermost chambers!

6

'Messina! Messina!' or the Parting of the Ways

THE LANGUAGE OF DIPLOMACY, when it talks of those moments in history which were 'seized' or the opportunities 'cast away', shows a fondness for using homely analogies drawn from locomotion. Not always have they proved to be felicitous. As, for example, when Neville Chamberlain looked across the Channel in 1940 and announced, just before the German armies burst into France, that Hitler had 'missed the bus' . . .

The critique of Britain's European policy, in the crucial decade of the 1950s, when a new design of cooperation between the old nation-states in the West was being fixed and settled, is persistent in these allusions to the European bus, boat or train which Britain is said to have missed.

In 1950, when Jean Monnet had produced the Schuman Plan for the Coal and Steel Community as the nucleus of European unity, he expressed his conviction that the British were not a people to board the train standing at the station, but would join it only if they saw it begin to move. His analysis was in keeping with Britain's tradition and reputation as an eleventh-hour nation accustomed to Balance-of-Power politics, a view which had been confirmed in him by the British rejection of his overtures for joint Anglo-French action in 1949.

In that watershed of a weekend in June 1950, when the Schuman Plan was revealed – and Britain refused to participate in the negotiations which followed – Monnet had this recorded exchange with Stafford Cripps, the Chancellor of the Exchequer.

'My dear friend,' Monnet said (when Cripps asked him if France would go ahead with Germany and without Britain), 'you know how I've felt about Britain for thirty years, there is no question about that. I hope with all my heart that you will join from the start. But if you don't, then we will go ahead without you; and because you are realists you'll adjust to the facts when you see that we've succeeded . . .'

Now, only four years later, it was Jean Monnet, and the American policy which had endorsed his concepts of federation as the path to unity in Europe, who appeared to have suffered perhaps a mortal defeat. The attempt to solve the problem of rearming Germany by extending the logic of the Coal and Steel Community into the field of defence collapsed. That was 'a bridge too far'.

The official British scepticism about the impractical idealism of the European Federalists appeared to be vindicated. With the fall of the European Defence Community, the initiative Britain had lost, with the advent of the Coal and Steel Community, swung back towards her. And this is the context in which the belief that Britain 'missed the bus' in Europe finds its most liberal distribution. This bus was the one which was waiting at Messina in June 1955.

In this improbable location in Sicily, the Foreign Ministers of the Six who had failed with the Defence Community's ambition of an integrated European Army met and issued an invitation to Britain to take part on any terms and conditions she wished in exploring European unity in a new direction. One suggestion was the objective of forming a general common market.

As France and Germany had successfully begun to forge their new unity in the Coal and Steel Community, Britain's older European constituency, the smaller nations, had begun to look over their shoulders. The Dutch – and that ubiquitous figure in Britain's European odyssey, the Belgian Foreign Minister, Paul-Henri Spaak – were prime movers in the audacious resolutions adopted at Messina which had been purged of the supranational language and ambitions which Britain had declared 'unacceptable' to her in the past. It was hoped thereby to enlist Britain in a fresh start and re-examination of 'unity in Europe'. The junior minister in the Foreign Office under Anthony Eden at that time, and with responsibility for European affairs, was Anthony Nutting.

NUTTING: I think it was the last and the most important bus that we missed. I think we could still have had the leadership of Europe if we had joined in Messina. I remember Spaak saying to me some time afterwards (the Treaty of Rome had been signed and we were outside the European Economic Community), 'You know, you have no conception of how much we needed your moral leadership in Europe. We were people all of whose countries had been occupied or had been (in the case of the Germans, and Italy) under a fascist government. It had been the patriotic duty of everybody during the war in those countries to oppose the government, to oppose authority, to lie, to cheat, to do everything which it was your patriotic duty not to do. Suddenly to reverse it, suddenly, when the enemy was defeated, to get out of the way of lying and cheating, withholding taxes, engaging in black-market activities and all that – it was a tremendous moral crisis in our countries. We felt that we needed the moral leadership of Britain who had never had to make these choices, never had to do these underhand things as their patriotic duty. You, who were untainted by this, you could have led us, you could have given us that essential leadership which we needed . . .

But, he said, 'you missed the bus and then when you tried to come in afterwards because you realised that we'd got something good going that you wanted to join, well, then, of course, not unnaturally the price was rather high . . .'

IT WAS BECAUSE the subsequent price was high (and it remains a subject of contemporary argument) that a rueful light has shone subsequently on British diplomacy at the time of Messina.

But the defeat of the federalists and the downfall of the European Defence Community had been so absolute a rejection of that model of European integration that it is plain a complacency settled upon its opponents. In the Foreign Office there was a feeling that in so far as Europe was concerned British policy had 'got it made', and that St George had slain the federalist dragon. The rise so early of what would prove to be so important a phoenix as the one which took shape at Messina and emerged as the 'European Common Market' – that was dismissed as improbable.

This is how, in the view of one of its younger members, the British Cabinet looked at Europe in the aftermath of the Defence Community's collapse in 1954. The President of the Board of Trade then was Peter Thorneycroft.

THORNEYCROFT: Those who believed that we were eventually going to find our place in Europe didn't cease in that belief. Ministers would change, opinions would change. We were not without friends, and we quietly went on with our work. I was concerned, at that time in 1954, more particularly with persuading the Conservative Party of the virtues of free trade. I think it's worth dwelling on that because at that moment there was another battle going on. Remember, the Conservative Party trading policies at that time really stemmed from Imperial Preference. This was the Ark of the Covenant to the Conservative Party. I remember the Blackpool Conference of the Conservative Party in 1954 when Leo Amery (who was the great protagonist of the old school, of the leaders of the Imperial Preference group) had put down a motion condemning the General Agreement on Tariffs and Trade. I remember the discussion in the Cabinet. I said I wished to oppose this Motion, and the Cabinet said I would lose. We had the debate round the Cabinet table, and Winston Churchill, at the end of it, said: 'Let him try!' I won the debate and, in a way, it was an important thing to happen because it was the defeat of the 'old guard'. It was the end really, emotionally, of the old concept of Imperial Preference inside the Conservative Party. We were free from that moment to move forward into the wider, freer world of the General Agreement on Tariffs and Trade, and the rest.

CHARLTON: But you rightly infer that the 'pro-Europeans' like you and Macmillan in the Cabinet were a tiny minority. You were also repeatedly outvoted. What is your assessment of where British policy stood later in 1954, as the handover to Eden as Prime Minister is coming in 1955, and with it also the effort to relaunch the idea of 'Europe' at Messina?

THORNEYCROFT: It was in a way a lull, really, because the European struggle, which in some ways was the important one both from the point of view of foreign policy and of trade and commerce, was put aside. I mean, we couldn't advance any further. It was in limbo.

CHARLTON: But Stalin is dead; he died the year before. The Indo-China war is coming to an end in the first phase of the Geneva Conference. Do you have the feeling that with the defeat of EDC, coupled with the apparent lessening of international tensions, the drive and energy behind European integration had, for the moment, dissipated?

THORNEYCROFT: The Europeans were still very interested in what was going on. But as far as this country is concerned, we went into retreat. A lot of our subsequent problems, of course, stem from this. At the very moment when we ought to have been shaping the European Community, we were on the sidelines.

CHARLTON: Why were we?

THORNEYCROFT: We stood aside because there was no strategic decision in the British Cabinet to play a part in Europe; and they felt that if they went in they would be committed to it.

THE LAST POINT WAS a familiar strand of concern in the official advice, which had previously led to rejection. As early as 1947, when Britain was one of sixteen nations studying the feasibility of a Customs Union in Western Europe, the Foreign Office and Board of Trade had warned that participation, beyond the preliminary stages of examination, would imply commitment by Britain to the outcome. It was rejected by the British in consequence, and that rejection by Britain was then sufficient for the Customs Union concept itself to founder.

Now, in 1955, British policy over Europe was, Lord Thorneycroft says, 'in limbo or retreat' as the themes of economic integration, arising out of the meeting at Messina, were about to present themselves once again. Sir Anthony Nutting's memory of Anthony Eden's personal responses to these ideas carries us across the threshold with the new Prime Minister, from his time in Opposition, when the Schuman Plan so dramatically confronted Britain, to the new moment now of Messina.

NUTTING: Having said all that I have said about Eden's Atlanticism, I do remember that there was one very significant – I suppose you could call it a hiccup – when the Coal and Steel Community project was first announced and Bevin refused to do as the Dutch did and say, 'Well, we'll go along and see what it looks like, and if we don't like it pull out.' I remember we were walking in the garden of Anthony's house in Sussex. Anthony suddenly stopped and said, 'Do you know, I think this is so serious, our refusal to go into this and see what it's all about – and show willing – that I think this could be the beginning of World War Three!' I was absolutely astonished! I thought this must be the wildest exaggeration. But when I asked him, did he mean war with Russia, no, he thought this was a golden opportunity missed for bringing the Europeans together, bringing the age-old enemies, France and Germany, into one movement and one European community; and that we should be there. He seemed to think then that we should be participating in some way. But when we were actually invited to participate, and when he was challenged himself, he said no. The Coal and Steel Community was already formed before we got into office in 1951, but when he was invited to associate himself with the European Defence Community, the European Army project, it proved abortive, largely because we would not join it, and therefore the French refused to ratify it.

Later, when the European Economic Community began to take shape and the conference at Messina took place, I begged Anthony to let me go as an observer, just to sit there, just to show some presence. But no, he would not have it. He completely turned against *any* participation once he got into office himself.

CHARLTON: Now, is one just to dismiss that as what one says in Opposition as opposed to Government, or has he deeply reconsidered his whole stance and come to some new position?

NUTTING: I think he'd already gone off the boil a bit before that. After all, what followed in the wake of the Coal and Steel Community, was all the debates about a European *political* community, at the Hague and in Strasbourg, in which Macmillan and Duncan Sandys and Churchill himself took part. Eden did not want to take any part in that. He did not want to pronounce on it at all. He wanted to leave all his options open. I think probably, when he thought it through in his purely tactical way, he saw a leap into Europe as being a leap away from America. I don't think Eden really understood economics well enough to realise that there was a considerable importance, from a purely economic point of view, in Britain joining this Economic Community and becoming founder members of it. Secondly, he certainly was not enough of a strategist to see that this was possibly the best, and almost certainly the last, opportunity that would present itself for Britain to exercise political leadership in Europe, and that with the old Empire and the colonies all about to become independent this was to be the new role for Britain.

The argument he used was that, if I was sent as an observer to Messina, this would raise hopes which we could not possibly fulfil – that I would be in a very invidious position. Not that he perhaps minded much about the personal side, but that Britain would be in an invidious position, sitting there in the role of an observer and saying nothing! Therefore we should either join in the conversations as founder members or not at all. As he was not prepared to join as a founder member, therefore we had better not join at all.

CHARLTON: No advance therefore from the position we'd adopted essentially over the Schuman Plan?

NUTTING: Absolutely none. He did as Bevin did, and he said let's see how it works out. It'll probably come to nothing, just as the European Defence Community did.

WHILE EDEN HAD BEEN forced to give a guarantee that Britain's army would remain on the Continent, and in that sense (and in terms of Britain's ultimate destiny as a member of the European Community) British policy seemed, in the words of the old hymn, to 'nightly pitch its moving tent a day's march nearer home . . .', Anthony Eden now turned away and continued to assert vigorous views about the validity and ability of Britain maintaining her world role.

At this time Britain not only had an army on the continent of Europe but also on the Suez Canal. There were 800,000 men in uniform – half of them national servicemen. The cost of these commitments was made more demanding by the determination to maintain a nuclear arm as well. The Conservatives in power had confirmed the original decision by Clement Attlee to make the atomic bomb, and had now taken its logic to the next step – the development of the hydrogen bomb.

But the British 'position' was all the time being challenged or reduced. The American refusal to support this position in the Middle East – where Britain was still 'putting troops into this or that oasis, and a sheikh here and a ruler there' – and by withholding that support undermining British power and influence – all this was a cause of continuous friction and resentment. The Australians and New Zealanders, reflecting the realities of the new power balance in the Pacific, had entered into a new defence pact with the Americans, ANZUS, in 1951. Eden's and indeed Churchill's efforts to include, or associate, Britain with this new arrangement had not succeeded.

These were, no doubt, among the more important stimuli to a quickening of resolve in Eden not to accept what was seen as a misguided and premature reduction of Britain's status which was neither in Britain's interests nor the long-term ones of the Western alliance as a whole. After Churchill, when Eden followed, there was continuing support for this wider outlook from the Foreign Office, and also that twin pillar of British policy in Whitehall, the Treasury.

As the issue posed by Messina came to the fore in 1955, the Under-Secretary of State at the Treasury was Sir Frank Figgures.

FIGGURES: The structure of government – and after all the departments of state react to the structure of government – had changed a little. Winston Churchill had retired. Anthony Eden was Prime Minister, Harold Macmillan was Foreign Secretary, Lord Butler was still Chancellor. But obviously things were moving. The significance of the International Monetary Fund, and of the General Agreement on Tariffs and Trade, was becoming greater. We were moving more nearly towards a *world* economic community, which is very important. It is extremely important in Treasury thinking; in so far as Treasury thinking is dominated by any one thing, it must be dominated by the Reserve situation. And the American influence, whatever all sorts of people might have been saying, American influence was very concerned that the world community should be built up and not undermined. So that must be counted an extremely important strand of policy in Treasury thinking at the time. Much more important than the narrow question of relations with Europe.

The Commonwealth situation, and the problems with the Commonwealth, was changing over these years. The earlier concepts, that one would revert to some form of Imperial Preference, which the Conservative Party in Opposition had wanted to do, had been found to be quite impractical. Therefore economic ties, commercial and industrial ties with the Commonwealth were tending to become slightly less important. The sterling problem itself was moving, steadily and inexorably, to a really rather critical situation, but the mid-1950s weren't a troublesome period. Indeed, it might almost be called annus mirabilis as far as we were concerned – 1954 and 1955! So, no, I don't think there was a significant change in the attitude of the Treasury as a whole to the European affair.

THE COINCIDENCE OF ECONOMIC recovery under the Conservatives with the relaunching of the 'European idea' at Messina was no encouragement (in the short term, at least) to any serious reappraisal of Britain's position. Rather the opposite. This was allied to the fact that the most significant factor governing foreign policy in the decade of the 1950s, while the Conservatives held office, lay in the conceptions and the objectives of Anthony Eden. Eden's principal Private Secretary at the Foreign Office, refreshing his memory from the diary he kept of his time with Eden, was Sir Evelyn Shuckburgh.

SHUCKBURGH: I think all those people who were the bosses in the Second World War found it impossible to believe that we didn't still have great influence really beyond what we did have. Eden was aping Winston a great deal. There'd been so much of this going about as top people, deciding everything for the world, I thought they'd find it very difficult to get unaccustomed to that.
CHARLTON: And you too?
SHUCKBURGH: I suppose we all overestimated the role that we played. Yes, I suppose we did.
CHARLTON: Was there any feeling that the 'imperial mission' which Britain had, the Empire on which the sun never set, that this mission was over and that Britain was returning to some kind of pre-imperial destiny in Europe?
SHUCKBURGH: I can only say, from what I remember of my thinking, that we

were overstretched, and that we musn't be overstretched. We ought to get away from situations which we couldn't maintain – like the Canal Zone, and so on. But even when we had done that, we would still be a really great, remarkable people, whom everybody would be likely to respect and want leadership from. I think that's perhaps where we stuck somewhat. Although I'm not sure we wholly exaggerated, because I still think there was an element of truth in this: that we are able to exercise more influence in foreign affairs than if we'd been the Dutch, so to speak, who also had a great Empire once.

It is extremely difficult to reduce your status. It always is. I remember Eden was trying to get out of the Canal Zone – being sniped at for being a 'scuttler' on that. You can't go round giving up too many things at the same time because, you see, you've got to carry the country with you. I do think we were going through the great difficulties of knowing that we were overextended, but not really being able to do it all in the order or speed at which, if you'd been just a thinker, you might have suggested was right.

CHARLTON: How much time did Eden think Empire and Commonwealth had to run? How much time did he think he had?

SHUCKBURGH: I think he thought he had time. He had a high opinion – rightly – of his skills as a diplomat. In all these negotiations conducted over Persia, over Egypt, and so on, he really thought he would be able to bring about the necessary adjustments of our position, and even reach solutions. He was always believing that solutions could be found, and that he could find them. I think he thought there was time.

CHARLTON: It was Arthur Creech Jones, I think, the Colonial Secretary in Attlee's Government, the previous government, who considered that Empire and Commonwealth had another fifty years to run. If you had said to Eden that it was all going to be over by the sixties, and we were going to be forced to apply for membership of the European Community, what might his reaction have been?

SHUCKBURGH: I think he would have said it was feeble and defeatist, and typical of me.

CHARLTON: There was no sense, then, of Britain being somehow returned to a pre-imperial position? That Empire being over – it had in fact been an aberration, and that Britain was a European power. Do you remember discussing this sort of theme with him?

SHUCKBURGH: Yes. I can't answer that. But of course there was the other dimension, which was the American dimension, and it would depend whether they were getting on very well with the American President or not. Sometimes there was very strong resentment of the Americans in that government. That was one of the things that built up, I think, towards Suez. It was not that they did not get on well with Dulles, I don't think, but it was that they began to feel that they were not receiving the equal high treatment they thought was their due as one of the three Great Powers, you see, from the Americans at certain stages.

I think Eden enjoyed himself much more in larger international forums and larger international operations – dashing about to see the Chinese and all that. I think he enjoyed that more – certainly more than the economic side of Europe. He was not really interested in that.

CHARLTON: Maxwell Fyfe's view was that, because Eden was not part of the Churchill/Duncan Sandys launching of the European movement at the Hague and Strasbourg – that he was not invited or felt unable to take part – it was a root cause of Eden's subsequent distrust, dislike, misunderstanding of what had actually happened in Europe?

SHUCKBURGH: I wouldn't like to deny that. I think it could be true. I don't remember him ever expressing that view, but it was an area in which he was not expert. It was not his area and I think it very likely that what you say is right. His eyes were on other things, not on that. And it could be that's partly it. I think there was also, perhaps, a sort of thought that being 'European' was a rather upper-class privilege in England, and that a more popular line was the Kiplingesque line. I mean, Eden certainly considered himself a very civilised man, and was very interested in the Latin, historical and Christian background to Britain – and wanted to encourage that – but I think as a politician he probably thought that was not very well understood by great masses of the British. What was better understood was New Zealand lamb, and links with India and America.

CHARLTON: And with hindsight does it appear to you that there was any very important disadvantage in the fact that the war had rather cut the Foreign Office itself off from Europe – that we'd had five years or more out of Europe, and that therefore we'd rather lost contact with and were out of touch with the strength of feeling there behind this impulsion, this wish to 'unify'?

SHUCKBURGH: I would say this, that I agree with what you've just said. It was, of course, an error of judgement, but it wasn't an error of judgement by our leaders necessarily. I think the whole nation felt like that. Once, later on, Eden said to me, would I write some letter and defend him and his position over the EDC, saying it was not true he was against the European idea. I said to Eden, Look, personally I would not, if I were you, try to deny this. I think you were reflecting British opinion when you were cautious about this – not wanting to put British troops under foreigners and not wanting to take risks with sovereignty. I think you really reflected your own country and, I said, personally I would *not* apologise for it. I mean he *wanted* to apologise. My view is that the British were simply not in the mood to go along with the Europeans.

I know there were important people in the Foreign Office who were so pro-American they would not disagree with Eden. There were others who had this view I have described to you of our great role in the wider world. I was not a very important person then. I think I probably said I don't believe these Germans and French are really going to do it, or would not be able to bring it off, and we'd better keep our options open and our hands free. They'd never brought anything off before, and after all the history of Europe didn't suggest it was going to be easy to bring off something like this, did it?

THIS GENERALLY SCEPTICAL British disposition had been carried over therefore, and was now part of the general context in which Britain was about to make her responses to a renewed invitation from Europe – this time to start afresh, and as a founder member of the Common Market. But the picture is not complete without a brief reminder of the American attitude to Britain and 'Europe'.

The British could claim, rightly, that this was not always consistent or clearly stated or indeed openly declared. Sir John Colville, Churchill's Private Secretary, says it was not raised directly with Churchill during either the

Truman or Eisenhower administrations. There was a division in policy-making circles in the United States and a debate within them (which went on for some years) about whether it was in the best interests of the United States for Britain to take the path of European unity. Eisenhower, while he was still Supreme Commander of the NATO Alliance, had made almost an 'intervention' with his Guildhall Speech in London in 1951 (at the time of the Schuman Plan), intended to encourage a change in British attitudes. There followed the protracted wrangle over the European Defence Community. It is true that Eden, in justifying Britain's decisive abstention, was able to make use of a remark to him by Eisenhower that British participation in the EDC would, at that stage, be 'premature' – but Eisenhower had become (as Supreme Commander) and remained (as President) a convinced European. At the time of Messina he was at the very apex of US policy. The head of 'policy planning' at the State Department in the Eisenhower administration was Robert Bowie.

BOWIE: He really did have an interest in the European unity idea and in its achievement. I think the Guildhall Speech in 1951 was very much a reflection of his own thinking. It was a very eloquent plea for Europe to unite for the benefits, both political and economic, and in terms of leadership. I think he stated this as a personal plea to the British; he thought he had special standing with the British because of his close contacts during the war and his known friendship with the British; and in making the speech at the Guildhall he intended to say to them: You really are not reacting as you should to the opportunity offered by – for example – the Schuman Plan, which had been launched just about a year before.

CHARLTON: So it's true to say that there is an important difference of emphasis. Dean Acheson, in the previous Administration, had been largely agnostic about this. He could see the British reservations and to some extent sympathised with them. Would you say that had subtly but importantly changed with the advent of Eisenhower?

BOWIE: I think Dulles, too, was strong in his belief that this was a useful idea which the United States should support; and so I think that both the combined effect of Dulles and Eisenhower's personal interest probably did make a difference in the degree to which the United States made clear that it did support this movement.

CHARLTON: But would you say that when the Eisenhower Administration came in, its own beliefs and thinking, coupled with the thinking as it evolved in the previous Administration, added up by this time to a clearly formulated idea on the part of US policy-makers that Britain's true destiny lies in Europe?

BOWIE: Yes, I think that's a fair statement. I think by that time the feeling was that Great Britain had not taken the proper measure of its own actual potential in the world as it existed, and that it was perhaps holding back from joining Europe for reasons which really were outdated. That the belief, somehow, in the Commonwealth and the 'special relationship' with the United States – and indeed the larger global role, which was certainly an image in the minds of a good many of the leading foreign-affairs people in Britain – was essentially no longer a valid picture of Britain's possibilities. Therefore Britain was making a mistake in not joining this effort to construct a European system.

THIS AMERICAN PERCEPTION was wholeheartedly opposed by Anthony Eden. Eden's belief in his own long-established, and only recently confirmed and acknowledged, diplomatic authority – following his rescue of the Western Alliance from the wreckage of the EDC – can only have reinforced his own determination, allied with that of the Foreign Office, to fight a successful rear-guard action for Britain, as the unwelcome irritant to the Foreign Office of European integration, so lately thought to be quiescent, suddenly arose again.

In May 1955 Eden, now Prime Minister, had won the general election with a large majority of fifty-seven and four clear years to rule. On 7 June 1955, the Foreign Ministers of the Six (including France), after their meeting in Messina in Sicily, issued an invitation to Britain to take part in a fresh attempt, starting from scratch, to explore European Unity in a new direction.

The six governments, who were acting on an initiative from Holland and Belgium – the 'Benelux' countries – supported by France, 'wished to emphasise that they were unanimous in their hope that the British government would participate in this work in the closest possible manner'. And 'this work' meant in practice that all the countries would agree to set up committees working in Brussels in the ensuing months to thrash out the whole issue together. The chief of the Belgian delegation set up at the Messina conference in 1955 was Jean Charles, Baron Snoy.

I have referred already to Britain's 'older constituency' in Europe, which is to say the one which predates Empire and Commonwealth, in the Low Countries. There, the memories of a time when Britain *was* a European power are perhaps less atrophied than they have become in Britain itself. In the library of his country house not far from Brussels, the Baron has the original letters written to his ancestor by Elizabeth I of England – and signed by her with that famously intricate flourish – recording her gratitude for facilities and safe passage granted her armies commanded by the Earl of Leicester in the sixteenth century. Now, in 1955, those same underlying realities of an ancient balance of power within Western Europe were dictating an interest in Britain's attitude. Baron Snoy, who was Spaak's principal aid, was, like him, a strong advocate of political and economic cooperation with Britain. At Messina it was the Belgians together with the Dutch who had taken the initiative in holding any new door which might be opened to unity in Europe, open also for Britain.

SNOY: I remember that at Messina we were, of course, in a very difficult position, because it was six months after the rejection of the EDC Treaty. We knew that on the French side we ought to be extremely cautious about asking them to abandon something of their sovereignty. Therefore we presented as a Benelux formula at Messina a great number of possibilities to start the merger again of the principal European countries. We proposed at Messina either the Transport pool, or the Electricity pool, or the Nuclear-energy pool, or perhaps a merger on Customs duties and commercial policy. And we didn't know if we should select a Free Trade Area formula or a Customs Union formula for these last ideas. Everything was open. The British were invited to sit with us to discuss the merits of the different kinds of systems we ought to accept.
CHARLTON: And invited as a full and equal partner?
SNOY: As a full and equal partner.

SO IT WAS THAT what became known as the '*relance*', the relaunching of the European idea, began. As Baron Snoy says, the Benelux initiative at Messina put forward the concept of a Common Market, to be achieved in stages, as one possibility. This was the suggestion of the Dutch Foreign Minister, Beyen, who at once came to London to explain the intentions of the Messina resolutions at a series of meetings presided over by 'Rab' Butler, the Chancellor of the Exchequer. He also delivered the formal invitation to Britain to take part. The head of these affairs in the Dutch Foreign Office during the Messina period was Dr Ernst van der Beugel.

VAN DER BEUGEL: There had been a very strong feeling in Holland that the cooperation of the British was indispensable, more from a political point of view than from a purely economic. But there was no consensus, even in Holland, on this; and Beyen, who was the Foreign Minister who handled this matter, belonged to those who hoped that the British would come in, but who were absolutely determined to go on if they would not come in.
CHARLTON: What can be said about the responses that he got, first of all from Macmillan, who was Foreign Secretary?
VAN DER BEUGEL: I think that when he talked to Macmillan he got the impression that there was a chance. There was disappointment when it proved not to be true.

THE FORMAL BRITISH REPLY was written by Foreign Secretary Harold Macmillan, and said that, as the Six would no doubt be aware, there were special difficulties for Britain in any proposal for a European Common Market. But what kind of Common Market was, following Messina, an open question. Whether a Customs Union, with a common external tariff (which Britain had consistently opposed since the earliest post-war years as incompatible with the Commonwealth interest), or a Free Trade Area was a matter for argument. The Six plus one, Britain, would repair (it was suggested) to Brussels. There under the coordinating chairmanship of the Belgian Foreign Minister, Paul-Henri Spaak – a generous Anglophile who had been a wartime exile in London – they should together try to find agreement. The odious preconditions for negotiations with Britain which had made the case for rejection of the Schuman Plan for Coal and Steel five years earlier (i.e. a willingness to yield national sovereignty to a common high authority) were conspicuous by their absence from the Messina invitation. There were no preconditions.

The six months which followed the Messina Conference, from June until November 1955 (while the 'Spaak committees', as they were known, worked out the design for what became the Common Market), assumed in retrospect great importance for Britain. Their consequences did no less than alter the future course of British history.

The European countries appointed significant political figures, as in the case of Spaak, to the work of the Brussels committees, which began in July. The British did not. They sent neither a delegate nor an observer, but a 'representative'. In diplomatic terms it was an ambiguous status. It signalled the continuation of past policy, suggesting 'close association' but in the end 'detachment from' full involvement in Europe. It showed that Britain still considered initiatives over European integration in economic rather than political terms; as had been the

case with the Schuman Plan five years before, so too now. Following Messina the British representative sent to Brussels, to attend at what would prove to be the birth of the Common Market, was a senior civil servant – an Under-Secretary at the Board of Trade, Russell Bretherton. At the meeting in Messina itself Bretherton had been the lone official British representative, Eden having refused permission for a Minister, Nutting, to go. Bretherton had been briefed, before departure for Messina, by the political head of the Board of Trade, Peter Thorneycroft.

BRETHERTON: I did discuss it with him before I went, to some extent, and had a talk, half an hour's talk, quarter of an hour's talk, with him before going to Messina. At that time Thorneycroft was certainly not beyond the general line of 'help', and 'be as helpful as you can, don't seem to want to make us wanting to stop things – but no commitments'.

AND WHEN, A MONTH AFTER Messina, in July 1955 the study of the Messina proposals began in Brussels, the nature of Britain's representation remained unchanged. Bretherton was again sent to represent the United Kingdom.

BRETHERTON: As to the level of representation, we were not represented by a Minister because we were not in any way politically closely involved in this, you see. It was an economic, primarily an economic affair, and so it was quite natural to send somebody from the Board of Trade or the Treasury; the Board of Trade was the most obvious, I think. It so happened that I had been the Board of Trade representative on OEEC for a year. It was known that I had got a certain amount of European background because I had been, in an entirely different capacity, at the Marshall Plan conference in 1947, and again at some of the discussions on the economic side of NATO later on; therefore I was, I suppose, a rather natural sort of person to send – at that sort of level.

I must say that, when Spaak summoned the meeting of what we called the Steering Committee on 1 July 1955 to get the thing going, I was a little startled to find that, besides Spaak himself who was presiding, the German representative was Dr Walter Hallstein, the Foreign Minister, and the general level was that sort of thing. And there was I – an Under-Secretary from the Board of Trade!

Never before, or since, have I been called Your Excellency!

CHARLTON: Are you telling me that London did not appreciate the political character of the whole thing, or at least you didn't until you actually got there, to Brussels?

BRETHERTON: No, I don't think we appreciated it. At least, I didn't appreciate the political nature until I got there. This was all part of the London view, which was that they took the Messina resolutions, as they were, as economic matters. First of all, of course, we were very much in two minds about whether we *wanted* Europe, on the economic side, to get closer together or not. The line that HMG had taken all the way since 1947, since the Marshall Plan conference practically, was that OEEC, the Organisation for European Economic Cooperation, was the centre where we wanted and thought European affairs ought to be discussed.

CHARLTON: What were your instructions when you went to Brussels?

BRETHERTON: I took the Chancellor's reply to the formal invitation. Officials advised on this in a body called the 'Mutual Aid Committee', which looked after the whole of this sort of European relations and reported and recommended to Ministers. I took the Chancellor's formal reply after cursory preliminary discussion in the Mutual Aid Committee at official level, and that was all. I was my own witness, I mean. That was the main thing – and, of course, a knowledge of what HMG's policy was. The appraisal made by the Foreign Office and others, I think at the time of Messina, immediately after Messina, was that nothing would happen. There would be meetings, no doubt, and a show, but nothing more than that. Although not everybody believed that, that was the official Foreign Office view; they in fact circulated an 'Intel' to that effect.

FROM THE OUTSET the official British responses to the invitation to participate fully and without conditions in writing some new prescription for economic integration – the Common Market being only one of the suggestions at Messina – seem to have had a rather world-weary ring to them. Inevitably so, given the constraints imposed by Bretherton's threadbare instructions.

BRETHERTON: On the whole it was felt that we couldn't really stand out for complete non-participation in the whole thing. There were several reasons for that. One of them was that we were in trouble in OEEC because we had been pressing the Europeans – all of them – too soon and too hard for convertibility of sterling, which the Europeans thought would have a pretty bad effect on mutual relations, and on trade between their countries, and so on. Secondly, because the Foreign Office anyhow had divined that our policy in Europe was to be helpful and cooperative but entirely without commitment, and if we could operate that policy in these circumstances that was the one to operate.

CHARLTON: The Messina resolutions were purged of the 'idealistic ambitions' we had found impossible to accept at the time of the Schuman Plan. Words like 'supranational' are carefully left out. So how is this direct invitation to the UK seen by us this time, without such language and much more cautious about 'federal' ambitions than hitherto?

BRETHERTON: I don't remember that anybody made that point at the time certainly, and I think it was assumed that behind it were the federal ambitions, although I think everybody also agreed that the federal ambitions were not shared by everybody in Europe, not just ourselves.

CHARLTON: Spaak says in his memoirs that it was an earnest of their hope that we might yet find our way to take part with them, and above all their wish to prevent the Europe which was taking shape being confined to the Six. Did we share that view?

BRETHERTON: Well, you see, I don't think we thought that Europe *was* taking shape in those days.

CHARLTON: Did we accept that what they called, in the famous fourth clause of the Messina resolution, a Common Market, did we accept that the form this was likely to take was open for genuine discussion and argument?

BRETHERTON: Certainly. Certainly. Of course, if we had been able to say, or had said without meaning it like the French, that we accepted 'in principle', agreed 'in principle', we could have got whatever kind of Common Market we wanted. I have no doubt of that at all.

CHARLTON: Therefore, the fact that we chose not to participate in the end, and therefore not to influence the final outcome, is absolutely fundamental, and that decision was taken in advance?

BRETHERTON: Yes. It was the result of an established policy which, as I say, was cooperation without commitment.

'COOPERATION WITHOUT COMMITMENT' was a dusty answer with which to arm Russell Bretherton when the Spaak committees, setting about their task in Brussels, were 'hot for certainties' about Britain's attitude to a Common Market, be it in the nature of a Customs Union or Free Trade Area, and with Paul-Henri Spaak himself considering that he was 'holding the door open' for the United Kingdom. Another witness who was both at Messina and involved with the subsequent months of discussion and activity in the Spaak committees throughout their time in Brussels was Spaak's *directeur du cabinet*, Robert Rothschild.

ROTHSCHILD: When we had met in Messina, we had no preconceived ideas. Later on we realised that the agreement on the Benelux memorandum came because nobody knew very much about it! There were no terms and no conditions at that time. Our minds, the minds of all of us, were totally open. Let me remember the strange procedure which was decided first of all at Messina. When the memorandum was accepted, when it was decided that we would have talks about a Common Market, and that the British ought to be there, Adenauer, certainly, suggested that one man, and Spaak had suggested that one man, a politician, should be put in charge of the experts. We used to say that the experts were people who found the problem to each solution, rather than the solution to each problem! Spaak had in mind a former Belgian Prime Minister, van Zeeland, and much to our surprise Adenauer, I believe, suggested Spaak should do it himself. His first reaction was to say No, because he was Foreign Minister and he thought he would not have the time, but he was pressed to do it and by his own people, and he did accept it.

So here we are, in Brussels, with Spaak in the chair and all the governments sending, usually, either top civil servants – but brilliant ones like Robert Marjolin of France, or semi-political figures. Most of them were people in favour of it. Marjolin was very much in favour, Gaillard and Maurice Faure were very much in favour of it. The Germans who were sent were very much in favour, the Dutch were of course, the Italians were. That group of people was made up, as I say, of top civil servants or political figures. The British sent a man from the Board of Trade, Bretherton, who was obviously not a top man in the British establishment, but who was a very pleasant fellow and very courteous.

One of the first things Spaak suggested was that it would be a research group without entailing any responsibility for the governments; that the work would be done totally informally. Of course, we knew that all of them were in touch with their governments, but this gave them a freedom of expression they would not have had if they had had to ask for instructions every day.

Bretherton came to those first meetings – I still see his face in front of me in spite of the number of years which have passed. He usually had a rather cynical and amused smile on his face, and he looked at us like naughty children, not really mischievous, but enjoying themselves by playing a game which had no relevance and no future. And then very soon he disappeared. He never came again. I must say that when he first came he said he was an 'observer', which was not very relevant, because at that stage we were *all* observers. As I said, it had been decided not to commit anybody. And then, one day, he disappeared and never came again. It was very strange.

As ROTHSCHILD IMPLIES, the negative constraints of Bretherton's instructions and therefore Britain's representational attitude were ill-received, particularly by the more enthusiastic Europeans in Brussels.

BRETHERTON: I spent all my time, in fact, in the Common Market Committee (the main one which was presided over by a Dutch professor), and it was a very good body really. Everybody there, including myself, was prepared to talk very frankly. What we were concerned with was, in fact, looking at the difficulties and problems and forms of a Common Market. A Free Trade Area wasn't ruled out.

At that time a Free Trade Area of the Six or Seven, or whatever, was looked at to some extent. We met in a building in Brussels in an extremely hot room in what turned out to be a very hot summer, which made a difference. We met steadily from, usually, Tuesday to Friday in every week from 1 July until 9 August, if I remember rightly. Spaak had intended – and said at the beginning – that he was going to work right through the holiday period. But when we got into August this was more than could be stood even by the Europeans, and a lot of people found that their daughters were getting married or their grand-mothers were getting buried; and eventually he agreed that we should have a break. Originally, I think, only for ten days, but in fact it lasted until 1 September.

CHARLTON: Have you read what Spaak said about you in his memoirs?

BRETHERTON: No, I haven't read Spaak's memoirs.

CHARLTON: May I quote it to you now?

BRETHERTON: I should be most interested.

CHARLTON: 'Throughout our talks', Spaak says, 'Mr Bretherton's attitude was one of discreet scepticism.'

BRETHERTON: Yes.

CHARLTON: 'While the representatives of the other powers went about their work with a will, he remained silent for the most part.'

BRETHERTON: That is not true.

CHARLTON: 'And when he did join in, it was only to express doubt about whether his country could accept whatever idea looked like being the basis of agreement at any given time.'

BRETHERTON: I would defend myself against those charges. What I did do, of course, was to discuss the technical aspects of the thing, and in particular the point that was a very important one that, if you were going to have a Customs Union, which was what all of them rather assumed was the form, there were great difficulties about that for us because of our Imperial Preference arrangements tying up with the Commonwealth. And I did say (and other people, I think, accepted it) that a Free Trade Area would be a good deal easier. But the French didn't like that, and everybody I think at that time saw troubles about it on the technical side; and also I think they felt that this Free Trade Area wasn't a close enough thing from a European *political* point of view. I think that point did come in there, certainly.

CHARLTON: How did you report back during your time with the Brussels Committee?

BRETHERTON: One of the difficulties about this, of course, was that we had no Ambassador in Brussels at the time. He wasn't there. There was no economic attaché as an appointment. There was a political chargé d'affaires, Basil Boothby, who was very good and very helpful and did, in my view, a great deal. But the telephone communications were awful and even the bag did not arrive in under about four days. This was perfectly true, it was awful. It was very difficult.

CHARLTON: Did you feel rather cut off, would you say?

BRETHERTON: Yes. I came home every weekend, usually a Friday night or Saturday afternoon, and I got back to Brussels in time to start work again on Tuesday morning. More often than not that meant going back on Monday. Sometimes, I think about twice or three times in the whole affair, I managed to attend a Mutual Aid Committee on the Monday before I went! I would ring people up of course when I got back on Monday and talk to them. But that was about all.

BRETHERTON'S INSTRUCTIONS OF 'No Commitments' left little room for manoeuvre. The Cabinet Minister who briefed him on his departure for Brussels was the President of the Board of Trade, Peter Thorneycroft.

THORNEYCROFT: This reflected the attitude of the Government at that time. We were not participating in these talks; we had not taken a decision to go into Europe. The Foreign Office, who really decide what we do abroad, were opposed to the whole concept of the thing; and I should think perhaps we were rather lucky to have got anybody of Bretherton's ability to at least be there.

CHARLTON: Can I quote you, though, what Spaak said about him? That 'nothing could have more clearly outlined the attitude of the total British in-difference to Europe than the series of negative interventions made by this luckless representative in the debates of the Brussels committee.'

THORNEYCROFT: Yes, yes. Well, no doubt he was a very loyal and able

official, but he was sent there with a brief not to commit this country to anything, which was the Cabinet's decision. One can't place any responsibility or
blame on Mr Bretherton's shoulders. He was a keen European and one of the
most brilliant officials I've ever had the privilege of working with.
CHARLTON: But you sent him with a set of negative instructions?
THORNEYCROFT: Oh, he had a completely negative brief – he was bound to.
The Cabinet had really decided against the European concept.

AS THE WEEKS PASSED in the summer of 1955 and Britain continued to withhold any signal of positive commitment to the work of the Spaak committees in
Brussels, where the experts were studying the Messina resolutions for a Common Market and Euratom, important personal efforts were made by the Dutch
and the Belgians (acting, in part, as emissaries of the Six) to try and persuade a
change of mind in London. Spaak himself came to London to see 'Rab' Butler,
then Chancellor of the Exchequer, and also the Foreign Secretary, Harold
Macmillan. And if the British had been considered to be 'detached' in Brussels
they were apparently found to be coldly distant in London. Spaak was accompanied on these visits by Rothschild.

ROTHSCHILD: Spaak spent thirty to forty-five minutes in this conversation
with Butler, trying to convince him that the idea was a good one and that we
should have the British government with us. And it was obvious that he was not
convincing Butler. I still see him, very immobile, holding one hand with the
other hand and looking at Spaak without saying a word, and the colder he
became the warmer Spaak became, and the warmer Spaak became the colder
and colder Butler obviously became. After a while we realised that it was no use
going on. Very friendly, we said goodbye and we went off. It was a beautiful day,
and we walked along the street and suddenly Spaak was rather gloomy, turned
round to us, and said, 'Have I been obscene?'
    We were rather taken aback by that question. 'Why obscene, sir?'
    'Well, I don't think I could have shocked him more when I tried to appeal to
his imagination than if I would have taken my trousers off.'
    And that was the sort of conversation that we had with Butler. Macmillan was
a very different man, of course. I don't remember exactly the details but, to
make things short, we had the feeling that Butler was very opposed, Eden was
very opposed, and Macmillan less opposed. Macmillan was easy; Spaak was a
man of imagination, and as I said, of a certain warmth, of great warmth. He saw
the future of Europe in many fields – military, economic, and financial integration. That was what he tried to appeal to with the Ministers. Eden obviously
saw that integration was a wonderful thing – for the Continentals, but not for
the British.
    I remember one speech he made at that time in public somewhere, where he
said, 'I feel in my bones that we are not Europeans.' To which Spaak said,
'That's a funny place to have thinking.'

ROBERT ROTHSCHILD REFERRED TO Anthony Eden's key speech in the
United States – at Columbia University in 1952 – three years before Messina.
Eden had said, about the frequent suggestions that Britain should become more
closely linked with a Federation on the continent of Europe, 'We know in our

bones that we cannot do it.'

The attitudes of the smaller countries were reflecting a profound disappointment with the British outlook. Britain, however, was listening not so much to
their advocacy but to the voice of France. The British view – that nothing much
would happen in Brussels and that the Messina resolutions should not be taken
too seriously – was bolstered by the belief in London that France would go no
distance at all, given her traditional protectionist policies, towards a Common
Market. This general British conclusion ultimately proved, of course, to be a
near-fatal lack of insight into the vitality of the underlying will on the continent
to make a common cause and a break with the past. The Foreign Office maintained its line in the knowledge that Bretherton, the man on the spot in
Brussels, was beginning to express some disquiet in his reports and, towards
the end of the summer of 1955, beginning to urge contrary policy advice.

BRETHERTON: The policy advice that I gave, certainly in the latter part of the
period, after the holiday (and to some extent, I think, before), was that this was
much more serious than they thought it was. I kept on saying that. In fact, of
course, they laid on quite a considerable study in London of the economic
advantages of our going into a Customs Union; and the disadvantages to us if
there were one and we were left out.

IT WON'T BE UNTIL 1986, under the 30-year rule, that the findings of that
study could become known publicly. But there is private evidence that HOPS, as
it was called – 'The Home and Overseas Policy Sub-committee' of the
Cabinet, chaired by R. A. Butler – later came to the conclusion that, while it
was probable that Britain stood to gain economically from going in, the balance
of advantages as seen from London was insufficient to compel any rethink of
policy.

After the holiday season in the late summer of 1955, the Spaak committees in
Brussels were coming to the point where decisions would be called for and
treaties prepared. Britain and Europe were approaching a parting of the ways.

BRETHERTON: I had then, and I have now, a great admiration for Spaak; I
liked him and I got on personally, I think, very well with him.
CHARLTON: When you started telling London what he was up to and it was
more serious than you had imagined or they were imagining back home, what
responses did you get?
BRETHERTON: Well, here again, you see, most of this was taking place in the
holiday period and I don't remember that I got any or much response. One
point, because it bears on the business, I said that I think this is very much more
serious than you think. I did write a letter which I have and could quote – in
September – saying that I thought it was serious.

But the big question was the French. At that stage Clappier, the French
delegate (whom I also knew very well in the OEEC), came and made a verbal
statement – I suppose he must have had authority for doing it – that the then
French government was very anxious that we should be involved in this, that if
we would say clearly that we wanted to go in and take part – not necessarily precisely in the Customs Union, but in some close relationship to the affair – he
thought that France would come along pretty fast. But if we continued to say we

weren't committed, the French would do nothing and he thought the Italians wouldn't either. Now you've got to remember that this was one French government, and in February 1956, or six months later, of course they had some elections and the Mollet government came in, which was much more European in its approach.

CHARLTON: Yes, and Mollet was Anglophile. I find that fascinating. In other words, this Clappier remark was thought back in London to be very significant . . .

BRETHERTON: No, I don't think anybody took any notice of it. The general view then, in London, was still that nothing was going to happen, and that anyhow this rather strengthened the view that the French would wreck it in any case.

CHARLTON: Not allow it to happen.

BRETHERTON: Not allow it to happen. I mean, that accorded with our deeply held view. I think probably Clappier's position, what he told me in September 1955 was perfectly correct. I don't think there was anything funny about it, but they did change their governments. Then I think they sat down, or perhaps they had sat down before, and really thought out what they might get out of this from a purely French point of view – which was in the first place agricultural support in a big way and of a kind which we certainly could not have agreed to, and later on, of course, the inclusion of their colonies, which was not discussed at Brussels. We said we did not want to discuss this point except in relation to the difficulties of a Customs Union, and the French said they did not want to discuss it; and it wasn't discussed at all in the period I was in Messina.

CHARLTON: Can I put a personal question to you? While faithfully executing the instructions you had been given on behalf of the British government, did you yourself begin to change your mind while this conference was going on?

BRETHERTON: Oh yes.

CHARLTON: Were the opportunities available to us which we should, in your view, have accepted?

BRETHERTON: Well, I think it all depended on that. I said quite frankly in the letter I wrote, which I can quote to you if you like: 'If we are prepared to take a firm line, that we want to come in and will be a part of this, we can make this body into whatever we like. But if we don't say that, something will probably happen and we shan't exercise any influence over it.'

CHARLTON: Our position before, over Coal and Steel, had been the opposite, for example. As we could not have made that into something which we wanted, we rejected it. I mean, you were giving absolutely 180° contrary advice three or four years later. After Messina, you were saying that the attitudes now were more 'flexible' and there was the possibility of accommodation with which our interests coincided.

BRETHERTON: I think the balance of power, so to speak, was very different You see, the 'Coal and Steel' was France and Germany. In this one there was Benelux and Italy, who were on our side all the way through and wanted us in desperately. The Benelux people had an essentially low-tariff free-trade liberal attitude; the Italians wanted the same; and the Germans, of course, were in the wider field – they were certainly very anxious to have a pretty liberal kind of organisation. I am sure that if, in fact, we had been able to say from that time, 'We want to come in', and we negotiated, we could have got something very much more what we wanted. Except possibly agriculture – that might have been very troublesome, certainly. Before we broke up for the holidays, which after all was quite early in these affairs, I did report to London that there had been an approach to me, on a personal basis, from the head of the French delegation, Clappier, to the effect that France would be prepared to go quite a long way and quite quickly in the direction of a Common Market, but *only* on one condition – namely that the United Kingdom was also taking part or in some way closely associated with the operation. Then, on the other hand, if the United Kingdom seemed to dissociate herself France would make no move. And the Italian delegate said much the same thing.

I summed up by writing that 'we have the power to guide the conclusions of this conference in almost any direction we like, but beyond a certain point we cannot exercise the power without becoming responsible for the results'. I don't think anybody took any notice.

IN CONSEQUENCE THERE IS little to make one suppose that Britain gave any serious consideration to joining any form of Common Market in this vitally important period of its gestation. Bretherton received no further instructions, or at least there was no change in those he had. 'They were', he says, 'clear enough instructions after all. But the thing is, they did not meet the bill.'

In September 1955, with British policy still standing unchanged at 'no comment', a meeting of Foreign Ministers was called at Nordwijk in the Netherlands to review progress of the 'Spaak Committee'. The British Foreign Secretary, who was then Harold Macmillan, with his avowedly pro-European credentials, was invited. He did not accept.

BRETHERTON: The background of all this, you must remember, is that there was no Press interest at all. Public opinion was not interested. Most ministers were not interested. Macmillan, although he plays it up a good deal in his memoirs, took no active part in this. The Foreign Office line on it was that nothing would happen, and anyhow our first care should be to preserve our relations, our 'special relationship', with America. That was a bit odd when the Americans were pushing this themselves.

There was a ministerial meeting of the Six early in September to which

Macmillan was invited. He had some other fairly important engagements and
he didn't go. He said that he would send an official instead. Spaak and the Six
Ministers said: No, we won't accept an official – you must send a Minister, or
not at all. But this was still in the holiday period.

IT WAS ALSO EVIDENCE of growing impatience with Britain's demonstrably
negative attitude, as London continued to preserve an unconcerned detachment.
    From the outset much of the steam behind the relaunching of the European
idea had been supplied by the tenacity and creative energy of Jean Monnet.
Monnet was a very close friend of Spaak's and had been closely concerned with
the drafting of the Messina resolution. Monnet had calculated that, despite the
rebuff to his concepts which had been made so manifest with the defeat of the
Defence Community, France could not afford to say 'No' a second time. That
calculation differed, as we've noted, from the British assessment. It was based
on the knowledge that the *rapprochement* with Germany implicit in the Coal
and Steel Community had gone much deeper than was supposed in London.
An effort by Bretherton during the holiday period in London to get more
leverage in his instructions was unsuccessful. Monnet's authority was un-
questionably reinforced as Britain maintained a refusal to any commitment to
the outcome of the work in Brussels.
    One who had personal experience of that was the Director-General of
economic and military affairs in the Dutch Foreign Office throughout the time
of Messina to the signing of the Treaty of Rome, Dr Ernst van der Beugel.

VAN DER BEUGEL: Monnet's personal influence was tremendous. As to the
British, Monnet took a very clear decision that you should never make a compromise and that the British would come in if the *fait accompli* was created. He
exerted his influence in two ways: one you will probably know, the second you
might not. One was, of course, the 'Monnet committee', which was composed
of the parliamentary leaders of the Continental parliaments. It was my personal
experience that, when the Dutch tried to score a point in Brussels, we were
immediately summoned by the parliamentary committee with the 'Monnet
message', and they told us to stop being difficult and just to go along. That was
one channel. The other channel was the Americans; at that time, 1956-7, it was
still the Eisenhower administration. Monnet was on the closest possible terms
with Dulles and with the network of the Eastern establishment. The US
Ambassador came to see me and said that he hoped the Dutch government
would change its position, and so forth and so on. It was the greatest influence
possible.
CHARLTON: It would seem obvious, then, that at this time the British were in
effect bypassed, that they became less relevant and less important, if you have
American support plus the Continental will.
VAN DER BEUGEL: Yes, but that was the position: the Continental support
plus American support. Monnet was not 'French' in the sense that he wanted to
have the British out. Not at all. Monnet was absolutely honest that he wanted to
have the British in. But he wanted to have the British in after the *fait accompli*
was created. He didn't want to compromise.

BY NOVEMBER 1955, it was clear that the expert committees could go no further without political guidance from their governments. As all the delegates (Russell Bretherton included) returned to Brussels, Monnet, together with Spaak, had managed to engineer a change in procedure which would bring matters to a head. Monnet's personal assistant, the man who eventually drafted the Treaty of Rome, was Pierre Uri.

URI: During the first phase of the Spaak committees in Brussels there were several committees, and plenty of people who really had no notion of what it was all about! You really could not make a distinction between the British and the rest, and honestly, during that phase there were on each of the issues either seven answers – the Six and Britain – or no answer at all. But there was seldom the feeling that the British were really dragging their feet.

All of a sudden the decision was taken, by Spaak I think, inspired by Felix Gaillard, that all the committees should be disbanded, and that it was a waste of time, and that now everything could be really concentrated in a small group – the chairman Spaak, the chiefs of the delegations, and that was all, with just one expert for each, according to the topic, and one reporter. That was how I was chosen as a 'rapporteur'. Spaak asked Monnet who could do the job and Monnet, I think without hesitation, told Spaak Pierre Uri could do the job. And that is how I received the wholly important mission of having to conceive the Common Market.

I told Spaak this is the method I propose to you. I mean, there are lots of things which need purely verbal agreement, and other important key issues, which have either seven answers or none, so I am going to prepare a working document which can be either one page or a bit longer, ten pages, and on each of those issues offer one solution, which is connected with the answers I give in the other documents. Once we have agreed these key points, it would be a series of papers. I think it was either eleven or thirteen, I can't remember very well. Then we have 'The Report'. They said they agreed. That is how we worked. But this was the change of method, and it provided the occasion to say to the British, 'Are you interested or aren't you?'

The change of procedure, going over from those various committees, with people, not all of them being very 'compétent' or imaginative, to just a small group, with the chief of the delegation being able to call on one expert each time according to the topic, the Chairman and one general 'reporter', all gave the opportunity to say to the British, 'Now this is beginning to be serious! Do you want to be in, or do you want to stay out?' To some extent we *did* have the feeling they were dragging their feet, but anyway we now had the chance to make it all more effective and come to a faster conclusion.

Then there was a rather dramatic meeting. It was the last meeting of the co-ordinating committee before we went over to the new method. Bretherton, who was a Chief Representative, had to read out aloud the brief which he had received from Whitehall. It was said to us that it had been written in long hand by the Prime Minister, Anthony Eden himself. And I can assure you that Bretherton read it in the dullest possible way. He was under instructions, and he was a faithful civil servant. But I think his heart was not in it, and he did not want to associate himself with it, I thought. It was very sad. I must say, later on when he saw what we produced, the so-called Spaak Report, he said, 'This is a damned good report. I wish we had been in it.'

RUSSELL BRETHERTON HIMSELF does not confirm what Uri and his colleagues appear to have thought, or been given to understand, that Bretherton
read from a brief in Anthony Eden's own handwriting. But this moment in
November 1955 when Britain said, in effect, no to a Common Market she had
been invited to design was obviously 'dramatic'.

BRETHERTON: I had perfectly clear instructions, which were to make a speech
saying that we are very interested in all this and so forth, but clearly we couldn't
take part in it, and we hoped that as much as possible, at any rate of the fringe
things like transport and the other things, should go back to OEEC. Spaak just
blew up at that point.
CHARLTON: Did he?
BRETHERTON: Yes. It puzzled us at the time why he blew up in just that way,
because he knew this would be our position. At least he ought to have known.
But I think he was misled, because Beyen had been to London the week before
and had seen the Chancellor [R. A. Buttler].
CHARLTON: This is the Dutch Foreign Minister [Beyen].
BRETHERTON: Yes. It transpired afterwards that the Dutch Foreign Minister
had reported that the British attitude was about to change, and I think Spaak
thought I would come to Brussels to this meeting with some new instructions;
and, of course, I hadn't got any.
CHARLTON: It is interesting that when you were writing home saying that it is
more serious . . . we ought to be taking it more seriously, which is the inference
from what you say . . . one might have expected your instructions perhaps to
have been altered or reconsidered in some way. Do you feel the Cabinet gave
concentrated attention to this possibility, that the whole thing might break up
and Spaak might . . .
BRETHERTON: No, I don't think the Cabinet took much notice of it at that time.
My instructions for going to the meeting in November were certainly much more
rigid, and the Foreign Office instigation added even stronger weight to the 'put-
it-all-back-into-OEEC' argument than before. And those are what I had. For the
first time I had what really amounted to almost a written instruction, I mean something almost to read out, you see, which I had not had before, and didn't want.
CHARLTON: When you say Spaak blew up, can you slow down the explosion
and just remember what he said?
BRETHERTON: As soon as I had spoken, Spaak just said, 'Well, I am
astonished and very hurt at this. You are just sticking to your guns. England has
not moved at all, and I am not going to move either'. And he then went on and
said, 'Well, clearly, you can't take part in the completion of a Final Report on
this' – we told him before that we couldn't, in fact, agree to take part in 'recommendations' – 'that will be done, completed by the Heads of Delegations only –
and you, of course, will not be on that delegation any longer, on the steering
committee or anything of that sort . . . I will report it myself,' I think he said,
'before Christmas.' In fact, he didn't produce a report until about February.
CHARLTON: In his memoirs Spaak uses the word 'withdrawal' himself,
because he feels that because our position was inflexible it was we who withdrew rather than . . .
BRETHERTON: Yes . . . In fact it was Spaak who said, 'You must not attend
any more.'

CHARLTON: And he says this: 'This wait-and-see attitude by Britain persisted until the famous meeting in Venice in April 1956, and when we resumed our negotiations for the Common Market, the British representative was nowhere to be seen and his government did little or nothing to either justify or explain their absence. . .'

BRETHERTON: Well, this is a very biased, weighted thing. The point was, we had been invited to Brussels by Spaak and we were there at his invitation, and he changed the structure of the thing at the November meeting, as he explained. So that in fact we should not be there, could not be there. He said, in fact, that his 'final report must be completed by people who are committed to recommendations'. We were not committed, of course, and we were not invited, and we never went again.

AND THERE, IN HIS OWN WORDS, Russell Bretherton is in effect rereading the burial service over Britain's first encounter with the Common Market. He reminds us that there was a British 'veto' long before the more notorious one pronounced by General de Gaulle – the British refusal of 'Europe' in 1955.

The week before this dramatic meeting in Brussels, the last at which Britain (in the person of Bretherton) was represented, there was a last-minute attempt to enlist British membership of the Common Market. The Dutch Foreign Minister, Beyen, came to London a second time. The first had been in June, immediately after the Messina conference, when he explained its purpose and results to a series of meetings presided over by the Chancellor of the Exchequer, R. A. Butler. Now six months later, a week before the British with-drawal, he came again to see Butler. Beyen left this meeting apparently with the

R. A. BUTLER

impression that Britain was likely to change her mind. Therefore when Bretherton read out his coldly dismissive brief from London, bad temper and mistrust were piled on disappointment in Europe; and it explains, perhaps, Spaak's outburst.

Ernst van der Beugel, of the Dutch Foreign Office, says that Beyen was 'offended' as well as disappointed with the reply given in Brussels to his eleventh-hour visit to London. Lord Butler now speaks for the first time publicly about this encounter (and indirectly about the intangible influence of personalities upon policy), recalling, in his late seventies his decisions as Chancellor of the Exchequer in Eden's government at the time of Messina and the Spaak committees which followed in Brussels.

BUTLER: The Beyen business I remember quite well, because I was rather surprised that the Dutch Foreign Minister should take such a big part. I got very bored with him, and so did everybody else; and so in the early part we, I'm afraid, rather cold-shouldered him. Then on the second occasion when he came over, which was more businesslike and there were all these talks, I think it possible that I listened. And the word 'listened' is very important, because what I mean by that is that I was not combative, or against, or rude; and I think that may have given him the impression that he had made an impression. But after he had gone – I consulted with my colleagues – I had not betrayed my country in any way by wrong words, but I think that I had been sensibly sympathetic to him, and had overcome (on the advice of some of my advisers) my personal repugnance to him.
CHARLTON: Repugnance? Why repugnance?
BUTLER: Well, he was a very pushing man. And he was always telling you what to do. I was sort of looking rather to the bigger nations, you see, and he rather took the lead, you know.

THE NEW RIGIDITY in the instructions Bretherton took back with him to Brussels for the November meeting in 1955 suggest to me that the Foreign Office, anticipating that the next stages would imply commitment to the outcome, foresaw the chance to break. Under the thirty-year rule, the documents which will throw more light on this will not be available for some years yet. The detailed considerations which led to the British withdrawal from the formative discussions which led to the Common Market therefore remain obscure. The Permanent Under-Secretary at the Foreign Office then was Sir Harold (now Lord) Caccia, who has felt unable to help. Stated at its simplest, this is the quintessential reason as given by 'Rab' Butler who, with Anthony Eden, took that decision.

BUTLER: The fact is that Britain at that time was not proposing to go into a European alliance – I can say that quite definitely.

ODDLY ENOUGH, THERE IS an interesting and total discrepancy in the rival accounts of the technical reasons for the British withdrawal. Russell Bretherton broke in with vehement protest about this word 'withdrawal' when I put it to him.

BRETHERTON: It wasn't a decision to withdraw. We were thrown out. This is a complete misconception. We were perfectly prepared to go on being what we had been, namely an observer. But Spaak laid his plans. It became clear at that meeting in November that he had laid his plans on the basis of producing his own report, his final one which was in fact a blueprint for the Common Market. He said, and obviously quite rightly, that if you are not prepared to play on that, clearly you can't take part in forming the final report and we don't want you there. That is what he said.

BUT BRETHERTON'S EXPLANATION of Britain's withdrawal and subsequent absence from this point onwards is put into context by Spaak's principal aide during this period, Robert Rothschild, who maintains there was no question of Bretherton's being 'thrown out'.

ROTHSCHILD: One day he disappeared and never came again. It was very strange.
CHARLTON: The British version of this, of course, is that there was no withdrawal by them, but they were excluded.
ROTHSCHILD: No, that's absolutely not true.
CHARLTON: How can a discrepancy like that . . .
ROTHSCHILD: Well, I challenge you to show me any document – in diplomacy most of those things are done in written form – I challenge you to give me any document which would prove that, at any time, certainly the chairman, and as far as I know, any of the participating governments, did anything to exclude him.
CHARLTON: Well, perhaps it rests upon Spaak's own attitude. There is evidence that Spaak lost his temper with what he regarded as the British prevarication, that we were attending but not really contributing. A decision had to be made, this thing was only heading in one direction, it was going to end in an agreement – I'm trying to paraphrase Spaak's views – and, in the end, he just lost patience and said: 'Well, if you're not in it, we'll go ahead without you,' or words to this effect. And the British took that as exclusion. First of all, do you agree with that?
ROTHSCHILD: No, I don't. Let me, first of all, tell you that in a number of years – and I spent many, many years with Spaak, through practically all my professional life – I very, very seldom saw him losing patience unless he wanted to shock. He was a very good *comédien*, and during the negotiation in Brussels, at the latest stage, he once or twice made scenes; but they were put-up jobs for the result. Certainly he was very, very pro-British – sentimentally. He liked most of the British statesmen. He had relations of close friendship with Anthony Eden; he liked Macmillan; he had great respect for Churchill, whom he'd met many times during the War when he was in the government-in-exile. And he would have been more patient with the British than he would have been with the Belgians. I never saw him lose his patience; I never saw him do anything in the chair which could be construed by Bretherton as trying to get rid of him.

It's always been a mystery to us why Bretherton was taken away like that. Of course, we often came to London and we saw the Ministers and we realised that they were not interested. They were opposed to it.
CHARLTON: Are you saying that Spaak would have been willing for the British to have gone on as they were, 'observing' without taking a decision?

ROTHSCHILD: That's right. Until the meeting in Venice in April 1956 certainly. They could have told us what they wanted. They never told us what they wanted. They never said we don't like the idea of the Customs Union, we don't like this or we don't like that. They were gone by that time and we had no longer an English colleague at the table. That's really the truth as I see it.

CHARLTON: Well, there's a total disagreement of the two views! I must say to you that the only British view I've heard, at first hand, is that something happened when, because the British felt they could not advance their position or go along with the general direction of things as a result of the Spaak committees, they were excluded and . . .

ROTHSCHILD: I really challenge you to give me any clear information as to how they were excluded. Of course, it is a long time – but I've lived the last twenty-six years under the impression that, one day, they decided not to be in it any more! This is the first time I've heard any claim they were excluded. Because there would have had to have been a discussion about their exclusion. Who would have decided to exclude them? The Chairman could not have done it on his own! As I said, *all* the governments around that time were keen to have you with us. So there would have been a discussion about it. We would have tried to find a way to keep them. That I do not remember at all.

PERHAPS, AFTER ALL, both accounts may be reconcilable in this explanation of Bretherton's disappearance from Brussels given by Peter Thorneycroft, who as President of the Board of Trade was his political boss. Lord Thorneycroft accepts that Britain withdrew Mr Bretherton.

THORNEYCROFT: I think he was withdrawn because, in the circumstances in which he was placed, he was beyond being able to make any useful contribution. But to sit for ever at a conference where you're really not able to speak on behalf of a government with any authority or with any positive proposals is not a very enviable position or a very useful one.

   At that time we could have got – we can't rewrite history, you don't absolutely know what you would have got – one could have had arrangements about agriculture. Perhaps controversial, perhaps not wholly acceptable in this country, but very, very different to the Common Agricultural Policy that exists today. The assistance to European farmers would probably have been more on the lines adopted in this country. Special positions could have been negotiated for some part at any rate of Commonwealth imports and so forth. We threw away a great opportunity.

THE NEGOTIATIONS WHICH LED eventually to the creation of the European Common Market lasted from the meeting at Messina in June of 1955 until the Treaty of Rome was ready in May of 1957. Often, as Spaak himself wrote in later days, they were 'on the brink of failure'. But they succeeded.

   After the 'withdrawal' of Bretherton to London in November 1955 the United Kingdom took no further part in them, and Britain was no longer represented at the deliberations of the Spaak committees which led to the Spaak Report.

BRETHERTON: After November? Well, we were no longer at Brussels. The only link we had after that was a very curious and rather characteristic one.

The one that got away: the Messina conference in Sicily, June 1955 (left to right, Johan Beyen, Gaetano Martino, Joseph Bech, Antoine Pinay, Walter Hallstein and Paul-Henri Spaak).

There had been arrangements, while we were at Messina, by which Spaak committee papers – the stuff that was produced by the Secretariat – was passed to the Embassy for transmission to London – usually rather late, very late. And that was not stopped. So we went on getting the more important papers. They were just sort of passed under the counter to the Embassy who passed them back to them! This went on until about February in 1956.

CHARLTON: I infer from that that this was Spaak?

BRETHERTON: I presume, and we all thought that it was Spaak, yes, still trying to get us in, and he was decent, I think, to do it for us.

CHARLTON: Spaak had another go, didn't he? He wrote to Eden personally in February 1956 and got a reply back saying once more that the OEEC was the route Britain intended to pursue, and Spaak said that while Eden's letter expressed goodwill it showed him – Spaak – that there were still fundamental differences of view between Britain and the Continent. So I put it to you that this really was the parting of the ways between us?

BRETHERTON: Oh yes, they were in that sense. Of course, a great many people, perhaps the majority in London, still believed that nothing very much would happen in the end! You see, the actual negotiations – Spaak's own report, which was a sort of blueprint for a Treaty, it wasn't more than that, was not produced until February 1956; and then the negotiations between the Six were conducted very secretly, mostly down in the south of France somewhere, and the final decision to go ahead was taken in Venice in May or April of 1956.

There was something of a shock after Brussels, in November certainly, within the Establishment, although not very widely still. Also, what was then still the Federation of British Industry, which had also been watching this fairly closely, woke up and came to see Frank Lee, the Permanent Under-Secretary of the Board of Trade, and talked about all this. And I went and talked to them at considerable length, and they started testing British industrial opinion, which previously of course had been presumed to be rather protectionist and would be against anything of this kind.

About a fortnight, or perhaps a bit more, after the final meeting for us in Brussels in November, I got a letter from Frank Lee passing on some very nice things which had been said about me at one of the ministerial committees and I replied to that. He had said he realised this had been a great strain and so on. I replied saying yes it had been a strain, but that I had enjoyed it very much and the only thing about which I was unhappy was because of the line we were now taking. Because I thought that we greatly underestimated the amount of steam that there was still behind these sort of ideas in Europe.

WHAT 'THE LINE' WAS, that caused Russell Bretherton concern, we shall take account of in the next chapter. It led to a sudden and swift change for the worse in the atmosphere between Britain and the Six.

THE BRITISH WITHDRAWAL from the Spaak committees in November 1955 began the overture to a long period of mistrust and tension between Europe and Britain. Marked by the milepost of Bretherton's withdrawal from Brussels, such opportunities as were then open to Britain to make the kind of Europe she later wanted slipped inexorably away. In consequence the price next time would be higher. The European bus – or boat or train – was on the move again, and British diplomacy had waved it away, confident it was most unlikely to reach its declared objectives. There was no clear perception that a general Common Market would emerge, and so soon, as a serious rival to Britain and the Commonwealth.

Why did we not go on with our participation in the efforts to form a Common Market in 1955? A valedictory to that fateful summer, autumn, and winter should properly come from the man who as Chancellor of the Exchequer had, next to Anthony Eden, the widest knowledge and was most directly concerned in a decision which marked the parting of the ways between Britain and Europe.

BUTLER: Well, I can tell you, better I think than probably anybody living, because I was at that time Chairman of the OEEC. At that time Britain was regarded as the normal chairman of Europe, and I was in the chair for nearly four years running, and I spoke French and German. The French government, at that time, if you remember, was in disarray. They always arrived late, and we thought that we were very important.

When we heard that the Six were meeting in Messina, we attributed it largely to the Dutch Foreign Minister, Beyen, who was very important at that time. We were all inclined not to take it seriously. I remember giving almost my final dinner in Paris to the OEEC – I suppose it was about sixty or seventy people – and making a remark saying that excavations were proceeding at Messina at which we were not taking part – I wasn't very rude, but – at which we were not taking part.

CHARLTON: 'Archaeological excavations', you said.

BUTLER: Yes! I always remember that because it was, in my view, a definite lack of foresight on the part of myself, and a much bigger lack of foresight on the part of the Treasury, and a very big lack of foresight on the part of the Foreign Office. But the fact is that the advice we were getting, and from our Ambassador in Paris and all that, was that we should just let it go, you see? That is how the bad start, the late start for Europe, really started. I ought to have said: 'Well, let's get on to the new horse', you see. But I did not. And I wasn't blamed at the time at all, and I have not been blamed very much in history. But my own feeling is that that is where we started to go wrong in regard to the European Economic Community of today.

CHARLTON: It's a revealing phrase to me, the one you have just used, or quoted, to me when you made that speech to the Europeans, that you had heard of some 'archaeological excavations at Messina'. Now, that rather does suggest that you were looking at this new attempt to relaunch 'Europe' as digging up a past that you thought had been buried once and for all with the collapse of the Defence Community. Now is that fair?

BUTLER: Well, I'm telling you exactly what I said, because I have a very good memory. I have as you know written a lot of notes and written a book, but I have never put this in before because I have never been asked. I am not particularly proud of it, but I don't think it was a great sort of shame for a statesman because I was never asked by anyone to do anything else! But I think it was a mistake: and I don't think either the Foreign Office, which was a huge organisation, over which I have presided, or the Treasury, which is an almost bigger one, were in favour at all.

CHARLTON: What about Anthony Eden?

BUTLER: Anthony Eden was bored with this. Frankly he was even more bored than I was.

CHARLTON: Thought it was irrelevant, an irritant?

BUTLER: Well, he thought it was going too far. To do Anthony justice, of course, he had a certain amount of, not exactly genius, but he had a certain amount of flair in foreign affairs. I think he thought the French were a bit difficult.

CHARLTON: That they would not go ahead with it.

BUTLER: Yes, he did. He had very considerable flair in foreign affairs which we all know about. Much more than he had later with Suez, which was awful, but in the earlier part of his career he had a lot of flair.

CHARLTON: Can you remember how the decision to withdraw Mr Bretherton from Brussels was taken.

BUTLER: I think it was taken through – well, it is best to talk in simple English! Through boredom by the Government, that is why it was taken.

CHARLTON: But it was not a decision taken in the Foreign Office alone?

BUTLER: No, no, no, no.

CHARLTON: And it was a Cabinet decision?

BUTLER: No. And it was not a decision which was widespread through the Cabinet, or through the whole government machine. Perpetually you come back to the combination of the Treasury and the Foreign Office.

CHARLTON: But you took that decision, or helped to take it, yourself? Can you remember on what grounds, precisely?

BUTLER: Well, we just thought it was not going to work. That's where we were wrong, you see.

CHARLTON: But Harold Macmillan tells us, in his memoirs, that in September 1955, at which time we were still being represented by Bretherton at the work which was going on in Brussels to form the Common Market, he wrote to you saying this: that he had heard that there was 'talk that we might be disengaging ourselves', and he says this: 'I am sure that you would wish that all the necessary consultation should take place before any such steps were taken'. Now, one possible inference of that is that full consultation did *not* take place before that decision?

BUTLER: Well, I remember Harold being in touch with me, and of course nobody can possibly underrate Harold's intelligence, I couldn't myself. And I think that is what I call an intelligent letter. But the fact is that it was not received by the Treasury or me, or taken very seriously. We may have made a mistake over that, although I don't think, at that time, Harold was quite convinced that the modern EEC was going to emerge. The fact is, as I have said, that Britain at that time was not proposing to go into a European alliance and I can say that quite definitely. And therefore, although Macmillan may have been looking ahead, I do not think he differed from the rest of us in thinking that it was not the time to break the link. That is a very fair way of looking at it.

CHARLTON: You and Anthony Eden, at the time of Messina, if you both took this decision that Bretherton should come home and that we do not go any further, must have had some conversation together about it? Do you remember what passed between you?

BUTLER: The extraordinary thing is, you see, that it is partly a weakness of the British governmental and Cabinet system, that big ministries, especially the Foreign Office and the Treasury, are so busy, and so much plugged with files, that they do depend on their immediate advisers a lot. And there is no doubt that the immediate advisers of Anthony and myself were advising us *not* to go on with this. So whenever I met Anthony, the sort of conversation was simply, 'Nothing doing', you know. That is really what happened, which I think was shortsighted, and if Anthony was alive today he would agree with me.

THE YEARS WHICH IMMEDIATELY followed Britain's passing up of her invitation from Messina to join the Europeans and her withdrawal from the Common Market negotiations ushered in more painful and increasingly visible constraints upon her former freedom of action. They witnessed a last attempt by Britain to have it both ways, with the launching and failure of a British alternative to full membership of the Common Market which also put forward an alternative design for all of Europe – the Industrial Free Trade Area, IEFTA. They included the climacteric event of Suez in 1956, the downfall of Anthony Eden, and with him a particular vision of Britain's role and position in the world. They include the return to power in France in 1958 of 'nemesis', in the shape of General de Gaulle. They were years of dilemma and perplexity. They were years in which the chair in Brussels was empty and Empire was unpossessed.

7

A Last Step Sideways

As MAY NOW BE SEEN, with the bright illumination of hindsight, it was at the end of 1955 that Britain turned down the last best chance she had of making the kind of European Community she later wanted.

Astonishingly, Britain had probably come closer to the consideration of throwing in her lot with Europe at the time of the Schuman Plan in 1950 than she had done five years later with the better opportunity of the Common Market. By withdrawing, after six months, from the negotiations in Brussels which followed the Messina conference, the United Kingdom had refused the invitation from France, Germany, Italy and the Benelux countries to help design, as a founder member, the future Common Market. 'Once to every man and nation comes the moment to decide' – and Messina was not perceived by Britain as the moment or the opportunity.

The Prime Minister, Anthony Eden, who probably exercised the biggest influence over that decision, had positively rejected the European concept for Britain. 'Rab' Butler, who was Chancellor of the Exchequer at the time, made a significant point, in the previous chapter, about institutional behaviour and Cabinet government. We have his authoritative word for it that the decision was not widely spread through the Cabinet or the government machine, but that it was taken on advice from the top of the two big ministries, Foreign Office and Treasury – and in effect, it would seem, by Butler and Eden alone. The attempt to recruit Britain and the continuing efforts in Brussels to establish a general Common Market in Europe were regarded by both Eden and Butler (in Lord Butler's own words) as 'a bore'! A bore, and therefore an irritant and a nuisance.

And yet, following Messina, the efforts to 'relaunch the European idea', as it was called on the Continent, could not by then be so readily dismissed as the precipitance of over-eager theorists (which is, more or less, how Britain viewed both the Schuman Plan for the Coal and Steel Community of 1950 and the Defence Community proposal which followed that and failed). Those 'Spaak committees' in Brussels – as the British representative to them, Russell Bretherton, had reported home after a while to London – were showing the revival of an all-important tenacity and seriousness of political purpose, though they had yet to demonstrate consolidated success. But, as Lord Butler has reminded us, there was little apprehension in the Cabinet, and neither he nor Eden believed that the continuing efforts in Brussels would succeed and, because of that, come to sway the whole life of Britain.

The issue of the Common Market did not receive the Government's concentrated attention in 1955, and therefore the British 'refusal of Europe' in such a form can hardly be seen as that serious, considered thought of the nation which, in the end, prevails. British public opinion went on in unsuspicious confidence and only began to wake up when the Common Market was already a probable event, with the signing of the Treaty of Rome in 1957. The European concept made little appeal in government, party or opposition, or the country or the Press. Harold Macmillan says in his memoirs of the Messina decision that 'we were all looking back to the struggles and traditions of the past . . .'

Therefore Britain, as it entered 1956, saw no necessity for choice. But events in the four years which now followed were to force it upon her. They included the abortive invasion of the Suez Canal and the humiliation and national self-judgement which went with it; Anthony Eden's departure after his breakdown; and the failure of the first all-out effort by Britain both to take account of the political and economic development of 'the Six', and to envelop and extend it with a counter-proposal for a Free Trade Area. By 1958, with the recall to power in France, from more than a decade of brooding retreat at Colombey-les-Deux-Eglises, of General de Gaulle and the coincidental putting into effect of the Treaty of Rome and the Common Market, Britain found that Europe was not just being organised without her – but against her.

We might begin an account of these years with an echo from Lord Butler's reflections on the Messina decision, as he remembered how he and Anthony Eden looked at things at the time they said 'No' to joining the European Community as founder members in 1955.

BUTLER: I think the mistake we made in the early days was that by that time we were already dismantling our Commonwealth in every way, in some cases already in trade preferences, and because nowadays what the Conservatives stood for in the old days, with Joseph Chamberlain and protection, is quite out of date, isn't it? All that has been dismantled, and I think it was rather short-sighted that we did not realise that something was starting which might make a *new* combination, you see? For example, there was a comparatively low tariff wall, it does not have to be jumped now, does it? It did in those days.

CHARLTON: The coincidence of these two things – of a genuine invitation, one that we could have, should have, found perhaps much easier to accept than the Schuman Plan or the earlier opportunities to take a lead in Europe immediately after the war, which is passed up –

BUTLER: Yes.

CHARLTON: And at the same time Anthony Eden in particular seems to wish to reinforce the whole imperial dimension, particularly in the Middle East. I'd like to hear you talk about that – the development of a real tension between ourselves and the Americans, for example, and Eden's determination, would you say, to reassert the British position and British authority?

BUTLER: In some ways Anthony Eden has never been really fully studied, because there has been so much abuse. For example, I read an introduction by A. J. P. Taylor to a new book on Eden, which is so rude that you can hardly read it. And, that is not fair. You see, all that is because of Suez. Well now, in his early days Eden was, I think, a slightly old-fashioned Foreign Secretary, and he did almost exactly what the older men in the Foreign Office – 'the Knights' you might call them, at the top – told him to do. Therefore, he was, on the whole, very successful. But there is no doubt that the trend you mentioned, the sort of 'imperialistic' trend, and the extraordinary British – and rather typically British – characteristic of being nervous of foreigners, was present in his mind, which you can hardly believe in a Foreign Secretary. But he was slightly old-fashioned. The more I study the views of Eden the more I find. He lived, you see, in a colossally old mansion, which his family had been in for 400 years – and he was much more of an old-fashioned aristocrat even than Halifax. Extraordinary! But he didn't say so himself because he was young and he fought in the first War. He was gallant, wasn't he?

CHARLTON: But was there any real resistance to Eden's view and determination to go on playing a world role in this country, that he was *not* going to be pushed into Europe by the Americans, that he wasn't going to be barged out of the position the British had built up?

BUTLER: Well, you see, he inherited the old tradition, didn't he?

AT THE END OF 1955 the Prime Minister reshuffled his Cabinet. Rab Butler was replaced as Chancellor of the Exchequer by Harold Macmillan, and Selwyn Lloyd went to the Foreign Office. This has usually been seen as Eden wishing to have a more compliant figure, and incidentally a less avowedly 'European' one, in the Prime Minister's former domain of foreign policy, where Eden's own authority was in consequence now augmented.

However, in the important months covering Messina and the meetings of the Spaak committees in Brussels, while he was Foreign Secretary, Harold Macmillan does not appear to have taken, or insisted upon, any particularly forward position, in advance of his colleagues, over events in Brussels. Only later, when he was Chancellor and after Russell Bretherton had withdrawn from Brussels, did he begin to change.

The British having pulled out, Spaak, the Belgian Foreign Minister, produced his now famous 'Report' out of the work of the expert committees. It suggested that the proposed Common Market should take the form of a Customs Union, not a Free Trade Area. For a brief period following withdrawal, British policy reacted to developments in Brussels with outright hostility. When coupled with the British refusal, the disappointment in Europe turned to resentment. Spaak himself later noted that, as he saw it, 'little by little the British attitude changed from one of mildly disdainful scepticism to growing fear'. In seeing increasing British hostility to the Brussels talks, Spaak added this, 'Having first refused to take part in them, they now made them out to be a danger to European unity.'

Robert Rothschild had been present with Spaak throughout this time of conception and gestation of the Common Market, from Messina onwards.

ROTHSCHILD: The feeling was that when the thing began to take shape, and especially after the Treaty of Rome, the Treasury and the Foreign Office at that time were beginning to fear that, contrary to their expectations and if it all worked, there was a force growing upon the Continent of which they were not part. So the alternative was either to become part of it – which we were hoping, and of course we were vindicated because in the end you *did* join it – or destroy it. To be very candid, after a while we began to feel that Her Majesty's Government was decided to try to bash the whole thing.

CHARLTON: What's the evidence of that?

ROTHSCHILD: Well, conversations, pressures, and mostly the proceedings of OEEC under the chairmanship of Reggie Maudling. We saw extraordinary things. The Labour members and the Labour governments of Norway and Denmark aligning with the Conservative government of Great Britain against the 'dirigisme' of the Common Market. It took months of negotiations there and, you should remember, the subject of the conversations in Paris at the OEEC at this time was to find an association between the new Customs Union and the countries which were remaining outside it, which would later unite and form themselves into EFTA, the Free Trade Area zone.

THERE WAS ALSO, it would seem, a rather more incandescent phase of active British hostility and opposition. This was immediately following the decision in Brussels which had led to Russell Bretherton's withdrawal and return to London, and to the decision that the Common Market would take the form of a Customs Union, not a Free Trade Area. This period itself was short-lived and lasted for a few months only, but the atmosphere it engendered between Britain and Europe was chill, and the after-effects proved more durable.

The reason why this phase of overtly active opposition to the Common Market proposals *was* so shortlived – the firm and interested support of the Americans for economic integration in Europe – is suggested in this recollection of Russell Bretherton himself, then Under-Secretary of the Board of Trade.

BRETHERTON: We made, of course, a very ill-judged and, I feel, unfortunate approach to the Americans, saying we think this is all going to form a Customs Union, or not a Customs Union but something very protective and damaging, and won't you help us to stop it? To which we got an *extremely* dusty answer!

SPAAK HIMSELF LATER MADE use of a memorandum, written by Britain to the German Government in December 1955, which sounds this particular note in British responses. It stated that Britain found the Common Market envisaged was neither compatible with her economic and political relations with the rest of the Commonwealth, nor could it be reconciled with her Free Trade policy. Britain warned that 'nothing should be done to provoke a clash between the interests of the Six and the OEEC countries'.

Declaring that it had always been his view that candour was the best means of avoiding friction and resolving difficulties, in February 1956 Spaak despatched to London the leader of the Belgian delegation during the work in Brussels of the Spaak committees, and his principal aide in those negotiations, Baron Snoy.

SNOY: The political accord had come in January 1956 between the Heads of Delegation, and Mr Bretherton had already left us. He left us, in fact, in December 1955, when it was decided that we should propose a Customs Union instead of a Free Trade Area.

I was sent in February 1956 to London to meet the Chancellor of the Exchequer, Mr Macmillan. We had a lunch together at the Belgian Embassy and I explained everything to him, what we had decided for the Spaak Report of the Heads of Delegation, and his answer was, 'You have commenced a very fine undertaking and we shall help it; but as for a Common Market, your Common Market, it will kill our trade, and we will have to fight against it.' It was a very

Britain attempts to repulse the Common Market with 'Plan G'. Peter Thorneycroft argues its merits, Paris 1957.

major position, and I reported to Spaak that we had very little hope to get on that side.

THE FIRST FEARS THAT there *would* now be an integrated Europe were taking root in Whitehall.

BRETHERTON: Thorneycroft, immediately after the breakdown in November, was obviously very worried and certainly stirred up his colleagues in the Cabinet. I don't know exactly how he did it. Thorneycroft, I think, took a large part in this. What we did was, really, to feel that we had better *do* something about this and prepare a plan which we *could* accept. That led up to the Free Trade Area which was, of course, for the first time, a Free Trade Area between the Six and ourselves.

CHARLTON: In industrial goods only?

BRETHERTON: In industrial goods. And 'Plan G' – for a Free Trade Area – was what came out of that. By that time there were many, or at any rate a majority of the Cabinet by the spring of 1956 was in favour of getting back into some sort of really close relationship with what was going on. And that was the best plan we could get. It produced frightful shrieks, of course, from what was still then the Dominions Office, I think, and its Minister!

CHARLTON: I've rather passed over that in talking to you, but at Messina do you believe, or in the Spaak committees in Brussels, that some sort of association with the Commonwealth would have been possible, in addition? That we could have got something with which our long-held position in the Commonwealth could have been reconciled?

BRETHERTON: That was never discussed there, no. It's very difficult to see in what form. It could have emerged in the form of a Free Trade Area and that was discussed to some extent. I think we probably could have got it if we had said we will come in on a Free Trade Area but we will not come in on a Common Market. If we had said that I think we would probably have got it or something like it, close to it anyhow. But of course it was not possible.

NOT POSSIBLE BECAUSE, as we must recall, Lord Butler said the Cabinet had not made the necessary strategic decision, and 'the fact is that Britain, at that time, was not proposing to go into a European alliance – I can say that quite definitely'. Lord Thorneycroft, who was then head of the Board of Trade and Bretherton's boss, looked up some of the records to reinforce his own memory of how he 'stirred up' his colleagues, following our withdrawal.

THORNEYCROFT: Could I quote a bit of what I was saying to the Cabinet and my colleagues at that time?

> All courses [I said] raise issues of complexity and considerable controversy. The most tempting course is to do nothing. If we can contrive a policy with Europe, however, to deal with the situation, we can justify it, expand it, and defend it. We shall be in a central position from which we can repulse attack. If, on the other hand, we just leave things to develop we run into grave dangers. In Europe we shall forfeit any claims to leadership. In the Commonwealth we may find ourselves at the end of the day clinging to the remnants of imperial preference. Nor can we hesitate for very long. Certain tactical moves are open to us but tactics depend on strategy, and until we can agree upon our broad strategic concept generally, tactical arrangements may not only be ineffectual but could be really dangerous . . .

And I then went on to argue the case for having a Free Trade Area in materials and manufactures, and special arrangements which could have been made in agriculture. But of course they've been made on lines very different to those that *would* have been made had we participated. It was a very great mistake.

If we had gone in then, our position was strong, our reputation high. We were wanted by our friends and colleagues, perhaps not with the fervour of the Hague conference but still wanted very much. We could have played a great part in it, and the resultant community would have looked quite different, or very different to the one which exists today, and would be geared far more in British interests.

CHARLTON: So it was a diplomatic catastrophe, in retrospect?

THORNEYCROFT: Yes, it was a diplomatic catastrophe from that point of view.

THORNEYCROFT'S WORDS TO HIS Cabinet colleagues early in 1956 heralded

the first stirrings of a new policy and a somewhat belated concentration upon Europe. It was not yet a move into Europe. That decision had been taken – and we were against it. But it would prove to be a last attempt by Britain to square the circle with the Continental Europeans and Britain's traditional interests in the Commonwealth by an alternative design for European cooperation. What was called 'Plan G' would now emerge. Britain would propose a Free Trade Area, in industrial goods only, between the Six intending to form a Common Market, treated as a whole, and Britain plus the rest of Europe – the Industrial Free Trade Area.

Before we examine the conception and eventual failure of 'Plan G' we should follow the Europeans one vital step further – to Venice, in May 1956. There the Foreign Ministers of the Six met to receive Spaak's Report and its recommendation that the Common Market should be in the form of a Customs Union. This was the time of decision of the National Governments as opposed to the delgations of experts which had been meeting under Spaak's chairmanship in Brussels. A qualified invitation, despite her withdrawal from Brussels, was extended to Britain to take part in the drafting of the Treaties if she accepted this Report. Britain did not do so, and did not go. The strategic decision had been made at the time of our withdrawal not to become committed.

In his own memoirs Paul-Henri Spaak recollected that his colleague Baron Snoy called this meeting in Venice the 'miraculous' conference. Snoy once again was present as Belgium's Finance Minister.

SNOY: The Venice conference was a conference of one hour and a half where the utmost decisions were taken for the future of Europe. I went to Venice, and Spaak had probably the same feeling as I had, that we would meet a tremendous French opposition to the Report of the Heads of Delegation, called 'Report Spaak'. It happened through good chance that the French had the chair; so Pineau arrived, took the chair, and he started the conference by asking: 'Well, we have here a report of Mr Spaak – could Mr Spaak comment on that report?'

Mr Spaak answered: 'My report has been in the hands of the governments and the Ministers of Foreign Affairs for three weeks. I suppose everybody took the time to read it very clearly, and I have no comment to make.'

The Venice Conference of May 1956. In 1¹/₂ hours the decision to form the Common Market was confirmed. Britain – invited – does not attend.

So poor Pineau asked the members of the Conference: 'Would anybody comment on the "Report Spaak"?' Nobody asked for the floor. So Pineau said: 'Being Chairman I have to give the answer of the French government first'. And he gave the advice that the French government was in favour of the 'Report Spaak, provided there would be a new chapter written about colonial and overseas territories . . .'

I remember having said to Spaak: 'Now for God's sake, let nobody take the floor again.' And that was what happened. After an hour and a half everybody went out to the *laguna* saying, We have only to make the communiqué. And I never expected such an important conference to go through with all the acceptances of all the decisions written in the 'Report Spaak' – provided we should find a solution for Algeria and the colonial and overseas territories, which was a difficult matter, I agree, but not insuperable.

IT WAS BECAUSE THE British thought these difficulties *would* in the end prove insuperable, allied with France's long tradition of protectionism in trading, that it was considered in London that the French 'would go no distance at all towards a Common Market'. But the French were about to make a radical reappraisal and a shift in their policy.

It is important to remember what the situation of France was then. Economically, it was in all kinds of crisis, unable to accept foreign competition and with a protectionist tradition. In short the Common Market presented it with a major challenge and forced far-reaching internal changes in order to meet open competition with Germany. As a result of this, during the 1960s – the period of maximum dynamic growth within the Common Market – France emerged with a completely new economic infrastructure. From all this Britain had elected to stand aside. The defeat and humiliation of France in Indo-China in 1954 and the growing insurrection in North Africa no doubt helped to concentrate the French mind for this fundamental change. Whereas Britain's orderly transition from Empire to Commonwealth, and the dimension and nature of her overseas relationships, offered no strict analogy and imposed no similar sense of urgency.

But Lord Butler, who opposed the suggestion at the time, has said that the mistake Britain made was not to make her own move into Europe at this same period, when the British trading position with her overseas Commonwealth was notably declining. By her withdrawal from the Messina invitation and the Brussels committees Britain did not exploit the chance to make the fundamental new arrangements which, in the British absence, France set out to secure for herself.

As we have seen, at the last moment – the stage when the Common Market Treaties were being prepared, after the agreement reached by the Six in Venice to go ahead in principle – France suddenly raised the issue of her overseas territories as a condition of entry to a Common Market. The man who drafted the Treaty of Rome, steering its way through the shoals of Agriculture, of Customs Unions and Free Trade Areas and overseas possessions, was Jean Monnet's principal assistant, Pierre Uri.

URI: There was no question but that agriculture would be in it – everybody was agreed on that. It was not forced on the others by the French. Of course, the French would never have accepted something which did *not* include agriculture but there was really no discussion between the Six on that point. The difference between the Customs Union, with common policies, and the simple Free Trade Area is mostly the difference over the inclusion or exclusion of agriculture. But there was no disagreement on that point. When I was, or had been, in charge in Brussels of preparing that report I had said that there were only two things on which I want to summon a small group. One is agricultural policy, and the other one is all the social problems – adjustment policies, wage policies, social security – those kind of things. We had, I think, two meetings on agriculture, and that is how we came up with that particular chapter in the Spaak Report, the chapter I had written. After those meetings, and this is the one thing where I did not change a word, it was such a delicate matter, the chapter on agriculture was the agreed paper – and I did not change a word.

CHARLTON: But would the final 'deal' sketched at Venice in April 1956, and open to the French, of inclusion of what was left of the French Empire and the special provisions for French agriculture – would those same provisions, broadly, have been possible for the British Commonwealth, do you feel?

URI: You know, the provisions about the French – there was nothing so noble about them. France was giving up the preferences it had enjoyed in its former Empire. There was one thing which was immediately recognised. If this had no special access to the market, there was no reason why France should bear all the burdens of all the financial aid. On the whole that wasn't so difficult.

CHARLTON: And as far as the British were concerned?

URI: As far as the British were concerned they were not there any more! They weren't there. But *had* they had been there, provided they accepted the main and the key idea – that we were all really working together for a common project – I think they would have got the same deal as the French did. Provided you start from an objective situation, that we have a preference in our Empire which recognises that there is a compatible means of membership in a European Community, that there are no preferences any more in the market, and that those countries are going to be open to our partners on exactly the same basis as they are to us – and obviously the corollary of that is the share or the sharing of the financial burden – then there is nothing abnormal about it.

Personally I regret the British not coming in earlier, because the European Community is too much bent on Africa and not enough on Asia. I know these are enormous countries. India is such a big lump in the developing world, but personally I regret the certain lack of balance between Africa and Asia in the preoccupations of the European Community, and this is probably due to the fact that the British had not been in from the start.

IT IS WORTH DWELLING for a moment on the possibilities of agreement with France in these years just before the return to power of General de Gaulle. Pierre Uri's drafting of an agreed chapter on Agriculture was not the Common Agricultural Policy of today. The latter was not negotiated by Adenauer and de Gaulle until after the Rome Treaty was signed, and was not therefore a part of the Rome Treaty. If Uri's view might be thought to be the result of his own close involvement with Jean Monnet's particular vision, it is supported by this rather more detached calculation of what was then official policy in the French Foreign Office.

Hervé Alphand, Ambassador of France and twice Director-General of the Quai d'Orsay, spoke similarly of 1955 and 1956.

ALPHAND: I think the invitation to the British was made with the intention of bringing Britain inside the Community and to discuss with Britain the articles of a Treaty, and then, had Britain accepted, the Treaty would have been different probably. I think we would have had to take into consideration probably the special interests of Britain with overseas Commonwealth trade and the existence of the sterling area and so on. The Treaty would probably have been different.
CHARLTON: And France would have acquiesced in that?
ALPHAND: Probably.

BUT AS IT WAS, with Britain standing back the future Common Market, and in particular the Agricultural Policy, would be an accommodation reached with the Germans over the essential interests, principally, of France.

Another who was intimately involved throughout the period of Messina, leading up to the Rome Treaty, had a more personal recollection of how it was that France resolved the issue of her own 'Commonwealth', her overseas possessions, the 'territoires d'outre-mer' – by her decision following Messina to make her own radical move back into Europe and into an integrated European Community. The Director-General of Economic and Military Affairs in the Dutch Foreign Office at this time, in 1956, was Ernst van der Beugel.

VAN DER BEUGEL: What made the situation so difficult was that the Treaty was ready. And the French came up with the *territoires d'outre-mer* at the very, very, very last moment, which created a great shock to the others. I remember very well a Sunday on the Quai d'Orsay when – that was the first time the Prime Ministers were called in, for the thing was negotiated in the garden of the Quai d'Orsay, between Adenauer and Mollet – I still see them walking through the garden arm in arm. And the Germans paid; essentially the Germans paid the bill. But at the very, very last moment – the Treaty was ready – the French then said, the Treaty will not pass the Assembly if we don't bring in the *territoires d'outre-mer*, which was a very nasty way of negotiating what they knew six months in advance. The French put the pressure on right at the very last moment.

CHARLTON: Yes, which is the soul of the whole European idea really. The Germans were willing to pay almost any price. The British appear to have been convinced, until very late in the day, that Germany would not pay that price. Macmillan's memoirs are quite extensive on this whole subject; but he says somewhere in his diary that 'the Germans have sold out completely to the French', in a tone that seems rather offended and surprised. As late as 1957-8 the British appear to have been caught napping by Dr Adenauer's will and determination.

VAN DER BEUGEL: With one marginal comment, that British foreign policy did very little to influence the Germans. There was a total absence of the notion that Germany was – or was going to be – the key country in Europe. British diplomacy was totally focused on France and neglected the Germans. But the analysis that Adenauer was in the pocket of the French – that analysis in itself is right.

THIS FACTOR WAS, and is, such a determinant in post-war Western Europe that it's hard to see whether it might have been otherwise. Ernst van der Beugel thinks there is an additional factor involved: a failure of British policy over Germany. Sir Con O'Neill, a distinguished Foreign Office official who served in Germany and later led Britain's negotiations at the time of our eventual entry to the Common Market, agrees.

O'NEILL: I've always seen it as profoundly disappointing and one of our greatest mistakes – though perhaps we couldn't have avoided it – that we allowed our relations with Germany to become so infinitely less important to Germany than are Germany's relations with France. Now I may have taken a superficial view – I probably did – but I was a little bit surprised that things went as they did. At the time I was in Germany, in Bonn, the first three and a half years, 1949 to 1953, I thought our relations with the German government were increasingly good. But we didn't ever really appreciate how 'un-British' in his outlook, how unappreciative of the British, how hostile to the British, Adenauer really basically was from the start. And how, as a Western European, he didn't understand England. He didn't like England very much. He regarded us as some kind of maritime pirates, jolly good at swiping chunks of Africa and looking after our own interests, but not very reliable in a European context.

ONCE MORE ONE HAS recourse to Harold Macmillan's memoirs for this vital period in the middle 1950s as the Community is being formed. He says that the settlement by France and Germany of the protracted dispute over the Saar coal region should have been a clearer warning to British diplomacy that the reconciliation between them had gone much deeper than London supposed. Offered the choice of becoming part of Germany or France at a referendum in 1955, the inhabitants of the Saar opted for Germany. But what is significant is that France accepted this outcome so soon after the war. It was proof of the strength of the new ideas animating Europe. Therefore this episode should have diminished British expectations that the Germans, although historically 'free traders', would support the new design about to be put forward by London as an alternative to the Common Market – the Free Trade Area. Particularly as Dr Konrad Adenauer and his Foreign Minister Dr Hallstein made the political aspects of European integration paramount.

O'NEILL: They welcomed it. They were prepared to go a very long way towards it. Adenauer in particular thought that this was the way of exorcising Germany's 'Prussian' complex, as you might say, mastering the 'Eastern tradition' in German policy and cultural attitudes, and anchoring Germany firmly to the Christian, one must say to the Catholic, West. Hallstein probably shared those views. I think, in a way, he was less of an ideologue than Adenauer; but I don't think Hallstein thought very much of the British, I'm sorry to say. And he must have supported to the full Adenauer's increasingly firm view that the right thing was to anchor Germany's future in the closest possible relationship with France.

Now here, as on so many occasions, I was wrong in my appreciation at an earlier stage. Because it was very conspicuous and undoubtedly the case back in 1950-2 – the period we were negotiating these very complicated Bonn Conventions which put an end to the Occupation of Germany and were a kind of Peace Treaty – that it was the French who were fighting for every conceivable restriction, limitation and humiliation on Germany; and we and the Americans who were fighting to lift, to abolish, change and get rid of all this.

It made no difference. The Germans understood it. The Germans realised that the French had every conceivable ground for suspicion and hostility, in search of security. They realised they were in for a fearful row with the French over the Saar, which eventually was solved, and from Germany's point of view happily. It did not fundamentally spoil their relationship with the French, that the French tried to preserve all the privileges of Occupation. It did not improve *our* relationship with the Germans that we were prepared, generously, to get rid of them – because Adenauer and Hallstein had concluded that Germany's future must lie above all with France.

BRITISH RELATIONS WITH ADENAUER, who so changed Western Europe after the last war by leading Germany into a quite new and historically un-precedented partnership with it – looking West and not East, had hardly been propitious from the outset. In a perhaps unusually significant episode Adenauer had been dismissed from his post as Lord Mayor of Cologne in 1945 by a lone British brigadier, locked up, and then exiled to a village outside the city. It's always thought to have rankled with him, and been reflected in or assisted some of his later judgements.

Germany's Ambassador to London for many years, who was the official spokesman in Bonn for the Adenauer government in the fifties, was Karl-Günther von Hase.

VON HASE: I have studied this question very carefully and I wrote a little piece about it in a book on Adenauer. You know he was a Rhinelander, and by the way after the First World War he was handled by the French in a very bad way. After the First World War it was the British who supported him and during even the Hitler time helped him to improve his situation and get back part of his pension, which Hitler had taken away from him, because of his opposition to Hitler as Burgomeister of Cologne. Then there was this incident when the British kicked him out after the Second World War as Mayor of Cologne – I think this incident was always overestimated. He was, of course, disappointed at the time. Later he always used to joke about it and never was really hurt by it. But it is a fact that he did not see in Britain the same partner, with the same kind of 'antennae' for European thinking, as he did in France with people like Monnet and de Gaulle, or in America for his policy with people like John Foster Dulles, John McCloy and Dean Acheson or other people. I think it was a certain tragedy. There was never any animosity on the part of Adenauer towards Britain, but his main interest centred around France, and he did not want to endanger, or to see put in danger, so to say, his *first* political achievement – cooperation and friendship with France – by some other power.

IT WAS ONE OF THE BEST KNOWN of American diplomats at the end of the last war, Livingston Merchant, who in paying tribute to Anthony Eden's diplomatic skills said of him that he detected an underlying characteristic which he found in every British statesman, with the sole exception of Winston Churchill – an 'almost instinctive effort in any conflict, great or small, to find a compromise solution'. Merchant went on to suggest that this had been the case particularly since the carnage on the Somme in World War One. It was after this, he felt, that Britain had 'the realisation that its role could no longer be that of a determiner of events but was one of a negotiator and a mediator'. To which one might add a 'bridge', and a maker of coalitions.

Certainly, the Cabinet having ruled out a move into Europe and being therefore unwilling or unable to contemplate the disruption involved in joining the Common Market, Britain put forward what it considered was now dictated by the forthcoming division of Western Europe – a necessary compromise.

And so in 1956 and 1957 we come to 'Plan G', the proposal for a Free Trade Area in Europe in industrial goods only – between the Six forming the Customs Union of the Common Market, to be treated as a single unit, and outside it Britain plus the rest of Europe. But the emergence of 'Plan G' put an end to the official air of detachment which had characterised British policy at the time of the Schuman Plan, the Defence Community and, most recently, with the decision not to go on with the Messina invitation to take part in the Common Market. Britain was constantly invited during those various episodes to declare her position and say what she wanted; but she had always refused to do so if it meant accepting any obligation for the outcome, were that to lead to any more exclusive involvement in Europe.

Plan G showed that the new partnership between Macmillan at the Treasury and Thorneycroft at the Board of Trade – both of them pro-Europeans – was unwilling to leave all the running to the Common Market countries, and that the time had come in 1956 – now almost posthumously late in the day – for Britain to put forward some comprehensive ideas of her own.

THORNEYCROFT: We had some plusses because Harold Macmillan comes on to the scene and wants to do something. He is partial and he puts forward a series of alternative options which are then studied in Whitehall. Broadly speaking, the option that is adopted is the Free Trade Area scheme, and he tries to get in on that basis with the Europeans. Already the difficulties have mounted up on us. Before they were tentative, but now they have a system of their own which they've negotiated and agreed; and the result is it's far harder to get a new concept in.

CHARLTON: Essentially, this free trade proposal you put forward is a device for what? To get entry for our industrial goods into Europe as it's organised but without the *quid pro quo* of agricultural imports from France here?

THORNEYCROFT: What I was saying from the Board of Trade, at that moment at any rate, was not that nothing should be done about agriculture, because something obviously would have to be done about agriculture. It was that special arrangements should be made about agriculture, which indeed they had been by the Europeans.

CHARLTON: But that was watered down in the final proposal, wasn't it?

THORNEYCROFT: I think so, yes. Probably watered down because of the pressure from the Commonwealth Office and from agriculture – I mean, one was fighting against strong lobbies here at this time.

CHARLTON: Therefore, when we came to put this plan to the Europeans, we were offering France, as I see it, only this: increased industrial competition in Europe, but without any outlet for her agriculture.

THORNEYCROFT: Yes. Mind you, we are an important market for France both in agriculture and in manufacturers. We were not without cards in our hands even then, and we're still getting in a lot of agricultural produce from France.

CHARLTON: I just wonder whether the thing appeared to you to be flawed from the beginning or whether you thought it had a genuine hope.

THORNEYCROFT: I think it was all right as an opening position. I would have thought that in any serious discussion of it we would have been forced into an agricultural debate fairly early. But even there it is, after all, what we were forced into years later.

CHARLTON: And the point is you, at that time, would have gone the whole hog and made agriculture part of it?

THORNEYCROFT: Oh, we would have had to, absolutely. I mean, no doubt about it. We would have had to come to some arrangement. They would have been better than the ones we've got at the moment.

CHARLTON: Yes. Spaak says that he warned Macmillan at the time that this wasn't going to work, that if we thought this was . . .

THORNEYCROFT: Spaak was right. But it was probably all right, as I say, as an opening debating position. But they could have gone on. The Europeans would say: 'Well, this isn't perhaps quite going far enough, you've got to do something about agriculture'; and an agricultural solution could have been worked out.

But remember that all the time we were still not absolutely in the clear with our Commonwealth partners; we had to carry them with us. So don't underestimate the difficulties of those concerned at that moment.

CHARLTON: But when would you say it was apparent to you that we had left it too late to write our terms of association with the new European Community?

THORNEYCROFT: Well, I think that point occurred to me from the moment when we didn't participate in the original negotiation.

WHILE, TO JUDGE FROM what Peter Thorneycroft has said, Plan G had a rather forlorn expectation of success from the beginning, it was nevertheless pressed by Britain with vigour. It meant that, in parallel with the new-found confidence of the Six following the 'miraculous conference' in Venice – the words were Snoy's – where by April 1956, 'the utmost decisions were taken for the future of Europe', there was now this major, rival and first British initiative competing for consideration and adherents.

To accompany the launching of Plan G there was an important change in representational attitudes. This time a political figure was put in charge, the Paymaster-General, Reginald Maudling, rather than a senior civil servant with the status of 'observer', as had been the case with Russell Bretherton. While the Six went ahead, ploughing their own inspired furrow towards the Treaty of Rome at separate meetings, there was now also a rival focus. British diplomacy sought, in Paris, to resuscitate the relevance of OEEC and use it as a framework in which to conduct the separate set of negotiations to solve the problem of how to associate the British-sponsored idea of a Free Trade Area with the new Common Market in prospect.

The OEEC elected as chairman, to preside over this examination of whether the Free Trade Area proposal could be made to work, Spaak's close associate, the Belgian Finance Minister Jean-Charles Snoy.

SNOY: I must say that, at that period, a certain number of people thought that the British were always trying to kill the negotiation of the Common Market through their interferences and their interventions in the discussions about 'Association' in the OEEC. Personally, I never shared that feeling. I was myself the Chairman of the Group Seventeen of OEEC, where we discussed the technicalities of a Custom Union or being a member of a Free Trade Area. We found all kinds of technical possibilities; but it would have meant very difficult discussions taking much time. It had been decided that we should not wait for a formula of Association to be found *before* the Six prepared and signed our Treaty.

It was perfectly understood that all the members of the OEEC wanted to be interested in their connection with the Common Market countries, and that we had to find some way to do it. I myself have a very clear memory of the fairness of the negotiation in the Group of Seventeen in OEEC. I would say that Thorneycroft and Maudling were very convinced people in negotiating that. I had much to do with them, and I was convinced they wanted a Free Trade Area.

Now did they want it to diminish the impact of the Common Market? To reduce or to paralyse to a certain extent the Common Market? That is the problem of intentions I can't go into! But I consider it was fair, and that we had a fair negotiation about the Free Trade Area, and that we were helped by the British in a number of ways. For instance, in 1957 when the Treaty of Rome was signed we were required also to push forward the negotiation in OEEC for a Free Trade Area – but we asked our British friends to avoid pressure during the period during which there was the problem of ratification in our various Parliaments. And they complied very gently, and very fairly, to reduce the tempo of the negotiations for the Free Trade Area *until* the principal ratifications had gone through.

In that period the change was this: from the Venice conference the British understood that there *would* be an integrated Europe, and they wanted then not to be absolutely outside it. So we had to find an association formula. The Venice Conference being in April/May 1956, already by July there was a decision of the Council of OEEC to study a Free Trade Area *with* the Common Market.

SUSPICIONS ABOUT THE NATURE of British intentions apart, there were strong hints in 1956 that the Europeans no longer wanted to wait for Britain. And there was another major constraint upon British policy, the attitude of the Americans and their continued support for Continental integration.

At the beginning of 1956, just after Britain had pulled out of the efforts to form the Common Market and tried to enlist the Americans in putting a stop to it, the Prime Minister, Anthony Eden, and the new Foreign Secretary, Selwyn Lloyd, visited Washington for a meeting with President Eisenhower and his Secretary of State, John Foster Dulles. There they were told that the Americans considered Britain was being 'ill-advisedly' hostile to developments in Europe.

This whole sequence, from the British refusal of the Messina proposals to the putting forward of the alternative British design for Europe of the Free Trade Area, is dismissed with scant mention in Anthony Eden's autobiography. Messina receives only a line or so; and of the visit to Eisenhower he says, simply, 'On Europe, we could not agree.' Significantly he added this: 'The Americans entertain the same enthusiasm for these new proposals about European integration as they did for the European Defence Community' – which suggests the Prime Minister believed the Common Market might suffer the same fate.

A diplomatic historian who has had a privileged access to the still-classified papers on both sides of the Atlantic affecting Anglo-American relations is Professor Richard Neustadt of Harvard.

NEUSTADT: I think you find that, all through the 1950s and well into the 1960s, right up until the time the British gave up the mission east of Suez, different members of successive American Administrations, and different parts of the career bureaucracy in the United States, weigh two glimpses of Britain differently.

I think that the most instructive comment I know of is not just a Dulles comment but a comment of Dean Rusk's who succeeded to the Secretaryship of State in 1961 and was there until 1969. He said in 1962 – I guess it was during the 'Skybolt' crisis – he said this to his own State Department officials, his 'Europeanists', chiding them, 'We must have someone to talk to in the World –

the British are the only people we can be *sure* of talking to in the World'. Now that's a matter for the British, as the only other people with a global mission, and the British as 'Anglo-Saxons'. Both those facets of the British role were terribly important to the people at the top of the American government. This is why, I think, one must be careful in assuming, in any part of this period, that the people at the top were as passionate about getting Britain into Europe as the permanent civil servants in the State Department, one level down. Moreover, the permanent civil servants in the Pentagon were never eager to see Britain in Europe – or at least I don't recall a time when there was any passion on that score from the military services. You had really, on this side of the water, just as on your side, sentiments that worked in opposite directions, and people don't really confront these sentiments – they live with the dichotomy.

CHARLTON: But I suggest that the attitude in Britain, after the collapse of the European Defence Community and the Messina resuscitation, is that it is more than a setback. It is that these people have been defeated, we have always opposed it, they have proved themselves to be a minority, these ideas are impractical, they cannot be transubstantiated and become reality. What about Dulles though? He has been personally supporting these ideas from their beginning, and it may be a guide to the strength of the movement for unity in Europe, and American support for it, to know how Dulles behaved in the run-up to the formation of the European communities?

NEUSTADT: My impression is that there is constant American support for these Continental moves. I don't think that support is seen in Washington as 'anti-British'. My impression is that there is division in Washington about how important it is to involve the British simultaneously. The Monnetists are saddened by British obduracy and by their not seeing their great chance – which the Americans see on Britain's behalf – to take over the European move-ment.

CHARLTON: There is that revealing bit in Anthony Eden's memoirs, when he is Prime Minister in his own right, and he has a meeting in Washington with the Foreign Secretary, Selwyn Lloyd, and they meet President Eisenhower and Dulles, the Secretary of State. It was in January 1956, just as the decision to go ahead with the Common Market is taken in Brussels and Britain has opted out. There are only two or three lines, but Eden emphasises the breadth of agree-ment with the United States over policy but mentions that 'over Europe, we dis-agreed'. Now, it is thought that Dulles and Eisenhower suggested rather strongly to Eden that he was being 'ill-advisedly hostile' towards the integration of the Continent including Britain, and they seemed to suggest to him, would you agree, that Britain *ought* to be, must be, a part of this?

NEUSTADT: My impression is that that was their position. I think one has to be careful about what that means in that period – the pre-Suez period, the pre-missile period. I think it was very attractive to one strand of American opinion, with which I believe it's fair to associate President Eisenhower. To think that European integration *was* necessary and desirable for reasons of recovery, opposing the Russians and containing the Germans – but to include Britain not merely as another government but as the earnest of this European entity, *sustaining allied relations with America*, and sustaining a global view. Britain was not merely to go in there, but to go in there and dominate it on behalf of joint British–American concerns.

CHARLTON: The British seem to have had a more sceptical view of their own possibilities in that direction than the Americans did. They take the view that they are being bundled into Europe by America – got out of the way!

NEUSTADT: That's right. I think there is a strand of opinion among American policy-makers, with which numbers of our civil servants could be associated and with which it is conceivable Dulles himself could be associated – but not Eisenhower, I believe.

I don't want to testify about Dulles. He's a subtle person masquerading as something of an unsubtle one! He is very much Eisenhower's Secretary of State and conscious of his dependence upon Eisenhower. So I find interpreting his personal views difficult. There certainly were some people who wanted, as you say, to bundle the British away, forget about them, 'they're pro-French', and so forth. But the dominant view, I believe, was that English membership and leadership is the way to secure Europe as an 'outward-looking partner taking world responsibility'.

CHARLTON: What encourages Eisenhower and Dulles in their belief that, if Britain *does* take part in continental integration, it *can* order things to the British – and to the American – advantage?

NEUSTADT: The American vision is that the British have an unparalleled civil service as well as a desirable world view; that – compared to the French, who are still recovering from the war, to the Germans who'd collapsed – if the British would go into Europe – and put their civil servants into Europe – they would naturally, out of sheer competence, dominate it, and dominate the organisations. That view was held when it probably had a good deal of substance to it immediately after the war. But it was maintained for years, indeed it became a British view. By the time Britain actually got in, of course, it did not prove out. But I think that right up through Harold Wilson – I think Harold Wilson believed that as late as 1967.

CHARLTON: Go in and run it?

NEUSTADT: Go in and run it!

IN THE SPECIFIC INSTANCE of Macmillan and Thorneycroft's 'Plan G', the Free Trade area scheme, the United States saw it as a step away from the principal aim of her statecraft post-war in Europe – the encouragement of the idea of a community which would stand on its own feet and overgrow the old antagonisms of the nation states. This was the recollection of the American ambassador in Paris at the time, and subsequently Eisenhower's Under-Secretary of State before becoming the Treasury Secretary, Douglas Dillon.

DILLON: I don't think we particularly objected to it [Plan G] as long as it did not impinge on the success of the Six, of the European Community. The priority in our policy was to support the European Economic Community, and then if this thing could work in addition to it so much the better. But I don't think that we felt it was a really important change. We did not think the significance of it was as great as that maybe placed upon it in the United Kingdom. But we were not 'opposed' to it. If we thought it was going to impinge on the successful functioning of the Six, then we would not have liked that.

CHARLTON: Well, of course the Six were suggesting that it did!

DILLON: To the extent that they did, that would have had influence with us. If it came to a choice between supporting one or the other we would have given our support to the European Economic Community, because we thought that it was more significant.

BUT NEITHER WHEN THE real test came did US policy strive officiously to keep alive the Free Trade Area scheme. Douglas Dillon's answer suggests that it was seen as of, literally, peripheral importance. Therefore the American judgment was that Britain had, by then, a diminishing relevance in shaping the radical changes taking place on the Continent from her position outside it.

There was another, and ultimately overwhelmingly important, strand of American thinking, because in the end it was triumphant. This was the close link between Jean Monnet and a handful of key figures in US policy-making circles. Foremost among them was George Ball, the American who next to Monnet himself was responsible for the eventual success of the European Economic Community and who would later become President Kennedy's Under-Secretary of State. George Ball suggests the essential political reason why there was little American enthusiasm for Britain's Industrial European Free Trade Area scheme, IEFTA.

BALL: The Seven was a concept of a Free Trade Area which would be, in effect, prejudicial to the American position without offering any compensatory political strength to the nations involved; and this seemed to me, to us, to be exactly the thing we didn't want. We didn't want the nations to move into arrangements which were discriminatory against American trade unless there were compensatory political advantages; and we saw no political advantages in this. Indeed, we felt that all this was going to do was to complicate Britain's ultimate relationships with the Continent, which indeed happened. I think the EFTA was a major tactical error from the British point of view.

BUT THE UNIQUE PATTERN of Britain's long-established relationships was still a powerful, if more and more a residual, obstacle. In addition to which, it was tenaciously held in Whitehall that just because the Six had proclaimed an intention to go ahead with a Customs Union called the 'Common Market' – and had made demonstrable progress towards that end – that didn't mean that it would necessarily succeed. On the British side, 'totally and centrally' concerned (to use his own words) in the later stages of the Free Trade Area negotiations, was the Under-Secretary of the Treasury, Sir Frank Figgures.

FIGGURES: There were certain things which you could do and certain things which you could not do – certain things which were excluded by the then inarticulate major premises of political life. Now, there's a very important point here; things in the event don't turn out precisely as they are expected to. The Treaty of Rome in relation to the Messina concept is one of these. The concept of Messina was that there would be created a thoroughgoing Customs Union. Now the concept of a 'Customs Union' is clear. It is almost like one of those things which exists as an idea in the mind of God, except that when you come to implement it, it doesn't look like that.
CHARLTON: Can I press you on that? That's what it became. But when it started that question was left quite deliberately open.

FIGGURES: It was not *de facto* open. What was *de facto* open was the rigidity of the Customs Union. Now it is a fact that, by the time the Treaty of Rome was negotiated and signed, no single case existed in which a member of the Community had to modify its tax or import structure with any territory with which it had previously had special associations. Now that's going very far. But if you take them one by one, you will find not a single case. In other words, the Customs Union was far from complete.

Now, of course if we had been told that that was the sort of structure which was going to emerge, we would have been able to say: Well, that's perfectly all right by us, there's no trouble about that one – or at least, at any rate, the major objections to a Customs Union, which were put, for example, very powerfully in one speech in the House of Commons by Mr Maudling. He said (I'm not quoting, because I haven't got the text): I don't find it conceivable that the day would come when we would have to have a tariff on produce coming from Australia and not a tariff on similar produce coming from Western Germany ... As he said that I'm sure he was expressing something which was more than an inarticulate major premise of politics in those days.

Now, if we had seen that that sort of structure would enable us to maintain the totality of that system, so that we would have maintained imperial preferences, so that we would have maintained free entry for Commonwealth goods into this country, a major objection would have disappeared. But, of course, I'm sure you will appreciate that if we had said: Well, we'll come in on the same basis as you, and that's what it means, the Treaty couldn't have been negotiated. Because that would have meant that the whole of the temperate foodstuff imports from the British Commonwealth would have come into a member of the Community free and for nothing. And that would have totally undermined all the concepts which were developed, both in the early stages and finally in the Treaty of Rome.

THERE, IN A TREASURY perspective, was the British dilemma restated. A dilemma which, even though it might be one to make the angels weep, was one for which the improvisations of existing British policy were proving increasingly inadequate, if not at this stage exhausted.

FIGGURES: I do not think the European Free Trade Area negotiations, which broke down if I remember rightly towards the end of 1958, were intended as a riposte. They were intended as an effort to get as nearly a united Europe as possible, in effect around the kernel of the Six.

CHARLTON: How do you believe or remember that we estimated our bargaining position at this time?

FIGGURES: I can only talk in terms of recollection. I believe myself that through this period we consistently exaggerated our bargaining position. It gradually slipped away, and I think we perhaps did not appreciate it quite quickly enough. I certainly think that there was a general expectation – not everybody shared it – but again, I think, it's important to appreciate that there are many views held by people on these things, people who get deeply involved in negotiations. There were some who said you *won't* get this thing through, you won't get it accepted; you'll run into this, and you'll run into that, difficulty. That was perfectly fair and you had to accept that. But by and large it was thought that it *was* gettable; it was sensible; it was workable. It was no good going for something which was *not* workable. We thought that, with certain difficulties, it *would* be workable. There were sufficient people who were anxious to get us involved in Europe to give us a fair chance of getting it. Yes, that's right. In which, in the end, we turned out to be wrong.

THE LIGHT THAT FAILED

Emmwood's view of how Britain's last great struggle with the Continent before applying to join the Common Market came to grief.

AND HAD THE FRENCH government not fallen Harold Macmillan, for one, believed Plan G *would* have succeeded.

1956 WAS NOT, however, remarkable in Britain for this confusing inchoate struggle over the political and economic future of Europe, but for a single event which had lasting reverberations – Britain's joint invasion with France and Israel of Suez. As Eden put it: 'What are we seeking to do? First and foremost, to stop the fighting, to separate the armies, and to make sure that there's no more fighting. We've stepped in because the United Nations couldn't do so in time.'

The Suez affair led directly to Anthony Eden's resignation (after his break-down), and his replacement as Prime Minister in January 1957 by Harold Macmillan, who had more than shared in Eden's determination to take military action at the beginning. The abandonment of the Suez expedition at US insist-ence, and under the pressure of obloquy at home and abroad, forced a divisive debate and an important revision of Britain's own perceptions of itself as a nation able and willing to sustain a world role. It was that role which Eden had, in reject-ing the European concept for Britain, resolved to uphold.

Some senior Foreign Office figures, like, for example, Roger Makins (Lord Sherfield) who had a large influence upon policy in the 1950s, maintain that Suez was almost the least among post-war crises. They point to the fact that, ironically, within two years the United States and Britain were acting, side by side this time, in another military intervention in the Mediterranean, the Lebanon in 1958.

But the implications of Suez for the way Britain looked at Europe, and itself, were more profound. The Americans and the Russians had combined to stop the British and French from carrying out something they had jointly and sovereignly determined to do in the Middle East. Harold Macmillan spoke in later years of London having to face 'the United States and the Kremlin in this strange coalition'. As he said at the United Nations: 'The United States forced us through offensive and humiliating resolutions – combining with the Russians to knock us about!' In sum, the rival philosophies of the United States and the Soviet Union professing anti-imperialism in common had the effect of suddenly making Britain's elected and preferred role as leader of a global Commonwealth of Nations seem less tenable.

The variety of considered reflections upon the role of the Suez episode in dictating a reappraisal of British policy more properly belongs to the time when Macmillan, having succeeded Eden as Prime Minister, set in motion the funda-mental reassessment which led to Britain's application to join the – by then – burgeoning Common Market, still three years ahead. But Suez did one thing at once. It was a forcing-house of argument and self-examination whose con-sequence was to diminish the plausibility of conducting an *independent* military and defence policy anywhere in the wider world. As one informed insider sub-sequently said: 'Suez presented the biggest challenge to Britain's leadership of the Commonwealth since the American War of Independence.'

This was written in a recent history of a major Department of State, the Commonwealth Office. The author, and that 'informed insider', was its former Permanent Under-Secretary, Joe Garner. Lord Garner makes, in his own mind, the radical link for the evolution of British policy between Suez and Europe.

GARNER: In my view, there's absolutely no doubt there were two major events which changed the British attitude. The first, I would say unhesitatingly, was Suez. It is the fashion, I know, in certain quarters to say that Suez was just a flash in the pan and didn't really matter very much. I think it was enormously significant and enormously symbolic. I think Suez more than anything punctured that Great Power illusion once and for all. We showed ourselves – we showed the world, which was more important – that we could not operate on our own on this sort of scale. This was a great shock. But we accepted it and we drew the conclusions. We took a little time to draw the *full* implications, no doubt, but I think, never after 1956 did we make quite the same claims to operate as a great power in the world as a whole. We realised that our status was different.

That was point number one. Point number two was the Messina Conference which, we thought, stood a very poor chance of getting off the ground. But by the post-Suez era it was clear that not only did the Common Market exist, it was enormously successful. It was prosperous and it was going ahead. And the question therefore faced us, what were we going to do! Our first attempts, of course, were to try and form an Association without the full extent of the Customs Union, but eventually it became clear to us that no Halfway House was possible. We were then faced with the alternative of union or nothing.

AMONG THE SIX, Suez became another stimulus in an accelerating process – the remarkable speed with which, following their declaration of intent at the 'miraculous conference' in Venice in 1956, the Six advanced to the signature of the Treaty of Rome in 1957. The junior minister at the Foreign Office with

The signing of the Rome Treaties which established the Common Market, 25 March 1957.

special responsibility for Europe in Anthony Eden's government, and who resigned over Suez, was Anthony Nutting.

NUTTING: I think as far as the French were concerned it had a very considerable influence. The French, of course, were furious with the Americans, so equally were we, but it made the French all the more convinced that they must go as fast as they could towards European integration because they could not, as they saw it, rely on the United States any longer. Then of course, when the whole thing collapsed, and we and the French fell out indeed, they felt let down by Britain as well. So in that sense I think it undoubtedly helped to speed up the pace of European integration. So far as this country was concerned it just left us in a total vacuum resenting everybody, resenting the French, resenting the Israelis, resenting the Arabs, resenting the Commonwealth, resenting particularly the Americans. British foreign policy was left in a sort of void really, for several years, until we picked ourselves up and said, Well, we've got to go in *some* direction.

IT WAS IN VAIN that Britain argued throughout 1957 and 1958 that the Free Trade Area proposal was a desirable evolution which, by accommodating the British dilemma, increased the prospects for European unity and therefore offered the more practical path, in the long term, to the result the Europeans had shown themselves willing to achieve at once. Acceptance of the British scheme would have slowed the momentum towards the accomplishment of the Treaty of Rome and the Common Market. It would also have posed, of course, a continuing challenge to the Community thesis. More than that, it was a *rejection* of the Community thesis.

Spurred on by France, which had made that radical reappraisal of policy which would not be commissioned by Macmillan in Britain for another three years – a reappraisal which meant France giving up much of her protectionist past and entering open competition with a rapidly reviving Germany inside the new Community – the Europeans, increasingly confident, were no longer willing to wait, or temporise.

The hope, or belief, in London that the Germans in the person of Ludwig Erhard, then Economics Minister, with his declared preference for the Free Trade philosophy, would swing the arguments Britain's way proved to be misplaced. Sir Con O'Neill, who has been called upon throughout for his analysis of the Anglo-German perspectives in Britain's post-war diplomacy, had this to say about our Free Trade Area initiative.

O'NEILL: I never had any personal involvement with these affairs at that time – I had, I think, come back from China – but we did not realise in this country, and I certainly did not realise at the time although I came to realise later, how deeply unpopular our Free Trade Area effort was. Not merely with de Gaulle – who was the man who eventually stymied it – but with most of the Community and, above all, with the Commission. It wasn't unpopular with the Germans. Erhard, you remember, became Chancellor. Erhard was all in favour of our Free Trade Area efforts, *but* for a reason we did not really appreciate. Erhard was in favour of it because he was afraid that we would skim the cream off trade with Scandinavia, Austria and Switzerland. He did not want discrimination to grow up against Germany. That is why he and the German government were all in favour of a Free Trade Area, not because they particularly wanted us in.

CHARLTON: We presumably undertook it in the belief that we could succeed. And I'd like to know why you think we thought we could succeed when we knew it was against American policy wishes. The Americans did not want this to happen because it discriminated against their economic interests without the political result they wanted, of closer political unity in Europe. So we were 'at war' really on two fronts, with the Americans *and* with Europe. Now why did we think we could succeed with this strategy?

O'NEILL: Well, we very nearly did succeed! I think we would have succeeded in creating the Free Trade Area but for the French opposition. Because German support was more or less enough, nearly enough, to neutralise French opposition. And, if you remember, the negotiations were broken off *not* by a common decision of the Six – that *they* would not take part any longer – but in a manner which became rather familiar on a couple of occasions later – by a unilaterial decision by the French that they would not play any longer.

CHARLTON: Then de Gaulle goes and sees Adenauer and gets his agreement to kill the negotiations, doesn't he? Why does Adenauer support de Gaulle over, one assumes, and against the advice of Erhard?

O'NEILL: Well, in the end, I agree, Adenauer *did* support him. Perhaps probably over the advice of Erhard. It was a very crucial moment. If you recollect this was the moment when Adenauer was getting very, very old and when ideas were in the wind for the Franco-German bilateral arrangement which grew up later.

CHARLTON: Their Treaty.

O'NEILL: The Treaty. And Erhard was overruled. But it wasn't a hopeless enterprise. It did very nearly come off.

CHARLTON: So once again we return to this fundamental political fact of France and Germany seeing eye to eye, and us not seeing that they see eye to eye?

O'NEILL: France and Germany being determined that they *must* see eye to eye, even when they don't, so to speak! Being prepared on both sides, but even more so on the German side, to sacrifice a lot to it. The Germans have always been scared – they still are – that they may somehow, sometime, be forced to choose between the French and the Americans. I'm sorry to say that we play very little part in that equation. So far, the Germans have managed to avoid that choice. They've managed to remain loyal to both their allies. The risk is still there for them.

THROUGHOUT 1957 AND 1958 the comparison between the two sets of negotiations in Europe was instructive. Both faced technical difficulties of great complexity and long historical standing. Those in Brussels, which led to the creation of the Common Market, succeeded because the negotiators there were animated by a common political will which in the end was strong enough to solve those problems. The negotiations which Britain conducted in OEEC in Paris to get Europe to agree to the Free Trade Area were caught up, as Spaak once described them, in a 'tangle of largely academic complications'. Be that as it may, they failed because in this instance the negotiators were *not* inspired by the same shared ideal.

The former Director-General of the French Foreign Office, the Quai d'Orsay, Hervé Alphand, offered this distillation of the French analysis of what Britain was trying to achieve.

ALPHAND: It was a normal reaction.
CHARLTON: To do what?
ALPHAND: Well, it was a normal reaction, not being a member of a club, to create another one!

WHEN THE EUROPEANS of the Six turned down the British concept of free trade in industrial goods only between the Common Market countries and the rest of Europe, the central concept of preserving all the British interests and at the same time uniting Europe in a looser, less organic way collapsed. Britain was left leading a peripheral alliance in Europe; and the division of the West between Inner Six and Outer Seven was reinforced rather than erased. The Continent was 'at Sixes and Sevens'.

Sir Frank Figgures, the Under-Secretary of the Treasury, became the Secretary-General of the peripheral alliance of 'little Efta', the smaller European Free Trade Area comprising the outer Seven.[1] He suggested these as the principal contributory strands in the tangled failure of the more all-embracing concept – Britain's last great struggle with the Continent before seeking full membership of the Common Market.

FIGGURES: There was one very important one, and it is quite difficult to evaluate it, but there was the total opposition to these ideas of ours from very many – not all – but very many of those who were most deeply involved with the Community. I don't mean only the national officials but the Community officials. They were very concerned that, if you showed you could do things along other simpler lines, the willingness of the members to put up with doing them in the rather complex ways they thought necessary would be undermined.

There was one specific point about this. You remember this was the period when Erhard was extremely important in the German government and there was a very strong body of opinion behind Erhard . . .
CHARLTON: Who believed in Free Trade?
FIGGURES: That's right. And they were very concerned that, if we had this Free Trade Area an important part of German opinion would have said, What the devil do we want all this structure for, when now here we've got everything which is necessary in this much simpler form. That particular view about Germany was not only shared by the Community officials, in the Commission, but it had its effect, undoubtedly, on many French officials and, I think, was also not without its influence on American officials. You will appreciate that, at this particular period, American officials were *extremely* important in all these matters. There was a time when the United States representative in Brussels was called 'the Tenth Commissioner'!

Now, there is one force, pretty important. The second one was the agricultural one. There was a general appreciation that agriculture was a devil of a problem to deal with. Nonetheless, the concept which was the best that *we* were putting forward was that the extent to which the United Kingdom market was going to be open to Europe was going to be jolly circumscribed! All those

---

[1] The Seven consisted of Britain, Norway, Sweden, Denmark, Austria, Switzerland and Portugal.

who had access to it already were not going to be damaged, nor was British agriculture going to be affected. So the amount left over, whether they were within the Community like the French, or outside the Community like the Danes, was going to be pretty small. This took a lot of the gilt off the ginger-bread – even for those who were keenest. The Dutch were quite keen on this, but the fact that they were not going to get much agricultural advantage must have diminished their enthusiasm.

I think, in the end, it was a feeling that the Community had a better chance of getting off on its own, if it did not have anything tucked around it. The Com-munity was felt to be a very uncertain, difficult exercise. Those who were most concerned to see it succeed, some for very limited, rather introspective, reasons and some for rather big and important reasons, did think it ought to have a chance on its own. So there we are. Three reasons which seem to me to be sufficient to explain why Plan G broke down.

BUT TO HAVE COME as far in the chronology as the actual rejection by the Europeans of Britain's Free Trade Area offensive in 1958 is to anticipate the event which made that rejection inevitable – as opposed to being merely, as it must have seemed, something on the cards.

During the critical time in which France was taking the plunge into the Common Market, the political situation in France itself, because of the colonial war in Algeria, was growing more precarious. And that was another reason why the architects of the Common Market were determined to make haste and not wait for Britain, while they had a pro-European in Guy Mollet at the head of affairs in France. On 1 January 1958 the Treaty of Rome, establishing the Common Market, came into effect.

In the ensuing months, France advanced to the brink of civil war. As the direct result of a military coup in Algiers, by June of 1958 General de Gaulle, after more than a decade in the political wilderness, once more assumed his long-deferred responsibilities for the destiny of France. The last months of that year brought things to a head. They marked the refusal of the British alternative for Europe and, with it, Britain's last attempt to sidestep the Common Market.

For the British this could not be seen as only the failure of a single and very large-scale initiative. It invited a deeper reflection; that it was the exhaustion or end of the road for a whole policy pursued from the earliest post-war years – 'Association' rather than 'Full Involvement'. Sir David Eccles, who had suc-ceeded Peter Thorneycroft (elevated to the Treasury) as President of the Board of Trade, signalled an earlier storm warning while the rival negotiations for Common Market and Free Trade Area were heading for their eventual show-down. In a speech he made to the Commonwealth Chambers of Commerce in June 1957, in which he indicated how Britain viewed – should the Free Trade proposal come to grief – the prospective exclusivity of the Common Market Six, Eccles said: 'Although it is not hostile or military in intent, six countries have signed a treaty in Europe to do exactly what – for hundreds of years – we have always said we could not see done without damage to our own country . . . If we're left outside this, or don't join this, the Germans would run it. Adenauer knows it and he fears it.'

This speech was widely remarked on the Continent and set an undertone as the two sets of negotiations proceeded. Eccles' bluntly-expressed sentiments

were akin to those Macmillan himself would address to General de Gaulle face
to face in the summer of 1958. On 29 June, in Paris, Macmillan was among the
General's first visitors on his return to power. In the Napoleonic code which
was familiar to them both, de Gaulle recounts in his memoirs how Macmillan
suddenly

> declared to me with great feeling: 'The Common Market is the Continental
> System all over again. Britain cannot accept it. I beg you to give it up. Otherwise
> we shall be embarking on a war which will doubtless be economic at first but
> which runs the risk of gradually spreading into other fields!'

Whereupon, the General has said, he tried to pacify the British Prime Minister,
'ignoring his overstatement', and asked him why the United Kingdom should
object to seeing the Six establish a system of preference such as existed inside
the Commonwealth. Thus the General aimed shrewdly for the Achilles heel of
Britain's 'Free Trade' posture – the surviving system of preferential trading
with the Commonwealth.

By November 1958 de Gaulle and the new government of France had
decided, in the General's words, to 'break the spell'. By making it clear that
France would not accept anything which did not include the common external
tariff and provisions for agriculture, the French effectively vetoed the British
design. It was de Gaulle's submission that the Six would be 'dissolved' in the
Free Trade Area sought by Britain.

In December Sir David Eccles proved to be the individual touchpaper in the
forum of the OEEC in Paris when months of mistrust and repressed irritation
between Britain and France suddenly ignited. The Belgian, Baron Snoy, was
present on this occasion as Chairman of the Council of OEEC.

SNOY: You made some mistakes, and I always criticise Eccles for the way he
handled the OEEC meeting. It was the end of 1958. The French had unilaterally said, at a press conference given by the Minister of Information, Jacques
Soustelle, that they did not want to go on with the Free Trade Area negotiation
because Free Trade Area meant different tariff systems for the members,
which was a definition they had accepted some eighteen months before! Then at
the meeting of OEEC, where it was possible to renew the negotiation, instead of
that Eccles had a very arrogant attitude, which was of course accepted by the
French who were taking, on *their* side, a very arrogant attitude – and we had a very
disastrous meeting of the OEEC!

I remember that there were a certain number of possibilities of compromise
agreement, but nobody wanted it. I understood that on the British side, there
was impatience – there had already been impatience in June, and I myself had
flown to London to speak with Maudling and ask him not to take the responsibility for a rupture. I told him it would be unsafe for you and that it is not a good
position for the British. And Maudling complied with my suggestions and we
had a rather good meeting in July 1958 in Paris at the OEEC for the discussion
on the Free Trade Area. Then, of course, I understood that, with the French
move of November 1958, the impatience of the British would become extreme.
CHARLTON: But what was the nature of Eccles' 'arrogance', and why were we
impatient?
SNOY: You were impatient because the French, of course, had taken a position

Britain sets out to organise the Outer Seven of Europe against the Common Market Six. Derick Heathcoat Amory, the Chancellor of the Exchequer, initials the Agreement with Reginald Maudling, President of the Board of Trade.

which was incompatible with the idea of Free Trade Area. The idea of 'renewing contracts' with the European Commission in the Six was that you had to start again a discussion about what was the definition of a Free Trade Area and what kind of result it would have. And Eccles immediately took up a point – I don't remember his words – but everything was broken after he had spoken.

THE BRITISH AMBASSADOR IN PARIS at the time was one of the Foreign Office's most distinguished luminaries in the policy field for over two decades, Gladwyn Jebb. Lord Gladwyn adds this personal anecdote about the last rites of the Free Trade Area proposal and the row which finally buried it.

GLADWYN: The French really made it quite clear that they weren't going to have anything to do with it, in spite of having led us to believe they would have some kind of solution. They then suddenly pulled themselves together and said they wouldn't. Then there was a frightful row and Eccles had pleaded the cause very eloquently and rather indignantly. And he had, more or less, a stand-up row with Couve de Murville.
CHARLTON: Can you remember the row?
GLADWYN: I wasn't there. No, I wasn't there, but I came in afterwards. There was a reception at the Quai d'Orsay for the British delegation to which I was invited. Eccles had just come in. Couve was in a state of great emotion, quivering with emotion, and he looked exactly like a sort of cat who'd been brutally assaulted by a bulldog and who had just gone on quivering. Obviously, you

know, it was a dreadful scene really. Not that he said anything impolite or any-thing like that, but it was purely the atmosphere which was exactly like that.

I think that Eccles thought that the French had more or less indicated they would agree to some kind of solution, I think probably, and then it was rather a shock to him, not unnaturally, when they just said, No, they wouldn't. That meant the end, the final end of all efforts of himself and Maudling.

CHARLTON: You've said that, in a flash, it was only then that we recognised what perhaps we should have recognised many years earlier.

GLADWYN: I think that's true, yes. I think we should have – several years before . . .

CHARLTON: That Europe was being organised, not just without us . . .

GLADWYN: No, but potentially against us, yes.

ALGIERS IMPINGES ON THIS STORY of Britain and Europe in an oddly dis-connected but interesting way. Events there, in 1958, had been the cause of the return to power in France of the single figure who would now come to fill Britain's European universe for the decade to come, General de Gaulle. Long years before, in the 1940s, before the outcome of World War II had determined Europe's immediate future, Harold Macmillan had been in Algiers too, rubbing shoulders with the French, when he was installed (as it was said) as 'Viceroy of the Mediterranean' by Churchill.

Then it had been Britain's finest and France's darkest hour. This time in 1958, while Macmillan and de Gaulle were each at the head of affairs of proud nation-states, the fortunes of war were about to be reversed. France had ended the decade of the 1950s with a clear calculation and a new purpose. It was firmly dismissive of any further compromise with British attempts to have it both ways. And often that voice of France spoke through someone else who had been in Algiers in the wartime years, and who was now de Gaulle's Foreign Minister, Maurice Couve de Murville.

COUVE DE MURVILLE: We believed that the good direction was the Common Market and not the Free Trade Area. I would say, philosophically, because the Common Market was more in our tradition than Free Trade. France has never been a free-trade country, and it believes more in organisation. The Common Market was not only free trade for industrial production but also a future agriculture common policy; and that's a thing to which we were very much attached, for the reason simply that agricultural production is important in our country. So we could not accept the British idea. We accepted the Common Market, and inevitably a sort of conflict was to appear between Britain and the Common Market countries.

CHARLTON: Macmillan seems to have placed a lot of reliance on Ludwig Erhard's view prevailing. Why do you think he was wrong?

COUVE DE MURVILLE: He was wrong to rely too much on Erhard simply because the Germans, when it came to a real decision, were bound by the fact that they had signed the Rome Treaty. They were bound to stick with their partners. They couldn't go their own way against the others.

CHARLTON: But did you regard it as a rather balanced situation at this time, or did you see Macmillan's proposal as a rather desperate move by the British to . . . ?

COUVE DE MURVILLE: I would rather qualify it as a desperate move in order to prevent the entry into force of the Rome Treaty. I mean it was the last, the last effort to avoid what they considered and which was in fact – at least temporarily – the break between Britain and the Continent.

THE BRITISH THEMSELVES would claim that the Free Trade Area scheme was more important, and more creditable to their European thinking, than that; and that its existence probably caused the economic policies of the Common Market to be less inward-looking than they might otherwise have been. But throughout this decade of the 1950s, now drawing to a close, Britain had been overwhelmed by her own outdated vision of Europe. The inheritance of a set of ancestral ideas induced a pervasive scepticism which blighted the judgement of what the Europeans intended or were capable of achieving.

Jean Monnet's prophecy that the British would make the fundamental change in their traditional policy towards the Continent only when they saw the new Community was working was about to be fulfilled. It was. And they would.

8

The Channel Crossing

WHEN HAROLD MACMILLAN SUCCEEDED Anthony Eden as Prime Minister in 1957, he took a piece of No. 10 Downing Street notepaper and wrote out, in his own hand, these words from a Gilbert and Sullivan opera, *The Gondoliers*: 'Quiet, calm deliberation disentangles every knot . . .' This jaunty philosophy he stuck with a pin to the green-baize door which separated the Cabinet Room from the Private Office in No. 10. It became the signature tune of the Macmillan years of government, which lasted from 1957 until 1963. He made it a watchword for all at Downing Street as he set out to restore the lost national self-confidence of Britain and keep the country buoyant in the sea of troubles which flooded in upon it in the bitter, divisive aftermath of the Suez failure – and after what was becoming obvious by 1958: the breakdown of the European policy.

In Macmillan's own case, as he has confided to us in his memoirs, 'quiet, calm deliberation' often masked some 'sickening anxieties'. As far as the European issue was concerned, his motto masked also a new sense of urgency which was taking hold with the belated but growing awareness that time was no longer on Britain's side.

Macmillan found the broad sweep of history and its Toynbeean perspectives attractive to him and instructive. Some years after he had stepped down from office himself he reflected for the BBC upon the great change he was now about to accomplish for Britain in these words.

MACMILLAN: When I was a boy the Europeans ruled the world. A civilisation which started about 2500 years ago was centred on the Mediterranean, spread to Gaul and Britain, with smaller numbers of people centred around the North Sea, and the Mediterranean ruled the world, the whole world. And what did Europe do with those years? They did what the Greek city states did. They tore themselves apart in two terrible wars, lasting ten years of my lifetime, in which they destroyed each other – for the Africans, the Asians, the Russians and all the rest to see. But they lost their supremacy. So I've always thought that Europe is not all that important economically; I think we argue too much about the economics; we may have to pay more, I don't know about that. It's important politically because it's the only hope of restoring the influence of Europe; and Britain should play her part in that.

IT WILL NO DOUBT remain a question of lasting historical inquiry and interpretation why it was that Britain so completely changed her mind between 1955 (when after Messina she had withdrawn from the talks which founded the

Common Market and thereby passed up a major say in the form it assumed) and 1960 (when that decision was put into reverse). No one is more closely informed about the context in which this historic decision was taken than the man to whom Harold Macmillan entrusted the ensuing negotiations and who, ten years afterwards, as Prime Minister himself, succeeded in taking Britain into the European Community.

In Edward Heath's view, was there perhaps one controlling factor which, in the end, decided Macmillan to make the Channel crossing and strike out for Europe in 1961?

HEATH: First of all, you must remember that this was a Cabinet decision. It wasn't just a Prime Ministerial decision. The great majority of the members of the Cabinet felt strongly that our future lay with Europe, and many of them (including my generation) had made up our minds about this a long time before. What we found was that it hadn't been possible to bring it about. When, therefore, there seemed to be a further opportunity of bringing it about, naturally we were in support of it. I think that's a very important factor. It wasn't just Harold Macmillan. Macmillan, of course, had been one of the leading politicians in the 1940s in the European movement, and in the Conference at the Hague, and in urging Churchill to work for this in the new post-war world. That didn't alter the fact that, although some Cabinet members took a slightly different view and perhaps were more concerned about particular aspects of the negotiations (like the future of British farmers under the Common Agricultural Policy), it was a Cabinet decision in which the great majority were firmly and strongly behind making an application to join the Community.

CHARLTON: When did that majority occur? Because it wasn't there at the time of Messina, when we turned it down.

HEATH: You can't say it occurred at any one particular point. I think that, as we had our discussions in Europe from the summer of 1960 onwards, and saw what the attitudes of the different countries were and what the possibilities were, then gradually the Cabinet recognised that they would move to a point at which they would have to decide whether or not to make an application. And I felt that as we moved along so their minds were gradually being made up. I'd have thought the question which had to be asked was why, after the late 1940s and the great meeting in the Hague, did those who had taken part in this movement, and spoken so prominently in the Conference, then appear to do so little for the next decade about getting Britain into the Community.

CHARLTON: Do you have an answer?

HEATH: I think it's a combination of answers. I think, first of all, when the Conservative Party came into power in 1951 it was so preoccupied with the economic crisis that it didn't have very much time for thinking in European terms. I think there were others, too, who discouraged Jean Monnet in 1950 when he came to discuss the Coal and Steel Community. There were those who thought, like Anthony Eden, still in terms of the 'three circles' of which we were at the centre; and being in the centre, it did not involve being a member of the European Community. It meant working very closely with the Commonwealth, although they were independent countries, and working closely with the USA. So it's a combination of those attitudes. There were also some, of course, who didn't believe that the European Communities were going to last, that they

Britain opens negotiations for membership of the European Community. The French Foreign Minister Couve de Murville with Edward Heath, Lord Privy Seal, and Christopher Soames, Minister of Agriculture, Brussels 1962.

were purely ephemeral and after a short period of months or a year would then disappear. It was when they were proved to be wrong that it was recognised that this was a major development in European unity.

EDWARD HEATH LEAVES US in small doubt that he considers Britain's European diplomacy for most of the decade of the 1950s to have been an aberration – an interruption to the logic established by Churchill and Macmillan in their promotion of the movement for European unity, from which they had then held back and, most notably in the case of Anthony Eden, never accepted. In this sense the Cabinet's approaching reversal of policy, as the decade of the 1960s began, was not the result of any sudden reappraisal but rather the resumption of the former path from which Britain had strayed.

Mr Heath, who had made a remarkable (because it was an almost uniquely 'European') maiden speech in the House of Commons over the Schuman Plan in 1950, when he had advocated full and immediate participation in the Coal and Steel Community, considers it was 'a gradual making up of minds', confronted by an inexorable accumulation of signs and portents which pointed the way to Europe.

By 1958, with Anthony Eden's departure and the failure under Macmillan of what proved to be Britain's last attempt to sidestep the issue posed by the successful creation of the Common Market – the rejection by the Six (at the instigation of General de Gaulle) of Britain's alternative scheme of an industrial Free Trade Area – Britain faced exclusion from the markets of Europe and from consultation over Europe's decisions. In consequence, the European issue was becoming for the Prime Minister the dominant theme. The stakes had become very high. Britain's whole trading position and her role and place in the world were all, and at once, seen to be in question. Two factors, not foreseen by the Foreign Office in recommending Britain's negative decisions over Europe in the 1950s, had by the time the decade ended become heavyweights in a new balance of considerations. They were the competitive failure of British industry, and the return to power in France of Charles de Gaulle. The Foreign Office line had been that – even if the Continental Europeans brought off the unity to which they aspired and about which London remained determinedly sceptical – it would always be possible for Britain to change her mind and join later. But by 1958 both views were becoming dramatically less tenable. The Common Market was a demonstrable success; and de Gaulle had closed the door on Britain's efforts to go on having it both ways.

In short, the existing policy had failed. It had failed to prevent the creation of a new, powerful, and rival economic system to that of Britain and the Commonwealth. More exactly, by the end of the 1950s it had failed to find some hyphen, or bridge, between the two.

The evidence is that, by itself, the breakdown of the European policy with the collapse of the Free Trade Area scheme was not sufficient to make the Prime Minister contemplate initiating the vital change. On the contrary, the evidence is that throughout 1958 and 1959, his long pro-European credentials notwithstanding, Mr Macmillan was still doing what he could to avoid it. This is how he looked at the situation in 1958 in the immediate aftermath of his defeat by General de Gaulle in the matter of the Free Trade Area. Harold Macmillan's senior Foreign Office aide and Principal Private Secretary throughout his government was Sir Philip de Zulueta.

ZULUETA: I think he was rather depressed and rather worried. He did have a conception of Europe – not quite de Gaulle's conception of Europe 'from the Atlantic to the Urals' – but at any rate a Europe comprising, not just the Six, but including Scandinavia and Switzerland and Greece and the Iberian peninsula. He thought of Europe in a much bigger sense – like the Roman Empire really, if you like. So he did not like the idea that there were more divisions being created in Europe, and which he saw might happen with the Six and the non-Six.

I don't think, at that stage, he really seriously thought that Britain simply ought to join the EEC. At least that is not my impression, my recollection. I think again, for the reasons we had had in the past, there appeared to be very great difficulties, primarily Commonwealth difficulties – and also difficulties with our own agricultural policy – which appeared to be too difficult to overcome at that moment.

EARLIER MENTION HAS BEEN MADE of the confidential survey of the European policy commissioned among the major Departments of State in Whitehall, which was completed just *after* Britain's withdrawal from the Messina negotiations in Brussels in 1955. This appraisal was in the hands of Sir Burke Trend (later the Cabinet Secretary) reporting to the sub-committee of Cabinet known aromatically, it seems, as HOPS (Home and Overseas Policy Studies), presided over by Rab Butler. It was on the basis of this report – hostile to the seeking of full membership as far as I have been able to ascertain – that Britain took her stand over the first attempts to form the Common Market.

It was this report which had armed both Anthony Eden's and Rab Butler's rejection of Europe in the face of Macmillan's more enthusiastic attitudes in 1955 to the relaunching of the movement for European unity. It remained the basis of British policy now, with Macmillan, as Philip de Zulueta tells us, 'depressed and worried' by the failure of the Free Trade Area.

ZULUETA: A document of that sort, once it has gone through all the imprimatur of the various committees and so forth, is in itself fairly definite. I mean that there is no point then in reopening it. If any civil servant or anybody else starts saying, Well, let's look at the question of Britain joining the EEC, somebody will say, But haven't you heard of the Trend Report, or whoever it may be? And so it does, in a sense, stop discussion. And that is its purpose. It is to bring the matter to a head and decide it, one way or the other, for the time being.
CHARLTON: So it more or less precludes urgent reconsideration of any particular aspect, does it?
ZULUETA: Yes. I mean it would be something which could only then be reopened, as indeed this issue was ultimately reopened, by the Prime Minister himself – if you continue with the same government, obviously. It would not be reopened otherwise unless the Prime Minister, at any rate, agreed to reopen it.
CHARLTON: And the assumptions that Britain *had* to make some sort of choice, as the Europeans and the Americans saw it – Mr Macmillan seems to be rejecting all this as late as 1959, would you agree?
ZULUETA: I think he would have liked to have found a way of avoiding it, yes. I think that's right.

ONE HAS TO LOOK, therefore, between 1958 and 1960, for one or more additional considerations which, allied with the process described by Edward Heath as 'a gradual making-up of minds', tipped the scales for the Prime Minister and brought the minds of others around to come to a wholly new conclusion about Britain's place in Europe. One of these new considerations was to be added to the deeper reflections which were following in the wake of the Suez affair. Suez had been more than a demonstration – it was proof – that Britain was no longer mistress of all that she held to be vital and which was accessible to her by sea. Not since the capture by Japan of the great naval base at Singapore during the war had there been such painful confirmation that an era in which Britain had been a maritime great power was indeed passing.

Harold Macmillan cast the aftermath of Suez in a European dimension. France and Britain had been met with the unnatural combination of Russia and the United States. It seemed, he wrote in his memoirs, to be a 'portent' and

'alarming' – 'never before in history had Western Europe proved so weak . . .'
So, more than the deflation of national pride, Suez had for Britain – as Edward
Heath corroborates – this fundamental implication.

HEATH: That we were no longer able on our own, or even with France, to
carry through a political-military policy in any part of the world. Suez was followed, of course, by a very considerable anti-American feeling.

THE ANGLO-AMERICAN RELATIONSHIP, while it was quickly repaired in the
warmth of the personal friendship between Macmillan and Eisenhower was
thereafter never perhaps quite the same.

Hard on the heels of the more considered reflections of what Suez had
portended came one of the additional and symbolic strategic issues which led
Britain to make the change of course in 1960. It arose out of the major defence
review conducted in 1957 and it concerned nuclear weapons. The start of
Harold Macmillan's Prime Ministership in 1957 also ushered in the wintry dawn
of the age of the intercontinental missile. In that year the Russians fired into
orbit around the Earth the first man-made satellite, *Sputnik*.

The *Sputnik* was greeted with a wild surmise. It was visible from opposite
ends of the Earth in what seemed an instant. It was out of reach and coercive,
high and mighty. An Australian concert audience in the Sydney Town Hall
could emerge at the interval on a summer night and watch it travel the night sky,
devouring distances which had seemed illimitable; as it fell below the horizon
they could know that the rocket was coming up in winter over the cities of
Europe. More perhaps than by Suez itself, the whole military and strategic context for Britain was transformed by this event. The British Defence Review of
1957 took account of both. It marked the start of a new era. As a result of it the
Government decided to develop and maintain a British nuclear deterrent. The
British hydrogen bomb was to be carried on a long-range British rocket,
capable of striking any presumed enemy and called Blue Streak. Yet within
three years of this major strategic decision the Government abandoned the
project. It was too costly, and already informed military judgement considered it
obsolescent.

The chain of nuclear decisions made after the cancellation of Blue Streak
threw a long shadow in terms of Britain's European diplomacy. They were
later seized upon as the basis for the fundamental differences which arose
between Macmillan and de Gaulle, and which now lay just over the horizon.
But Suez and the missile age together acted as a powerful wrench on Britain
from her traditional moorings as a maritime power accustomed to exercising a
worldwide and independent influence. The enforced cancellation of Blue
Streak threw into sharper relief the questions which were being posed by the
evident inadequacy of purely national resources – on the scale of those then
available to Britain – to keep station in the new world after the war. The
corollary of that was undoubtedly to give the theory of the large internal market
(upon which the European Community's Common Market is based) a wider
appreciation and respect in London. The abandonment of Blue Streak was stark
proof that a purely national nuclear deterrent was going to be very difficult to
sustain.

One can see emerging, with growing plausibility, the new coalition of ideas born of economic constraints and the consequent loss of political freedom, particularly as at this very time the Common Market had become a fact and Western Europe was embarking on a period of unprecedented growth and prosperity.

HEATH: I think the economic argument was important in the minds of a large number of people. There were some against entry into the European Community, who would argue that it was an even balance as to whether we would go in, or whether we would lose, or whether the situation would remain the same. I think, again, the majority felt that on all grounds we ought to benefit. And if we couldn't benefit by going into a Community in which tariff barriers against us (and other protectionist devices against us) were going to be dismantled and finally abolished, then we certainly weren't going to succeed in the outside world in which they remained against us.
CHARLTON: But would you give those economic factors greater weight than the political consideration that something was growing up in Western Europe?
HEATH: It varied very much with different people, different backgrounds. Obviously the industrialists in the City of London looked for the economic factors. I think a lot of the politicians looked at the political consequences.
CHARLTON: Yourself?
HEATH: Well, I have always put the political consequences first. And that doesn't mean to say that I in any way underestimated the economic opportunities. I thought they were very great indeed.
CHARLTON: Did you mean it to be something which stood on its own two feet, independent between the Soviet Union and the Americans, having a character and personality of its own? Many people think that a 'Third Force' Europe inevitably meant neutralisation. How did you see it?
HEATH: I saw it as a development which would give Europe a firm basis for political stability, which would therefore prevent any part of it from wanting to move towards the East and the Soviet bloc. This particularly applied to Western Germany wanting reunification with the East. Of course, I recognise that, as it became more and more powerful, economically strong, then Europe was bound to play a much larger part in world affairs. But this was not going to make it neutral as between East and West; of course not; and it was not going to make it anti-American. We both had the same interests and therefore we would be working together. It might be that in the long run we could persuade the Soviet bloc to become more liberal, but that was obviously a very long-term affair. It was summed up really by President Kennedy in 1962, when he said the Atlantic Alliance is bound to be based on two pillars, one on each side of the Atlantic. Of course, you can't have a very satisfactory basis if one pillar is much taller and rounder than the other pillar. You've got to have a balance. It's rather interesting that we're just getting into that stage now.

THE ENFORCED CANCELLATION of Blue Streak is not seriously disputed as a new reality which began to concentrate the mind of the British government wonderfully. Rab Butler, when I asked whether he would call it a critically important factor leading to reappraisal of the old policy, said simply, 'Yes, I would'.
    However, in this particular instance the need for a decision pointed, unhelp-

fully, in two directions at once. To Europe, in terms of place and the fraternity which comes with the sharing of a common dilemma. To Europe also, and the recovery in the long term – through the broader economic base of the European economic system – of the capability to conduct an effective European political and military strategy. For by this time Britain's economic crises were coming to her like some undulant fever, with the bouts recurring at shorter and shorter intervals. Then, again, it pointed to the United States, in terms of an immediate replacement for Blue Streak, which had proved to be the last sputtering candle of an all-British independent nuclear deterrent. The Americans alone had the technology and the equipment to maintain Britain as a nuclear power. In both dimensions, therefore, the nuclear issue assumed for Harold Macmillan in 1960 the greatest importance.

ZULUETA: The problem which we had, and have, on advanced defence and advanced weapons is that, whereas the United States can probably afford to start off work on half a dozen – ultimately taking them a long way down the line and finally finding that one, or maybe two, can be pursued – our difficulty is, and was, that we probably can't afford to pursue more than one, or at most two. Therefore, of course, you may get it going because you are taking a decision on whether to go ahead with an idea which won't be realised for between five and ten years and it is extremely difficult to do!

Macmillan believed very strongly that the existence of a British 'Independent' deterrent was tremendously important, not only for us but also for Europe, because it was a trip-wire, or call it what you like. At any rate, it was something which prevented us from suffering from some deal maybe done between the United States and the Soviet Union, which everybody hoped would never happen and probably wouldn't. But nevertheless, it was a slight danger perhaps in the back of his mind. And of course it was the view which de Gaulle subsequently took rather more strongly and vociferously. I think also there was an element of the feeling that the prestige of having a nuclear weapon of your own enabled you to have a seat at what was laughingly called 'the top table', which meant that you had perhaps rather more influence on world affairs than you would have otherwise. This also was important.

CHARLTON: But does Macmillan, at the time the Defence review is undertaken – and it's a very profound one with implications for these famous and hitherto unassailable obligations to the Commonwealth – is he thinking of Europe at this time? Is this an approach to Europe in essence, or is he undecided? Could it still be an 'independent role' for the country at heart?

ZULUETA: Well, I think, like all Prime Ministers, he wanted to keep as many of his options open as long as he could. Which, after all, is essential.

CHARLTON: But still at this stage he had not thought of a fundamental reappraisal?

ZULUETA: I don't think so. I mean, that's not my recollection.

HOWEVER, THE CRISIS imposed by the cancellation of Blue Streak sensibly increased the uncomfortable general knowledge that, in 1960, Britain was scrambling. Scrambling in the wake of developments in Europe; scrambling by suddenly having to shop off the peg in the United States for the very symbols of independent nationhood and the means of remaining an effective nuclear power. It inevitably augmented a feeling, coming as it did within only three years of a major overhaul of defence priorities, that Britain lacked a coherent policy.

In order to plug the hole left by Blue Streak, the Prime Minister turned unequivocally to the United States, and there to his old wartime friend and companion-in-arms, President Eisenhower. He reached an agreement with Eisenhower in 1960, in which he secured as a substitute for Blue Streak an American missile called Skybolt, somewhat less ambitious in strategic capabilities, but which could be carried by the manned bombers of the RAF. Mr Macmillan also had an unspecific promise of the Polaris submarine missile for the indefinite future. (Polaris was then emerging as the ultimate in global strategic weapons.) In return the Prime Minister agreed with the President that the USA could establish the American nuclear submarine base at Holy Loch in Scotland for their own Polaris submarines. These necessarily hurried decisions predisposed the defence politics of Britain for many years ahead. Skybolt and Polaris were to become the totems of great and fundamental argument, first between the British and the Americans, and above all between de Gaulle and the Anglo-Saxons – the General seeing in the ease of the Macmillan–Eisenhower partnership the wartime hegemony of Churchill and Roosevelt, his own exclusion from which he so bitterly deplored.

If, then, it was not Blue Streak, what was it in 1960 that might be called the last milepost on Britain's Damascus road leading her to seek entry to the European Community? The evidence is that it was a political event. In 1959 Macmillan was labouring mightily in the desolate vineyard of East–West relations to launch, as an independent British inititiave, what would today be called '*Détente*'. He had worked to bring about an annual meeting of the leaders of the Western and Eastern blocs, and had got Eisenhower and Khrushchev and de Gaulle and Adenauer to agree to a first summit meeting to be held in Paris in May 1960. The context was that of the greatly increased tensions brought about by the start of the missile age, and nuclear testing in the atmosphere. The immediate objective was a ban on such tests as a start on disarmament. The Prime Minister was acting in the face of very considerable opposition from both the Americans and the French, who were sceptical that a basis for agreement existed, and the suspicions of the Germans who thought that any compromise with the Russians would be at the expense of German interests at a time when the Russians were resuming the threat of Stalin's old challenge to the whole Western position in Berlin.

The leaders of East and West duly assembled in Paris. Whereupon the elaborate edifice Macmillan had built collapsed. An American spy plane, the U2, looking for the new Russian intercontinental rockets, had been shot down over the Soviet Union. The plane, the pilot and his pictures were in Russian hands. Overlooking the fact that the Russian satellite was flying over everybody's national territory, Khrushchev created such a furore over the U2 incident that the Summit never really began. It was a fiasco. It suggested clearly that Britain was playing a role no longer commensurate with her power. It was his perception of the failure of the Summit which, in the opinion of the Foreign Office aide who was very close to the Prime Minister throughout these years, was of decisive importance for Harold Macmillan.

May 1960: the failure of the East-West summit after the shooting down of U2. General de Gaulle, Harold Macmillan and President Eisenhower.

ZULUETA: My own opinion is that the failure of the 1960 Summit was really crucial in the development of his concept in Europe, because at that Summit it became apparent that he really couldn't, by himself, bring irreconcilable American and Russian positions closer. General de Gaulle just washed his hands of it and said the whole thing had been decided in advance in Moscow, anyway, and there was no point in arguing, and really wasn't intensely worried on the subject.

CHARLTON: How do you remember Macmillan reacted to the failure of the Paris Summit?

ZULUETA: Well, I've never seen Macmillan so upset and distressed, because (as he says, I think, again in his book) it was the failure of something that he'd been working for, the collapse of something which he'd been working for for several years, namely some kind of a *Détente* between the Soviet Union and the United States, with Britain and France, but particularly Britain, acting as the go-betweens, if you like. He found that it couldn't really; and I think this led him to think very much again about what the British position was in the world. The colonial empire was, if not gone, rapidly going, the Commonwealth obviously not being really strong enough, coherent enough, as an economic force. So what does Britain do? How does she play a part in the world? What does she do in the future?

CHARLTON: You were a close observer at this time, a trusted confidant as well as a senior official. What do you remember of Macmillan's own personal odyssey from this moment onwards? What were the strands, what became the controlling factors? Was there a moment, do you think, when he decided?

ZULUETA: I don't think there was a day on which he suddenly decided, you know, Europe is the thing. But certainly he moved, from then onwards, really rather fast in the direction of feeling that this was the right road for Britain to follow, and that Europe was going to be united, and that without being part of it Britain would neither be important on its own nor play a part in a wider grouping.

AND SO, IN THE FIRST HALF OF 1960, Harold Macmillan directed that all the assumptions upon which British foreign policy had stood since the Second World War were to be looked at afresh. In the wake of the rejection by General de Gaulle of the British proposal of the Industrial Free Trade Area in 1958, Britain was by now conducting essentially a holding operation in Europe, as the political competition for the future between the Six of the Common Market and the Outer Seven countries of EFTA intensified.

The European Free Trade Association was an attempt by Britain to avert the danger of seduction of the other countries, one by one, into the Common Market orbit. Now, at Macmillan's behest, the whole British situation and position was to be subjected to analysis and profound re-examination. At the official level this was done under the supervision of the new head of the Treasury, Sir Frank Lee, who had moved over from the Board of Trade. All the relevant departments of state in Whitehall were involved at many levels. Christopher Soames, one of the few who have seen the results of that still 'most confidential' inquiry, was soon to be given by Harold Macmillan an appointment of critical importance as Minister of Agriculture.

SOAMES: The Prime Minister had asked for a paper on Europe – first of all on the pros and cons, and secondly on the possibilities. And the paper came out really saying that there were more pros than cons in the interests of the country, but that the difficulties were enormous and that probably the country wasn't ready for it yet. And, in particular, our agricultural policy wasn't going to fit in with what the Continental one was likely to be. This was going to affect a lot of our relationships with the Commonwealth and all that, and the difficulties seemed very great. This paper didn't have very wide circulation, but enough to those on the need-to-know basis.
CHARLTON: This was Sir Frank Lee's paper?
SOAMES: That's right. I mean, this is my memory of it; it's a long time now since I read it. It looked rather bleak at that time for those who felt that we ought to be going in and that we were missing a bus. Well, we had indeed missed it, because the Treaty of Rome had been signed and we hadn't been there. We'd gone in with the other grouping – the European grouping of EFTA, which was tiny compared with the Community in terms of trading importance. As I say, it looked rather bleak.

THE PAPER PRODUCED BY Sir Frank Lee's interdepartmental inquiry was closely linked with the deliberations of the special sub-committee of the Cabinet known as HOPS. Macmillan appointed as chairman of this Cabinet committee a figure who was of crucial importance to him in the handling of the whole European question, R. A. Butler. It had been Rab Butler who, as Chancellor of the Exchequer, had principally taken the decision (together with Eden) to say 'No' to the invitation to take part in the formation of the Common Market at the end of 1955. At this time, in 1960, he was Home Secretary, and soon to be appointed First Secretary of State. This is Lord Butler's recollection of the significance of the role played by HOPS and its findings.

BUTLER: Well, as usual I'll tell it to you from the inside. I think the first reason that I was appointed was because the Prime Minister felt that I hadn't been any too well treated, and he was always friendly with me. At that date the succession to the leadership was not settled by any means; and at that date in many ways I was the senior, right up to the end, in the succession. But I think they thought: here is a job, a big job for Butler in the Cabinet. That's the first point; and the much more important point was that they wanted the correlation of the hitherto backward Foreign Office and hitherto backward Treasury (except, fortunately, for Frank Lee) to be brought to the front. Frank Lee of course developed more and more in favour, and at the Board of Trade he was always behind it.
CHARLTON: But how would you summarise the findings of that committee? Were they neutral?
BUTLER: That committee didn't meet as often as history either may or may

not relate; but it did bring together the facts, and it did lead to Harold Macmillan's eventual decision that we must make the further bid for Europe. There is no doubt it did. You see, it was the only committee at which you could produce a memorandum next morning because it is already composed from the minutes and things, you see. So in that way I *did* help Europe.

THE SITUATION HAD BECOME not unlike some paraphrase of Macaulay's *Lays of Ancient Rome.* Those who had been 'behind' were now crying 'Forward!' Macmillan himself was already standing on the farther shore of the European argument. In the appointment of Sir Frank Lee as the new head of the Treasury, the choice had been made of the man who would be foremost in leading the attack within Whitehall, and later in Europe itself, to produce the basis for a successful reversal of policy. Lord Butler, when he spoke of the hitherto 'backward' Treasury and Foreign Office, clearly infers that the view of Macmillan's Cabinet at this time was that Whitehall had been too inflexible in its thinking and too rigid in its advice. Sir Frank Lee's role (both the man and his appointment) had therefore a profound importance. One of his closest colleagues at this time, in Whitehall and during Lee's time at the Board of Trade, was its Second Secretary – Sir Herbert Andrew.

ANDREW: He was a human dynamo! He had an extraordinary capacity for work. He was fluent, quick and never devious. He was open and easy in discussion. He never took a line that pounced on his opponents or tried to whittle them down. He argued patiently and cheerfully. I think he was not a political economist of any rigid or fervent views; and to some extent I think Frank judged, as I think many people do in Whitehall (the likeable ones!), he judged the men as much as the argument. He was a great leader of men, and he was always a most exciting person to work with, and work for.

But he was, of course, a civil servant through and through, and I think he became interested in the European idea when Ministers became interested in it. He rarely wasted his energies on things that Ministers were *not* interested in! But once this came over the horizon, he went into it to see just how far we could move, and what we could do, and what the main stumbling blocks would be, in an extraordinarily quick and perceptive way; and the kind of headings under which our application – Mr Heath's opening speech which was published as a White Paper, I think – and all that – all the breaking down of this large and vague and forbidding subject into some kind of workable unit was very largely Frank Lee's work – and it was done in a very short space of time.

CHARLTON: Presumably it is of the greatest significance that he becomes the keystone, the lynchpin of our whole negotiating structure?

ANDREW: Yes. I don't think there was anyone else about at the time who could have done it.

CHARLTON: But his impact on Whitehall must be rather profound? After all he had had many predecessors and they have chosen to think differently – albeit in different circumstances. It would seem that, with Lee, the whole thing changes?

ANDREW: He, in effect, was told to look at things again. And he looked at them again, to see what the possibilities were. No, there was no one else. I think the people who were good all-rounders in Whitehall at the time were too rigid in their views one way or the other – too rigid in their thinking. And Frank had the confidence of the Treasury and the Foreign Office to a greater extent than any other person from outside those departments does.

CHARLTON: Yet it would seem to me that he doesn't look at it quite like an agnostic – or if he does he rather quickly becomes a true believer?

ANDREW: That is, I think, to take a view of the great civil servant which Frank was – which is not quite the role they're playing. He looked at it to see what was the best that could be made of our position. That involves, I suppose, appearing to have a certain enthusiasm for it. But I think if Frank had been told to think of conclusive reasons why we could *not* go in, then he would have produced a very convincing table of things.

CHARLTON: What encourages me to ask is something he says to one of the senior Americans, to George Ball, in 1961. Ball regarded it as a most significant moment; Lee says to him that he does not shrink from the political implications of the European Community. Now Ball is a known protagonist of European integration, a colleague and friend of Jean Monnet's from the beginning. I just wondered whether Frank Lee had advanced to that stage?

ANDREW: I think it is fair to say that Frank *did* believe in it, but not the phrase 'true believer'. It implies a man whose mind is closed to any alternative. He believed in it in a very English way – in terms that 'something was possible here' rather than 'something *must* be done at any cost'. I don't think he would have said that we should pay any price. I think he felt that we could pay, in political terms, quite a stiff price.

THE ATMOSPHERE IN WHICH the reappraisal of policy in 1960 was conducted in Whitehall was one of some continuing scepticism that the success of the Europeans, while manifest, would prove durable. Herbert Andrew recalled that, in Whitehall, few people held an absolutely clear view, but that there was still a feeling that the demolition of the old tariff barriers within Europe would cease, and that endemic protectionism might suddenly erupt, whereupon the whole European enterprise, striking that ancient continental rock, would founder.

While this view was held with diminishing confidence, Europe was seen as a lesser importance, by some even as trivial, compared with the issues of world trade and world finance which were thought to be dominated by the dollar and the Americans. Looking back, this view which had its origins in Keynesian thinking had become an obsession, which (according to Sir Herbert Andrew) had lasted too long in Whitehall. Sir Herbert Andrew, Second Secretary at the Board of Trade, later led the trade negotiations for Britain's entry to the Common Market.

ANDREW: We rather prided ourselves, I think, on 'thinking bigger' than the Europeans – I speak here entirely from my impressions of the time rather than from anything in our policy or from anything that anybody said or wrote. We were the one country in Europe which had not been beaten; and to take a collection of losers and join them, and turn our backs on the rest of the world, seemed to us in a curious way – looking as we look at it now, it seems curious – to be turning our back on the future. I think this is quite important, not so much in the arguments that people used but in the emotions that were behind it. I remember in 1960 Frank Lee wrote a piece about Europe and ended with the quotation from Pitt: 'We saved England by our exertions, now to save Europe by our example'. Or something to that effect. I wrote a piece producing some counter-arguments which ended with the bit from Shaw's *Apple Cart* where King Magnus says we're all melting down into a world of wops. And that didn't seem to me at the time – I changed my view later – to be the right thing for us to do.

CHARLTON: Sounds like an echo of the argument Churchill used about the European Defence Community, 'a sludgy amalgam'.

ANDREW: Yes, it is, yes, yes. I think there was the same thought there.

IN JULY 1960 Macmillan carried out a Cabinet reshuffle which had, in view of the men he choose, an unmistakable significance for the treatment of the European issue. Three new appointments were made in areas which were critical for any decision over Europe, and which would need to be carried before any major reappraisal: the Commonwealth, the Conservative Party, and Europe itself. The Opposition, the House of Commons, and the Country would come later. Because the Foreign Secretary, Lord Home, had his seat in the Upper House, the Prime Minister needed a Cabinet member in the Commons. He moved Edward Heath to the Foreign Office, with wide responsibilities as Lord Privy Seal for exploring the whole issue with the Europeans. Duncan Sandys (who from his house in Pimlico had organised the 'European Movement' Churchill had led at the Hague Conference in 1948) went to the Commonwealth Office. Christopher Soames (who had married Churchill's daughter Mary, and had been the old leader's Parliamentary Private Secretary, and was serving as Secretary of State for War) took over as Minister for Agriculture. All three had strong pro-European beliefs. It ensured that, in any re-examination of the whole question, it would be lent a more sympathetic ear than it had had in the past. The intentions of the new moves, clearly intriguing to all concerned, were not openly declared by the Prime Minister at the time. For example, upon accepting his new job from Harold Macmillan in July 1960, Christopher Soames tried to draw him out.

SOAMES: I remember asking him at the time – I didn't know about the other two – but when he put me into Agriculture, I said: Are you putting me there because you want me to edge towards Europe? I mean, is this what you're thinking in terms of? And he said: Well, he didn't think it was possible, alas, at that time, because he'd seen the Frank Lee Paper. It all looked rather difficult, perhaps too difficult for the present . . . So I went away for the summer holidays and ruminated about my new job and took a lot of papers away with me. And I decided then that we were going to have to change our agricultural support policy anyway, because we couldn't afford to go on. The subsidies were too great. A greater share of the farmer's price had to be borne by the market. And this was going to be what the Continental system was to be based on, so I didn't see why this should stop us. I didn't agree, then, with this Paper.

CHARLTON: That's an absolutely crucial point, if I may interrupt you for a moment. You're saying that the Agricultural Policy was not changed because you had collectively determined to edge towards Europe, but it would have had to be changed anyway because the level of support necessary for our own domestic policy was beyond the ability of the country to carry.

SOAMES: Well, it was very high. It was higher than was in our interests. It had to be paid for out of taxation; and also it was so difficult to determine what the sum was going to be. I remember in fact that it was in that very year, 1960–1 I think, that I had a supplementary estimate of £100 million (which was then a great deal of money; probably the equivalent of a billion today), £100 million for the cost of agricultural support, because the bottom fell out of the grain market, and the bill for subsidies became enormous. So it seemed to me indeed (and this happened after I thought it was going to, I'd seen it coming as it were) we were, at any rate to some extent, going to shift the burden from the taxpayer to the consumer, to the market place. This was going to happen. I remember saying to the Prime Minister: We'll look rather silly if this is the reason we don't join – and then we go and do it ourselves.

I knew Harold Macmillan as a man who had very much an overall strategic political concept, and I know in my heart that he always wanted this country to be a part of the Community, a leading part of the Community. He thought that's where Britain's destiny lay. I'm sure, looking back on it – although he mightn't have said it when I asked him a direct question, he might have said 'No' because he used the Frank Lee Paper – there's no doubt in my mind he was thinking that this was what he needed to do, this was what was necessary to do, to take Britain into Europe.

LORD SOAMES ALSO RECALLED that at this time the Prime Minister had handed him a paper, which he himself had written, about the future of Britain. This set of personal reflections noted the fast-receding position of Britain as the heart of an Empire and Commonwealth. It emphasised the rapid changes affecting the British position everywhere, and it ended with Macmillan concluding for his part that Britain could no longer carry the necessary weight, economically or politically, outside Europe. It seems clear that the Prime Minister was letting fall some elegant 'cues' in the path of at least one of his new triumvirate of Ministers.

The major overhaul of British policy was confidently in train. The chancelleries of Europe braced themselves for the next round. And it was with a Shakespearian 'Now let it work' that the Foreign Office awaited further developments from the yeast of Europe's dangerous division. They were quick in coming – and from an unexpected direction, the one for which Edward Heath had been given special responsibilities.

HEATH: In the previous summer, the view had been taken that the European Free Trade Association had been established; and that certainly for some considerable time ahead there was no possibility of making any further progress. Then, to everyone's surprise, in August Dr Adenauer proposed a meeting between himself and the Prime Minister. The Prime Minister and Lord Home went to Bonn. After that the Italian invitation followed; I went and had talks with Rome; and that was followed in September by talks in Paris. Then the exploratory talks were completed with all the other countries. It was on the results of that that the Prime Minister decided it was timely to make an application to join the Community.

THE SIGNIFICANCE OF the new ministerial appointments was therefore at once apparent. The talk is no longer of close forms of association with Europe, but of full membership of the European Economic Community. So often accused of 'missing the boat' and ignoring its opportunities, there were this time clear indications of an important shift by London. Dr Adenauer's invitation was construed as 'movement', a bit of 'give' in a situation which had become hard and set. It had come following the failure of the Summit between East and West in Paris, which Macmillan had arranged and which, it has been suggested, had a decisive impact on his own thinking about Europe. While the Prime Minister had deplored, in a showdown at the time, 'the Germans selling out everything to the French' (as he put it) when they had gone along with de Gaulle's determination to reject the Free Trade Area proposal, Macmillan now detected, in these suddenly warmer intimations from Dr Adenauer, a moment to be seized.

HEATH: I think Dr Adenauer's invitation was made because he felt that Europe was in fact going to drift into two camps, and in view of his attitude towards the Soviet bloc this, from his point of view, was very undesirable. He may not have wanted to increase the size of the Community, but he certainly didn't want to have half of Western Europe going in one direction and half in the other.

DR ADENAUER HAD THEREFORE let it be known in his present mood of disenchantment that he wanted a Europe which included the United Kingdom. The opportunity his overtures signalled was not lost on any of the newly appointed Ministers. Christopher Soames had concluded by the autumn of 1960 that British agricultural policy could and should be changed, and that now might be the time to say so. When he heard of the Adenauer–Macmillan meeting, Soames headed at once for Downing Street.

SOAMES: I put this point to him, and I said this: Brussels shouldn't stand in your way – and if you're going to talk about Europe to Adenauer, do have this in the back of your mind. Now is not the moment to go into details, but I think I'm convinced myself that we're going to have to change anyway. And it rather flowed on from there . . . I told him my thinking on how we'd have to change the agricultural policy. He then asked Rab Butler to come in, who was then deputy Prime Minister and was rather the keeper of quite a number of Conservative consciences, including the conscience of the countryside. We talked, the three of us. And I think that Rab – in fact I know he did – saw that this was probably right thinking. If we had to change, well, then, let's change in a way that was in the best interests of the country.
CHARLTON: Now, Butler played a crucial role over the Messina meetings a long time before, and he's never been pro-European. Did his opposition at this point collapse in the face of what you said about the need to change the agricultural policy, or . . .
SOAMES: Yes, I think it did really. I remember very well: we spent an hour (I'm not sure whether we had lunch together), just the three of us . . . I know Macmillan said, I'd like you to talk to Rab about this; let's have a talk, the three of us; and we did . . . I'm not saying that he immediately saw it; but I think he went away and chewed it over – and he's a careful thinking man, Rab – and

he thought it over, and he said, I think, Yes, I accept this. But mark you, this sort of fell into Harold Macmillan's lap.

IT HAS BEEN POINTED OUT already that Rab Butler was, in terms of party and country, a crucially important figure to Harold Macmillan in heading for Europe. He carried great weight in the Cabinet; and in the arts of Cabinet government, as elsewhere, the Prime Minister made his moves with subtlety but with clear purpose. In giving to Butler 'that big job inside the Cabinet' the Prime Minister had deeply involved him in the reconsideration of British attitudes that was taking place. By locating him at the very centre of these activities he made it, presumably, more difficult for Butler, had he so chosen, to oppose the intended change or challenge Mr Macmillan's leadership of it. Here is the personal odyssey of 'a careful-thinking Englishman' at that time of incipient historical change by Britain over Europe.

BUTLER: Well, you see, the funny part is that at first, before 1959, I was doubtful about the wisdom of going into Europe, and I was actuated by the fact that all my life I'd represented a farming constituency; and all my life I'd been connected in one way or other with the NFU, National Farmers' Union. I couldn't conceive that the farmers – who, I still believe, although not a majority in politics, are at the bottom of the Conservative Party – I couldn't believe them wanting to yield their annual price review, as you remember it was called, to French and Germans, especially to the French. I knew the French, having lived in France, and I was partly educated in France, I knew of the enormous political power of French peasants in agriculture, which still exists today, and that's why Giscard was always so jealous at our meetings when farm prices came on. You see, I thought that we should be done in. But then I had a long talk with Harold, and he brought me round very cleverly. He asked me to go and talk to some of the branches in the North, in Yorkshire, and I'd been talking in Essex and other parts, and although I had a fairly rough time I did put the case, and eventually the NFU came out very much in favour. That affected me.

CHARLTON: Were you speaking against your own convictions . . . Macmillan having got you to have another look at this question of being in Europe?

BUTLER: Well, I was doubtful because of the farmers, and therefore the more I met them, the more I thought I'd be able to make up my own mind. Although one or two of the meetings, especially the one in Essex, were a bit rough I began to see that the farmers thought that they would get just as good a deal (as it turned out, in fact, especially with Peter Walker, one who's been very clever, the present Minister).

CHARLTON: But the Agricultural lobby, of course, was very powerful then?

BUTLER: Well, the funny thing about it is that it wasn't so much that the lobby was powerful – because it's very small, isn't it – but *I* was powerful, that is to say, I was a farmer and I thought that we were going to lose on it. Then I still turned a little bit to my past in the OEEC in Paris, where I'd been so proud of running it without any trouble, that I hesitated . . .

I'd always foreseen that de Gaulle was going to be a great nuisance – because I met de Gaulle when he first came over, with Winston, and you know how rude he was to him. De Gaulle, of course, had a most wonderful patriotic record for

his own country, but he didn't want us. The reason he didn't want us was – a
very simple reason, you see – that he thought we might take the lead from him.

IT WAS WITH VARYING DEGREES of apprehension or comforting illusion that
de Gaulle was perceived as a possibly insurmountable or, alternatively, a
negotiable obstacle. Encounters with the Constable of France were at this stage
some distance further off.

Before such a momentous decision could finally be recommended by the
Cabinet there was the question of US attitudes. As we have seen, American
support for the economic and political integration of Western Europe had been
remarkably consistent throughout the years after the Second World War. By
the end of 1960 the Eisenhower administration had ended as the US had
elected a new President, John Kennedy. Macmillan had been exercised by the
disparity in years between himself and so youthful a figure; the need to be seen
to be open to new ideas and fresh thinking probably assumed a certain
additional importance.

Kennedy had appointed as Under-Secretary of State someone who, in retrospect, must be seen to have exerted a considerable authority upon the fundamental choices made by Britain. This was George Ball, of Cornish ancestry, a
lawyer born in Illinois. He proved to be among the most influential of the
Americans concerned with the making of policy who had come to Britain and
Europe through those Western windows in the light of the Lend-Lease agreements and America's entry into the war. He was a man of prodigious and
muscular energies, with an aroused intellect. He had subsequently become
deeply involved in the economics and the politics of Europe from the Schuman
Plan onwards, as Jean Monnet's lawyer and his intimate friend. As the winter of
1960 turned to the spring of 1961, both London and Washington were preparing
for Macmillan's visit to Kennedy; Ball had come to London for that reason.
And in the light of an all-important answer which he returned at a critical
moment in the last stages of the reappraisal of British policy, and later was
instrumental in persuading the young President of the United States to repeat,
George Ball's interventions rank alongside those of Monnet himself at earlier
stages of European unity.

It was on this visit to London in March 1961 that Ball received an invitation
from an old and personal friend, Sir Frank Lee, the new Permanent Under-
Secretary of the Treasury, to come to a meeting at which he found Edward
Heath was also present.

BALL: It was at this meeting that we were told by Lee and then by Heath that
Britain was considering seriously a change of policy, and was examining it.
Then the question was put to me: How would the United States react if Britain
should make the decision to apply for membership in the European Community? The fact that Lee was the one who initiated this was, as far as I was
concerned, an indication to me that policy was being rethought – because I
knew his views, we had had long talks about it in the past. He was very frank in
what he said, and he was very frank in this March meeting (as I knew he would
be because I knew generally what his views were). He said that as far as he was
concerned they were perfectly prepared to accept the idea of moving towards
some kind of a federation. I was both surprised and elated. Both Frank Lee and

Ted Heath made it quite clear what the motivating reasons were; and, as I remember them, perhaps the dominant one was the feeling that Britain could simply not afford to be outside the new dynamism that Europe was achieving through the building of the Community. If it did, there would be a certain atrophying of the industrial strength of Britain – and American investment would come to the Community, it wouldn't come to Britain. It would be, in other words, outside the mainstream of policy.

CHARLTON: So the dynamic (or relatively dynamic) economic growth on the Continent has had its effect?

BALL: It had already had its effect, and to this extent it was a kind of validation of the Monnet thesis about what British reactions would be. Also (and they were quite explicit in saying this) EFTA was not proving to be an adequate counter or an adequate substitute for membership in the European Community.

Now, I was put on a bit of a spot, because I had never discussed this matter with President Kennedy except in a very generalised way. I had written some 'task force' reports in which I had strongly recommended an American support for Europe. So when I was asked specifically by Heath and Lee what the American attitude would be, I replied that I don't know whether I'm making American policy or interpreting it, but I will tell you quite frankly what it is – and I did it with some personal trepidation because I didn't know what kind of hell I would get from the President when I got home . . .

CHARLTON: So you didn't have a mandate?

BALL: I didn't have a mandate at all, but I was quite prepared to give them an answer because I felt that there was only one policy for the United States – and I must say that the President supported me fully. I was in no trouble at all.

CHARLTON: When the Prime Minister comes to Washington for his meeting with the young President, what advice do you give to Kennedy about how to deal with Macmillan? While you have had a meeting which excites and exhilarates you in London – the British are coming round – you still have to deal with this presumably very important and not unsubtle political figure who has come to Washington to talk to the President.

BALL: Well, what I told – or wrote to – the President primarily at that time was: If Macmillan asks this question and we reply, we should reply in rather specific terms; that if the British (and these were almost the words that I had used in the March meeting, which I again used and which I told the President were what I thought a proper American appraisal must be), that if Great Britain were to make application for membership in adherence to the Rome Treaty, and do so in the recognition that the Rome Treaty was not a static document but indeed was a process leading toward greater and greater unity, including political unity, and might even ultimately lead to some kind of confederal or federal system for Europe – that I thought this would be a great contribution to the cohesion of the West and indeed to the strength of the whole non-Communist world. But that we would not favour any British move if the intention of that move was to water down the Treaty of Rome, or to try to transform the Community into anything that would be simply a loose consultative arrangement.

So that when Macmillan did come over, and almost the first question that was put to the President by the Prime Minister was the one that had been put to me in London, the President said, 'I'd like George Ball to answer that'.

CHARLTON: And that question is what? What exactly had Heath said to you in London?

BALL: How would the United States feel if Britain were to make a decision to apply for membership in the European Community?

CHARLTON: And Macmillan put the same question to Kennedy?

BALL: Exactly the same question to Kennedy, and Kennedy then said, 'Well, I think I will ask George Ball to answer that for you'.

CHARLTON: And Kennedy having called on *you* at this meeting to put the American position can have left Macmillan few doubts whether Kennedy was, in fact, a supporter?

BALL: I think he left Macmillan in *no* doubt; and I think Macmillan himself felt enormously pleased by this.

GEORGE BALL HAD BEEN DELEGATED in the presence of, and by, the American President to give a vastly important reply to Harold Macmillan's question. How was it that John Kennedy came to take up his position over Britain in Europe? He had had to make up his mind within three months of his inauguration as President. The Assistant Under-Secretary of State in the new American administration, and deputy to George Ball, was Robert Schaetzel. He had special responsibilities for American policy in Europe.

SCHAETZEL: One ought to go back a little bit to the Stevenson report. After Adlai Stevenson had made an unsuccessful effort to become Democratic candidate, he withdrew and became part of the successful Kennedy effort. Kennedy, I think, as a political gesture – a domestic political gesture rather than a quest for foreign policy insight – brought in Stevenson to do a report on foreign affairs for him. Stevenson turned this report over to George Ball, and George had a group which included Tom Finletter and David Bruce. And I was working directly to George on that. It was a report which really did what a report on foreign policy in my view ought to do – which was to try to put things together in a kind of strategic package, to give a man a picture to start off with, a check list of items of things which are desirable.

Given George Ball's long association with Jean Monnet, it was quite natural that the theme of this would be the importance of uniting Europe and that this is where American policy ought to come down. It was delivered to Kennedy the day after the election in Florida. The only thing I know for certain is that he spilt scrambled eggs on it! But the point is, that report is the document he read from November to January; and on which he had time to read and an opportunity to reflect. He was apparently impressed by it.

George Ball, bear in mind, was a very forceful character in all this! He was sort of 'given' European Affairs by Dean Rusk – who was not much interested in the area. George took that over gladly and he ran with it! He became in effect Secretary of State for European Affairs. So that with George in that position – and Kennedy I don't think ever thoroughly understood this, but he had a kind of sympathy for it and at critical points would say the right thing – but there was a detachment to Kennedy about this European idea which was very different from Eisenhower's quite evident commitment to it.

CHARLTON: Which only makes Ball a more significant figure really?

SCHAETZEL: I think Ball was absolutely crucial in the whole thing.

CHARLTON: The available record shows, I think, that the British were hanging on, hoping that the new Kennedy administration would not take up the involved and, as they saw it, emotional commitment that Dulles and Eisenhower had had to Jean Monnet and to 'Europe'.

SCHAETZEL: I'm unable to recall having an explicit feeling that the British had this anticipation of a more congenial group with whom they might be working! Except, if anybody had asked me the question I would have said that I would anticipate it! No one particularly knew what Kennedy's position on these issues might be. He had had this association with Britain; his father had been Ambassador there and so forth. I think it was a not unreasonable hope for any British government to have, that this was a fellow they could either get on their side or manipulate. I think they overlooked the fact that Ball was an extremely strong individual at the very beginning, knowing a lot more about European politics than anybody else around.

I think all of us shared – not because we were tutored by Monnet – but shared for, I think, many of the same reasons the feeling that it was just wrong for Britain to be out. It was wrong for two absolutely crucial reasons. One was the belief that Britain had a contribution to make to this process which was absolutely unique – the whole gift of 'carpentry' in government which exceeds that, I think, of any country on the Continent, including the French. So we felt that there was a positive contribution to be made by Britain in the construction of Europe, and the strengthening of Europe, which would make it better able to carry out the global tasks that people in support of this policy believed would be one of the end results. The other is a negative. That was, as long as Britain was out, Europe was incomplete. There were divisions within Europe – most notably with the Netherlands and with the Italians – each country fearing it was going to be dominated by these powerful countries, France and Germany. These two considerations were always in mind and were always the goal. So that while we were fighting the British because of what we felt was their bloody-mindedness on 'Europe', on the other hand the hope that was always there was that they'd come out of their slumbers and see the thing straight, and then we'd get to work!

CHARLTON: What survives in your memory of the cardinal meeting in London, in March 1961, between Frank Lee and George Ball – with Ted Heath there too?

SCHAETZEL: This was one of my more vivid memories. There was this long-term, intimate relationship between George Ball and Sir Frank Lee going back to their wartime association and Lend-Lease. Neither George nor I had been forewarned at all. I know I wasn't, and I don't think George was, but Frank Lee announced, and obviously this wasn't casual, that a decision had been taken by the government to seek membership of the Community and, in a sense, invited the American reaction.

Ball's reaction, and mine, was total surprise! In other words, after all these years of British fighting and spoiling, this sudden decision, announced without any forewarning, was a very exciting event indeed. Ball's response was essentially enthusiastic. 'Don't worry – nothing would please the American government more!' I, reacting as his assistant and a bloody-minded bureaucrat, sort of demurred by saying, Well, this is your personal view! Or something to that effect. Trying, I think, to protect George from saying something which he was not in a position to say until after there had been discussion in Washington! But George Ball was absolutely right. I may be rationalising the whole episode, but this was very early in the new Administration, and the pecking order of the various characters was not by any means clear. Ball's position then was not what it became in, say, the latter part of the Administration or the Lyndon Johnson Administration. But he was very strong and forceful. He had no difficulty when he got back to Washington.

CHARLTON: I think, from what I've heard so far, there are a handful of people – but in vital positions – who were completely committed to the policy of uniting Europe and to the form that unity was taking?

SCHAETZEL: That's right. I'm happy to have been among the people who were from the very beginning firm supporters of the idea of a United Europe. I suppose the policy statement which has gotten the greatest attention was President Kennedy's speech in Philadelphia in July of 1962 which spoke of the twin pillars and of Atlantic partnership. It's sort of interesting, just as a footnote to that, it moved Dean Acheson, the 'corporation lawyer', to say when Monnet would talk about equal partnership – Acheson would splutter and say, 'I've spent most of my life in a firm made up of partners and I've never seen an *equal* partner yet!'

But yes, the Monnet idea – the strong institution with a gradual transfer of sovereignty from the member states to this; and something which is frequently overloooked by the critics – no desire by the United States to dominate the entity. Now, that was the belief of the 'Believers'. I would say that the other forces in American policy probably did not prevail because, first of all, they were not equal believers in whatever their policies were. They tended to be 'observers'. In other words, they were not committed much, one way or the other. And it was like watching a horse race. If the horse won, fine! I think perhaps that would describe Kennedy and Rusk, McNamara, McGeorge Bundy and others. There were very few who were *enthusiastic* supporters of this policy.

Whether it was conscious or inadvertent, or through association or osmosis, George Ball and, I think, the people working with him in a way were reflecting the pattern of Monnet's genius, and the way he was achieving things within governments. Those of us who worked with Monnet became enormously impressed by this man's skill in having, on the one hand, a large idea – which he pursued tenaciously – and yet an infinite capacity to manipulate, to move, and to persuade governments of that from the bottom on up. It was an idea which was fairly simple but very important, which when it was once fixed in one's mind then an awful lot of things just automatically fell into place. Once the concept and the strategy were clear, then you didn't need any new orders. An alert bureaucrat knew that he had to attack on this and defend on that. And that was really the Monnet tactic. That meant that a very few people were in a very powerful position. They had the idea itself and they were positioned at strategic points.

FACE TO FACE, the British Prime Minister had consulted the American President and he was now armed with the knowledge that the United States positively welcomed a decision by Britain to attempt to enter the European Community. Macmillan returned to London to address the formidable task of urging a revolutionary change of principle in attitudes to Europe upon his Cabinet, the Commons, the Commonwealth and the country.

A 'Vicky' cartoon of the period shows Macmillan as Laocoon, the centrepiece of one of the most famous of all classical sculptures. In it 'MacLaocoon', a figure of surpassing bodily pain and passion, is depicted wrestling mightily in the toils of monstrous constraints which coil around him like vines of iron – de Gaulle, Adenauer, Europe of the Six, and the Seven, NATO, the Commonwealth, Khrushchev, and the H-bomb. 'Vicky' was highlighting, with a classical anology, what had by now become the popular image of Macmillan, and which had produced his sobriquet 'Supermac' as common currency in the Press.

Following the visit to Kennedy, by the summer of 1961 the pace over Europe was quickening, but there was still no firm policy approved by the Cabinet. As a result of Sir Frank Lee's review of policy in Whitehall, carried out at Macmillan's request, the vastly intricate skein of British interests and trading relationships had been 'reshuffled'. The main threads were now laid before Cabinet ministers for their consideration.

The keenest reservations were entwined around the issue of Agriculture. This was so both in the United Kingdom, where it was of crucial importance in Conservative Party politics and also because the potentially rival figure to Macmillan's leadership and the new direction over Europe – R. A. Butler – was centrally concerned and had to be securely won over; and also in the Commonwealth where it directly affected the historical, albeit unsettled, relationship with 'the British farms abroad'.

One of those most closely concerned in the new look at policy in Whitehall, particularly in this all-important sector of Agriculture, was Eric Roll, the Deputy Secretary of the Ministry of Agriculture, brought into the post when the review was undertaken. Lord Roll was subsequently the senior official and deputy leader (under Edward Heath) of the negotiations in Brussels for British entry to the Community from 1961 to 1963. Sir Frank Lee's review, under the thirty-year rule, is still of course obscured from public view. However, we might properly suppose that Lord Roll knows of its detailed considerations intimately. They were considerations which made the case, of course, for what was a turning-point in British history.

ROLL: Take the economic side first. I think the recurrent balance of payments crises, and the increasingly obvious lagging of the British economy and of British industry, behind other countries in productivity and other things, is one factor. You know, a sort of feeling that, well, we can't really go on like this! That was number one. Number two, the Commonwealth connection. In the economic sphere this was becoming more and more difficult to maintain in its full state. If you take, for example, what became such an important issue in the negotiations – namely, the foodstuffs from the temperate zone (which works in together with our own agricultural problem), the maintenance of the markets for, say, New Zealand dairy products, or Australian meat, or wheat, was beginning to create more and more tensions, and more and more conflicts as our *own* agricultural interests increased. As, for example, our desire to trade with *other* countries – for American wheat, Canadian wheat. We were partly being pushed by them, and partly because, for our own reasons, we wanted to be freer to deal there. All that had become much more difficult to maintain.

Now, on our own agricultural front there was the system of deficiency payments. This was a very ingenious one, and a very suitable one for our situation
because it provided support for the farmers while at the same time enabling us
to import from wherever we wanted to – the cost falling on the taxpayer and not
on the consumer. That was becoming increasingly difficult; and each price
review – I happen to know this from my own experience – was becoming
increasingly difficult from a ministerial point of view. The interests, if you like,
of the Chancellor of the Exchequer and the Minister of Agriculture were getting further and further apart, and the cost of the system more and more
difficult.

On the political front, again, the process of Commonwealth independence
and transformation into the new sort of Commonwealth was gathering pace – it
had almost been completed by then in all its essence. Here again conflicting
tendencies were beginning to be seen. Some of the Commonwealth countries,
for certain purposes, wanted us to hold fast to the Ottawa System[1] and to the
political connections. Others, for their own reasons, wanted to be freer in
economic matters and so on.

You could say, although this is an overdramatic way of putting it, the stage
was set – both on the political and the economic fronts – for facing up to this
underlying dilemma much more clearly. At the same time, I think the American
attitude had become much more clear-cut in support of European integration.
Therefore the argument that we were risking pushing the Americans into
isolation became less and less tenable. It was perfectly plain that the most
vigorous and powerful exponents of American foreign policy were very anxious
that we should join in, and very anxious to see European integration succeed.
Furthermore – and this is where Monnet has been proved right again and again,
and certainly on this point – there had always been a certain doubt in the minds
of people in Whitehall and Westminster whether the efforts of Monnet and
Schuman and Pleven and all the rest of them were going to succeed, and therefore that was another reason for holding back. Why get into a vessel which was
being sort of put together and may prove to be totally unseaworthy? Monnet
always used to say the best way of convincing the British to come in – since they
are realists – is to make a success of it. As soon as they see it is going to be a
success they'll *want* to come in! By 1960 more and more people in London were
beginning to be convinced that this thing *was* going to go on and we'd better be
in.

Perhaps I might give you one interesting example of this, which I think was
important at the time. Agriculture was of course alongside the Commonwealth,
probably the most important single issue. John Hare (Lord Blakenham), then
the Minister of Agriculture, commissioned a study, under instructions from the
Prime Minister I suppose, on what the consequences of the Common Agricultural Policy would be. Well, you know, civil servants, even when they cease to be
civil servants, are under certain constraints, so I can't tell you too much about
that; but the interesting thing about it was that this study in Whitehall, which
was a very elaborate one, produced an enormous report. I was chairman of the

[1] The Ottawa System took its name from the Imperial Economic Conference at Ottawa in 1932
where 'imperial preferences' between the Dominions and the United Kingdom were codified and
established. Britain, for instance, introduced tariffs on non-Empire wheat and butter in return for
the Dominions increasing the preferences they gave to British goods.

working party which produced it. This was taking place at the time when the Six were working out the Common Agricultural Policy – in other words, we were trying to assess the consequences of something which did not yet exist and which was still being formed.

But I remember my own conclusion, which I presented to ministers with this 'working party' report. I took the view that we could not square the circle. It was *impossible* to have a common agricultural policy, or indeed an agricultural policy of our own, which could be totally satisfactory to the Exchequer, to the consumer, to the Commonwealth, and to the British farmer. You just could not reconcile all these four interests!

CHARLTON: Therefore, what was the recommendation you made?

ROLL: My recommendation was that the quicker we got *in*, the more chance we would have to get as much reconciliation of these factors as was possible.

I mention that, simply because it was rather indicative of a number of things that were happening at the time in regard to what was taking place on the other side of the channel. In other words, people were beginning to see that this *was* going to happen, and more and more people were saying, Well, if it *is* going to happen and if it *is* going to be successful, can we really afford to be out of it? And if the answer is, We can't *afford* to be out of it, isn't there a case for saying we want to be in on the *formation* of this, so that we can be sure that it contains fewer embarrassments than it otherwise would.

CHARLTON: But the decision to change direction for this country, after 300 years or so of the 'imperial' experience, must still have been a bit of a shock in Whitehall? At least one imagines it must have been?

ROLL: I believe that even the most ardent protagonists of negotiating and, if at all possible, getting in from Macmillan's 'hour' – whatever they may have felt about political union and 'federalism' as a sort of distant idea – did not think this was a real issue. I believe, therefore, that there was always this feeling that – however successful the European Community was going to be, and that we ought to be in it because it *was* going to be successful – it would fundamentally be an *economic* union, and its political consequences would be very slow to appear.

Obviously once you get into bed economically, other things will happen! But I mention this because, I think, this was said to be the ultimate safeguard. This is why all the question of sovereignty was rather pooh-poohed by most people, because they did not think it was going to be a real issue. I think they proved to be right. In the event, even if we had not joined and if the Six had been on their own, I believe it is very doubtful if the federalist idea would have got very much further.

I remember at the Commonwealth Conference in September 1962, when Macmillan made his great exposition – I was sitting behind him in the row of officials at Marlborough House – and he started off by talking about 'This great problem of nationality and sovereignty which must be in everybody's mind . . .' – marvellous performance it was – and suddenly he seemed to go into a sort of trance! He threw his head back and started to philosophise about what really constituted nationality: and he argued this back and forth with himself, aloud. He finally came to the conclusion that 'language' was really the essence of nationality. I can tell you that most of the people around the table, who shall be nameless, the Commonwealth Prime Ministers, did not know what on earth he was talking about! It was rather typical because I don't think, fundamentallly, he thought this was really something that was going to happen in the next twenty, thirty, forty, fifty years – this 'federalism'. It was a long way off. Therefore we were not really taking such a great risk, and if, in the end, in thirty years' time or a hundred years' time, we did have a federal Europe, so what?

CHARLTON: So can you compare then the findings of the Home and Overseas Policy Committee's review, as between the one which Burke Trend [Lord Trend] undertook and which produced the hostile recommendations at the time of Messina to full involvement in Europe, and the one carried out by Sir Frank Lee? How strong was Lee's recommendation for Europe?

ROLL: You will have me up under the Official Secrets Act if you're not careful! But I don't know that I would qualify the work of these committees and their reports in quite such stark terms as you did. Whitehall, generally speaking, and in the absence of a clear-cut ministerial decision, is very much apt to put alternatives – a very proper thing for officials to do – and point out the likely consequences of different courses; perhaps with a loading this way or that way but, in the end, leaving the decision pretty open.

I think the economic arguments were both positive and negative. Negative, in the sense of what we ourselves were likely to have to put up with and looking ahead to the consequences of balance of payments forecasts, industrial development forecasts, growth, productivity and all the rest of it, on the one side. And positive, the opening up of great markets or, again negative, what competitive power they were going to have compared with us. It prevailed in the end. This is really all it did, with the addition perhaps of the argument that NATO still seemed in pretty good shape at that time as far as the French were concerned. Since we had NATO, since the Americans themselves were very keen on European integration, since federation was a long way off in everybody's mind, it is not surprising that, in the end, the economic balance of the argument prevailed. But also, in the end, these things are matters very much of political judgement; I mean political in the widest sense of the word.

I don't think it is a case of the official advice saying, You jolly well have to negotiate with Europe! That's not the way it is done. It presents the arguments. The arguments seem to point in the direction of negotiation. You are not saying, 'We are going to go in', full stop: but a negotiation to see what the terms could be; which is the way it was presented at the time, and, indeed, the way it was. Of course you could say, in retrospect, that once you've said that, you're virtually committed.

BY THE SUMMER OF 1961 Macmillan had put his tactical mastery of the opinions and passions of such men to the test in the Cabinet. A final meeting of all the ministers took place at Chequers. The die was cast.

SOAMES: It was for me a *fait accompli* before it started. What we did was, we really worked out how we would get there. I think that it was understood by then that this was where we were going; and then Heath was put in overall charge of the negotiations. But the Chequers meeting finalised the ministerial decision, the Cabinet decision, as it were.

CHARLTON: Do you recall the combination of those two things – Cabinet and Chequers – as being dramatic in any way, or was it decided rather quickly?

SOAMES: The Chequers meeting was quite long, half a day or a day. It was open to people, you know, to put their point of view, but undoubtedly it was agreed. It was there that it was agreed. But it never crossed my mind that it wouldn't be. Because who was speaking against it? I mean, the Commonwealth Secretary, Duncan Sandys, wanted it: I thought it was right; Heath thought it was right. And, above all, the Prime Minister thought it was right. And Rab Butler thought it was right. (And so did a lot of others.) It was then decided that we would go for it.

THE CABINET TOOK ITS DECISION on 27 July 1961. Four days later, on 31 July, the formal announcement was made in the House of Commons of the Government's intention to apply to accede to the Treaty of Rome. Britain had set out to make the Channel crossing.

The British decision was, in essence, a political one. The recovery, the maintenance, of a sufficient sovereign power and influence in the second half of the twentieth century had been judged, after 'quiet, calm deliberation' – Harold Macmillan's calculated misnomer for this period of urgent, enforced reconsideration of Britain's whole position in the world – to lie in membership of the European Community.

But 'what country, friends, is this?' The magnificent vagueness of 'Europe' would now be put to the rigorous proof of protracted negotiations. The glow and force of the conception had to be communicated to the public mind, to the Commonwealth – and to General de Gaulle.

9

The Great Refusal

A FEW MILES FROM Hyde Park Corner in London, where the Plantagenet and Tudor monarchs once hunted in the deer parks – and on what is today a royal golf course – a singular impression has been made in the earth of England. It is a small crater, which has been preserved against the encroachment of seasonal growth for more than sixty years now. It forms no intentional part of the architecture of the venerable golf course or its activities, and it has not been tended for that reason alone. This curiosity is marked with a small marble headstone which records, with an eye on history, that the hole in the ground was made by a German bomb dropped, not in the course of the Second, but during the First World War of 1914–18.

It is almost inconceivable that such an event, which incidentally caused no loss of life, would be at once commemorated and for so long remembered anywhere else in Europe! That eight-foot-diameter hole must have an extra dimension, something which must reflect more than the sense of outrage or indignity aroused, presumably, at the time. It might, I think, be seen as an eccentric little monument to something even less welcome than that early, intrusive bomb itself – to the shock that was felt at the ending of a prolonged historical immunity. It is a mark, I believe, of the beginning of a fitful public awareness that, in that sudden dwarfing of the geography of Europe, the long and privileged exclusiveness and seclusion of Britain was breaking down. But it is also a reminder of how that immunity was cherished, and the tenacity with which it would still be defended as Harold Macmillan moved to reverse Britain's historical policy over Europe.

The decision of the British Cabinet on 27 July 1961 to make a formal application to join the European Economic Community was, as the Prime Minister said, a turning-point in British history. It signalled the return of Britain to the active pursuit of involvement and ambitions on the Continent of Europe. Such an involvement had been sedulously avoided for 400 years, since Mary Tudor lost the last of Britain's continental possessions, Calais, in the sixteenth century. For four centuries after that symbol of national disgrace and painful humiliation Britain had fought as hard to steer clear of close involvement in Europe as she had once fought to maintain it. But now, in 1961, that another empire and other possessions overseas had been lost, and that Britain had quit India and was being hustled out of Africa by what Harold Macmillan called 'the winds of change', he had judged that a fitful public awareness must be brought to accept that Britain had come full circle.

Macmillan had obeyed Churchill's injunction to a Prime Minister that he 'must bind the Cabinet to him'. Now he had to deal with what Disraeli had once so memorably referred to as 'the sublime instincts of an ancient people'. In a performance of consummate political skill and artistry he won over his party for the attempt to move forward into Europe at the Conservative Party Conference at Llandudno in 1962. Even today, listening to the recording of his speech, it is possible to 'feel' that audience slowly warm and, in the end, cheerfully submit to him. The Prime Minister, with every phrase and every pause alike honed and sharpened to concert pitch, drew upon an avuncular memory of the Music Hall to help persuade an uneasy gathering that Britain had hesitated over Europe long enough.

MACMILLAN: Perhaps some of the older ones among you may remember a popular song, now I think recently revived: 'She didn't say Yes (*laughter and applause*), She didn't say No (*laughter and applause*), She didn't say Stay (*his voice rising as the audience joins in*), She didn't say Go! She wanted to climb, but she dreaded to fall. So she bided her time, and she clung to the wall! (*prolonged laughter and applause*) . . .

WITH THE AID OF that inspired piece of theatre, delivered in an easily breakable code, Macmillan laid before the faithful a new appraisal of Britain's postwar policy; and in the same breath beckoned them to strike out with him on the road to Europe.

Two years earlier, in 1960, Britain had passed a more sobering landmark. That was the year in which Macmillan had set in motion the re-examination by Whitehall which had now led him to attempt this historic reversal of traditional policy; and it was also the year in which, for the last time, Britain remained the richest state in Europe per capita of population. The Community countries had begun to forge ahead. But there had been another landmark. The whole world was forced to take account of it. The British Cabinet, when it made its decision to apply for membership of the Common Market, did so in the brooding presence of a fundamentally challenging new fact which had begun deeply to impress public opinion. This was the dawn of the age of the intercontinental missile – of which that small sixty-year-old crater, in what was once a hunting forest near London, had been the harbinger.

One cannot help but be struck by the impact which this doubly forbidding combination, suddenly made apparent, had on those who had previously opposed and contested the relevance of the European idea to Britain. It was a harsh enlightenment, revealing Britain sensibly diminished and Europe itself loomed over.

A crucial 'late vocation' in Macmillan's Cabinet, swayed by the context of this particular period, was the Deputy Prime Minister, 'Rab' Butler. Only six years before, at the time of Messina, Lord Butler had shared Prime Minister Anthony Eden's rejection of the whole notion of Britain as a member of an integrated European 'Community'. 'In our bones we know we cannot do it', Eden had said to the Americans in 1952, and stuck to that until he left office after Suez in 1956. Now, in 1961, Macmillan was saying, in effect, 'In our minds we know we must!' 'Ours is an island story', Anthony Eden had maintained in the 1950s, and Rab Butler had been an 'Eden' man. One of the most fascinating figures in contemporary British political history, Lord Butler, then in his seventy-eighth year, had these reflections upon Eden's (and his own) position.

BUTLER: I think he underestimated something very important, which I am now going to bring in; that is the – not exactly throwing away – but the alteration in our imperial status, which started in 1947 in India and proceeded at a great pace between 1950 and 1960 in Africa and the rest of the world. That is one of the most profound changes in the history of the world. The Romans never did anything like it. And you see, it is one of the reasons why Africa is so terribly disturbed now. It was one of the great moments, I think, in English history. And that is why many of us after that, including Anthony, suddenly said, Oh well, we just can't be an island – or an aircraft-carrier for America – which was an expression that we hear used. We must go in with Europe, and make 'Europe'.

You see, Europe in number is over 300 million; and I thought at the time, when we went in, how exciting to have the large European Community, which is bigger than America and which could stand up to Soviet Russia. That is why I want still more power given to Europe.

CHARLTON: Do you say that there was – in view of your own disarming confession that you were plainly wrong in 1955 – that there was a failure of the political class in this country? A failure to encourage the British people into a belief that their circumstances were totally different?

BUTLER: Yes. When you say I make a disarming confession, I definitely do, because I now think I ought to have been more far-sighted. But on the other hand, absolutely no force was urging me the other way, either in British public opinion or in British ministerial opinion. So it was not, so to speak, my fault. But I think that, being a prominent citizen and having a brain, I ought to have looked further ahead. I also think that Anthony ought to have. I think Harold [Macmillan] *did* look ahead, but it was not until a little later that he became more devoted, you see!

HAROLD MACMILLAN DREW STRENGTH for this 'devotion', and comfort from the anxieties which his call for so radical a departure undoubtedly caused him, in his belief that he was correctly interpreting almost a Law of History. In his own later reflections, in a fine chapter of his memoirs, he gives prominence to the pregnant forecasts of the English philosopher historian, Arnold Toynbee.

Writing in his monumental *A Study of History* in the 1920s, Toynbee had seen, in the predicament of what he called 'the pygmy states' of Europe, a phenomenon which had historical precedents. Europe, through its 'creative energies', had called into being a brave new world on the periphery of Europe – an 'expanding constellation' of a new order of Great Powers, of an 'overwhelmingly average calibre', which were bidding to dwarf or dominate it. Toynbee saw in this predicament an age-old challenge to statesmanship. As it had been for the city states of Ancient Greece, and for the Italy of Machiavelli, so too must it follow, as the night the day in the case of Europe. If the pygmy states at the centre do not take preventive action, the giant states on the outside are destined to overwhelm them 'by sheer weight of metal'.

Sir Arnold Toynbee (who incidentally had been among the first inhabitants of a garret in the Foreign Office devoted to post-war planning in 1942) had identified a process in the history of civilisations which, for him, could be considered almost a Law. It applied to a category which he called 'Creative Minorities', and he called this process itself 'Withdrawal and Return'.

Harold Macmillan, one can imagine, was plainly intrigued by the way

Toynbee then proceeded to break this process down, as he flung an arm across the centuries and civilisations, in a manner which must have had resonance with a Prime Minister contemplating the reversal of a tide of many centuries of accustomed practice and behaviour! The first step in this process, Toynbee argued, is the extrication 'whether voluntary or not of the creative minority from previous entanglements', in order to carry out its creative task. The last step is its return 'to general life of the Community from which it withdrew'.

In English history one such cycle of withdrawal and return might be said to begin with the loss of Calais, and with it the last of the British possessions in Europe. That, Toynbee proceeds, was followed by typical phases of origination, of which Shakespeare's England stands as the exemplar; of construction, during which period North America was populated by an English-speaking people, and which included the innovations of responsible parliamentary government and the British Commonwealth. These British transplants having taken root, Toynbee foresaw as being imminent, if not already taking place, another 'extrication' and a return to the community from which, in historical terms, the British had temporarily withdrawn in order to carry into effect this creative urge. He noted acutely that, in all cases, the process of 'return' in history is apt to be 'painful and humiliating'.

Informed by the rumbling thunder of such judgements handed down by a great British historian, Harold Macmillan may be seen as a statesman who felt called to the duty of averting the danger to which Toynbee had alerted Europe after the First World War. He was a creative individual, from among that creative minority, the British. In the performance of his task the Prime Minister, and Britain itself, were brought once more face to face with – France. Macmillan knew that if he were to succeed he had to have a sufficient understanding with General de Gaulle. He sought that in his epic, but elliptical, encounters with the French President during two long meetings, in the Châteaux of Champs and Rambouillet, during 1962.

The two men had had a close association in Algiers during the war. Algiers then was Allied HQ in the Mediterranean. Macmillan, appointed by Churchill, was there, as has been said, as 'Viceroy' of the Mediterranean and the guardian of the political aspects of the Anglo-American wartime partnership, at the time when it was first forged in a theatre of operations. Algiers was also, of course, part of the French Empire. It was the stage on which the struggle for eventual power in France was played out. Those were the days of France's humiliation.

The roles were now, in a sense, reversed. This time it was Macmillan who had a claim to make, and who was 'demandeur'. These talks at the 'summit' between the Prime Minister of Britain and the President of France were the first, and therefore fascinating, strategic explorations by the British, for four centuries, of a future in Europe. This is how Rab Butler responded to the invitation to look back upon the perhaps inevitable ambiguities and confusion which arose out of them.

BUTLER: I am using a lot of language that has never been used before, you know. I think that when Macmillan was appointed by Churchill to be the Resident Minister in North Africa, he did a wonderful job. A lot of that job was with de Gaulle, and a lot of that job was with the French. He thought he had

Macmillan's last meeting with the General before the veto of Britain's first bid to join the Common Market, Rambouillet, de Gaulle's official country residence near Paris, December 1962.

more control over the French than de Gaulle. Winston praised him very much for North Africa, and that is why Winston eventually decided that, as Harold was ten years older than me, he might as well be Prime Minister, and I could follow on later. He admired Macmillan very much, Winston. And Macmillan was very much what we call 'Sous l'Empire' – under the empire of the French. I think he thought he had them all in his pocket, and he didn't! That is what went wrong at Rambouillet. He didn't have him in his pocket at all. I don't think anyone had de Gaulle in their pockets really.

CHARLTON: What would you say was the absolutely controlling factor, in Macmillan's mind?

BUTLER: I think the controlling factor in Macmillan's mind was that – having known him all my life, I think he is a very forward-pushing fellow. I don't mean pushing in a nasty way, but he's a very ambitious and forward-looking fellow. And I think he thought that there really would be no future if we kept out of this. That's why de Gaulle's first veto was such a terrible disappointment to him. And why, in my view, his visit to Rambouillet was an absolute flop – because he never persuaded the gentleman at all – and he thought he did! In some ways, you see, Macmillan is an actor, and he acted beautifully with de Gaulle at Rambouillet. But unfortunately de Gaulle didn't act back, you see!

LORD BUTLER IS NOT ALONE among the few who were in any position to know who felt that Harold Macmillan had an exaggerated idea of his own persuasive powers as far as General de Gaulle was concerned, and that he

believed this would make agreement easier. As is now history, he wrongly supposed – he certainly hoped – that they shared a concept of Europe. Among its
essentials was a British belief that a Western European economic system must,
in the end, be dominated by Germany in the absence of a counterweight and
inclusive British presence; and that, when it came to the role of the nation
state, the British were just as antagonistic to the ideas and supranational
aspirations of the Federalists as General de Gaulle had shown himself to be.
Together it was hoped these things would assist Macmillan in his attempt to
persuade the General that a moment in history was now at hand; that Britain's
Pauline conversion to the European idea had become a necessary, mutually
desirable event which might not recur – a tide to be taken at the flood or
shallows and miseries would, in the end, ensue.

   During their wartime association in Algiers Macmillan had worked successfully, against the violent antipathies of Roosevelt and the anxieties of Churchill,
to have de Gaulle acknowledged as the leader of Free France. Some years ago
Harold Macmillan spoke to Robert Mackenzie and the BBC about this
particular time, and about the General and his veto of Macmillan's bid to enter
Europe.

MACMILLAN: A great man and I had a great affection for him, and I think I
helped him a lot in Algiers, for which he had an affection for me. But of course
he lived in the past. He lived in a world in which he thought a single country of
Europe could dominate the world, Napoleonic, Louis XIV. But what is Europe?
What do we call the Europe we're talking about? It's a little peninsula that sticks
out into the sea from the great Asian plain. Now, when we talk about Europe
we're talking about *half* of Europe. Half of Europe, the other side of the Iron
Curtain, is gone. We're only talking about what is left, the few countries of the
old European civilisation that are left. The idea that one of them can dominate
the others is just living in the past!

BE THAT AS IT MAY, as they say in the Courts of Justice, Macmillan was under
few illusions that Britain was now in a precarious, vulnerable position diplo-
matically, negotiating as between the Commonwealth and Europe. Throughout, the Prime Minister clung to a central hope or belief that, if specific
objections from de Gaulle could be met – these notably were presumed to be
arrangements for agriculture and a 'more equal' voice for France in the Atlantic
Alliance, then the last obstacles to Britain joining the European Community
would be cleared.

   Harold Macmillan's diaries reveal the importance of the 'Algiers experience'
for de Gaulle. They show that the Anglo-American hegemony of the war had
frequently been discussed between them. Macmillan, at one of their meetings
before the British decision to join the Community had been taken, had, with
some irritation asked de Gaulle why he 'harped on this to such an extent'. This
is partly, no doubt, what he meant by saying that de Gaulle 'always looked back'.
The great wartime conferences – Teheran, Yalta, Potsdam – at which the
future of Europe was settled – and from which France had been excluded –
stuck in de Gaulle's throat, they were a constant galling memory for him. He
was now about to show, in his treatment of Macmillan, that he had a lesser
memory for Vichy France and for the fact that it was Churchill who insisted at

Yalta – against Stalin and Roosevelt – that France be given a zone of occupation
in Germany and a veto through membership of the Security Council of the
United Nations. These were decisions which made possible the recovery of
position by France after the war.

That General de Gaulle did not, when the time came, extend to Harold
Macmillan and his difficulties, and those of Britain, a reciprocal generosity in
Britain's now more humble hour was to the Prime Minister a matter for a last-
ing, stinging reproach. These are the words in which, some years later,
Macmillan chose to make it.

MACMILLAN: He also had a real hatred of the Americans, and a kind of love-
hate complex about the British. The truth is – I may be cynical, but I fear it is
true – if Hitler had danced in the streets of London, we'd have had no trouble
with de Gaulle! If we'd given in to Hitler, we'd have had no trouble with de
Gaulle. What they could not forgive us is that we held on, and that we saved
France. People can forgive an injury, but they can hardly ever forgive a benefit.

THAT BLISTERING AND TRENCHANT verdict of Macmillan's, which he gave to
the BBC, like his other comments, during an interview in connection with the
appearance of another volume of his memoirs, *Riding the Storm*, has helped to
reinforce a ready British disposition to see the General's exclusion of Britain from
the European Community, at her first serious attempt to join it in 1963, as largely or
even wholly retributive.

Today, however, seen at the less emotional distance of some eighteen years,
British objectives, it seems fair to say, lacked the clarity which was needed in
order to negotiate the most important hurdles. Macmillan knew all the time that
he had probably sought in vain to convince de Gaulle that now that Britain and
France 'had no more Empires they had no more rivalries'. Their differences
over what, in France, is called 'a *European* Europe' went beyond emphasis. This
was, to de Gaulle, fundamental.

The General's Foreign Minister, who conducted the official negotiations for
France over Britain's application, was Maurice Couve de Murville. 'Couve', as
he is widely known in Europe, had had an early formative introduction to the
history and practice of British diplomacy before the war in an English house-
hold. He had been tutor to Sir Harold Nicolson's children at Sissinghurst in
Kent. I once heard it wondered out loud in Foreign Office circles, at a more
than usually jaundiced moment in Anglo-French affairs, whether M. Couve de
Murville's frequently troubled relationship with the British might possibly be
put down to his days under this, at times no doubt, difficult roof, and attributed
to his having undergone the 'Sissinghurst experience'!

Maurice Couve de Murville was another who had been in Algiers and
London, and with de Gaulle and Macmillan, during the war. Almost de
Gaulle's first visitor at the Matignon, when he returned to power in France in
1958, after his years in the wilderness, had been Harold Macmillan. Couve
agreed that, beginning then, the British Prime Minister could have entertained
few doubts that they saw the future of Europe with a difference which was
fairly profound.

COUVE DE MURVILLE: That leads us to the political field. You see, the difference between the French and the British, in that regard, has always been how they consider their relationship with the United States. It is very simple and clear for the British, for them that raises no problem. The Americans are their cousins, they speak the same language, they have the same civilisation. It is quite normal that cooperation is complete and that the strongest one – in the past it was London, at present it is Washington – takes the lead; and nobody feels hurt by that situation. For the French it is different. They do not speak the same language as the Americans, they are not of the same origin, and they've always had, let us say, a very strong feeling of their national existence. This does not mean that the British do not also have that! And therefore, for us, it raises the question of relationship, not with a cousin, but with a foreign country. I think that is really the philosophical basis of the difference. You must add to that, of course, the question of the national interest, which is always pre-dominant in foreign policy. The national interests of the French people are not necessarily the same as those of the United States. With the British it is a little different, because there is much more unity in the common interest. So that really is the basis of everything as regards to the foreign policy of Britain and France.

IN 1962 THE SITUATION was that the General was in sight ahead, like some dark but unpredictable cloud, while Macmillan was hurdling the lesser but still very formidable fences on the way to what he knew must be a final and exacting encounter with him. In public a relentlessly optimistic view was projected of the eventual outcome, it being held that to do otherwise would risk undermining the whole enterprise. The Cabinet having agreed the previous summer, the nature of application was debated in both Houses of Parliament and approved.

In Brussels Edward Heath had charge of the overall conduct of the British negotiations. They were perhaps the biggest in history, in their extraordinary range and diversity. But the British application for membership of the Common Market was being hammered out, all the time, within narrowing constraints. The Americans had given an importantly qualified approval to Britain pressing ahead, and as the time for decision approached there were some suspicions and anxieties about the exact nature of the British intentions.

When the Prime Minister had gone to see President Kennedy, on the eve of his momentous decision in 1961, to ask if the Americans were in favour of Britain joining, and for the help of the United States in making it possible, Kennedy had not given the answer himself but had turned, in marked manner, to his Under-Secretary of State, George Ball. It was Ball who, in the presence of President and Prime Minister, gave the official American response. The answer essentially was yes, provided Britain did not seek to water down the design of integration provided for in the Treaty of Rome.

It has been important to recall on more than one occasion that George Ball had been, over many years, an effective supporter and influence in American policy-making echelons of European integration, dating from his association with Lend Lease. It is of more than passing interest that the Secretary of State, Dean Rusk, a Rhodes Scholar who had been at Oxford during the famous 'King and Country' debate and who knew the British well, left the conduct of this policy in Europe very largely to Ball. The latter's insights and experience of the developments which had led to the formation of the Common Market had authority, and were acknowledged. It bears repeating that George Ball must be seen to have had an important hand in the post-war destiny of the British, as that destiny came to be shaped by the establishment and eventual enlargement, to include the United Kingdom, of the Common Market. Following Macmillan's meeting with Kennedy in 1961 at the White House, Ball recalls these further exchanges with the Prime Minister.

BALL: I believe it was the following evening, at a dinner at the British Embassy. Macmillan got me aside twice in the course of the evening, and one of the things he said was: 'Yesterday was one of the great days in my life, with the new Administration and the new President. And', he said, 'I want you to know that we are going to do this. We are going to have trouble with de Gaulle, but with your help we are going to *do* it, and we are going to go in.' He seemed extremely exhilarated, repeating 'this has been a great day', 'one of the great days of my life'. And of course I was enormously pleased. So I said to him, well, you know, I had some talks with Sir Frank Lee and with Edward Heath when I was in London (see page 246), and he said, 'You don't think I would have talked that way to the President yesterday if I hadn't known all about your conversations in London!'

CHARLTON: But your advice to President Kennedy, saying, in effect, OK but don't let them try and water down the whole thing, is according to my information founded on a certain sense of unease that Macmillan might try – that his conversion is in some doubt?

BALL: Well, I don't think we were so concerned about Macmillan. We were concerned that the whole British political process, I mean, might result in a sort of compromise position where it would be 'We will go in, but we will only go in on our *own* terms, and we are going to transform the Community from being anything supranational, or any effort to build a *real* unity'.

CHARLTON: So your own tactics with President Kennedy were to get him to make it quite clear to Mr Macmillan that there could be no easy compromise, that the British *had* to accept the political implications?

BALL: That's right. This was the advice that I gave him consistently over a very substantial period of time, and I must say he was very good about it.

CHARLTON: That the way to deal with the British was to force them to face up to this issue, or stay out?

BALL: Yes.

THE RECORD AVAILABLE in the United States of George Ball's subsequent exchanges with President Kennedy, after Macmillan's decision, shows that he was soon sounding warnings to the President, reflecting the basic concern he has already outlined about Macmillan's possible final position.

BALL: We then watched, obviously with very great interest, to see what the British government did about it. We watched the speeches in Parliament. A very brave, bold speech, I thought, by Heath, and a very forthright speech, I guess, by Alec Douglas-Home. And at the same time we were aware of the counter-offensive that was starting in Britain, and we did not know quite what would happen. When the application was finally made it seemed to us to be in rather luke-warm terms. I had the feeling that Macmillan, by that time, was telling Parliament and the British people that Britain was making an application but there would not be any nonsense about supranationality or anything of that kind: that this was a *commercial* arrangement. I was a little disturbed about it, but he had to manage the thing from a tactical point of view and this was his decision. I still believe that he believed in Europe, because the one thing I always found with Prime Minister Macmillan was that, in private conversation, he was very moving and eloquent about the need for unity, based on his war experience. His buddies had all been killed, he had a decimated unit he was leading, and the old rivalries had to be put to an end, and there *had* to be the building of a real European structure.

CHARLTON: It's interesting though, isn't it, that there is still no agreement, despite what you believe you've achieved in helping to bring about this fundamental conversion of the British, there is still no real agreement about what Europe is to be with Britain in it?

BALL: No, although with individuals yes. With the British government collectively, certainly not. I think that there was still, and the whole Macmillan tactic it seemed to me, as I wrote to President Kennedy at the time, was to move crabwise into the Common Market, sideways, and not to face the basic issues as to what the genius of the Institutions was, that they were an attempt to move towards political unity. Mr Macmillan gave simply a kind of tradesman's view of the Community.

FOR THIS REASON George Ball continued to urge upon the President that Britain should be advised to negotiate transitional arrangements only, leading to full acceptance of the Community as it stood, in the first instance, if there were to be the successful outcome the Americans certainly wished for.

Throughout 1961–2 Britain conducted an exercise of immense complexity. The deputy leader of the United Kingdom delegation, led by Edward Heath, in Brussels – and the senior official – was Eric Roll. This, in Lord Roll's view, was what determined the character of the British negotiation and its heavily detailed and protracted nature.

ROLL: The crucial thing there was that the French were not prepared to have, as it were, a collective negotiation with the Community, on one side, and the British, plus the others who also wanted to come in, on the other. Partly because I suppose, I don't know what was in their minds, I can only conjecture, partly because they thought that the Dutch, and the Belgians certainly, possibly the Italians and perhaps even the Germans, would be a little more forthcoming; and therefore they would find themselves in the position, if it *was* a collective negotiation, of being seen to be the bad boy. They wanted to have a negotiation in which each member country was still represented on its own. The other reason, no doubt, was that the only way in which you could have had a collective negotiation was to give far more power to the Commission, and that traditionally the French were not prepared to do anyway, and certainly not on this score!

CHARLTON: To what extent was the negotiation with Europe also, in parallel – and at the same time, a negotiation with public and party opinion at home? That we are educating Britain itself – and that determined this step-by-step and very long process?

ROLL: But indeed, you've put your finger on a most vital point, which accounts both for the length of the negotiations and for their difficulty – because you were addressing a number of audiences at one and the same time. You were addressing your negotiators across the table, and the Press coverage was terrific. It had ready access to officials and ministers, so anything that was said in Brussels was very quickly and generally known. You were at the same time talking to the Commonwealth all the time, in London, to their representatives in Brussels, in the Commonwealth capitals and at collective meetings. You were talking to the farmers and the consumers. You were talking to the British public at large. You were talking to the House of Commons and the House of Lords. Each one required, if you like, a somewhat different presentation. I don't mean for any sinister reason but simply because their interests and concerns were different. When in Brussels you were being tough, you risked antagonising those at home whom you wanted to win over in the Cabinet and the House. When you were being too forthcoming in Brussels you were risking antagonising those who were expecting you to keep battling on all the time.

So, all in all this was a very, very difficult situation, and made it, of course, very easy for anyone who was really thoroughly hostile to the whole idea to play on that.

CHARLTON: To what extent was protracted negotiation also an attempt by Britain, at one minute to midnight, to organise Europe as she wished it? We have announced that we've accepted the principles of the Treaty of Rome, but can one also see it as an attempt by us to recruit to our side the states other than France, at the very time when France has succeeded, in parallel negotiations, in organising it as France wished?

ROLL: Yes, and indeed shortly after the breakdown came the signing of the Franco-German Treaty. But no, you're putting it in slightly too sinister terms if I may say so. Once you go into a multilateral negotiation of that kind – and it was the French who insisted on it being multilateral – obviously one of the techniques, if you like, the art of negotiating in that way – rather than just sitting opposite one person trying to buy a house or sell him a carpet – is that you try to, shall I say, in quotation marks, 'exploit' the differences of view of people on the other side. And in many matters, for instance in agricultural policy, attitudes to Commonwealth trade, and in questions concerning the Budget, the interests of the Six were not always exactly the same. We naturally tried to make the best of that if you like. We had support on this issue from the Dutch, on that issue from the Belgians, on another one from the Germans, as indeed you would wish to use any differences of view inside the French camp itself.

CHARLTON: Yet given all that had gone before, would you agree we never quite succeeded in ridding either the Americans or the interested Europeans of a suspicion that we were still trying, not to join the club, but to remake it?

ROLL: I think after the negotiation had broken down – and we all know how that happened – many people, or some people at any rate, were saying, Ah well, the British were too tough, the British were trying to push things this way and that way. Obviously the difficulties which we had in reconciling all these interests did not suddenly disappear just because we decided to negotiate. They were still there. Naturally we found ourselves torn this way and that way, and naturally we tried to find a solution each time which would give us, if not the best of all possible worlds, at least a tolerable mixture. But I do not think that any of us in Brussels, from Ted Heath down, had the slightest feeling, or indeed the wish, that we could fundamentally change the structure of the Community. Unless we failed miserably to convey this back home, which I do not think we did, I don't believe that Harold Macmillan or Rab Butler or any of the other ministers primarily concerned were under any illusion.

BUT SUCH HOPES AS THERE WERE that the six states of the Community, who were still in the process of pain and grief compromising among themselves, would now extend that compromise significantly towards Britain and the Commonwealth were not sustained. In those stern judgement seats of the Brussels negotiations the British little by little were made inexorably aware of the extent to which their situation was changed.

Another of the senior officials in charge of Britain's negotiations was Herbert Andrew of the Board of Trade. This diminutive Yorkshireman, usually wreathed in pipe smoke and exuding that unrushable tenacity which is held to be the cultural badge of his county, emerged as one of the more vivid 'characters' in Brussels during the course of Britain's immense negotiation. Upon retirement he took Holy Orders and is today the Reverend Sir Herbert Andrew.

ANDREW: Looking back, it seems rather absurd but, when we tried EFTA, the European Free Trade Area, with the non-members of the Community, we had the idea that it was a kind of negotiating contest. Many people did not believe that the Community would hold together. We were still, I think, influenced by the immediate past. While we'd had a good many hopeful moves in the years after the war, we had seen a number of policies fail, but we hadn't realised really that the *reason* they failed was because of our own relatively declining strength. There is this time-lag in all political things, as there is a time-lag in political thought. Most politicians I think tend to be trying to cure the ills of their youth rather than the ills of the present time. This is true of officials too, and certainly in Departments there is a kind of time-lag in the thinking.

The thing that really shook me about our negotiations to join the Common Market in 1961 was how little we counted in the thinking of the Community. How little we counted in the ideas that they had, and in their hopes for the future. Five of them were very glad to see us join. There was a certain stirring of sentiment among them, I think, but there was also a feeling that any new member would be a feather in their cap. But that we would have very much to contribute, to the extent that it was worth their while to alter substantially the arrangements which they had themselves laboriously made, this was not really on. We were not such a catch that they would go to very great lengths to catch us!

SIR HERBERT ANDREW WAS ANOTHER, therefore, who had come to cast, it would seem, 'a longing, ling'ring look behind' upon the invitations and opportunities passed up by Britain just a few years earlier. It was characteristic of what amounted to a national attitude of mind in Britain after the war that not just the political class itself, but that adjunct and critically detached observer of it, British journalism, had also been caught napping by the significance of the political evolution of Western Europe. This had left public opinion, in consequence, with only the shadow of knowledge with which to make up its mind on so large an issue.

The crucial developments in European integration had attracted the notice of only a couple of the quality newspapers and weeklies and had been written about with persistent or serious interest only to this, inevitably reduced, audience. In *The Times* coverage of it had, for the years in the fifties, been placed under the masthead 'Imperial and Foreign' News, which in retrospect must be seen as placing the issues at arm's length rather than suggesting they might be of direct, more intimate relevance. The archives of the BBC, in their turn, reveal only a cursory interest in the comings and goings which took shape eventually as the European Community. British public opinion was being called vicariously, by the unfolding of the negotiations in Brussels, to an almost posthumously late vocation, while on the level of national self-interest it has been argued since that, if it was Britain's overriding concern to get into the European Community *before* it became settled in its ways, then it was mis-conceived tactically to become involved in so long and detailed a negotiation. Harold Macmillan had given the task of trying to square this set of circles to the Lord Privy Seal, Edward Heath.

HEATH: The major question which, I suppose, history will argue about is what one might call the 'Monnet line', and the line which we ourselves followed. Jean Monnet always believed and urged – right from the beginning – that we should just say, outright, Yes, we will become a member of the Community. This would have saved two years' negotiations. In fact, it would have saved quite a lot of the first year's exploratory talks. Then we could have adjusted ourselves *inside* the Community, and got the Community to adjust at the same time. The problem about that was really parliamentary and public opinion. The difficulty was that at the time public opinion and parliamentary opinion didn't really understand the real nature of the Community. I am afraid there are still many who don't.

Monnet was quite convinced that no Community can exist unless it does take full account of each of its members' requirements. He always used to say that if you push it too hard it will break. But the interests of the individuals in the Community now are such that they don't *want* it to break up. Therefore they will be prepared to adjust in order to meet the special needs you have, which were not taken account of when the Community was first formed ten years previously. But the fact was, it was not possible to persuade parliamentary and public opinion of that. We knew that perfectly well.

CHARLTON: Did you have a personal view about a very long-drawn-out negotiation? Whether it held dangers? I mean, weeks spent on bacon and egg subsidies, things like that, whether the principal issue was rather lost sight of in that process?

HEATH: Yes, and of course the longer you continue in a negotiation the more likely it is that the public will get tired of it or bored by it and say, What is the point of going on with this? That was always a danger, and a very big danger. That was why we tried to get the whole outline of the negotiations settled by the first week in August 1962. We were almost successful in that, but not quite. You see, the Ministers and the Commission ceased to meet in the Community after the end of July. In fact we did keep it going into August, beyond their normal time. If we'd been able to settle everything by then, we could have gone to the Party Conference in October and said, Here you are, here is a complete outline of all the arrangements. Then we could have gone to the House of Commons when it met after the Party Conferences and said, This is the agreed broad outline. We can have as long a debate as you like about it, and if you accept this outline we can move forward very quickly on the details and settle the agreement for ratification.

CHARLTON: Do you believe that the Party and the House of Commons would have supported it at that stage?

HEATH: If we'd been able to complete the outline, yes.

CHARLTON: The other factor about that date, can I suggest, is that for the first time General de Gaulle gets a majority in the French elections – the Gaullists get a majority. Now tactically, if you'd been able to push the moment of decision forward, *before* this happened, then, it is argued, de Gaulle might not have been able to take the strong position – in fact use the veto – he did. Was that an active consideration in your minds at that time?

HEATH: Well, I was not to know, after I had tried to get them finished, that in October, he was then going to get his majority. So obviously it was not a major factor.

CHARLTON: No one was reporting from France that this possibility really existed?

HEATH: They may have been reporting the possibilities, yes, I would not question that – one would have to go through all the telegrams to check it – but from our point of view – after all, we had been carrying out the most strenuous negotiations for a full year and, for the reasons I've given, it seemed to be the best way of handling it – to get the complete outline. Then both Party and Parliament could see what it was and we could get a decision in the autumn which would have allowed us to move ahead with the preparation of the actual Treaty.

CHARLTON: Of course another suggestion made is that Couve de Murville, who was leading the negotiations on the French side, was deliberately prolonging them. That is, they are not protracted just because we are going into a mass of technical detail, they are also being deliberately prolonged by France in the hope that Britain will just give it all up?

HEATH: I would not describe it that way, no. The fact was that by the time we got to August I think everybody who had been taking part in the negotiations was tired out, if not exhausted. After all, on the last sitting the Chairman, from Luxembourg, collapsed and had to be taken out of the Conference Chamber! The three who were still taking an active part were Signor Colombo from Italy, who took over the Chair, myself and, for part of the time, Couve de Murville.

CHARLTON: I'm still not clear why it was not possible to bring the negotiation to a head round about August?

HEATH: Because of the mass of material which had to be covered.

MR HEATH'S AND MR MACMILLAN'S hands were tied. The Prime Minister had parliamentary approval for the change of direction, but for a commitment to Europe which was ambiguous and imprecise. In that interminable haggle in Brussels over bacon and eggs, over cricket bats and coconut oil, and, in one memorable instance in the long and detailed list of demands submitted by Ottawa, over 'the importation of clerical vestments from Canada', a political reality lay barely concealed like some tidal reef just beneath the surface – the absence of settled political agreement about acceptable objectives either at home, with the Commonwealth, or the Six.

In Brussels Heath was managing an enormous strategic enterprise, the extrication and return of Britain to Europe. The position of the negotiating team there seemed reminiscent of a Bairnsfather cartoon from the First World War depicting a harassed front-line officer in his dug-out, the sky above darkened by danger and bursting shells, the earth around him erupting, being asked on a field telephone from far behind the lines to account for the number of tins of raspberry jam issued to his unit in the previous month! And yet, of course, each of those items in that vast negotiation, humble, homely and familiar as many of them were, became in the absence of a sufficiently agreed political objective a coded symbol for argument about the future political orientation and nature of the European Community.

British public opinion, and that of the House of Commons, could not be advanced at this time beyond a readiness to accept the Community, not as it was, but rather as it would be shaped by the negotiations for British entry and 'without damaging the essential interests of the Commonwealth'. The harassed front-line officer, if we may so describe him, charged with winning the war in Brussels was Edward Heath.

HEATH: Of course, the other side of the coin was – and the Community felt quite strongly about it – that many in Parliament, and some members of the public and those who comment on these affairs, were asking for assurances of a kind which no country, individually, would ever ask of other countries. We were being told to ask for things in perpetuity whereas, if for example we were carry-ing on a negotiation over grain with the Australians, we would never dream of asking for something in perpetuity. So that was the other side of the coin which had to be handled and which was, at times, very difficult.

CHARLTON: There was no chance of altering the tactical approach? It still had to be cricket bats and coconut oil, all those things which took a very long time to decide?

HEATH: You see, each of the Commonwealth countries had its own special interests, and we knew that we would have to have a conference of Common-wealth Prime Ministers. They had been given the undertaking that they could have that, and that we would get their views upon it. Some would have said that we would have to have their assent; that was not a position I accepted myself. The Commonwealth had previously declared that individual member countries, of course, were free to make their own decisions. But if we were going to satisfy Commonwealth countries about their own particular interests, then we had to be able to tell them what agreement the Community was prepared to make about it. And this took a vast amount of time.

THAT DELAY, and the dangers it held for the securing of the principal objec-tives, was, one may safely say, a source of much frustration to Mr Heath. The political process, involving a joint advance by Britain and the Commonwealth, was applying heavy pressure on the negotiators to go down the path to Europe marked 'seeking exemptions'. That path had led to failure before.

At home the Beaverbrook press, the Crusader's sword drawn on behalf of the old relationships with Empire and Commonwealth, was painting the negotiations – which all the time was fulfilling their secondary intention of accustom-ing the population at large to the idea of a shift into Europe – as a series of humiliating surrenders by the men at the table in Brussels, like Herbert Andrew.

ANDREW: The Beaverbrook press line, of course, was a perfectly valid debat-ing point, because the technique of the thing, if you call it a negotiation – and I suppose we must – was that we dealt ourselves a very good hand of cards and then had to lose them one at a time! Knowing that we dealt ourselves, or the Commonwealth dealt us, a very large number of cards which really were worth nothing, because the other side just picked them up as soon as you put them on the table and said, Thank you for nothing – in that sense it *was* a permanent humiliation. I remember saying once in a Brussels café that I should have to leave the Board of Trade when this negotiation finished – however it finished – because I couldn't possibly ever face anybody in a trade negotiation again! Having, that is, given away, and not got anything in return – except something which is not a commercial prize in the negotiating sense.

IT WAS A FRENCH DIPLOMAT who told me of the very singular impression made by Sir Herbert Andrew when during the long British rearguard action – 'playing back' resolutely, as it were – this very English figure from Yorkshire would, at times, have recourse to elevated quotation, as he faced the Six signatories of the Rome Treaty in Brussels.

ANDREW: I think it must have arisen because I was reading the New English Bible at the time. The New Testament had just come out; I was reading it over breakfast before starting the day's labours. There is a piece in Revelations about the fall of the City of Rome! I adapted that slightly, after a somewhat earnest discussion when we had been talking about the level of common tariffs, which they were willing to negotiate down and had in fact done so, quite a long way, but which in certain respects we regarded as very high. We wanted to see them lowered in the interests of the Commonwealth. I made, I remember, a plea about that, if that is what you mean, with a slightly adapted passage from Revelations. 'The merchants of the earth also will weep and mourn for her, because no one any longer buys her cargoes, cargoes of gold and silver, jewels and pearls, casks of purple and scarlet, silks and fine linens' – those were the Asiatic textiles of the period! – 'all kinds of scented woods, ivories . . . spice, incense, perfumes and frankincense . . . All the glitter and glamour are lost, never to be yours again. The traders will stand at a distance for horror, weeping and mourning and saying, Alas, Alas for the great city that was clothed in fine linen, and bedizened with gold and jewels and pearls, Alas that in one hour' – and we had been talking in Brussels, you see, for just over an hour – 'Alas, that in one hour so much wealth should be laid waste'! That is what I read out to them.
CHARLTON: And tell me, how did these things spiritual go down in those very temporal surroundings among your negotiating counterparts?
ANDREW: I think they regarded it as a kind of harmless English eccentricity. I don't know. The Dutch asked me for a copy!
CHARLTON: What was the point you were trying to drive home with the help of Revelations?

ANDREW: That impoverishment would be the result if they pursued a high-tariff policy tending to regard the rest of the world as of no account. This was the feeling we had, and I think it was true of the French, I don't know if it is true of them now, but it was true of the old-style French official. One man who appeared at one stage in the French delegation, it was obviously something that he'd learnt, said that 'imports are a privilege that a country extends to another'. Now, you couldn't get any clearer definition, I think, of the difference between the old-style continental approach and the old-style English approach of free trade. But he was an official who'd obviously learnt his departmental doctrine when he was young and never forgotten it. I don't think the European countries and ourselves have got that divide any more. I think it is pure past history.

THE UNCERTAINTIES AMONG THE AMERICANS fundamentally were limited to how the British would work out the relationship with Europe. From the point of view of the United States itself, there do not appear to have been great anxieties, provided there would also be a move toward a general lowering of tariff barriers. This was something which George Ball had determined to fit into the final outcome as far as the United States was concerned.

BALL: I tried to argue that the ties that bound the Community nations together were not simply that they had a trade advantage among themselves. But let me say that at this point there was a certain apprehension amongst the good Europeans, the people around Monnet, that my idea of pushing them forward, toward a massive trade negotiation which would result in the lowering of tariffs, was some threat to the Community itself. There was a time when I even told President Kennedy perhaps we ought to postpone the Trade Agreements Legislation for a year because we were running into political opposition. On the other hand, there was an enormous advantage as a part of American tactics in being able to say that we would have to have a lowering of trade barriers generally, because otherwise the United States will suffer a major disadvantage in relation to the Community nations. So to an extent we were playing it both ways.

CHARLTON: What can you add now to what we know of the feeling of resentment against America which became apparent in Britain as the negotiations got under way?

BALL: Well, then the two issues which we had recognised were going to be obstacles became very important. One was the question of the EFTA nations; the other, which was very much more important, was the question of relations with the Commonwealth and to what extent the Commonwealth could be accommodated in the European structure. There was a third element which was to what extent might there be a consolidation of not only the preferences that existed under the Commonwealth system, but also the preferences that existed in the Francophone nations under the French community system.

I saw it from a practical point of view. If I were going to carry American support for the Community I had to make it clear that, while we were prepared to accept a *certain amount* of commercial discrimination, we were going to do everything possible to minimise that discrimination, by first eliminating the extension of the preferences beyond the nations that were actually members of the Community, but beyond that a trade negotiation.

CHARLTON: Yes, there of course is the Commonwealth issue, and also the resentment.

BALL: Although I thought of myself as an Anglophile. My father was born in Devon, after all!

CHARLTON: But Macmillan says in his memoirs somewhere, 'There was always Mr George Ball of the State Department who seemed determined to thwart our policy in Europe and the Common Market negotiations'.

BALL: Well, Macmillan indicates that I was a bloody nuisance, that I was always trying to put obstacles in 'our route to joining Europe'.

CHARLTON: Not joining Europe but in joining the sort of Europe he was prepared to join!

BALL: That's right, that's right. Of course, had Britain joined earlier it could have had a great many concessions that were impossible to get once the thing became frozen.

CHARLTON: Like what?

BALL: Well, I think arrangements with the Commonwealth. If it had joined before EFTA, then it would not have had EFTA as a complicating factor, and it wouldn't have had to worry about the Swedes or the Swiss or the Austrians. Beyond that, it could have established itself in a role where, so far as French agriculture is concerned, it would have been able to urge the position of its *own* agriculture and its *own* system of subsidies. It was very much more difficult for Britain to come along several years *after* institutions have been operating and have built up their own procedures and their own body of theology, and say, Now we want to change all this to accommodate it to us!

CHARLTON: I've always wondered about that, because it seems to me that even Monnet foresaw the need for Britain to make a break with the imperial past and devote its priorities to Europe, and as soon as you say that, you create problems for this emotional, historical and intimate relationship Britain has with the Commonwealth, particularly with the white Dominions.

BALL: Well, I'm not saying I don't understand the British point of view or that, if I'd been British, I might not have even been a part of it! But looked at from the point of view of the United States, we did not have to make these decisions. It was very easy for us to tell somebody else to make a decision. Had we had to do things that would have involved the derogation of *American* sovereignty, I think we would have been the stickiest people in the *world* on that score. But let me say this. Looking at it as objectively as we hoped we were, from outside, and trying to see what would have been in the best interests of Britain as well as of Europe, it seemed to me at least, and to many of my colleagues, that Britain would serve its *own* interests best in this way. I had a very strong belief during the whole of this period that Britain was going to have a very hard time resolving its problems of industrialisation if they were left within a strictly national context, but that in a broader context many things would have been possible. Messina was a great British mistake, I think. Now think what would have happened. There would have been no EFTA difficulty, accommodations *could* have been worked out with the Commonwealth at that time, and then Britain would have had the dynamism of Europe brought to bear on its economic and industrial problems.

CHARLTON: But now, as we are approaching the time of the 'Veto', to what extent do you think the British difficulties are attributable to these determinedly close and concerted links with America? Or are they, anyway, inevitable after the original British decision not to take part at the time of Messina?

BALL: Well, I always thought de Gaulle's objections were based on the fact that it would be a challenge to French primacy. But, had Britain joined pre-1958, in other words before General de Gaulle, one of the beauties of adhesion at that point was that it was in the days of the Fourth Republic which was fundamentally weak and therefore quite willing to make concessions.

THAT NOW, seven years later in 1962, was of course the rather brutal and fundamental difference. As the time for an overall decision drew nearer the situation was highly charged and dramatic. Harold Macmillan was, it would seem, under few illusions about the risks he was running, if not yet the eventual outcome. In 1962 the Prime Minister made an entry in his personal diary. He set down that the issue of the Common Market might prove to be 'the most exciting since the [repeal of] the Corn Laws in the previous century', and he wondered if, as had happened then, 'it might radically change all party allegiances and formations'.

Hugh Gaitskell, the leader of the Labour Party, found it less exciting. One of his recent biographers records that he considered 'it was always a bore and a nuisance' – almost word for word an echo of how, Lord Butler has told us previously, he and Eden looked upon it in the 1950s. At least, this was generally thought to be Gaitskell's public position. The Labour Party came out eventually against not the principle, but the terms of entry which Heath had, it seemed, been able to negotiate in Brussels.

At the Labour Party Conference in Brighton in the autumn of 1962 Gaitskell gave a qualified warning when he spoke of the dangers of a 'federal' Europe. But the qualification was swept out of memory by the responses his audience made to the striking by him of a single, emotional and reverberating chord, contained in this well-remembered extract from his conference speech.

GAITSKELL: Now we must be clear about this. It does mean, *if* this is the idea, the end of Britain as an independent nation state, the end of a thousand years of history! You may say, All right! Let it end! But, my goodness, it's a decision that needs a little care and thought.

GAITSKELL'S WIFE DORA is said to have remarked, when he sat down, 'All the wrong people are cheering!' The Labour Leader had been determined to avoid commitment on an issue which would sorely try the precarious Party unity. This was still being bandaged after the wounds inflicted upon it by the divisive encounters between Right and Left over unilateral nuclear disarmament and nationalisation. The major evolution which Macmillan fought successfully to get the Conservative Party to accept – to turn it towards Europe – also took place later, if more equivocally, in the Labour Party.

Hugh Gaitskell died in the same week in January 1963 as General de Gaulle said no to Macmillan's attempt to join the Community. Gaitskell had sent to President Kennedy a long personal letter setting out the objections of the Labour Party to the European enterprise. Kennedy gave this letter to George Ball, his Under-Secretary of State.

BALL: I think that brief arrived just at the time of Nassau, and Kennedy – I remember him tossing the letter to me and saying, 'Look, this is a letter from Hugh Gaitskell, you reply to it'. We never replied because by the time we got back to Washington a week had gone by and poor Hugh Gaitskell was dead. But it was, as I recall it, a rather legalistic brief about why it was not a good idea from Britain's point of view to join Europe.

IT IS OF PASSING INTEREST to note that Kennedy, having read Gaitskell's letter, then did as he had done in the presence of Harold Macmillan a year earlier – called upon Ball to give the American answer. Although never sent, that could have meant only one thing: there was no wavering in American support for British entry.

During the time Harold Macmillan was making his wholesale reversal of British policy over Europe, Gaitskell's subsequent successor as leader of the Labour Party had special responsibilities for the formation of policy. In this year, 1962, he was Chairman of the Party. Sir Harold Wilson gave this assessment of what, under his aegis, the fresh thinking and examination by Labour of the European question in 1960–1 had revealed.

WILSON: Hugh Gaitskell was very much against it. I was a little surprised but Hugh was a man of very strong views. He was a man who, in a few minutes, could give a definite answer, yes or no, and it wasn't going to be varied – when the slower-minded amongst us would like to spend a longer time coming to that view. I do remember very well having a drink with Hugh in the smoke room of the House of Commons about this time, and I said, 'Hugh, I've been having a number of meetings with our European colleagues' – I think I was Chairman of the party at that time – and I said, 'I'm beginning to think there is a lot more in this European thing than I had before. I know it will come as a shock to you!' He said, 'No, it doesn't. I'm beginning to have the same idea.' And so for a time we were moving into a much more 'communautaire' position, the two of us – with a lot of opposition, I do not need to tell you, in the Shadow Cabinet. I don't know whether he would have stayed with that position.
CHARLTON: Why therefore did he, and why did you, not wish to commit the Party to a position on Europe at that time?
WILSON: I think we were both of us a little 'all over the shop', sort of warm and cool. I was moving along those lines, but there was of course very, very strong feeling in the Parliamentary Party the other way. Later of course, when we came to office, it took a different position.
CHARLTON: Why?
WILSON: Partly because 'it was there' – the thing was 'there' and we ought to be there. What we did not know was what terms we would get. I thought, having been trained as an economics minister, that those who said we must be in at all costs were wrong. Equally, those who said we shouldn't touch it with a barge-pole were wrong!
CHARLTON: At the time you had this conversation with Gaitskell, you've had your developing contacts with the European socialists?
WILSON: Yes, I was heading our delegation to the various meetings we had. Occasionally he came too.
CHARLTON: What are the factors, in your own mind, bringing you both round

to this position, that Britain should be looking at this more seriously and with, I presume, the objective of going in?

WILSON: Yes, certainly. I think it was because we felt it was *not* such a hard-line organisation, and we found our European colleagues agreeably open-minded. In fact, of course, they took a very hard line throughout on the whole question of membership. We did oppose it, of course, as a Party when Ted Heath completed his negotiations, although we knew, and I said, there must be some freedom here. We have some passionately pro-Marketeers who will be very affronted and hurt; they are a minority in the Party but we must not pursue them with three-line whips and tell them they must not vote in accordance with the way they wish. And of course there were some Conservatives who voted with us against the Heath terms. I then persuaded the Party to say that we're not for it or against it – going right back to the Macmillan position in fact. That is, 'it depends on the terms'. We finally got it through that we would stay in, if we could improve the terms – and that is exactly what happened. That of course was many years later.

SIR HAROLD REVEALS THAT in the run-up period before the Brighton Conference in 1962 both he and Gaitskell were moving to a position *in favour* of British membership of the Community, but had had to take a more cautious position in terms of avoiding a split in the Party. The emotional overtones of Gaitskell's 'thousand years of history' speech and their intended effect have always been the source of interest and argument, to which Sir Harold Wilson added this recollection.

WILSON: I don't think any of us knew that Hugh Gaitskell was going to say that. If my memory is correct, we'd gone down there to Brighton, always on the Friday before the meeting to decide the Executive's attitude, the National Executive Committee's attitude, to the main issues coming up. Even on that Friday I was by no means certain that Hugh Gaitskell was going to take that line. And I certainly can't remember him showing us the text of that particular part of the speech.

CHARLTON: Did he say what he meant to say, did you feel? Did he know or realise it was going to have the effect it did?

WILSON: I think so. Hugh was very close, you know. I mean, he kept himself to himself. He had his own advisers, his own coterie – whether they were responsible – and of course Hugh always had a very great respect for Douglas Jay. Now Douglas Jay was, of course, and is, and has never changed, *fanatically* anti-EEC, against British membership. It is possible Douglas Jay had some influence on him.

CHARLTON: But are you saying that Gaitskell had decided against the thing in principle at this time? He's moved a good deal away from the position he'd discussed with you in the smoke room of the House? He's now really against it himself?

WILSON: He moved quite a lot, one way or the other. He was always, as I say, very certain he was right when he'd taken his decision and I was surprised in the House of Commons smoke room when I found him beginning to move the other way, having opposed it. We were in Opposition, he did not want to sort of split the Party further, all to no purpose. And it was a very reasonable line for an

Opposition to take, that it all depends on the terms.

AT THE SAME TIME, in parallel with Britain's protracted negotiations, the Community itself, far from being totally absorbed by them, was accelerating its own progress towards fulfilment of the goals of the Treaty of Rome. 1962, a year after the British application, saw the emergence, in broad outline, of the Common Agricultural Policy, with the principle of Community preference built into it with substantial fastenings! Agreement on agriculture was something which in historical terms, in Europe, had always proved elusive. Herbert Andrew agreed that it was 'another setback'.

ANDREW: We had to accept it, nor do I think we would have wanted to do anything to delay it. It was a very clear sign that they regarded the creation of the Community as more important than having us as members – which I suppose, ten years earlier, they wouldn't have done.

BECAUSE OF ITS IMPLICATIONS at home and for the Commonwealth, the Agricultural policy stood as the most emotional, difficult symbol of choice – the Gordian knot. Opinion was evolving in the Cabinet as the negotiations wore on and as the interests of the old Commonwealth, in particular the countries which had once been Britain's exclusive farms abroad, were publicly debated. When the CAP emerged in the middle of the negotiations there was a tremor; but the crucially important figure in Macmillan's Cabinet, Rab Butler, held firm.

BUTLER: But then, I thought my original fears therefore not unjustified. On the other hand, I felt once we were in we couldn't possibly come out. I never tried to come out. I never said a word to Macmillan or the leaders of the country about coming out. In fact I have never thought of it since.

THE CENTRAL ISSUE about the negotiation as a whole, mentioned earlier by Edward Heath – whether Britain would have been better off accepting the Community at the outset and working from within for the necessary adjustments – was posed in acute form by the Common Agricultural Policy's appearance so early. Heath was doing all he could to drive the negotiations to the earliest possible conclusion while the CAP was still an objective, or in its struggling infancy. But Britain seemed determined never to miss a chance of missing an opportunity! Christopher Soames had last-ditch arguments with the National Farmers' Union.

SOAMES: From the point of view of the farmers at home, those who were against it, Harold Woolley, who was the leader of the Farmers' Union, was dead against it – he never liked the sound of it at all. He was something to my mind of a Little Englander, and he used to say to me, 'You're asking us to get off one horse that we know and understand, we may not like it all that much but it's served us pretty well by and large – you're asking us to get off that horse and you aren't showing us the colour of another one to get on to! And I used to say, Well OK, of course there isn't, but it's much better that we should *be* there when the Common Agricultural Policy comes to be formed, rather than be *outside* it, and having it formed without us! Les absents ont toujours tort! Those who aren't there are always wrong! And this is indeed how it has proved. We've got this thing round our neck now and it's going to have to be changed. It's going to have to be changed because it doesn't fit the Nine, it doesn't fit today.

And of course it would have been undoubtedly a very different Common Agricultural Policy had we *been there*, which is perhaps one of the reasons why the General did not want us in.

THE MEETING OF Commonwealth Prime Ministers in London towards the end of 1962 was the last and widest river for Mr Macmillan to cross. That the Commonwealth should approve, and that it should not suffer unduly in consequence if it did, was the aspect of the decision which fell across all other considerations, for it touched, through the ties of kith and kin, both sentiment and emotion.

Residual doubts in the Cabinet were nourished at the last minute by the presence in London of that far-flung battle line from those former colonies, dominions and protectorates who for centuries had been linked by the now quickly-fading patterns of the Old Trade and the Old Flag. Lord Butler plainly found, even so many years later, and in his seventy-eighth year, the memory of this last day of decision harrowing, and spoke movingly of it.

BUTLER: At Marlborough House we got together the whole Commonwealth, and before it took place we had terrible talks with Bob Menzies, the Australian Prime Minister. Bob Menzies thought that we were traitors, and New Zealand did too. New Zealand did because of butter and sheep, you see, but Australia did on broader grounds of policy. Bob, as you know, was half a British statesman really. He was always coming over here! And he was dead against it. He gave great hell, you know, to Harold, and partly to me, and we decided it wasn't much worth going on. But then we persuaded Bob that, on the lines I have been talking to you, our Empire was gone, and a lot of our strength was gone, and had we not better join an economic unit where we could be a competitor with the USA and the USSR? And that was the final argument that appealed to Bob. Right up to that morning at Marlborough House, and I walked round that rather dim garden on the Mall with Harold about eight times, deciding whether we would cross or not, and Bob saw us and joined us. And in the end we all went back in to that wonderfully beautiful house – and decided to do it. But it was a very close thing up until the end.

A CLOSE-RUN THING, but like Waterloo itself decisive – for the present and for the far future.

Mr Macmillan was now ready for that last obstacle whose ultimate will was guessed at but unknown, General de Gaulle. This was Macmillan's own retrospective cryptic judgement of how de Gaulle must, at this moment, have judged the situation.

MACMILLAN: When we started the negotiations, before the last moment when de Gaulle turned it down, he did not believe that I could carry the Tory Party and the Commonwealth. I did carry both. Only when he found that I had succeeded in carrying it, then he just raised some technical question and turned it down.

Britain seeks the support of the Commonwealth in the application to join the Common Market.
Above: *Commonwealth Prime Ministers outside Marlborough House in London, August 1962.*
Left to right, Duncan Sandys, Archbishop Makarios, F. D. Goka (Ghana), Robert Menzies
(Australia), John Diefenbaker (Canada), Jawaharlal Nehru (India). Below: *The opening*
session of the Prime Ministers' conference.

IT WAS HAROLD MACMILLAN'S view, therefore, that General de Gaulle, who until Rambouillet had made plain no fundamental objection to British entry, was surprised by Macmillan's success and had then to find a pretext to close the gates of Europe on him.

It is history that the Prime Minister of Great Britain and the President of France, animated though they may have been by a common perception that the old nation states of Europe were 'overtowered' by super powers on either side, and linked by a somewhat distant but mutual respect from their days as wartime companions in Algiers in 1943, could not now – twenty years later – agree their views of Europe. Few can venture the reason why better than the Prime Minister who eventually succeeded where Harold Macmillan failed, Edward Heath.

HEATH: This again is one of the controversial points over which history will argue. They may well come to the conclusion it was because of the different historical backgrounds of the two men: that de Gaulle had a deep-seated view that Britain would look across the Atlantic all the time to the United States instead of to its friends in Europe – and that this was not going to be changed by Mr Macmillan being Prime Minister – whereas de Gaulle was concerned with the unity of Europe and particularly of the Community.

CHARLTON: Is that a judgement which you support?

HEATH: I don't personally, no. I can understand de Gaulle, with his background, holding that point of view. I can also see that he would have viewed some of the questions we raised, for example over the question of agriculture, as only confirming him in his view, that what we wanted to do was to create a Community in our own image instead of joining a Community which already existed. I suppose, in fairness to President de Gaulle, one could say that he had this question in his mind throughout. The answer may have fluctuated from time to time, but he finally came down on the side that we were not really thinking in terms of a *European* Community, but still really thinking in terms of an Anglo-American special relationship which wanted to have some relationship or other *with* the Community.

EQUIVOCATION, as that perplexed diplomat Hamlet remarked, will undo us. And as far as General de Gaulle was concerned it undid Harold Macmillan's attempt to take Britain into Europe.

In that last answer Edward Heath appears to reject one popular and widespread belief – that de Gaulle had, from the outset, determined to exclude Britain. If so, it must have been the very essence of the argument which Macmillan deployed to him, at their meetings in 1962, with which de Gaulle took issue. Mr Macmillan has given us in his own words what he considered this essence to be when he talked to the BBC upon the publication of his own memoirs.

MACMILLAN: I used to say to him [de Gaulle], you bring your history and your position on the mainland. What do we bring? We bring into this our friendship with America. That is an asset, not a liability. We bring what is left of our great Commonwealth and Imperial tradition. That is an asset – just as you bring in the French Commonwealth. It's a mean mind which thinks that you're less a good friend because you bring in another friend to help!

PUT LIKE THAT, Mr Macmillan would seem to confirm that, as events neared their climax in 1962, his own position was to conceive of British membership of the European Community as an addition to and not a substitute for the Anglo-American and Commonwealth links. When de Gaulle contemplated the aggregate of these final weights in the balance, modified though they may have been by the outcome of the negotiations, he chose to see them as enigma variations on the earlier British stance over Europe – trying to create an alternative, as Edward Heath believed de Gaulle saw it – a Community in Britain's own preferred image rather than the one which had taken root.

HEATH: De Gaulle was not prepared to have an alternative relationship, because he said, perfectly fairly, that what we would try to do would be to get the benefits without any of the obligations. If you live in a Community you have obligations as well as the opportunity to benefit. So in that respect he was taking up a perfectly fair position. But it was not commensurate with saying, Well, there must be some *other* relationship with the Community. He must have known that himself, that another relationship was not possible.
CHARLTON: So throughout, the conference with Mr Macmillan really failed to clear that matter up? Whether Britain was still trying to have it both ways, as I suggest de Gaulle may have seen it; that we were still not prepared to make the choice?
HEATH: It's here, of course, that you come to these very difficult nuclear questions, and to Macmillan's meeting at Nassau with President Kennedy. I do not think that President de Gaulle ever thought that Mr Macmillan was deceiving him on these particular items. Some argued afterwards that the veto happened because President de Gaulle was so angry that the British Prime Minister had double-crossed him or deceived him. I do not take that view at all. On the other hand, President de Gaulle can have taken it that it only confirmed his view that, when you came to a 'crunch' item, then the British would look across the Atlantic instead of to Europe.

IN STRATEGIC POLITICS the nuclear foundations for the conduct of foreign and military policy show up like a barium meal! An almost infallible indicator of where, at the last trump, sovereignty and allegiance lie, the subject of nuclear weapons came up at both Mr Macmillan's seminal encounters with the General in 1962. At their first meeting in June, at the Château de Champs in Paris, it was introduced by Macmillan, although in what terms and with precisely what intentions is still uncertain. The British papers will not be available, under the thirty-year rule, until the 1990s. However, it seems to be fairly generally agreed that it was at some time after this meeting that de Gaulle made up his mind to veto Britain's application to join the Community.

The Prime Minister concentrated upon a single objective with the French President, seeking to convince him of the seriousness of Britain's purpose, and by so doing get de Gaulle to yield the necessary concessions.

One who was present at these famously equivocal meetings, and who made the official record of their conversations (which, when necessary, he also translated for the two men), was Harold Macmillan's Principal Private Secretary, Sir Philip de Zulueta.

President Kennedy with Prime Minister Macmillan, Nassau 1962.

ZULUETA: Mr Macmillan tried at Champs to convince General de Gaulle that Britain was serious in wanting to join the Common Market, because the impression which we had got, rightly or wrongly, was that the General thought that this was all some rather complicated Conservative Party ploy for winning the next election. And I think that at Champs Mr Macmillan did in fact succeed in persuading the General that we *were* serious and that we really wanted it. I mean, the General kept on saying, 'What on earth do you want to bother with the Common Market for? It's all rather a waste of time more or less. Are you serious? And it's rather inconvenient if you are! I don't like the Common Market very much but I've got it and why on earth do you want to join it?' I mean, again it goes back to that paradox, 'You and we see things in rather the same way. Why do you want to join this rather tiresome organisation with which I am lumbered!' Whether he was being disingenuous is another matter, but that was really the general line of his argument.

CHARLTON: Did Macmillan think he was being disingenuous?

ZULUETA: No, not entirely. I think he half thought that and half didn't think that. It was clearly awkward for de Gaulle. I think that the General did not at all want to share the leadership of Europe, because the problems which Britain might be having – was having – about its future world role and so forth had obviously hit the French harder and sooner. The only way really that France was going to take the place at the top table which the General wanted it to have, and thought was her right, was by being the leader of Europe.

CHARLTON: Now, it is the nuclear offer isn't it at Champs which makes it clear to de Gaulle that Britain *is* serious?

ZULUETA: Well, yes. Not only that but the general way of approaching the whole subject.

CHARLTON: But our essential offer is to what, to Europeanise the British deterrent?

ZULUETA: Yes. Yes. In so far as that can be achieved.

CHARLTON: Well, you've said a great deal in those last few words. How far did Macmillan go, really?

ZULUETA: Obviously there was a limit to what was possible really, because of the whole very close involvement with the United States. I don't think he ever envisaged something which would be outside NATO. His concept would have been, I think, something inside NATO, where Britain would not have a better, if that is the right word, a better position or a more important position than the French.

CHARLTON: But Macmillan is offering something which was not really in his gift. Because the Americans controlled the essentials, the technical nuclear information?

ZULUETA: Well, there were elements which could have been offered.

CHARLTON: And which were offered by Macmillan?

ZULUETA: And which were offered. Well, not directly; they were hinted at. And also I think that there was a possible Anglo-French arrangement which might have been entirely acceptable to the Americans. I mean that they would probably have accepted something between Britain and France within the NATO context.

CHARLTON: What was its general character? What was possible?

ZULUETA: Oh well, it's too difficult to go into all that, but it was all to do with delivery systems and all that kind of thing, which one might have adopted.

CHARLTON: Doesn't de Gaulle's position at Champs rather dispose of the suspicion, long held in Britain, that the whole thing was a plot to keep Britain out? In other words, it is not until 1962 when it is really brought home to him at Champs that we are serious about this and that we *do* want to come in?

ZULUETA: That is my reading of it. One can't be sure but that is what I think was the case. Therefore he did not have to plot to keep us out before 1962 because he didn't think that we should ever really try to get in in a serious way. Conversely, of course, from 1962 onwards he then has to make up his own mind.

CHARLTON: When do you think he does make up his own mind, from what you saw?

ZULUETA: I should have thought he made up his own mind probably fairly soon after Champs, in the course of that summer. And I think that the mistake, or a mistake which we probably made, was to underrate the importance of the French elections in the autumn of that year, when the Gaullists for the first time got a parliamentary majority. Until that point the General was not strong enough for his own peace of mind in France, internally. Had we been able to – and we had a problem with our own public opinion, in the House of Commons, and everything else – it would have been better tactically from our point of view to have pushed the thing to the point of decision in July or August 1962. If we could have done that it would have been rather more difficult for the General to have given his categorical veto. I do think the French political scene played a more important part than people always realised.

CHARLTON: Of course, Macmillan earlier had pleaded with de Gaulle, hadn't he, to slow down integration in Europe until the British question was decided. Did Macmillan hold off at Champs trying to force the issue? A gesture to the French, trying not to antagonise them and the Europeans who were going ahead with their consolidation of the Community?

ZULUETA: I don't think that, after Champs, Macmillan had got the impression that de Gaulle was hostile. He got the impression, I think, that perhaps he had not made up his mind. And there was probably an element in Macmillan's thought that, you know, to push them too hard might push the General into a hostile reaction.

ANOTHER WHO WAS AT CHAMPS was de Gaulle's Foreign Minister, Couve de Murville. Couve's recollections, as the General apparently did most of the listening and Macmillan most of the talking, have a more pessimistic emphasis than those of Philip de Zulueta.

COUVE DE MURVILLE: How can I explain it? It was rather sad, enormously sad I would say. I mean, the feeling that these two old companions – because they were, after all, old companions – had difficulties in understanding one another. And, at the end, had difficulty in seeing their way to an agreement. It was not entirely negative but it gave, all the same, the impression that it could be very difficult to come to an understanding, and on both sides there was a sort of melancholy that they could not agree.

CHARLTON: As you say, it's not clear how much they understood one another. To what do you attribute that essentially? It's said, for example, that de Gaulle like Macmillan thought very little in specifics but more in rather lofty generalities. Was the negotiating style of the two of them the reason for it, do you think?

COUVE DE MURVILLE: Yes, but you know it was the same thing on both sides. They had no intention, no pretence to discuss economic topics: to say what would happen with, let us say, New Zealand lamb! It was not one of the big world problems that were in question at the time! No, they did not really discuss the substance of the matters, they discussed it in much more general terms. Macmillan was not very keen on economic problems, and de Gaulle had not the habit, either, to discuss freely the details of problems.

CHARLTON: But was it clear to you that the two of them were not really making clear to each other their relative positions? If I may say so, your English is nigh perfect, it must have been clearer to you perhaps if they were mis-understanding one another?

COUVE DE MURVILLE: There was a misunderstanding. I would say the main misunderstanding was more on the British side than on the French side. On both sides, from the beginning, everybody knew that it would be very difficult to come to any kind of agreement. In other words, it was more or less a desperate affair. But I would say that on the British side they did not understand very well why, and for a simple reason, I think. It is always very difficult to put yourself in the place of another man, and it was difficult for the British to understand that we were keen on keeping the system of the Common Market when they themselves found that it was a bad one! But they could not understand why we insisted in seeming to believe that it was a good system!

CHARLTON: General de Gaulle, am I right, saw Macmillan as 'demandeur', the man who was actually asking for something?

COUVE DE MURVILLE: Well, yes, yes. Macmillan hoped that things would all the same be possible. If he came to Champs it was because he knew that the negotiations were not going well and that maybe he could convince de Gaulle to make the necessary concessions for the negotiations to be made easier.

CHARLTON: Before he left London Macmillan had disavowed in advance any intention to raise the nuclear question, the defence issue. And of course many chose to recognise in that a technique in diplomacy – to disavow the thing which was perhaps uppermost in your mind! It is still not clear to me how this issue was raised at Champs.

COUVE DE MURVILLE: It was not raised as a natural question. No, it may have been mentioned in conversations, let us say in lunch conversations between the two men, but it was not a topic for discussion. It was not at all the same thing as the Rambouillet meeting. Of course, the reason why Britain wanted to enter the Common Market has always been for political reasons. And when you speak of politics it means also defence, that is true. But in the Franco-British discussions that was never mentioned. The discussion was always linked exclusively to economic affairs. Except in the Rambouillet meeting which was a different one.

CHARLTON: You see, some people I think feel that Macmillan would have been receptive to any sort of initiative from France or encouragement from France in this field, because at this time Macmillan wasn't sure what the response would be from the Americans in making it possible for Britain to continue as a nuclear power. The question of Skybolt was hanging over the British.

COUVE DE MURVILLE: But the British was a basically different approach from the French approach. We never imagined our nuclear deterrent as anything other than a French deterrent, which meant that we had to accept the effort and therefore the expenditure of doing it ourselves. Britain never imagined that its nuclear deterrent could be built without the help of the United States; that means inevitably without its being controlled by the United States. The approach was basically the opposite.

CHARLTON: But can you say that de Gaulle made it unequivocally clear to Macmillan at Champs that the essential qualification to be considered 'European' was not to be dependent in this field on the Americans?

COUVE DE MURVILLE: No. First of all, that was not discussed, this question of nuclear armament. Secondly, how could he say that, knowing the policy and the attitude of his partners in the Common Market? He couldn't have said to Britain that they could enter the Common Market if they adopted a policy in defence and foreign affairs completely opposite to that of the Federal Republic of Germany. I repeat once again that what was discussed at Champs was the conditions of entry by Britain into the Common Market.

CHARLTON: But as long as the ambiguity, or that particular question, was left unclarified or unstated by General de Gaulle, can Macmillan be forgiven for

leaving Champs with the impression that he had convinced de Gaulle of the
seriousness of Britain's conversion to Europe?
COUVE DE MURVILLE: He had not convinced. I don't think you can draw that
conclusion from what happened at Champs. From the beginning they realised
that it would be very difficult to come to any kind of agreement, and as things
developed the conclusions did not change.

THEIR NEXT MEETING, at Rambouillet in December 1962, six months after
the one at Champs, was Macmillan's last with the General before the veto in
January of 1963. In the interval, during the last and most difficult phase of the
negotiations, what Edward Heath has referred to as 'one of these very difficult
nuclear issues', which normally lie submerged, suddenly arose like some
volcanic island from the surrounding sea, to surface in the middle of Harold
Macmillan's intricate cross-Channel courtship of the President of France. It
was the result of a decision taken in the Pentagon in Washington by the
American Defense Secretary Robert McNamara.
     It will be remembered that in 1960, before the decision was taken to apply for
membership of the European Community, the British government had been
forced to cancel, on the grounds of cost and an unforeseen and premature
obsolescence, the British strategic rocket Blue Streak. Intended to be armed
with the British hydrogen bomb, Blue Streak was envisaged at the time as a
wholly sovereign and independent weapon, and the means of maintaining a
credible British nuclear deterrent. Now, in the new circumstances created by
the decision to cancel Blue Streak, Macmillan turned at once to the Americans.
He secured from President Eisenhower, in return for granting the United
States a base for its nuclear submarines at Holy Loch in Scotland, a promise of
a substitute. This was a nuclear missile called Skybolt, then being built for the
United States Air Force. At this same time the Prime Minister received an
imprecise promise of an offer in the future of what was then emerging as
perhaps the ultimate weapon, the Polaris submarine. Skybolt, it was agreed,
would be manufactured to the joint requirements of the American B52
bombers and also the V-bombers of the Royal Air Force. A decision had been
taken which deepened fundamentally the interdependence and intimacy of
Anglo-American strategic collaboration.
     But in 1962, following some disappointing trials, yet upon a pretext which was
at the time a matter for some British suspicion as well as concern, the new
Kennedy administration cancelled the Skybolt missile. Thus, at a stroke it
might be said, Britain had been unilaterally disarmed!
     Such 'suspicions' as there were about McNamara's Skybolt decision had
begun to circulate following speeches which the American Defense Secretary
had delivered in the summer and autumn of 1962 about nuclear weapons. At
Ann Arbor in Michigan in June of that year he had put forward views which
Harold Macmillan subsequently described as being compounded of 'vigour and
clumsiness', and which were a powerful condemnation of all *national* nuclear
forces 'except those of course of the United States'. This speech and others by
McNamara which followed up this theme just before Macmillan's fateful
rendezvous with de Gaulle at Rambouillet should for the moment divert us.
     The public deployment by McNamara of this new American position against
national nuclear forces, on the grounds that they 'lacked credibility' and were

an unnecessary duplication of great cost and effort, was taken as a general condemnation of existing British and French defence and foreign policy. The specific British suspicion was that, *should* Skybolt be deemed to have failed to meet its demanding technical challenge – while it was fired from an aircraft it was not shot downwards but up into the atmosphere in the manner of a much larger missile after launch from the ground – then its cancellation might not be entirely unwelcome in the United States if the corollary of it was the enforced withdrawal of Britain from membership of the nuclear club. It had now become American policy to encourage the integration of nuclear forces under American control within the NATO Alliance. The British Defence Minister dealing with McNamara's initiatives was that leading 'European', Peter Thorneycroft.

THORNEYCROFT: My response was negative, because I knew that there were powerful forces in America who were most anxious to contrive the end of an independent British deterrent and one way of doing it was to have some form of multinational or multilateral force. It was a sort of multinational navy going round the world, with French cooks and Japanese – everybody was in it! But it wasn't going to work because nobody would ever fire it! I mean, there would be a struggle, a mutiny in the crew before it went off! There were a lot of 'way-out' suggestions put forward for bringing everybody together, but their purpose was to prevent the British having an independent deterrent. My advice from the Chiefs of Staff and the scientists and everybody there in the Ministry of Defence was that we needed an independent deterrent, and every Government has accepted it ever since. Why did we have it at all? I think, before one talks about the effect it had on Europe or anything else – it was a fantastically expensive thing to do – the first thing one has to ask is *ought* one to have done it? You couldn't justify it as an instrument of foreign policy. You would have to justify it as instrument of deterrence.

On that, when I got to the Ministry of Defence I asked for a paper to be produced which should bear no relationship to the fact that I was a Conservative, or to anything that any Conservative minister had ever said, and which should get them to argue to me whether we *ought* to have an independent British deterrent. They produced a paper, and the Ministry of Defence and all the Service ministries and the scientists were quite clear that there is an impregnable case for having an independent British deterrent. That paper, or its successor, has determined the policy, not only of the Conservative governments but of Labour governments as well, ever since. Whether it's Wilson or Callaghan or one of the Conservatives, *all* of them in fact have been prepared to pay very large sums of money in order to have that.

CHARLTON: It's not so much spoken of in those terms by Macmillan, is it? I mean, Macmillan sees it as a seat at the table, an ability to influence great affairs?

THORNEYCROFT: Nye Bevan said you'll send us 'naked into the conference chamber' and all that, but this is the imagery of politicians. The reality is that you would not spend the vast sums of money involved unless you had an overwhelming deterrent and defence case. You couldn't get it through any cabinet.

CHARLTON: But your view, your interpretation of what McNamara said, was that his speech was directed at Britain too and not just at France?

THORNEYCROFT: Well, it would be directed against France as well. The

Americans, and I pay great tribute to them, and their overall deterrent is a
critical factor in having prevented major war in the world. Don't let's underestimate what their achievement has been. But there are many people in
America who would prefer that neither Britain nor France had an independent
deterrent of their own. I don't share that view because, in the last resort, a
Russian might just think it possible that America would *not* come to our aid. If a
Russian thought that then the deterrent effect of the American weapons would
be useless.
CHARLTON: That seems clearly to envisage that – you've got a weapon which
stretches into the next century as a credible weapon – that you perhaps all have
in your mind the possibility that one day the Americans will go home?
THORNEYCROFT: I think the important point to make is not so much that the
Americans may go home, but that is conceivable obviously – with human frailty,
a weak President, an atmosphere of retreat in America might bring that about.
But it's not so much what *we* think but what the Russians think. If the Russians
think the Americans are going home, the American deterrent ceases to be a
deterrent. And it's at that point, based on a *Russian* view, that we have to make
up our mind, I think, and have an independent deterrent of some kind ourselves.
That is the great argument for it.

ONE MAY TAKE THE RISK of identifying, as being among those Americans
Lord Thorneycroft considered would have preferred Britain and France not to
have pursued independent nuclear deterrents, President Kennedy's senior
adviser on Europe, the Under-Secretary of State, George Ball.

BALL: I don't think there was any great effort made to persuade Europe to
abandon the nuclear deterrent. There was a reluctance to extend to it any
American assistance in the construction of a nuclear deterrent, for any nations
other than Great Britain. This had a historical basis. The British had done the
initial work on the development of nuclear weapons and they were entitled
therefore to claim a special place, a special position, which was recognised in the
American legislation. There was a certain unease that developed among many
of us that this might be a source of trouble in the future, that it would encourage
the French to go forward with their Force de Frappe, and that later we would
be up against the problem of a German desire to play a nuclear role which,
obviously, would have been disastrous from the point of view of Germany's
relations with the rest of Europe.
    As far as France was concerned we were never happy with the Force de
Frappe, but of course this preceded even de Gaulle, this came in the Felix
Gaillard government in France. He was a great friend of mine, and when he
was Prime Minister I remember I once went to see Felix in Paris, and he
clapped me on the back and said, 'George, this has been a tremendous day! I've
just authorised the beginning of the construction of the French nuclear
capability!' And I told him that I felt it was a very great mistake and I was unhappy with it. But there was nothing we could do about it. I wasn't in the
government then.

IN DECEMBER 1962 the impending cancellation by the Americans of the
Skybolt missile thrust itself to the fore on the very eve of Harold Macmillan's

seminal final meeting: the one with de Gaulle on 15–16 December at Rambouillet, and three days later his talks with President Kennedy at Nassau in the Bahamas. At the first Macmillan would be making a last desperate attempt to get de Gaulle to yield to him and withdraw his opposition to Britain's 'terms' for entry to the Common Market. The other would be dominated by the battle with the American President to make it possible for Britain to continue as a nuclear power.

On 11 December in Paris, at a meeting of NATO Defence Ministers, Thorneycroft was left in little doubt as a result of his talks with McNamara that the Americans meant to abandon Skybolt. The British Defence Minister was with Macmillan when the confirmation came of the failure, by Skybolt, of an all-important test flight.

THORNEYCROFT: I remember seeing Harold Macmillan the morning we heard that Skybolt had finally failed, and he said, 'Well, what do you do?' And I said, 'Well, look, if I could – there would be an awful row – but', I said, 'if I could wave a wand and end up in three weeks' time with the Polaris submarine, it would be a wonderful arrangement for this country! It's a far better weapon and it is the only weapon really which is available and which can do the job'. And I remember him saying, 'Well, what we have got to do is to end up there.' And somehow or other we did. But there was a great controversy over this, of course, between the services, amongst others, because the Air Force wanted an airborne weapon and the Navy, of course, were prepared, rather happily, to go to Polaris.
CHARLTON: But reading what's available to people like me to read, it seems that you probably wanted Polaris anyway from the beginning, and the cancellation of Skybolt was seen as fortuitious really?
THORNEYCROFT: Yes. They offered us to go on with Skybolt if we wanted to. President Kennedy offered it to me across the table at Nassau. He said, 'Look, I'll give you all the expertise, the professionals, and then you can finish it'. He knew that I was under great pressure to go on with it. But I said that I was not prepared to buy the shares which his Defense Department had sold that morning! I thought that it was far better for us to go to something they had some *faith* in. I was sure it was right. We would have spent a packet of money on Skybolt and really got nothing at the end of it.

BY HIS INTIMATIONS THAT Skybolt would be scrapped McNamara had rather played into Thorneycroft's hands. But Polaris also carried wider and more significant implications than the rival considerations of the Services. It solved the British problem of a strategic nuclear deterrent for at least three decades ahead. It also enshrined 'Anglo-America' and the special relationship in a particularly vivid way. These new facts were sources of additional consideration and concern within the Kennedy administration. George Ball was one who saw that the step from Skybolt to Polaris was one which would, in his view, complicate the principal American design of British entry to the European Community.

BALL: McNamara did not have the same ideological approach as I had, because I thought that what we were doing was propelling Britain into a whole new generation of nuclear weapons, and that this was going to create obstacles among the European nations, which indeed – I do not know how much real effect it had – but it certainly provided a major excuse for de Gaulle's decision to exclude Britain from Europe at that time. So I was sorry from the point of European politics and the effect on the Alliance generally.

CHARLTON: How do you object to the way that McNamara handled that?

BALL: In the first place, he did not take my advice from the beginning. He had come to the conclusion that we should not go forward with Skybolt because he tended to look at things in the terms of cost-effectiveness. He thought that the state of the art was such, at that time, that it was not possible to build an air-to-ground missile which had any substantial range with the uncertain platform of an airplane as a launching pad. They had spent a lot of money but they hadn't been able to solve these problems. Therefore Skybolt ought to be scrapped.

I think his considerations totally eliminated the political implications of this. I think his thinking did! When he was going to London to see Thorneycroft, he called me in advance and said he was going to London to talk to Thorneycroft and he proposed to read the following statement at London Airport, which he then read to me. And I said, 'Bob, I think that's a great mistake. It's not proper to make a statement like that when you arrive in a country in advance of seeing the Minister, and anyway I think the substance of it is wrong! What it, in effect, says is Skybolt is no good and has to be scrapped. That is something which ought to emerge from a discussion and from negotiations. Why foreclose the possibility that it may be desirable to keep it alive for political reasons?' Well, all this he totally ignored. He went ahead and made this statement. And, as you may recall, it created quite a flap in London at that time!

CHARLTON: Yes. Am I right to suggest that essentially what is involved for you in that decision is that, *had* Skybolt been continued – and you wished to keep open some possibility of continuing it – it was a weapon-system which ran into a dead end after a certain period of time? Whereas the Polaris weapon, the submarines, prolonged Britain's nuclear strategic capabilities and her influence far ahead?

BALL: And prolonged the period of Anglo-American special relations in the field of nuclear weaponry, which, I had a feeling, was going to be a major impediment in trying to work out closer relations with France in particular, and which, over time, would be a real problem as far as Germany was concerned.

THE WHOLE HISTORIC ENTERPRISE, 'Britain and Europe', was now poised at brooding, but almost thrilling, uncertainty. Two all-important meetings were set down: with de Gaulle at Rambouillet for two days, 15–16 December, and after that Macmillan would cross the Atlantic to his meeting with President Kennedy at Nassau from 18–21 December. The Skybolt/Polaris decision could be taken only with Kennedy. Polaris was not yet secured, but first there would be de Gaulle. With France in the accelerated process of acquiring her own nuclear deterrent, the nuclear issue was one to which de Gaulle, it would later become apparent, had paid sedulous attention, and for whom it had a most particular significance. It became the dominant theme at Rambouillet.

It was after shooting pheasants in the rain and cold of the morning of 15 December that Macmillan sat down to talk to the General in the afternoon. They were alone except for de Gaulle's secretary, Burin des Roziers, and

Macmillan's secretary and chief adviser, Philip de Zulueta. Sir Philip took the official notes of their conversation. It was here at Rambouillet that the Prime Minister found himself to be without not just Skybolt, but also divested of his European hopes – that design for Britain to which since 'Messina', as Rab Butler considered, Harold Macmillan 'had become more devoted', and which he had so creatively and courageously pursued.

ZULUETA: I think the first thing to say is that it was pretty clear to me, and I think to Mr Macmillan, that the General was against our going into the Common Market. I mean that I cannot say that I was particularly surprised when he gave his veto, although I was rather taken aback at the precise way in which it was done. He was against it basically, I think, by then, and it was fairly obvious that he *was* against it.

CHARLTON: What do you remember personally from those moments when you're sitting there, taking the notes between the two of them? How does de Gaulle make this clear?

ZULUETA: Oh well, it just developed in the course of things. He didn't actually say so – I haven't reread the minutes for ages – I don't think he actually says so, but it's fairly clear from the way he approaches it that he doesn't really want it. The other point, of course, was that he was very sceptical, because Macmillan was saying that we knew we had to renegotiate the whole Skybolt position – you remember that the bombshell about Skybolt was really dropped by McNamara almost in the middle of this operation – and de Gaulle is obviously sceptical that we are going to get the sort of thing which Macmillan *says* he is going to have from the United States.

CHARLTON: Which is possibly Polaris, or probably Polaris, as a substitute?

ZULUETA: Well, yes. Macmillan said it would be either aerial or submarine. He insisted on the independence, whether it was aerial or submarine. Whether de Gaulle fully understood what he was saying in that sense I don't know. He probably did.

CHARLTON: Why do you think de Gaulle was taking that position?

ZULUETA: Because I think he was being briefed by his very able Ambassador in Washington, M. Hervé Alphand, who was probably getting his briefing from Mr George Ball and other people in the State Department.

CHARLTON: Which was that Britain would be excluded from . . ?

ZULUETA: Well, would *not* have a comparable offer been made to replace Skybolt.

CHARLTON: And de Gaulle interprets that, does he, as driving Britain towards Europe?

ZULUETA: I would have thought so, yes.

CHARLTON: That Macmillan would be forced to come to de Gaulle as a result?

ZULUETA: That would be my conclusion on that, yes.

CHARLTON: Was it also Macmillan's?

ZULUETA: I think so. I would think so. It was a very likely result. It would have been a very likely result.

CHARLTON: Which only makes this whole Polaris deal with Kennedy even more fascinating, that Macmillan was able to produce that in the circumstances?

ZULUETA: Yes, and of course the other thing which is interesting is that, for all the 'European' predilections, which you're quite right in saying the Americans to some extent had, it was the British actually who persuaded the Americans to offer to the French the same terms they'd offered to the British – and which de Gaulle found unacceptable. Now whether he found them unacceptable genuinely, or whether he *wanted* to find them unacceptable, I don't know.

CHARLTON: Is that still, for you, one of the unanswered questions?

ZULUETA: Yes.

CHARLTON: What do you think the answer is?

ZULUETA: Well, I think it's a mixture of the two. I don't think it really suited him to do a deal with the United States. De Gaulle was essentially a French politician, however great a statesman he may have been in other ways. It suited him to have an independent position for France.

BY THE NEXT DAY at Rambouillet a rising damp had begun to chill the chief participants and permeate their talks. The Foreign Ministers, Lord Home for Britain and Couve de Murville for France, were admitted following a long discussion which de Gaulle and Macmillan had had about the Skybolt issue in particular, and the deep-seated themes which lie buried in the nuclear issue in general. In his own recollections of this day at Rambouillet, Couve de Murville chose to make the direct link between the outcome of the British application to join the Common Market and the question of the nuclear deterrent.

COUVE DE MURVILLE: It was raised, of course, and it was raised between de Gaulle and Macmillan alone. They spent, I think, all the morning discussing that. We, the Foreign Ministers, joined after that and it was clear that it had not been very pleasant and that disagreement was total on this nuclear issue. With, of course, the consequence that it did not help the negotiation regarding the Common Market. As Macmillan spoke good French, it took part in French to a great extent on both sides.

CHARLTON: I'd like you to tell me something else. The meeting having begun with Macmillan summarising the British position, General de Gaulle then intervenes – you of course have seen the record of these conversations – and talks about Churchill and quotes the famous remark which is always quoted in France – made to de Gaulle by Churchill in June 1944 at the time of the invasion – 'Every time I have to choose between Europe and . . .'

COUVE DE MURVILLE: And 'le grand large!'

CHARLTON: 'Le grand large', yes, the open sea, the world at large, America. Then I will choose 'le grand large', says Churchill. Incidentally, do you remember that remark actually being made?

COUVE DE MURVILLE: No, but you know, it's like many so-called historic remarks which have never been made, but which do symbolise an attitude. And it's true that this remark is really symbolic of what has been, for centuries, the position of Britain. I mean Britain being part of Europe, or very close to Europe, and at the same time having its main interest overseas, in, as it was called in the old days, the British Empire. You see, the funny thing is that *all* the Common Market discussions of 1961 and 1962 developed on that theme, because the main issues, and the at times insoluble issues were (i) the existence of the sterling area and (ii) trade relations between Britain and the Commonwealth countries. And they were two things, two matters, upon which the British were, I may say, adamant; they did not want to accept the idea of dissolving the sterling area or of having their trade relations with the Commonwealth different from what they'd been ever since the beginning.

SOME ACCOUNTS OF THIS famous meeting have spoken of one moment in particular, 'an electric moment', when tension between the two was at its highest, the moment when Macmillan was perhaps made most acutely aware that his enterprise was probably foundering. Philip de Zulueta remembers the 'moment', as he has already indicated, as being something rather more widespread!

ZULUETA: It wasn't one sentence. It was de Gaulle's whole development of how he saw the role of Europe and how he saw the role of Britain, and that he didn't really see how they fitted in together and so on. It developed in the course of the conversation. It was clear that we were not at one.
CHARLTON: What was the atmosphere?
ZULUETA: Well, de Gaulle, as always, was a most charming and courteous host, but we were *not* getting on frightfully well from the point of view of policy.
CHARLTON: But perhaps you can help us more? When Macmillan leans back in his chair and says, 'In other words, there has been a *fundamental* objection from the very beginning to our entry', and more or less accuses de Gaulle of negotiating in Brussels in bad faith?
ZULUETA: Well, I don't think he does that! The one doesn't follow from the other. I mean, Macmillan is trying to argue to de Gaulle, 'Well, all right, yes but –' He is really saying, 'Look, it's no use your saying that *now* because if you really felt *that* you ought to have said it long ago!
CHARLTON: Why was that moment allowed to pass? We're told that apparently Lord Home intervened and changed the subject?
ZULUETA: It may be so. It may have been what happened. I do remember the Prime Minister saying something of the kind. Well, there was no answer to it, was there? It was true, as a statement. It was perhaps better to pass on to something else.

IF ONE MIGHT REASONABLY SUPPOSE that Zulueta's eyes were bent principally upon de Gaulle, Couve de Murville was watching Macmillan. Even now, twenty years later, it is not difficult to imagine that Couve's own air of languid, courteous detachment was itself part of the bedside manner – that distant fatalism and pessimism of Rambouillet where de Gaulle shut the gates of mercy on Macmillan.

COUVE DE MURVILLE: And then Macmillan was very sad and he almost broke down. I don't believe that he really understood the reasons for our attitude. He could not understand that they had lived in and thought about the world so much, for hours, that they could not meet. Which means really that he could not imagine that Britain could change! The fact is that an evolution has taken place, and Britain *has* changed enormously since the sixties. I mean from the point of view of the European Common Market.
CHARLTON: Can you confirm one of the myths about the conference, that de

Gaulle, when he saw Macmillan so crestfallen, quoted the words of the famous
Edith Piaf song, 'Ne pleurez pas Milord'?

COUVE DE MURVILLE: Oh no, no, no, he didn't say that. No. But he used the
words when he reported the meeting at our Council of Ministers, the French
Cabinet. I don't remember exactly how it came about but he concluded by
saying that, and that, after all, it was not tragic. Things were not ended for all
time, altogether. And therefore 'ne pleurez pas Milord'!

CHARLTON: But Macmillan knew when he left Rambouillet that he'd been
beaten? Defeated?

COUVE DE MURVILLE: He knew, yes. Not beaten, but that things were in a
deadlock. Because it was really finished. And the agony lasted for another two
months.

'AGONY' SEEMS RIGHT. Macmillan's own stylish, moving and exciting
account, given in his memoirs, of this tremendously exacting month of
December 1962 can leave his readers in small doubt.

After Rambouillet, the Prime Minister was deeply depressed and still having
to reflect upon the residual uncertainty about France's ultimate intentions. But
he was in consequence also faced with that 'heartless' necessity – choice – in an
even more acute form. Following a single crowded day at home in London, he
and his colleagues set out for Nassau, there to meet President Kennedy.

Macmillan had 'acted beautifully to de Gaulle at Rambouillet,' we should
recall Lord Butler saying, 'but the trouble was de Gaulle did not act back!' So
now the Prime Minister had to reassemble all his subtle armoury of historical
and sentimental persuasion and appeal. He had to bring it to bear at Nassau
upon the youthful President of the great power to which, culminating in the
outcome of the Second World War, so much of Britain's former world role had
been repatriated. The issues of Skybolt and Polaris had now been invested,
following Rambouillet, with an even more profound and symbolic importance.
Ahead they lay, more akin to Scylla and Charybdis, as the British and American
teams approached their joint rendezvous in those shoaling strategic waters!
Among the helmsmen of American policy with President Kennedy was George
Ball.

BALL: Kennedy was very fond of Prime Minister Macmillan and I think there
was a mutual feeling of great warmth. Macmillan had indicated to Kennedy
that, politically, it was very important for him to find a way out after the scrap-
ping of Skybolt, and that otherwise this would have created enormous problems
for him. My own view was that Kennedy simply responded to the despairing cry
of a politician in distress! A kind of fellow feeling. He wasn't going to let
Macmillan down, and he was going to help Macmillan out. He saw it basically
in those terms.

CHARLTON: How well prepared was Kennedy for this decision?

BALL: I don't think very well. I don't think this whole decision had been
prepared properly within the Government.

CHARLTON: The story that he was briefed at the last minute flying down in
the plane, is that true?

BALL: Yes, I think that is probably true. Flying down, yes, Mac Bundy
[McGeorge Bundy] and I went back and we both talked to him. And

Ambassador David Ormsby-Gore as he was then, Lord Harlech, also talked to him and told him very clearly, and quite properly, what Prime Minister Macmillan's concerns were. Kennedy had put his pyjamas on and was resting. So we were talking to him. But as far as the advanced preparation was concerned I really had not been involved in it, because Rusk [the Secretary of State, Dean Rusk] had been involved in it. At the last minute the decision was made that I should go to Nassau. I had rather strong views about it all but they had not particularly matured at that time.

CHARLTON: It's interesting that Rusk, the Secretary of State, does not go to Nassau, having done or been involved in the 'advanced preparation' – and for a decision which, after all, fills the British universe?

BALL: Yes, for the rather odd reason, actually, that he had a diplomatic dinner to which the whole diplomatic corps had been invited. The Nassau meeting date had been set rather quickly. Rusk had an obligation, he thought, not to disappoint the ambassadors by not being there, and it seemed too late to change the dinner. So, since I was his *alter ego* it was simply assumed I would go. And I went as Acting Secretary of State.

CHARLTON: It's quite extraordinary, though, that a decision of this magnitude is taken without . . . quite unprepared?

BALL: Well, I'll tell you one reason for it. I think there was a tendency on Rusk's part to leave this to Secretary McNamara of the Defense Department, on the grounds this was fundamentally a weapons matter. He did not have the same ideological compulsions that I had.

AT NASSAU THE BRITISH were taut and angry. Suspicions about the reason for the cancellation of Skybolt were unallayed. To view it in more emotional terms, twice now had the sword of independent action, the ability to carry out a military and defence policy, been struck from Britain's hands by her most intimate ally, America: Suez in 1956; Skybolt in 1962.

The Prime Minister faced the President. His position and that of the United Kingdom were now precarious. Rambouillet had failed; so had Skybolt. Macmillan had no substitute for the success of either, and in terms of practical reality the nuclear weapons at this level of strategic diplomacy were proving essential for its effective conduct. The Americans, strongly in favour of British entry to Europe, had no first-hand information about the frigid aftermath of Rambouillet just two days before. And so, at Nassau, Macmillan dissembled – lest, no doubt, the outcome with de Gaulle clarified American concerns and hardened them against giving the British what Macmillan was now going all out to secure – Polaris. 'Somehow we must end up there,' he had told Thorneycroft. He even told McGeorge Bundy, the President's National Security Adviser, for example, that he 'had had a very good talk at Rambouillet' with de Gaulle, who 'used to think that he did not want us in, but he's been seeing lots of Germans and now I think he does'!

However, the last-minute presence of George Ball at Nassau, whose advice throughout the British bid for entry had been closely followed and supported by Kennedy, meant that the risks and dangers of the nuclear issue for the European policy got their airing.

This fateful Anglo-American meeting opened with Kennedy first advancing the offer to which Lord Thorneycroft referred – a proposal to share the cost of *completing*, rather than cancelling, Skybolt. And, as Thorneycroft has recounted, when Kennedy made this offer across the table at Nassau, he turned it down, saying he was not prepared to 'buy the shares which the President's own Defense Department was selling that morning'! The British wanted 'something the Americans themselves had faith in'. That meant Polaris. Skybolt had been struck as a bargain between Eisenhower and Macmillan in return for Holy Loch in Scotland as the American nuclear submarine base. That bargain had epitomised the Anglo-American alliance. As for Skybolt now? In Mr Macmillan's own intervention, made in support of Thorneycroft in these exchanges, 'the lady had been compromised!' Violated by McNamara, and in public.

Well then, Polaris, said Kennedy, but Polaris tied in exclusively with NATO. It was at this point that Harold Macmillan's voice rose in diapason! He delivered a long soliloquy of polished and civilised eloquence. It cast something of a spell on those who heard it; their accounts, British and American, bear witness to its touching effectiveness. Macmillan insisted, as Zulueta has informed us he told de Gaulle at Rambouillet that he would, upon an ultimate British prerogative. This was the right to independent British control of Polaris in a moment of supreme national interest. The political point he forced home successfully with Kennedy was that Britain must have the *right* to independence. He would give a pledge to NATO that was both permanent and irreversible, embodied in Polaris; but before that there had to be the dignity befitting an old and honourable nation state, and America's staunchest ally, of the essential escape clause.

Based upon this compromise, the integration of Britain and her nuclear capability within the American-led alliance of NATO, but with, in the last resort, a form of independence, the Prime Minister succeeded in producing for Britain his extraordinary triumph of Polaris. The innate American generosity of spirit upon which Churchill had feelingly remarked early in the war had come to Britain's and Macmillan's rescue where the President of France had not.

Polaris predisposed British foreign and defence policy until almost the end of the century. But in terms of the priority which Macmillan attached to Britain joining the European Community it proved to be a two-edged sword. Kennedy had overruled the qualifications and concerns of the 'Europeans' in his own State Department this time, perhaps foremost among them George Ball.

BALL: I think Nassau was a major mistake. I thought at the time it was a mistake and I never changed my view.
CHARLTON: In retrospect, what is there to add about Macmillan's performance at this meeting? He seems to feel, doesn't he, that he can handle the Americans?
BALL: Well, I'll say he did! He did it very well. He got really what he wanted. My rearguard action at that time was to try to get something that would preserve the idea of a multilateral force. Again, I never saw this in the weapons context nearly so much as the political: giving the Germans some participation without letting them have a real, or the only, finger on the trigger. So we had some discussion on that. I remember, at one point, Macmillan turning to me and saying with some considerable disgust about my discussion of this matter, 'Well, you can't expect our chaps to share their grog with a Turk, can you!' And I said,

'Well, I thought that was exactly what happened on Nelson's flagship!'
CHARLTON: I don't follow that. What do you mean?
BALL: I mean that the crew of Nelson's flagship was not a British crew. It was gathered from the whole of Europe. It was a multilateral force.

PACE DEVON AND CORNWALL! From where, incidentally, George Ball's forebears came. *Pace* France, for whom under de Gaulle these ecumenical ideas were anathema – as they were for Thorneycroft and Macmillan.

Both Britain and France saw the American proposal for a multilateral force as putting an end to their own national deterrents. In maintaining to de Gaulle that he would insist upon the element of 'independence' for any substitute he might get from Kennedy for the fallen Skybolt, Macmillan had meant it to be inferred, as he had 'hinted' at Champs, that there would still now be prospects for Anglo-French nuclear collaboration in Polaris – once Britain was *inside* the Common Market. At that time well ahead of France in the nuclear field, Britain conceived Polaris and the link to American know-how as a possible bargaining dowry. Sir Philip de Zulueta says that 'it was actually the British who persuaded the Americans to offer the French the same terms as the British for Polaris' – that is, assigning the weapons to NATO but with the rider about 'independent control' in a moment of 'supreme national interest'. Kennedy hoped, for his part, that this might persuade de Gaulle not to pursue the huge cost of a wholly independent effort, by offering him a negotiation which might lead to coequal status with the British. This would fit the anti-dissemination policy of the United States, look ahead to the assumed future difficulty of German partici-pation with adequate safeguards in nuclear matters, and conform overall to Kennedy's 'Grand Design'.

This offer to France of terms similar in one respect to those agreed with the British at Nassau was dismissed contemptuously by de Gaulle. Couve de Murville offered this reason.

COUVE DE MURVILLE: At Bermuda [Nassau] the British obtained American help for the continuation of their military programme. The concession on their part was that their nuclear armaments would enter NATO – even if there was a clause which said that in case of extreme danger they could take a decision on their own. In other words, it was an agreement that was exactly in contradiction with the French position. The more so because, not only was there an agree-ment between Britain and the United States, but there was the beginning of a move to try to bring the other countries into the same combination with the 'multilateral force'. Of course it appealed to all the NATO countries. But, if you remember, among those NATO countries the French were the *only* ones to have even something modest in nuclear weapons. So it was an appeal that began with France! It was exactly in contradiction with *all* that we thought was necessary for us in terms of national defence. The Rambouillet meeting was dominated by that problem and would, and could, lead only to deadlock. There was no possibility of an agreement because that would have meant that either Macmillan disavowed what he had done in Bermuda, or that de Gaulle accepted exactly all that he had refused since he came back to power in France in 1958!
CHARLTON: It must have been a temptation for you, though? The British take

the view that they have achieved for France at Nassau what I think the British always insist that they achieved for France at Yalta. Just as at Yalta Churchill fought hard to have France recognised as one of the powers to take part in the post-war settlement . . .

COUVE DE MURVILLE: That's true. That's true. It can't be denied.

CHARLTON: And there is always a feeling, I'm sure you will agree, that France's gratitude for that has been lacking. Then Macmillan comes back from Nassau with the same deal for France that he has for Britain, the offer of the nuclear weapons . . .

COUVE DE MURVILLE: Yes, but there was a slight difference between the two! We *wanted* to have a part in the occupation of Germany in 1944, but we *did not want* to have a part in the American domination of the nuclear weapons of its Alliance.

YET THE SKYBOLT ISSUE was that 'technicality' which, we should now recall, Mr Macmillan suggested was raised only at the last minute by de Gaulle when the French President saw, to his surprise, that the Prime Minister had succeeded in overcoming the objections of the Commonwealth, and in carrying the Conservative Party forward with him to an almost revolutionary new position contrary to its traditions. The nuclear issue posed by Skybolt was used, in Macmillan's view, as an excuse which, if it had not existed, would have had to be invented by de Gaulle. That does not appear to be the view taken by Edward Heath, the man who, some ten years later as Prime Minister himself, succeeded in leading Britain into the European Community.

HEATH: I don't think the evidence exists that de Gaulle treated it purely as an excuse. He did, after all, think very deeply about these things. And again I think it's difficult for the French to take up the position that this was 'betrayal', when Polaris was to be used, in the first instance, for the security of Europe. And of course the President could say, Well, when it really comes to the point, you go to the Americans. You were going to have Skybolt, you find that they can't provide Skybolt, and *instead of looking for alternative European solutions* you then ask for Polaris and you make this agreement. The fact that Polaris was then, afterwards, offered to the French did not alter the President's position at all.

CHARLTON: Well, that only puts more weight and interest, I suggest, in the conference at Champs in June 1962, when the nuclear question was discussed. Now, is it possible to say what, positively, Macmillan suggested to de Gaulle was possible in nuclear cooperation between Britain and France at the conference?

HEATH: I don't think it is, no.

CHARLTON: But there were elements which were a departure from previous practice and which would take account of the new political entity in Western Europe, with France and Britain leading it?

HEATH: Yes.

CHARLTON: And therefore when we come to Rambouillet and Nassau and the Polaris conference, that is seen by de Gaulle as a retreat from that position?

HEATH: That is quite possible.

NOR DOES MR HEATH appear to agree with Harold Macmillan's verdict that the decision to veto Britain's entry was because, as the Prime Minister saw it, 'de Gaulle always looked back, to the past'. That the French President thought he could dominate Europe, that he saw in a French-led Europe the hegemony of a Louis XIV or Napoleon, and that British membership would destroy the chances France had of leading Europe.

HEATH: I don't think it was narrowly based in that respect. He also must have realised that German strength was already greater than French strength at that point. Therefore there were many things in which France could give leadership – as *we* can today. Any member of the Community on certain things, on certain matters, can give leadership. What he could not possibly have expected was what I think you're describing as Napoleonic, which was domination.

THOSE IMPORTANT DIFFERENCES of emphasis conveyed by Edward Heath, particularly concerning nuclear weapons, tell us perhaps a good deal about his own subsequent success with France where Macmillan failed. They reveal a further evolution of British policy over Europe in Heath's mind compared with Macmillan's. Perhaps a special relationship with France to complement the *natural* one with the United States? But that is another story. Who knows how far, had he succeeded, Mr Macmillan might have gone in building up Europe as a great power, and with Britain having a great voice in that power?

But until he *did* get Britain into Europe Harold Macmillan had determined that he could give up nothing of the old and vital arrangements while he explored possible new ones. That was the exquisite dilemma of his last desperate attempt to convince de Gaulle to yield. To resolve that ultimate difficulty required a mutual confidence and understanding the two men were unable to establish.

On the afternoon of 14 January 1963, in one of those stiflingly overheated salons of the Elysée Palace in Paris, the International Press Corps had made their twice-yearly descent upon a Press Conference of General de Gaulle. There it was that the great axe fell on Harold Macmillan's attempt to make Britain a member of the European Community. Speaking without a note of any kind near him, arms upraised when necessary to emphasise his doubts, his expression a parade of grimaces and concerns, there could be, by the time it was over, no room for doubt. It was a public Rambouillet, and a repeat of the judgements made there by de Gaulle. He did not actually *say* 'No', but it was an avalanche of negatives. 'One might sometimes have believed that our English friends . . . were agreeing to transform themselves . . . It cannot be said it is yet resolved . . . Will it be so one day? Obviously only England can answer . . . after a profound change . . .'

And on the vexed nuclear issue there was this: '. . . above all deterrence is now a Russian as well as an American achievement . . . No one could say . . . where, when, how and in what measure American nuclear weapons would be used to defend Europe . . . [Polaris] does not serve the principle of having our own deterrent force at our own disposal. To put our weapons into a multilateral force under foreign command would be a contravention of this principle. True, we would be able, theoretically, to retain the power in a supreme hypothesis. But in practice how could we do this in the unparalleled moments of the atomic apocalypse . . .'

In that litany of dissenting judgements, resting upon his thesis that Britain was 'not yet ready' for Europe, lay the 'veto', the Great Refusal by France under de Gaulle of Britain's first determined effort to find her place in the new Community of the old nation states of Western Europe, whose very survival she had done so much to ensure.

10

Epilogue

FOR THE BRITISH there was 'great and grievous' disappointment –
Macmillan's own words. There were two more meetings in Brussels in January,
but the French chairs were empty. Agreement was reached with the remaining
Five of the original Common Market on almost all the outstanding items in that
vast negotiation.

But the terms of the Treaty of Rome are quite clear. Any member has a veto
and the others can do nothing about it. On 29 January 1963 Edward Heath was
told formally that negotiations were at an end. It was all over.

HEATH: If you go back to the time of the negotiations, then a large part of the
French people were in favour of their succeeding. They were disappointed
when the negotiations were vetoed, because they thought they were going to be
successful. I think, too, they felt it would be a feather in de Gaulle's cap,
another feather, to show what France could do. If he had not vetoed and the
negotiation had been successful, he would have gone down in history as the
man who created the *real* Europe, which contained Britain. Now he will go
down in history as the man who prevented that happening for a decade, with all
the consequences for Europe, and for Britain herself. If you look at his record
in foreign affairs, although he was active world-wide, I don't know that
historians are going to think a great deal about his ventures in Quebec. No one
remembers his ventures in Latin America, in Africa. They will give him credit
for getting out of Algeria, in the same way that they will give Nixon credit for
getting out of Vietnam, and us credit at various times for getting out of places.
But it will not be positive approval. They will give him approval for restoring to
the French their self-respect and what has happened as a result of that.

Internationally he could have gone down as the man who created the real
unity of Europe which has been the endeavour of so many throughout the ages,
which has existed since Charlemagne, and now was going to be the most potent
power in the world to come. But that he denied himself.

HEATH AND THE BRITISH DELEGATION went home from Brussels resolved
that bitter feelings should not mislead them into making statements which
might prejudice the future, and in the conviction that this could not be the last
of it – the certainty they felt that they would return, as did the Yorkshireman Sir
Herbert Andrew of the Board of Trade.

ANDREW: I don't think de Gaulle had any sympathy from the others. As far as
I could see in Brussels the other delegations were as distressed, in fact more

The Great Axe falls. The General says no to Macmillan's attempt to take Britain into Europe, the Elysée Palace, 14 January 1963.

distressed, than we were. They were more emotionally shocked, I think, than we were. After the final announcement of the veto there, the German member was very upset. He came out to me, and I said, Don't worry. We're the bulldog breed, you know. We shall come back. We always come back, which I thought was not a bad thing to say to a German.

AMONG THE RUSH OF immediate reflections was the Prime Minister's own. Harold Macmillan noted in his diary, ten days after the shattering blow de Gaulle had dealt him, 'the great question remains, "What is the alternative?" to the European Community. If we are honest, we must say there is none – had there been the chance of a Commonwealth Free Trade Area we should have grasped it long ago.'

The British sat down to wait. In Zulueta's words, 'we were consoled by the fact that all men are mortal – even de Gaulle'. In the post-war years the very success of another vast undertaking, the global task of devolving, peaceably and painstakingly, so much of Britain's former power and influence, absorbed and deflected much of the national energy and attention.

Sir Frederick Hoyer Millar, now Lord Inchyra, entered the diplomatic service in 1923. After serving as Ambassador in Germany from 1955, he came home in 1957 to take charge of the Foreign Office. He was Permanent Under-Secretary for the four years from 1957 to 1961, the years of 'reappraisal' in which, after Messina and the founding of the Common Market and Suez, Britain made the turnabout in her historical stance.

After the General said 'No'. Edward Heath, Duncan Sandys, Christopher Soames and the German Foreign Minister, Dr Schroeder, Brussels, January 1963.

INCHYRA: One was so busy dealing with the day-to-day operations, one did not have much time to think about Britain's European policy. In those days it was mainly concerned with the problems of Germany and Berlin, of getting NATO firmly established and seeing that the Russians didn't get away with it! Beyond that, I don't know that we had any clear European policy, except that it was quite obvious that our earlier, world-wide responsibilities and activities were coming to an end. Obviously we were turning more and more towards Europe. One had to find another focus, but I would not like to say that we had any clear, defined objectives there – except to get closer to Europe.

One should have been able to make the time in an ideal world – in an ideal Foreign Office if you like – one would have had bodies, individuals, planning and taking a long-term view. We did try, as far as we could. There is always a danger, of course – one can see it so often in America – that the planners become operational. Then you have the devil of a job to stop them interfering with the day-to-day work. But it is quite true, one of the great difficulties is always to plan ahead and get a clear view of what the world may be, or what you would *like* it to be, in say ten years. One is continually being distracted by what's going to happen in the next five days! One was always being distracted by the day-to-day horrors – having worries about what the Russians were going to do, trying to align one's attitude with the Americans *and* the French, all sorts of horrors in the Middle East, in Cyprus, in the Far East too. Purely administrative problems take a hell of a long time.

You may have had a short Cabinet committee meeting perhaps, and they would get sidetracked into deciding whether to send troops into Jordan or something like that. That's the whole trouble. All these things that ought to have been looked at from the long-term point of view, carefully weighing out where our interests lay – then you always get sidetracked by some immediate decision on oil or something. There probably should have been a clearly pre-conceived plan, but I don't believe there was.

After Suez, the days when we thought we could go it alone, or whatever we called it, or when we really ranked as a sort of major power, if not over were jolly nearly over. One had to reconsider one's position and one's whole ability to influence things, say in a place like China, and things in the Far East. It is quite extraordinary now, when I think back not so much to the time when I was in the Foreign Office, but in earlier days when I was in the Private Office, before the war. It's quite inconceivable that all these discussions about the Near East and Jerusalem should go on without us being directly involved; equally inconceivable that all this business about Vietnam and Thailand could. We were always right in the middle of things in those days, and all that was quite gone.

I think it was fairly obvious by 1957 that our future lay in Europe, from a political point of view, but of course there were a great many economic difficulties to be overcome first. My own feeling was, and I became more and more convinced, that from a radical point of view one *had* to go in, otherwise one would be, relegated is the word, I think, to the second division. That is what I think is so wrong now. Everybody complains that they're not getting something out. We never went in to get something out. We went in to prevent our being kicked down really to a lower league.

Before 1957 the European countries had been clamouring for us really to go in and give them a lead. By 1957 and 1958 they were beginning to take a lead themselves. The French and the Germans were getting on very much better together. I think de Gaulle, and Adenauer for that matter, really felt they knew as much about how to run things as we did by then. So I think our power of attraction to the European countries was diminishing all the time.

CHARLTON: And when in 1958 the Treaty of Rome comes into effect, can you remember the feeling in the Foreign Office the day the Treaty was signed? What did you all think of it?

INCHYRA: Yes, everyone was rather sceptical about that, whether it would really work.

CHARLTON: Even when it was signed?

INCHYRA: I'm rather afraid they were, really. It depended a terrible lot on whether you were looking at the political side of the Foreign Office, who were perhaps rather in favour of it. The economists were much more doubtful as to (a) whether it would work from the economic point of view, and (b) what effect it would have on our own economy.

CHARLTON: And our concept of the Free Trade Area which we launch after the Six have gone ahead? Why did we think that could succeed?

INCHYRA: I don't know why we did it really, because it was fairly obvious it wasn't on from the point of view of the Six. They weren't interested in a Free Trade Area in manufacturers; all they were interested in was in protecting their agriculture, and lowering and getting a common tariff. I suppose it was trying to save something out of the mess. But it was obviously a second-best solution and one which, one ought to have realised at the time perhaps, was really a non-starter.

I wouldn't have thought that there was a critical moment when we suddenly decided to turn a corner and go off at right angles. I would have said merely that the slope we were on got steeper. I don't think it would be unfair to say that the new Prime Minister, Harold Macmillan, gave a considerable impetus to the movement. He was very definitely of the opinion that in our interests we ought to be full members. When you know that is the Prime Minister's view, you take some care to accommodate yourself. I think it was the general feeling that we'd rather missed the boat for quite a long time. After all, there were several opportunities immediately after the war, and in all those post-war years. If we'd taken the initiative we could really almost have written our own ticket, I think.

CHARLTON: I know the Foreign Office is not supposed to become emotional or excited about these things, but it just seems to me that this particular moment when we apply for membership of the European Community, when one looks back on it, is an enormous decision, historically, isn't it? Now do you, in the vaults of the Foreign Office, the guardians of the true flame of a whole position for this country, see it like that?

INCHYRA: No, I think you're quite right in that one did not realise at the time what a momentous decision it was and all the implications of it. One merely thought that, from a political point of view, here was a chance of saving a little of the position we've lost. And if we don't take this opportunity we shall be of no more account than a small, peripheral European country – and you've got to hop on the bandwagon while you can. There ought to have been a long-term plan, thought out in the 1950s perhaps, for this; and working on this as the culmination of a long series of discussions and Cabinet recommendations. In point of fact nothing of the sort, I think. Perhaps it was the fault of the machine. It just doesn't work properly.

BUT GENERAL DE GAULLE proved to be only an incident in a journey for Britain. It was a journey begun by Winston Churchill with his call for a United States of Europe, by his summons to 're-create the European family', with his wish to see 'the economy of Europe studied as a whole', and in that belief of his, expressed to Anthony Eden at a surely remarkable moment in 1942 – just after El Alamein and with the outcome of Stalingrad undecided – when victory over Germany was to him first in sight, that 'Europe must be Britain's prime duty and her prime care'. It was a journey which halted its advance and turned aside, to be relaunched wholeheartedly by Harold Macmillan, and which finally carried its objective under Edward Heath.

During the short span of British history measured from the Second World War until General de Gaulle's veto, Britain had pursued an obsolete concept – the leadership of an enlarging Commonwealth, and with herself at the centre of (in Churchill's own formulation) three intersecting circles. That global role proved to be inexorably transient. But to the British, accustomed to their long and stable supremacy in many fields, painfully difficult to accept. Painful to recall for Lord Butler.

BUTLER: We saw the Prince of Wales say the other day that Britain is not a first-class power. I wish somebody had stopped him. He oughtn't to say things like that. But the fact is that it's partially true, you see, and we have changed incredibly from what we were. Especially, of course, in naval power and the control over the seas. Absolutely. I mean, Mahon and all these great historians of our naval past are out of date – but we really did control the oceans, didn't we?

CHARLTON: I think *that* to future generations is going to be one of the great difficulties to understand. Why is it that a great maritime power, above all one that is accustomed to the uses of power through naval supremacy, does not make the political adjustment after the last war, when it's obvious among all facts that naval supremacy is no longer what is going to dictate the world balance?

BUTLER: You see, naval supremacy really ended with the Battle of Jutland. Terrible story I think, the Battle of Jutland – our shells not working and our armour not working and having no real success. I'm just reading this new life of Beatty.

CHARLTON: 'Something's the matter with our bloody ships today'?

BUTLER: Yes. Beatty is all very well, but honestly he wasn't up to Nelson. The fact is that after that there was a complete revision. Even Admiral Scheer, the German, wrote after Jutland that the conquest of the High Seas by great vessels can't go on, if you've come to the submarine and merchant shipping. The two German admirals, Scheer and Hipper, saw that neither side could win, really, on the sea. And you see, that's been an absolutely terrific reversal of the British tradition, hasn't it?

CHARLTON: But why did we not see it, if not after Jutland, then after the fall of Singapore, for example?

BUTLER: Well, we certainly got an awful shock in Singapore. That was awful.

CHARLTON: The Australians make fundamental adjustments because of that. They sign the ANZUS defence treaty with the Americans, they turn to the Americans after the war; they were no longer buying British as they had done; they were opening up to Japan and to the Americans.

BUTLER: Well, you see it all happened so quickly. First of all, we did not realise the almost complete loss of our maritime supremacy, that the Grand Fleet no longer meant anything. We did not realise, at first, the last breath of our prestige and of economic power, and in some cases military power, by the transfer of power, starting with India which had been done so very, very quickly – much too quickly – by Mountbatten. Much praised, but done too quickly by Mountbatten, all done in five months. But I think that what you're talking about is absolutely vital to the future understanding of British history, because we did not adjust ourselves from being a world power and an enormous maritime power depending upon the resources of the sea. Some of the great historians – I mentioned Mahon – had already established that as the beginning of our greatness. And we had not reflected upon that. That was what probably our greatest imperial historian, Sir John Seeley, had been describing in *The Expansion of England*. And we did not start in a smaller way, by getting into an idea which I still think must be realised – namely that we are now part of an economic unit which is absolutely able – if it really got together – to stand up against Russia and the United States.

EMERGING FROM THE SECOND WORLD WAR with a rightful feeling of achievement, but with an unjustified measurement of her own strength and power, induced Britain to misjudge the relevance to herself of the drive for unity in Western Europe. But in doing so, while the Community was in the making and others were being forced to make more radical accommodations, it is difficult not to conclude that the British as a nation sought to prolong a more comfortable interlude. It led Britain to forgo a chance, most likely the one at Messina in 1955, of seeing to it that the European Community which developed then did so more in accordance and in sympathy with her own preferences.

Many years later, in Paris, I spoke to the man who had first tried to enlist Britain for the leadership of Europe. While often taken to task in England for what was considered a simplistic belief, that a proposition had only to be self-evidently true for it to become practical politics, he had however done more with an *idea* to unite Europe, in that crucial decade of the 1950s, than those in history who had tried to do it by force of arms. That former British civil servant, old Jean Monnet.

MONNET: I never understood why the British did not join this, which was so much in their interest. I came to the conclusion that it must have been because it was *the price of victory* – the illusion that you could maintain what you had, without change.

The Contributors

THE BIOGRAPHICAL NOTES on the contributors are intended to show those details which bear upon the matter of their various interviews. A few other facts have sometimes been included, but the notes are not intended to be complete. The contributors are British unless otherwise stated.

Abbreviations used include: Admin – Administration; Amb – Ambassador; Assoc – Associate; Asst – Assistant; Bd – Board; BoT – Board of Trade; Brit – British; Chm – Chairman; Coll – College; Commr – Commissioner; Conf – Conference; CRO – Commonwealth Relations Office; Cttee – Committee; Dep – Deputy; Dept – Department; Dir – Director; Div – Division; Econ – Economic; Educ – Education; Exec – Executive; FO – Foreign Office; Gen – General; Govt – Government; Gp – Group; Ldr – Leader; Mil – Military; Min – Minister; Nat – National; Off – Office; Parl – Parliamentary; Perm – Permanent; Pol – Political; PPS – Parliamentary Private Secretary; Pres – President; Princ – Principal; Pte – Private; Rep – Representative; Sec – Secretary; Tech – Technical.

ALPHAND, Hervé (1907–   ). Dir Econ Affairs, French National Committee in London, 1941–4; French Amb to OEEC 1950, to UN 1955–6, to USA 1956–65; Sec-Gen French FO 1965–73.

ANDREW, Rev. Sir Herbert (1910–   ). Second Sec BoT (General) 1955–60, (Overseas) 1960–3; BoT member, UK delegation to Common Market conference 1961–3; Perm Under-Sec of State Educ & Science 1961–3.

BALL, George M. (1909–   ). American. Assoc Counsel, Lend Lease Admin, 1942–3; Foreign Economics Admin 1943–4; Dir US Strategic Bombing Survey, London, 1944–5; pol adviser to Adlai Stevenson; Under-Sec of State for Econ Affairs 1961; Under-Sec of State (to Dean Rusk) 1961–6, US Perm Rep to UN 1968.

BARCLAY, Sir Roderick (1909–   ). Served Brussels, Paris, Washington, London; Princ Pte Sec to Foreign Sec 1949–51; Asst Under-Sec FO 1951, Dep Under-Sec 1953–6; UK Amb to Denmark 1956–60; Dep Under-Sec FO 1960–3; UK Amb to Belgium 1963–9.

BATTLE, Lucius D. 'Luke' (1918–   ). American. Special Asst to Sec of State (Dean Acheson) 1949–53, 1961–4; Exec Sec, US State Dept 1961–2.

BEUGEL, Ernst Hans van der (1918–   ). Dutch. Sec Econ Cttee Dutch Cabinet & Dir Bureau of Marshall Plan 1947; Dir-Gen Econ & Mil Aid Prog 1952; Sec of State Foreign Ministry 1957–8; Amb & Special Consultant to Min of Foreign Aff 1959.

BOWIE, Robert (1909–   ). American. Special Asst to Mil Governor, Germany,

1945–6; Prof of Law, Harvard Univ, 1945–55; Gen Counsel Special Adviser, US High Commissioner Germany, 1950–1; Dir Policy Planning Staff, US State Dept, 1953–5; Asst Sec of State for Policy Planning 1955–7; pol adviser to John Foster Dulles.

BRETHERTON, Russell (1906–). Ministry of Supply and BoT 1939–45; Under-Sec BoT 1946–8; Cabinet Off (econ section) 1949–51; Under-Sec Materials 1951–4, BoT 1954–61, Treasury 1961–8.

BUTLER, Rt Hon. Lord ('Rab') (1902–82). Under-Sec of State, India Off 1932–7, FO 1938–41; Min of Educ 1941–5; Chancellor of Exchequer 1951–5; Lord Privy Seal 1955–9; Ldr House of Commons 1955–61; Home Sec 1957–62; First Sec of State 1962–3; Dep Prime Minister 1962–3; Foreign Sec 1963–4; Master Trinity Coll Cambridge 1965–78.

CARR, Rt Hon. Lord (Robert) (1916–). PPS to Foreign Sec 1951–5, to Prime Minister 1955; Parl Sec Labour & Nat Service 1955–8; Sec of State Employment 1970–2; Home Sec 1972–4; Lord Pres and Ldr House of Commons 1972.

COLVILLE, Sir John (1915–). Asst Pte Sec to Chamberlain 1939–40, to Churchill 1940–1, 1943–5, to Attlee 1945; Pte Sec to Princess Elizabeth 1947–9; Jt Princ Pte Sec to Churchill 1951–5.

COUVE DE MURVILLE, Maurice (1907–). French. Member, French Cttee for Nat Liberation, Algiers, 1943; Foreign Ministry 1945–50; Perm Rep to NATO 1954–5; Amb to USA 1955–6, to Germany 1956–8; Foreign Minister 1958–68; Prime Minister of France 1968–9.

CULLIS, Michael (1914–). Ministry of Econ Warfare (Spain, Portugal, London) 1940–4; Head of Austrian Section FO 1945; Special Asst Schuman Plan 1950; Scandinavia 1951–8; Malta 1959–60; Dir Arms Control and Disarmament FO 1967–74.

DILLON, Douglas (1909–). American. Amb to France 1953–7; Under-Sec of State for Econ Affairs 1957–9; Under-Sec of State 1959–61; Sec of Treasury, USA 1961–5.

FIGGURES, Sir Frank (1910–). Treasury 1946; Dir Trade & Finance OEEC 1948–51; Under-Sec Treasury 1955–60; Sec-Gen EFTA 1960–5; Third Sec Treasury 1965–8, Second Sec 1968–71; Dir-Gen NEDO 1971–3; Chm Pay Bd 1973–4.

FRANKS, Rt Hon. Lord (Oliver) (1905–). Ministry of Supply 1939–46, Perm Sec 1945–6; Provost Queen's Coll Oxford 1946–8; Amb to USA 1948–52; Chm Lloyds Bank 1954–62; Provost Worcester Coll Oxford 1962–76.

GARNER, Lord (Joseph 'Joe') (1908–). Dominions Off 1930; Pte Sec to successive Secs of State 1940–3; Senior Sec UK High Commission Ottawa 1943–6; Asst Under-Sec CRO 1948–51; Dep High Commr India 1951–3; Dep Under-Sec CRO 1952–6; High Commr Canada 1956–61; Perm Under-Sec CRO 1962–5, Commonwealth Off 1965–8; Head of Diplomatic Services 1965–8.

GLADWYN, Lord (Gladwyn Jebb) (1900–). Entered diplomatic service 1924; Ministry of Econ Warfare 1940; Head of Reconstruction Dept FO 1942; Counsellor FO 1943 (attending Quebec, Cairo, Teheran, Dumbarton Oaks, Yalta, San Francisco & Potsdam conferences); Acting Sec-Gen UN 1946; Asst Under-Sec FO 1946–7; UK Rep Brussels Treaty Commission 1948; Dep Under-Sec FO 1949–50; Perm Rep to UN 1950–4; Amb to France 1954–60.

GORDON, Lincoln (1913–). American. Pol economist & diplomatist; Consultant US State Dept European Recovery Program 1947–8; Econ Adviser to Averell Harriman, Special Asst to President 1950–1; Minister for Econ Aff and Chief of Mission to UK 1952–5.

GORDON-WALKER, Rt Hon. Lord (Patrick Gordon Walker) (1907–80). Parl Under-Sec of State CRO 1947–50; Sec of State CRO 1950–1; Foreign Sec 1964–5; Sec of State Educ & Science 1967–8.

GREWE, Wilhelm (1911–). German. Chief of Legal Div German FO 1953–4, of Pol Div 1955–8; Amb to USA 1958–62; Perm Rep NATO 1962–71; Amb to Japan 1971–6.

HALLSTEIN, Walter (1901–82). German. Ldr German delegation to Schuman Plan conf 1950; State Sec Federal German Chancellery 1950, Foreign Off 1951–8; Pres EEC Commission 1958–67.

HASE, Karl-Günther von (1917–). German. Spokesman German FO 1958–61; Head W Eur Dept 1961–2; Spokesman German Federal Govt 1962–7; State Sec Defence 1968–9; Amb to UK 1970–7.

HEALEY, Rt Hon. Denis (1917–). Sec International Dept Labour Party 1945–52; British delegate to Consultative Assembly, Council of Europe, 1952–4; Shadow Cabinet 1959–64, 1970–4, 1979– ; Defence Sec 1964–70; Chancellor of Exchequer 1974–9; Dep Ldr Labour Party 1980–83.

HEATH, Rt Hon. Edward (1916–). Dep Govt Chief Whip 1952–5, Chief Whip 1955–9; Min of Labour 1959–60; Lord Privy Seal with FO responsibilities 1960–3; Industry & Trade Sec 1963–4; Ldr of Opposition 1965–70, 1974–5; Prime Minister 1970–4.

HIRSCH, Etienne (1901–). French. Asst Dir of Armaments, Algiers, 1943; Pres French Supply Council, London, 1945; Head of Tech Div, French Planning Commission, 1946–9; negotiations for Coal & Steel Community 1950–2; Pres Euratom Cttee 1959–62.

INCHYRA, Lord (Frederick Hoyer Millar) (1900–). Served Berlin, Paris, Cairo, Washington; Perm Rep NATO 1952; UK High Commr Germany 1953–5; Amb to Germany 1955–7; Perm Under-Sec FO 1957–61.

JACOB, Lt-Gen. Sir Ian (1899–). Mil Asst Sec to War Cabinet 1939–45; Chief Staff Officer Min of Defence & Dep Sec (Mil) to Cabinet 1952; Dir-Gen BBC 1952–60.

MACMILLAN, Rt Hon. Harold (1894–). Minister Resident Allied HQ NW Africa 1942–5; Min of Housing & Local Govt 1951–4; Min of Defence 1954–5; Foreign Sec 1955; Chancellor of Exchequer 1955–7; Prime Minister 1957–63.

MAYHEW, Lord (Christopher) (1915–). PPS to Lord Pres 1945–6; Parl Under-Sec of State FO 1946–50; Min of Defence (Navy) 1964–6.

MILLARD, Sir Guy (1917–). Asst Pte Sec to Foreign Sec 1941–5; Brit Embassy Paris 1945–9; Pte Sec to Prime Minister 1955–7; FO 1962–4; Amb to Hungary 1967–9, to Sweden 1971–4, to Italy 1974–6.

MONNET, Jean (1888–1979). French. Dep Sec-Gen League of Nations 1918; Chm Franco-British Coordination Cttee 1939; Member British Supply Council, Washington, 1940–3; Commr for Armament, Supplies & Reconstruction, French Nat Liberation Cttee, Algiers, 1943–4; Gen Commr, Plan for Modernisation and Equipment of France 1946; Pres Preparatory Conf, Schuman Plan 1950; Pres Coal & Steel Community 1952–5.

NEUSTADT, Richard (1919–). American. Pol scientist; Special consultant to the President 1961–3, to Bureau of the Budget 1961–70, to State Dept 1962–9; Prof of Public Administration, Harvard Univ since 1965.

NITZE, Paul (1907–   ). American. Dep Dir Off of International Trade Policy 1946–8; Dep to Asst Sec of State for Econ Affairs 1948–9; Dir Policy Planning, US State Dept 1950–3; Asst Sec Defence 1961–3; Sec of Navy 1963–7.

NUTTING, Rt Hon. Sir Anthony (1920–   ). FO 1940–5; Parl Under-Sec of State FO 1951–4; Min of State FO 1954–6.

O'NEILL, Sir Con (1912–   ). FO 1943–6, 1947–57; Asst Under-Sec FO 1957–60; Amb to Finland 1961–3, to EEC 1963–5; Dep Under-Sec FO 1965–8, 1969–72; Ldr British delegation to negotiate entry to EEC 1969–72.

PLOWDEN, Lord (Edwin) (1907–   ). Ministry of Aircraft Production 1940–6; Chief Planning Officer & Chm Econ Planning Bd 1947–53; Chm Atomic Energy Org 1954–9.

ROBERTHALL, Lord (Robert Hall) (1901–   ). Ministry of Supply 1939–46; Adviser BoT 1946–7; Dir Econ Section Cabinet Off 1947–53; Econ Adviser to Govt 1953–61; Chm OEEC Gp of Econ Experts 1955–61; Principal Hertford Coll Oxford 1964–7.

ROBERTS, Sir Frank (1907–   ). FO 1937–45; Brit min in Moscow 1945–7; Princ Pte Sec to Foreign Sec 1947–9; Dep Under-Sec FO 1951–4; Amb to Yugoslavia 1954–7; Perm Rep to NATO 1957–60; Amb to USSR 1960–2, to Germany 1963–8.

ROLL, Lord (Eric) (1907–   ). Brit food mission to N America 1941–6; Under-Sec Treasury, Central Econ Planning staff 1948; Min, UK delegation to OEEC, 1949; Dep Head UK delegation to NATO 1952; Under-Sec Agriculture 1953–7, Dep Sec 1959–61; Dep Ldr UK delegation for negotiations with EEC 1961–3; Perm Under-Sec Dept of Econ Affairs 1964–6.

ROTHSCHILD, Robert (1911–   ). Belgian. Belgian FO 1952, Chef de Cabinet 1954–8, 1961–4; Amb to Yugoslavia 1958–60, to Switzerland 1964–6, to France 1966–73, to UK 1973–6.

SCHAETZEL, Robert (1917–   ). American. Special Asst to Dir, Office of Trade Policy, State Dept 1945–50, to Asst Sec of State for Econ Affairs 1950–4; Member Presidential Task Force 1960–1; Special Asst to Under-Sec of State 1961–2; Dep Asst Sec of State for Atlantic Affairs 1962–6; Amb to EEC 1966–72.

SHERFIELD, Lord (Roger Makins) (1904–   ). Asst to Macmillan at Allied Forces HQ Mediterranean 1943–4; Brit min in Washington 1945–7; Asst Under-Sec FO 1947–8, Dep Under-Sec 1948–52; Amb to USA 1953–6; Jt Perm Sec Treasury 1956–9; Chm UK Atomic Energy Authority 1960–4.

SHUCKBURGH, Sir Evelyn (1909–   ). Head Western Dept FO 1949–50, Western Organisations Dept 1950–1; Princ Pte Sec to Foreign Sec 1951–4; Asst Under-Sec FO 1954–6; Asst Sec-Gen (Pol) NATO 1958–60; Dep Under-Sec FO 1960–2; Perm Rep to NATO 1962–6; Amb to Italy 1966–9.

SNOY ET D'OPPUERS, Baron Jean-Charles (1907–   ). Belgian. Sec-Gen Belgian Min of Econ Aff 1939–60; Pres Council of OEEC 1948–50; Chief Belgian delegate for negotiations on Treaty of Rome 1957; Chm Steering Bd for Trade OEEC 1952–61; Pres Interim Cttee for EEC & Euratom 1957–8; Perm Belgian Rep EEC 1958–9.

SOAMES, Rt Hon. Lord (Christopher) (1920–   ). Parl Pte Sec to Churchill

1952–5; Sec of State for War 1958–60; Min of Agriculture 1960–4; Amb to France 1968–72; EEC Commissioner 1973–7; Lord Pres 1979–81.

SPAAK, Fernand (1923–   ). Belgian. Sec Econ Div Coal & Steel Community 1952–4; Exec Asst to Jean Monnet 1954–8; EEC Amb to USA since 1975.

THORNEYCROFT, Rt Hon. Lord (Peter) (1909–   ). Pres BoT 1951–7; Chancellor of Exchequer 1957–8; Min Aviation 1960–2; Min Defence 1962–4; Defence Sec 1964.

URI, Pierre (1911–   ). French. Econ and financial adviser to French Planning Commission 1947–52; Prof Nat School of Public Admin 1947–51; Econ Dir Coal & Steel Community 1952–9; Econ adviser EEC 1958–9.

WILSON, Sir Duncan (1911–   ). FO 1941–55, Dir of Research 1955–7; Asst Under-Sec FO 1960–4; Amb to Yugoslavia 1964–8, to USSR 1968–71; Master Corpus Christi Coll Cambridge 1971–8.

WILSON, Rt Hon. Sir Harold (1916–   ). Pres BoT 1947–51; Ldr Labour Party 1963–76; Ldr Opposition 1963–4, 1970–4; Prime Minister 1964–70, 1974–6.

ZULUETA, Sir Philip de (1925–   ). Pte Sec to Eden, Macmillan and Douglas-Home 1955–64; Asst Sec Treasury 1962.

Index

Note

1 Only the more substantial references are included.

2 Britain and other countries that occur frequently in the text are not shown in the Index.

3 Life peers, in cases where their style differs from their original names, are listed according to how they actually figure in the text.